CW01430020

Language and the Grand Tour

The Grand Tour was the classical continental trip to France and Italy, under-taken by young aristocratic men in early modern Europe, ostensibly for educational purposes. Using amusing stories and vivid quotations collected from travellers' writings, Arturo Tosi charts the rise of modern vernaculars and the standardisation of European languages. The travellers' writings pro-vide a valuable source of information about language contact, and illuminate how socialisation with the locals led, on the one hand, to conscious borrow-ings from prestigious foreign peers and, on the other, to linguistic disorienta-tion when confronted with lower-class speech and rural vernaculars. The first of its kind to approach the Grand Tour from a linguistic perspective, this book is a timely addition to this burgeoning area of study, presenting a unique case study of population movement, language change and education in early modern Europe.

ARTURO TOSI is Emeritus Professor at Royal Holloway, University of London. His previous books include *Immigration and Bilingual Education* (1984), *The Language of Italian Communities in the English-Speaking World* (1991) and *Language and Society in a Changing Italy* (2001).

Language and the Grand Tour

Linguistic Experiences of Travelling in Early Modern Europe

Arturo Tosi

Royal Holloway, University of London

CAMBRIDGE
UNIVERSITY PRESS

CAMBRIDGE
UNIVERSITY PRESS

University Printing House, Cambridge CB2 8BS, United Kingdom

One Liberty Plaza, 20th Floor, New York, NY 10006, USA

477 Williamstown Road, Port Melbourne, VIC 3207, Australia

314–321, 3rd Floor, Plot 3, Splendor Forum, Jasola District Centre, New Delhi – 110025, India

79 Anson Road, #06–04/06, Singapore 079906

Cambridge University Press is part of the University of Cambridge.

It furthers the University's mission by disseminating knowledge in the pursuit of education, learning, and research at the highest international levels of excellence.

www.cambridge.org
Information on this title: www.cambridge.org/9781108487276
DOI: 10.1017/9781108766364

© Arturo Tosi 2020

This publication is in copyright. Subject to statutory exception and to the provisions of relevant collective licensing agreements, no reproduction of any part may take place without the written permission of Cambridge University Press.

First published 2020

Printed in the United Kingdom by TJ International Ltd. Padstow Cornwall

A catalogue record for this publication is available from the British Library.

Library of Congress Cataloguing in Publication Data
Names: Tosi, Arturo, author.
Title: Language and the grand tour / Arturo Tosi.
Description: New York : Cambridge University Press, 2020. | Includes index.
Identifiers: LCCN 2019037282 (print) | LCCN 2019037283 (ebook) | ISBN 9781108487276 (hardback) | ISBN 9781108766364 (ebook)
Subjects: LCSH: Sociolinguistics – History – 18th century. | Europe – Civilization – 18th century. | Great Britain – History – 18th century – Historiography. | Travel writing – Europe – History – 18th century. | Travelers' writings, European – History and criticism. | Languages in contact. | Language and international relations.
Classification: LCC P40.45.E85 T67 2020 (print) | LCC P40.45.E85 (ebook) | DDC 306.44–dc23
LC record available at https://lccn.loc.gov/2019037282
LC ebook record available at https://lccn.loc.gov/2019037283

ISBN 978-1-108-48727-6 Hardback

Cambridge University Press has no responsibility for the persistence or accuracy of URLs for external or third-party internet websites referred to in this publication and does not guarantee that any content on such websites is, or will remain, accurate or appropriate.

To Judi, my wife

I took a couch to Ferney, the seat of the illustrious Monsieur de Voltaire . . . .

[he] opened the door of his apartment . . . I asked him if he still spoke English.

He replied, 'No'. To speak English one must place the tongue between the teeth.

and I have lost my teeth . . . .

(James Boswell, *The Life of Samuel Johnson*)

Contents

Figures

Preface

The linguistic history of Europe has been at the centre of a number of recent publications, many of which have been inclined to blur the sharp distinction between synchrony and diachrony. As a result, the chronicle of our European languages, which includes tensions, conflicts and mutual influence, has been enlightened by new studies concentrating on language attitudes, variation and change during a period that was crucial for the consolidation of multilingualism and the rise of modern vernaculars. Today this field is increasingly referred to as historical sociolinguistics or the social history of language, as both linguists and historians attempt to apply the tenets and methodology of contemporary sociolinguistics to the interpretation of the social functions of language in the past.

Since the early modern period is crucial in the history of Europe with regard to both the interaction between languages and their standardisation, this book starts from the assumption that the experiences of travellers on the Grand Tour can provide rich insights into social stratification in language use during that period. Not only do the travel writings of this mobile group provide a valuable source of information about language contact but they also illuminate how socialisation with the locals led, on the one hand, to conscious borrowings from prestigious foreign peers and, on the other, to linguistic disorientation when travellers were confronted with lower-class speech and rural vernaculars. By taking a sociolinguistic approach to exploring these written resources, it is hoped that the result will contribute to the description of the Grand Tour as a unique case study of population movement, language change and education in early modern Europe.

Acknowledgements

Many friends and colleagues have supported me with their enthusiasm during my research project, and the drafting of the manuscript. I have been lucky to receive positive appreciation and constructive criticism and I am indebted to all of them, either for helping me overcome some dilemmas or for helpfully commenting on earlier drafts of the book. I would especially like to mention Giulio and Laura Lepschy, Peter Trudgill, Peter Burke, Ivano Paccagnella and Peter Mackridge and to thank them for their stimulating discussions over the years. My gratitude also goes to John Gallagher for generously sharing with me some of his forthcoming works. Unfortunately his recent book was not published in time for me to take it into consideration before completing my manuscript.

I would also like to thank a number of colleagues in the Department of Filologia e Critica delle Letterature Antiche e Moderne at the University of Siena: in particular Maria Rita Digilio and Andrea Landolfi for their translation of some key passages from German. I am also grateful to Helen Glave and Jackie Willcox for their assistance with translations and proofreading, and to Helen Bilton for her great help with the indexing. I would like to thank the team of Integra-Pondicherry, especially Gayathri Tamilselvan, for their professionalism and flexibility in dealing with the proofs. It is a special pleasure to acknowledge the sympathetic interest in my project of Jean Hannah, who generously offered her professional assistance with the editing of the manuscript. Her constant willingness to discuss the imprecision of my second language, and her most helpful suggestions have greatly improved the readability of the book. Of course, all inaccuracies that have survived are my own.

I am also grateful to the Trustees of the British Museum and Windsor Castle Royal Collection, to the Curators of the Canterbury Dean and Chapter, the Paul Mellon Collection, the Archivio Storico della Città di Torino and the Istituto Nazionale per la Grafica in Rome for permission to use material held by them, and to the staff of the Warburg Institute Library in London and the Biblioteca di Archeologia e Storia dell'Arte in Rome for their assistance at various times.

Finally, I would like to dedicate this effort to my wife Judi for her help and support during the long gestation of the book.

Chronology

1738	Peace of Vienna, one of the last treaties drawn up in Latin
1740	The Hanoverian monarchy established in England
1745	Jacobite rising without French support
1750	Emergence of the Blue Stocking Society in England
1755	Samuel Johnson's *Dictionary* published
1756–63	Seven Years' War between all the great powers of Europe
1758	Rome 'crammed with Britons', according to Lady Montagu
1768	Laurence Sterne, *A Sentimental Journey* published
1770s	*Maccaroni* fashion established among young Grand Tourists
1775	Dr Johnson in Paris
1775–83	American War of Independence
1793	Otto Reichard, *Guide de l'Italie*, published
1798	Rome captured by Bonaparte's army and Italy under French rule
1779	The *Westmoreland* full of Italian art attacked by two French warships
1785	Forty thousand Englishmen touring the Continent, according to Gibbon
1786	*L'universalité de la langue française* declared by Antoine Rivarol
1789	Outbreak of the French Revolution
1793–1802	French Revolutionary Wars
1797	Leopold Graf von Berchtold, French edition of the *Patriotic Traveller*
1800	Mariana Starke, *Letters from Italy*, reputed to be the first modern guidebook, published
1802–3	Hostilities between the French Republic and Great Britain ended by Peace of Amiens
1803	American citizens free to travel in Europe
1807	Mme de Staël, *Corinne, ou l'Italie*, published
1815	Battle of Waterloo and Congress of Vienna
1816	First Channel crossing by steamer operated by the French
1817	Rome 'pestilent with English', according to Byron
1821	Regular Dover–Calais service run by the French
1821	Death of Keats and funeral from Piazza di Spagna, Rome
1832	The first Baedeker Guides in production
1836	John Murray, *Handbook for Travellers*, first published
1840–5	Ruskin and Dickens families, last Grand Tourists, in Italy by carriage
1846	Star rating for sights and accommodations introduced by the Baedeker guides
1847	*Continental Railways Guide* appeared
1850	Rail link London to Paris opened

Introduction

To most people, the expression 'Grand Tour' usually brings to mind an old-fashioned style of travel aimed at discovering the achievements of past civilisations. The archetypal Grand Tourists resided for a period in Paris and elsewhere in France, then headed south to Italy, where their journey into and around the Peninsula grew into a circuit of all its principal cities. Originally, only the French section of the continental itinerary was referred to by the term Grand Tour,[1] while the Italian portion was called *Giro of Italy*. Eventually, Grand Tour expanded in meaning to cover travels through a number of different continental countries, and *Giro of Italy* fell into disuse.[2] The term *Grand Tour* thus developed the particular sense of a classical continental tour for educational purposes.

Today, both a narrow and a broad meaning of the term Grand Tour coexist. In the narrow sense, the Grand Tour represents the culmination of the rich young eighteenth-century Englishman's education. In the golden age of that tradition, Grand Tourists were either aristocrats or wealthy townsmen who visited some of the cities and treasures of Europe, journeying in their comfortable horse-drawn carriages. Even in the previous century, many young noblemen travelled through the Continent, and most took up residence in university towns for specific academic purposes. These people were the protagonists of a phase that it is now often referred to as the 'origin of the Grand Tour'.[3] In both the seventeenth and eighteenth centuries, the majority of such travellers were young British gentlemen who, after a sojourn in France, continued their journey on to the Alps in order to reach Italy and spend time principally in Rome, but

---

[1] Some authors distinguish between the *Grand* and the *Petit Tour* of France. The *Grand Tour* included Lyons, Marseilles, Toulouse, Bordeaux and Paris; the *Petit Tour*, Paris, Tours and Poitiers. John Reresby, travelling with his tutor, wrote in 1654: 'In the month of April I began to make the little tour or circuit of France, and returned to Saumur after some six weeks' absence.' Kathleen, Lambley, *The Teaching and Cultivation of the French Language in England during Tudor and Stuart Times* (Manchester, 1920), 357 and 360.

[2] Both phrases were used for the first time in 1670 by the tutor and travel writer Richard Lassels who mentioned 'the Grand Tour of France and the Giro of Italy'. Richard Lassels, *The Voyage of Italy or a Compleat Journey Through Italy, in Two Parts* (Paris, 1670).

[3] See Michael G. Brennan (ed.), *The Origins of the Grand Tour, The Travels of Robert Montagu, Lord Mandeville, 1649–1654, William Hammond, 1655–1658, Banaster Maynard, 1660–1663*, (London, 2004).

increasingly also in Venice, Florence and Naples. The broad notion of the Grand Tour, therefore, refers to a stretch of time that covers almost three hundred years, consisting of two central centuries, a prelude in the late sixteenth century and an epilogue in the early nineteenth century.[4]

In addition to France and Italy, the tradition of the continental tour included other European destinations, such as the Low Countries, Germany, Austria and Bohemia, but not Spain, while Switzerland was sometimes incorporated as an alternative route to reach the other side of the Alps. One common idea about the Grand Tour is that the south of Europe was a magnet for northern Europeans. That was indeed the direction of the majority of travellers, but in addition to the British, there were German, Dutch and Polish people who also ventured south for educational purposes, and quite a few Italians headed north, often for no other objective than to discover the wider world. However, some commonplaces connected to the traditions of the Grand Tour are not justified on historical grounds, and it is best to clarify these now. The first is that the Grand Tour was inspired by an attraction to past civilisations, and the desire to discover how the classical heritage had survived on the Continent. However, the practice of going abroad to learn about foreign people, their techniques and industries was an older phenomenon which evolved into a form of proper economic and strategic knowledge-gathering as soon as ambassadors started acting like observers or even spies.[5]

Travel in order to gain commercial information became bidirectional, from the north of Europe to the south and vice versa, as soon as the practice of importing innovations from abroad spread during the early modern period. The case of the Anglo-Welshman James Howell is quite exemplary. Before he made a political career from his experience as a traveller, the first time he ventured abroad was as an envoy for a London glass company which sent him to Venice to learn new techniques there and hire workers from the glass-making factory at Murano.[6] The Italian Pietro Guerrini, an architect, was sent in the opposite direction by the

---

[4] A case might be made for other dates. Authors adopt boundaries for the Grand Tour that are relevant to their academic focus. See for example William Edward Mead, *The Grand Tour in the Eighteenth Century*; Paul Franklin, Kirby, *The Grand Tour in Italy (1700–1800)* (New York, 1952); Rosemary Sweet, *Cities and the Grand Tour, The British in Italy, c.1690–1820* (Cambridge, 2012). Stoye does not refer to the Grand Tour in the title, but explains that his study begins with the year 1604 because of the French Wars. John Stoye, *English Travellers abroad 1604–1667* (1952 rev. ed. New Haven 1989).

[5] Sophus A. Reinert, 'Mapping the Economic Grand Tour: traveling and international emulation in Enlightenment Europe', *Harvard Business School Working Papers*, 17–005 (2016) (online version), 3. The author explains that this 'neglected aspect of the Grand Tour' reached its peak during the eighteenth century, especially in trade, finance and politics: so much so that a traditional destination for artists, scholars and tourists such as Rome was supplanted for many travellers who had commercial, financial and political interests by the key city of Leghorn. 1–27.

[6] A destination like Venice also drew many apprentice diplomats, who were attracted by the politics of its unique republican tradition.

Figure 0.1 *A young man sets out on his travel.* ©The Trustees of the British Museum

Grand Duke of Tuscany, tasked with acquiring information about and illustrations of the achievements of other nations in the field of manufacturing ('quanto le altre nazioni abbiano d'industrioso e di singolare in ogni genere di fabbrica').[7]

Another enduring stereotype is that women never took part in the Grand Tour.[8] It is true that the challenge of travelling was seen by many aristocratic families as an opportunity to fashion the masculinity of their adolescent sons.[9] But when a continental tour came to be viewed as a way of making sense of the social and cultural differences exhibited by foreigners, not only did women play a major part in it, but they actually became as prolific as men in travel writing.

---

[7] His correspondence is remarkable, including from a linguistic point of view. For example, he found the mediation of interpreters both unsatisfactory and stressful, and after three years away from home, his diary was affected by regular contaminations from French. Some examples are *pussare* 'to push' for *spingere*, *turnare* ('to turn') for *girare*, *addrezzo* ('address') for *indirizzo*, *loaggio* ('loan') for *noleggio*, *argento* ('money') for *denaro*, *mondo* ('people') for *gente*. Francesco Martelli, 'Introduzione', *Il Viaggio in Europa di Pietro Guerrini (1682–1686)*, (Florence, 2005) vol. I, LXXXVIII, 139 and note 249.

[8] Geoffrey Trease, for example, in *The Grand Tour* does not discuss the question of how and why the feminine experience differed from the masculine: 'Women, of course, had never made the Grand Tour in a strict sense. Their educational needs did not call for foreign travels' (London, 1967), 191.

[9] See notably Michèle Cohen, *Fashioning Masculinity: National Identity and language in the Eighteenth Century* (London and New York, 1996).

The number of travel accounts written by women towards the end of the Grand Tour leaves no doubt about their intellectual motivation and interest in targeting their publications to a female readership.[10] Finally, while today many people believe that certain nationalities are more inclined than others to learn foreign languages, in early modern Europe we can find a great deal of evidence that such motivation depended on the cultural climate rather than national background.[11]

This book deals with the tradition of the Grand Tour in its broad sense and attempts to survey the linguistic experiences of all travellers – male and female – as gleaned from a selection of the immense range of documentary materials available. Although much of travel writing and other reference materials relating to language on the Tour concern a number of different nationalities, the majority of primary and secondary sources consulted for this study involve English as the native language of the travellers, and French and Italian as the languages of their destinations. This is not a matter of personal preference: the choice highlights the fact that, during the three hundred years of the period under consideration, by far the majority of the travellers were British, and the two countries that attracted them most were France and Italy. The discussion deals with a wide range of topics, which have been chosen to foreground attitudes to language, and changes in attitudes of this social group, or rather community, of young men and women who were inspired by the same cultural tradition. If the notion of 'community' implies too strong a sense of cohesion and solidarity among these travellers, one must remember that the heritage of the Grand Tour, transmitted from one generation to the next, was international in scope, as was the sense of a common purpose. Awareness of a common purpose is traceable to the early years of these travels, and is best expressed by the notion of a 'College of Travellers', as coined by the diplomat and politician Sir Henry Wotton. He used this phrase specifically to depict a group of people who went abroad looking for opportunities to improve themselves and their prospects.[12] Similar notions were expressed by others, for example James Howell, who referred to a 'moving Academy' or 'the true Peripatetique Schoole' to emphasise the intellectual benefits of travel.[13]

---

[10] See the significant number of entries in R. S. Pine-Coffin, *Bibliography of British and American Travel in Italy to 1860* (Florence, 1974), and the discussions in Brian Dolan, *Ladies of the Grand Tour* (London, 2001) and in Sweet, *Cities and the Grand Tour*.

[11] For example, the Dutch who embarked on the *Groote Tour* showed the same tendencies as the English about language learning. Much against the instructions in travel manuals, they stuck to their own company, and if they made an effort to converse with foreigners, it was with 'notable persons' rather than ordinary citizens. And when the English were in the Low Countries, they behaved in exactly the same way. C. D. van Strien, *British Travellers in Holland During the Stuart Period: Edward Browne and John Locke as Tourists in the United Provinces* (Leiden, 1993), especially 97–100. See also Anna Frank van Westrienen, *De Groote Tour* (Amsterdam, 1983), 341–3.

[12] Cited in Stoye, *English Travellers*, 93.

[13] James Howell, *Instructions for Forraine Travell* (London, 1642), 13.

The idea of travellers as a community of scholars on the move is clearly an early one in the tradition of the Grand Tour. However, precisely because this notion survived for so long and provided an element of continuity, it is useful to draw a distinction between different stages of the Tour, as shifts in cultural and political patterns during that period of European history influenced the motivation and linguistic training of the travellers in different ways before their departure, as well as their attitudes to language and usage while travelling. The main point is that, over its three-century duration, the evolution of the Grand Tour as a social institution was conditioned, year by year, by the general history of Europe.

Before the dawn of early modern Europe, travellers could usually be divided into those who travelled as an obligation – military, diplomatic, mercantile – and those who made a journey by choice. The latter were largely pilgrims and students. Pilgrims followed two main itineraries across continental Europe, either aiming for Santiago de Compostela in Spain, or making their way to Italy, bound for Rome, the capital of Christianity, or Venice, where they usually embarked for the Holy Land. Such pilgrimages from northern and central Europe declined with the Reformation, which, however, never really challenged the attraction of Rome and the desire to explore the magnificence of the Holy City.[14] The Italian peninsula also hosted a number of aristocratic and republican city-states which attracted much curiosity from early travellers for their strong political traditions. Some ancient Italian cities were also the home of the most famous universities in Europe, and even before the Reformation a great number of foreign students from most European countries sought residence in these places. In the second half of the sixteenth century, this movement of scholars slowed down, partly due to the practical obstructions created by the Counter-Reformation, partly because of the risk of indoctrination as perceived by the governments and religious authorities of some Protestant countries. The university of Padua, located in the Venetian Republic, was soon preferred for its liberal approach, whilst the older university of Bologna, situated in a Papal State, was under the close control of the Catholic Church.[15] The attraction of Italian universities continued during Elizabeth's reign in England, but the queen, who had been excommunicated by the Pope in 1570, decided to restrict free movement of her subjects to the Continent, and she felt it necessary to introduce a system of controls to monitor movement and regulate the education of the aristocracy abroad.

---

[14] On the attraction of Rome over the centuries, see Brian Barefoot, *The English Road to Rome* (Upton-upon-Severn, Worcs, 1993).

[15] Giorgio Fedalto, 'Stranieri a Venezia e a Padova', *Storia della Cultura Veneta, 3/1, Dal primo Quattrocento al concilio di Trento*, Girolamo Arnaldi and Manlio Pastore Stocchi (eds.), (Vicenza, 1980), 501–14.

A new approach to travel (called *peregrinari* rather than *vagari*), which differed from the experiences of pilgrims and itinerant students, emerged explicitly for the purpose of gathering empirical knowledge.[16] It was the university of Padua, with its international academic community, that conceived a new art or method of travelling, *ars apodemica*, involving the analysis of an activity on any given subject, and free from ecclesiastical influence. However, those who exported Padua's methodology to Protestant countries were German scholars, whose publications in Latin and the vernaculars spread this new approach to scholarship within central and northern Europe.[17] In this way, the formal doctrine of travel, that is to say a methodical approach to travel at the inception of the Grand Tour, emerged as a combination of the humanistic culture of Europe and the new Reformed mentality, which was more supportive of the notion of travel as an instrument of education. After the Counter-Reformation, the second half of the sixteenth century saw tensions between Catholics in France and Italy and Protestants elsewhere, although not enough to discourage the travelling plans of the most motivated travellers and students.

In England, the young men who managed to obtain a royal licence to travel on the Continent felt they were contributing to the cultural prosperity of their country while maintaining vital links with the main academies and cultural centres of Europe. From the early decades of the seventeenth century, in the intervals between European wars, it was common practice for male members of the English gentry to leave home and travel abroad with a programmatic set of introductions to continental aristocracies. The aim was to familiarise the younger generations with new ways of looking at the world, whether through conversation with famous people or through observing different cultures, with the ultimate purpose of acquiring mastery in the use of foreign languages. The challenges and privations experienced in foreign lands were regarded as a necessary complement to academic training and a prerequisite for any man of distinction embarking on a prestigious governmental career.

From the 1630s onwards, the general atmosphere surrounding religious controversies in the Continent eased. In England, the king had married a French Catholic, which made travellers feel much less worried about visiting Rome. In the Papal States, Inquisition officers were more discreet in their interrogations and more tolerant during investigations. In the middle of the seventeenth century,

---

[16] Justin Stagl, 'The methodising of travel in the 16th century: a tale of three cities', *History and Anthropology*, 4, 1990, 303–38.

[17] Stagl identifies about 300 books and booklets of instructions for travellers published in Latin and the vernaculars from the late sixteenth century to the end of the eighteenth century. The most influential works were those of Theodor Zwinger, Hugo Blotius, Hieronymus Turler and Hilarius Pyrckmair, who were all followers of Petrus Ramus's philosophy. These books of instructions included detailed suggestions to travellers about acquiring knowledge of a language, such as entering into a conversation, adapting oneself to new customs, and avoiding segregation with speakers of the same language, 309.

however, when England was torn apart by civil war, a large number of the nobility sent their children to be brought up in France to protect them from political and religious strife. Also around the middle of that century, some English travellers who reached Italy began to cultivate a passion for collecting art. A new class of traveller – people who were not necessarily close to the court but who were immensely wealthy themselves – felt that an art collection could become a strong indicator of social sophistication and political power. The first century of the Grand Tour proper was coming to an end, and perceptions about language held by most Grand Tourists were beginning to change. Latin was still appreciated for training in classical studies, but the emerging interest in the classical arts and cosmopolitan life was shifting the emphasis to the mastery of living languages. Italian was useful for travelling and assembling collections, while French was rapidly becoming the new language of international socialisation. This change in attitude to contemporary languages marked the transition of the Grand Tour from the seventeenth to the eighteenth century.

In the new century, continental touring became less systematic and more adventurous, as a taste for socialising increasingly developed while much of the stress on education fell by the wayside. Although travellers still learned foreign languages during their journeys, they ceased to make enormous efforts to become outstanding polyglots or even achieve the standard of a good linguist. Yet the fashion for travelling spread, and the number of Grand Tourists on the Continent increased. After the succession of the Hanoverians in 1714, Britain was free from internal political and religious conflicts but was at war with France, and these hostilities lasted for most of the century. This did not put an end to touring but it complicated the life of British travellers crossing continental Europe, who were forced to endure slow expeditions, especially through France and Italy. The boost in tourism in the eighteenth century was due especially to economic and cultural prosperity, which spread quite evenly throughout Europe. Both Great Britain and France made more money available to the new social elites, and tourism found fertile ground with the nouveaux riches. This was because the new middle classes in Britain and in France were not only wealthy but were increasingly envious of the exclusive habits and fashions of their aristocracies. Moreover, the output of daily newspapers and magazines increased conformism and spread consumerism. A minority of tourists still retained something of the original spirit of touring which had led early travellers to invest time in academic training or disciplines suitable for careers in politics, law and the sciences. But cosmopolitan socialites were on the increase: ambitious young men, dilettantes and connoisseurs in the field of art – for most of them the idea of the Grand Tour was to spend time in Italy assembling a personal art collection.[18]

---

[18] See Edgard Peters Bowron and Joseph J. Rishel (eds.), *Art in Rome in the Eighteenth Century* (London, 1997).

By the middle of the eighteenth century, the contrast between the prosperity in Britain and the decline of Italy, a country that had been so much celebrated by earlier travellers, exacerbated the attitudes of superiority held by fashionable tourists. They despised the locals of the same social standing and distrusted those from the lower classes, suspecting them all of subterfuges for exploiting tourists. They avoided foreigners on most social occasions and turned to their fellow tourists for company. Englishmen excluded locals from their own parties and felt no motivation to attempt conversations in foreign languages, let alone learn them.

It used to be commonly thought that the French Revolution killed the Grand Tour or, at least, that the revolutionary years were the beginning of the end of that institution. Certainly the upheaval of the Revolution brought many aristocratic traditions to an end and, above all, extinguished the cosmopolitan spirit that had spread amongst the European nobility in the century of the Enlightenment. If the French Revolution marked the beginning of the end of an old-fashioned style of travel, the Napoleonic wars into which the Revolution merged caused its final collapse. With the new system of faster roads, built by Napoleon to increase military mobility, followed by the rapid extension of the continental railways, Europeans experienced how train travel shrank distances within Europe. For the increasing number of Britons who crossed the Channel by a steamer and reached Italy by train, travelling was becoming a highly organised routine, carefully planned and implemented by the forerunners of mass tourism. The grandiose once-in-a-lifetime travel programme typical of the Grand Tour became unnecessary. Touring was suddenly something ordinary people could undertake, that is to say anyone with a certain amount of money to spend. Typical foreign visitors to Italy in the previous centuries, those of high birth with wealth, leisure time and knowledge of the country's art and history, were becoming rare. The new middle-class visitor, with a modest purse, restricted time, and either little prior cultural knowledge or an intense but specialised focus, was increasingly common. John Ruskin, who made the famous comment that 'the benefit of travel varies inversely in proportion to its speed', was one of the last of the Grand Tourists to travel in the old-fashioned style, and felt a true hatred for the railway system:

the poor modern slaves and simpletons, who let themselves be dragged like cattle ... through the countries they imagine themselves visiting, can have no conception whatever of the complex joys, and ingenuous hopes, connected with the choice and arrangement of the travelling carriage in old times.[19]

---

[19] John Ruskin, *Praæterita* ([1886] London, 1907), vol. II, 154.

Development of Travel Writing

During the early modern period, a great quantity of travel books were published in the main cultural centres of Europe. The output included a variety of publications, some of which enjoyed several national editions; others were translated into the major languages of the time, suggesting a rapidly developing interest in the new experiences made available through travel literature. Originally, personal impressions were of less importance than descriptions of the sights and monuments they encountered in the course of their travels. With time, however, interest also arose in the different people and cultures observed by writers. This perspective came to shape the image of our culturally diverse Europe which, over the course of centuries, contributed to the definition of national identities and the modern concept of 'otherness'. In addition to the large number of printed travel books, some of which have become classics in their national literary traditions, over the three hundred years of the Grand Tour, a wealth of unpublished manuscripts was left by the multitude of travellers, contributing to an immense repository of source material, with new items still being discovered today in public libraries and private archives. Within these vast and eclectic chronicles, it is useful to differentiate between the works of those travellers who placed what they encountered in their journeys at the centre of their narrative and the authors who focused primarily upon themselves, their memories and reactions. The former category includes reports of what to see and do in foreign countries, and this class has expanded into the broad category of travel guidebooks. The latter, where personal observations were the focus, comprises texts that were originally in the format of diaries and letters, many of which showed clearly that travelling as a leisure pursuit was coupled with the pleasure of writing about it.[20]

However, titles of travel books are not always a reliable guide to their contents, and classification based on the title, while possibly suitable for archives and libraries, can be misleading for readers and researchers. The vast body of travel writing from the early era of the Grand Tour consists of publications which the authors unassumingly called *Letters* or *Memories*, some of which include meticulous descriptions of towns and antiquities visited during a journey that was planned with the production of a resource for future

---

[20] This point is made by Pine-Coffin in his *British and American Travel*, 55–6, and by many other Grand Tour scholars. To give an idea of the appeal of travel books in this period, suffice it to mention that many were written by authors who had never been to the country in question. A famous case in point discussed by Sweet in *Cities and the Grand Tour*, 15, n45, is that of Thomas Nugent, author of what became a standard guidebook to Europe for many generations of travellers. Thomas Nugent, *The Grand Tour; Or, A Journey Through the Netherlands, Germany, Italy, and France*, 4 vols. (London, 1778), another is Madame d'Aulnoy, author of *Relation du voyage d'Espagne*, mentioned by Antoni Mączak, *Travel in Early Modern Europe* (Cambridge, 1995), 142–3. See Chapter 9.

travellers in mind. On the other hand, many books improperly entitled *Tour* or *Journey* offer no more than sketchy accounts of the movements and expenses incurred, motivated solely by reporting this to families and sponsors. There are also other and possibly more significant distinctions to be drawn. Some texts published as travel books were actually not written by the travellers themselves. This happened especially when journeys were sponsored by public institutions or relatives, and in many such cases the real author was a tutor or governor, or an experienced secretary appointed to take care of all the needs of a young traveller. As for the status of the various travel accounts, some were written by members of the nobility who went abroad in an official or semi-official capacity: i.e. diplomats, envoys, observers, secret agents or even spies. However, a large number of journals were genuine reports by young men sent abroad when the fashion of foreign travel spread, and a written account of their newly acquired knowledge was appreciated as evidence of an authentic experience abroad.

Until the Renaissance, travel accounts tended to be more scholarly than autobiographical, due to the fact that personal impressions of new lands or remarks about foreign people were deemed of secondary importance to descriptions of towns and an inventory of their monuments and antiquities. When interest in genuine accounts of personal experiences challenged the collecting of second-hand information or even outright fabrications about the wonders of foreign lands, travellers needed to create a new style for reporting their eyewitness testimonies about foreign lands. Their inspiration came from the narratives of pilgrims, the first true adventurers who travelled by choice and not through obligation. Even in the sixteenth century, especially before the Reformation, many pilgrims from all over Europe undertook difficult long-distance journeys in order to perform an act of religious devotion. The rhetoric and vocabulary they used to describe their pilgrimages offered an ideal model to writers of leisure travel accounts, and held the double advantage of being widely accessible while providing descriptions of the hazards of the journey that could serve as an example of the challenges faced by everyone on the road.[21] From the second half of the sixteenth century, travellers who drew on pilgrim narratives produced travel accounts which were not much different from earlier works, either in the narrative style – many titles were almost the same, for example *Report* or *Relation* or, more colourfully, Coryat's *Crudities* (1608) and Lithgow's *Painfull Peregrination* (1609) – or the itineraries covered – the final destination still being Rome or Venice, although not quite for

---

[21] The evolution of travel books and the different perspectives their authors took during the early modern period is too large a topic to enter into here, but for a useful introduction see Peter Hulme and Tim Youngs (eds), *The Cambridge Companion to Travel Writing* (Cambridge, 2002), especially William Sherman, 'Stirrings and Searchings (1500–1720)', 17–36, and James Buzard, 'The Grand Tour and after (1660–1840)', 37–52.

the same reasons.[22] There was no other type of travel narrative that could offer an equally useful model. Explorers by and large were not interested in writing, and reports by merchants attached to these journeys had a financial emphasis that contaminated the virtuosity of their correspondence. As for the diplomatic community, their diaries and letters contained eloquent statements serving a political function and well-informed expressions of familiarity with foreign people, including languages and customs. What changed the style of travel writing was the advent of an approach that turned the journey into a proper educational experience. Following instructions based on the *ars apodemica*, travellers could refer to a number of publications that suggested a method for a progressive construction of knowledge. These prescribed, above all, exploring classical *topoi*, linking the sources of knowledge of the past with the new expressions of modern civilisation. At the end of the sixteenth century, most readers of travel books were no longer pilgrims or ambassadors, but educated men who were often travellers themselves. Indeed, among the regions of Europe which had undergone the Reformation, England was developing a special interest in travel books, as its aristocracy was committed to knowledge acquisition, especially because political and diplomatic appointments required literary and linguistic training.[23]

A departure from the conventional description of foreign nations, which had been useful to medieval pilgrims and merchants, is clear from the new attention directed to what cities had to offer modern eyes. Travellers were now expected to establish links between the classical ruins of the past and newly discovered architectural techniques, if possible recorded in a sketchbook. Another suggestion was to examine the layout of urban developments enclosed by town walls, with a view to comparing the shape of cities with illustrations on maps and in guide books, something that was best achieved by climbing to the highest vantage point to gain a clear impression from above.[24] The situation changed over the course of the seventeenth century, when a large number of young travellers who were sent abroad by their families felt under a moral obligation to compile a personal memoir as evidence of their educational experience. Francis Bacon was fully aware that travel attracted a wide variety of people, and that the benefits of writing and reading a travel account were not the same for everyone. In his essay *Of Travel* (1625), he had a rather nice way of

---

[22] Thomas Coryat, *Coryat's Crudities: Hastily Gobled up in Five Moneths Travells in France, Savoy, Italy, Rhetia . . . Helvetia . . . Some Parts of High Germany and the Netherlands* (London, 1611) rpt. 2 vols. (Glasgow, 1905); William Lithgow, *Rare Adventures and Painful Peregrinations by W. Lithgow* (London, 1609), rpt. 1906.

[23] Joan-Pau Rubiés, 'Instructions for travellers: teaching the eye to see', *History and Anthropology*, 9, 2–3 (1996), 139–190. Rubiés reports that the new genre of travel books peaked between 1570 and 1630, when the main innovative feature of travel materials that were no longer aimed at pilgrims going to the Holy Land was the secularisation of knowledge,165.

[24] Stagl, 'The methodising of travel', 320.

Figure 0.2 *Bononia vetustissima* ('The ancient city of Bologna'), 1688.
Engraving from *Topographia Italiae* by Matthäus Merian (1593–1650)

expressing the advantage of keeping such records for everyone involved in
a tour: in order to bear witness to the education of the young or the experience
of the elderly. That wisdom made an impact on most travellers of his time, and
one of them, the not so young James Howell, in 1642 produced an eloquent
argument for the use of diaries:

He muſt alwayes have a Diary about him, when he is in motion of Iourneys, to ſet down
what [either his eares heare, or] his Eyes meetes with moſt remarquable in the day time,
out of which he may raiſe matter of diſcours at night, and let him take it for a rule, that
*Hee offend leſſe who writes many toyes, than he, who omits one ſerious thing. For the
Penne maketh the deepeſt furrowes, and doth fertiliſe, and enrich the memory more than
any thing elſe, Littera* ſcripta *manet,* sed *manant* lubrica *verba.*[25]

Also, around the middle of the century, travel sponsorship by The Royal
Society of England provided an impetus for travel writing and contributed to
shape the new genre. This learned society for the sciences issued guidelines to
incentivise travellers abroad to write accounts that would serve the public
interest. As this convention spread widely to most countries, traveller-authors
became more and more aware of what sponsors and publishers expected from
them. They knew what to look for in foreign countries, how to record personal
observations and how to write about this in a way that would engage readers.

[25] Howell, *Instructions,* 20.

But with the increase in travel literature, the genre ceased to be uniform. In the eighteenth century, some authors decided to stick to the traditional model and offer an objective account of the places they visited, while others were openly subjective and coloured their descriptions with personal opinions. A new category of professional travel writers was emerging, and their motivation to please readers was even stronger than that of drawing personal pleasure from their visits and observations.[26]

In the early days of travel, reprints and translations were the normal means of making successful publications available to readers in different countries and speakers of other languages. However, it was not unusual for translators to fine-tune a travel book to suit the tastes of another readership – if they felt that the content was too strongly biased by the opinion of the original author, they rewrote it entirely to meet the different perspectives of their audiences. But in keeping with the international culture of the Renaissance, the humanistic school of the *Res Publica Litterarum* encouraged the free circulation of written materials and enabled intellectuals to correspond with each other from great distances. Accordingly, readers of travel books could share their common interest across linguistic and cultural boundaries.[27] This came to an end with the Protestant Reformation and the Catholic Counter-Reformation. When religious prejudices became exacerbated, political suspicion and popular sensitivity suddenly increased with regard to the content of published materials, particularly travel books. This was also the time when many travel accounts began to mix the approach of pure travel guides with personal memoirs. Although writers claimed objectivity in order to appeal to an international market, the religious perspective assumed by some authors was a cause for concern and often for condemnation. The new climate of intolerance affected the process of reworking materials for a different audience. Not only did the reality of the Protestant north vs. the Catholic south make travellers uncomfortable on their journeys, but also the tensions between and within most European countries, which were increasingly divided by religious and political conflicts, disrupted writers' and translators' initiatives.

In the seventeenth century, one of the most important books on travelling in Italy was Richard Lassels' *Voyage of Italy* (1670), written in English but published in Paris, where it enjoyed the privilege of French and German translations. Lassels was a Catholic priest, and his book wielded some influence at the time, although his perspective was coloured by his extreme religious attitude. Towards the end of the century, even authors who were religiously

---

[26] Black, *The British Abroad,* especially xi–xiii, identifies waves of British hostility in such literature, from religious and ideological prejudices to travel snobbery that emerged in the middle of the eighteenth century. Jeremy Black, *The British Abroad: The Grand Tour in the Eighteenth Century* (New York, 1992).

[27] Marc Fumaroli, *La République des Lettres* (Paris, 2015), especially 33–55.

intolerant gradually produced less biased and more detached observations about other civilisations. As the touring fashion spread widely in the eighteenth century, travel books greatly increased in number, and quite a few began to include information of all kinds, from the amazing to the predictable. While some writers travelled in order to acquire specialist knowledge about architecture, art or antiquities, an increasing number visited the same places, admired the same sights and produced the same comments. For many travellers, the visit abroad was becoming more of an excuse to seek amusement than to learn through inspection and observation. Towards the end of the eighteenth century, most guidebooks were beginning to owe their popularity to the information they provided on the day-to-day running of a typical journey, with practical suggestions for routes and accommodation, rather than reflections on art and antiquities. This trend led to the production of a new type of book that was proving useful – a traveller's pocket guide, as opposed to a book meant for leisurely reading at home.

It seems typical of the tourist culture of the early modern period that, while religion had ceased to be an issue leading to persecution, it continued to be a matter of fixation. *A Tour Through Italy*, which ran to six editions between 1813 and 1841, providing a comprehensive and well-balanced account of all aspects of Italian life, was one of the most popular travel books of the time. It is interesting that its author, John Eustace, who was a Catholic priest, later in life regretted some of his more liberal opinions as expressed in this book. Indeed, throughout the duration of the Grand Tour, we find within the pages not only of descriptive travel books but also of personal memoirs that religion was both an issue of contention and an excuse for animosity. An English lady, Harriet Morton, felt it appropriate to name her book on Italy *Protestant Vigils* (1826), although its content did not deal with religious observations at all. Another visitor, Henry Digby Beste, as late as 1826 gave his book the title *Italy as It Is*, with a view to challenging Protestant prejudices. But the criticism of Catholicism continued throughout the century, sometimes in order to air pedantic arguments (as in *A Pilgrimage to Rome* by Michael Hobart Seymour, 1844), sometimes for the sake of controversy (*Rome Pagan and Papal* by Henry Wreford, 1845).

Unsurprisingly, the advent of railways and steamboats had such a huge impact on the Grand Tour that the titles of many books reflected the changing flavour of tourism, drawing attention to the new futuristic style of travelling. Some authors spelt out the advantages of rapid transportation, as shown in titles such as *A Trip to Rome, at Railways Speed* by Thomas Barlow (1836), *Journal of a Steam Voyage down the Danube to Constantinople* by Robert Snow (1842) and *Tour on the Continent by Rail and Road* by John Barrow (1852). As the Grand Tour declined, slower modes of travel were signalled overtly in book titles as a sign of eccentricity or of an old-fashioned taste for adventure: *A Ride on Horseback to Florence Through France and Switzerland* was written in 1838 by a woman, Mrs Dalkeith Holmes. When Joshua Lucock Wilkinson entitled his book *The Wanderer* (1798), referring to 'a ramble on foot', he possibly did not expect to inaugurate a fashion for travelling on foot by choice, in contrast to the poorer solo travellers in the past who covered thousands of miles on foot through necessity. The new trend of eccentric visitors touring on foot that emerged against the advances of modern transport resulted in books such as Charles James Latrobe's *The Pedestrian* (1830), George Hume Weatherhead's *A Pedestrian Tour Through France and Italy* (1834) and Arthur John Strutt's *A Pedestrian Tour in Calabria & Sicily* (1842).

Just as the mode of travel was changing rapidly, so was the flavour of travel book titles, as shown in *Change of Air* by James Johnson (1831), *'Mems' of a Ten Weeks' Continental Trip* by an anonymous author (1850), and most telling of all, *Rome Seen in a Week* by the prolific Italian author and publisher Luigi Piale (1853). The new mood of tourism filtered through into attitudes and emotions about travelling. Titles such as *Diary of an ennuyée* by Anna Jameson (1821), *A Spinster's Tour in France* by Elizabeth Strutt (1828), *Consolations in Travel* by Humphry Davy (1827) and *Solitary Walks Through Many Lands* by Henry David Inglis (1828) definitively signalled the dawn of the romantic age of travel. The evolution of the Grand Tour is best summarised by the titles of two travel accounts separated by some three hundred years of the history of this genre: Andrew Boorde's *Introduction of Knowledge* (1547?), which stresses travel as an educational experience, and Thomas Noon Talfourd's *Vacation Rambles* (1845), which is an obvious hymn of praise to the modern flâneur.

Language in Travel Accounts

Awareness of language, in the sense of conscious perception and personal views about language, emerges from travel writings in relation to two separate kinds of issue: experiencing a new language environment, and coping in a non-native language. From this perspective, sudden exposure to linguistic diversity abroad stands out as providing a major occasion for re-thinking language issues: in particular, the discovery that separate communities and diverse social groups used the 'same' language in very different ways. This is certainly more striking abroad than within one's own political and cultural boundaries. As for travellers' perception of their own linguistic performance abroad, the critical point was the realisation that knowledge of a foreign language was actually not quite the same thing as the ability to converse in that language with socially diverse groups of speakers. Indeed, the challenge of coping with a real-life situation abroad had little similarity to the comfortable experience of practising the foreign language with an instructor at home or at school. This true test of conversational competence brought with it the realisation that speaking a foreign language was like performing a different act of identity. Some travellers developed an awareness of the interplay between their native and non-native language; and a few also commented that it brought them emotional distress as well as personal enrichment. Of course, this incipient bilingualism was more evident in travellers who were engaged in writing about their travel experiences since they mainly used the foreign tongue for speaking but wrote in their native language. The revelation that a foreign language was a complex reality with little homogeneity and a myriad of linguistic forms, very different from the literary language, was cause for wonder and disorientation. The distance between the written language model studied at home and the multitude of phonetic variations in the spoken language heard on the road explains the great attraction for those localities with an international reputation for speaking the purest forms of a language. John Henley, better known by the appellation Orator Henley due to his interest in elocution, summarised this viewpoint in *The Complete Linguist, or an Universal Grammar of All Considerable Tongues in Being* (1719):

> As there is in every country some place where the living tongue is the most perfect, that is, among the knowing, both for standard and utterance, writing and conversation; as, for instance, Toledo is esteem'd the local standard of the Spanish; Blois of the French; London of the English; Leipsick of the High Dutch, &c, so Rome and Siena of the Italian; one for the delicacy of the tongue, the other for the justness of prounouncing.[28]

The international reputation of such cities rested on the fact that everyone was said to be a native speaker of the form of the language celebrated by teachers. This is why the most exciting prospect for most travellers was to secure a period of residence in one of these privileged cities. Most travellers were absorbed by acquiring the 'right' language rather than learning about its different varieties, and only some indulged in exploring the effects of conducting their everyday lives through two languages. But the very few who were seriously engaged in writing their travel accounts felt quite taken by the unusual experience of adapting their native language in order to describe the reality of a foreign culture. There was a mismatch between their daily efforts to communicate in one language and report about it in another. But disappointingly, most travellers did not take the opportunity to reflect on this. The main function of travel accounts was to share personal observations about foreign societies, while reflections on their bilingual experience were more likely to disclose private aspects of their public persona. Today there is a more general awareness that use of two languages can cause interference but at the same time also enhance linguistic performance. Even at that time, a small number of travellers seemed to be aware of this fact, and felt that it was right to address the mismatch in

---

[28] John Henley, *The Compleat Linguist. Or, an Universal Grammar of All Considerable Tongues in Being. A Grammar of the Italian Tongue*. Number. II. September, 1719 (London), II–III.

order to gain better control of their bilingual skills. Since early in the seventeenth century, when more stress was laid on the educational investment of
a Grand Tour, and travellers felt under close scrutiny from families and patrons,
the motivation for writing in a foreign language came from the genuine desire
to please the sponsors. Brennan offers the examples of some young men from
the Loire Valley, and many more are given by John Stoye, such as that of Cecil
William, who kept a diary in French and Sir John Harrington, who wrote formal
courtesy letters home in both Italian and Latin; Francis Windebank in 1607 and
Thomas Rowlandson in 1615, both of whom wrote in Italian from Italy as proof
of their industry, as did Henry Neville, who was there in the middle of the
century.[29] Unsurprisingly, in the cases of all these young men, the combination
of early knowledge about foreign countries and high-level mastery of foreign
languages earned them prominent positions in politics and the court.

In Peter Burke's 2004 study *Languages and Communities in Early Modern
Europe*, he makes the point that 'there is so much to be learned from the
descriptions of countries by foreign travellers, whose ears are sometimes well-
tuned to the distinctive qualities of local speech'.[30] This was certainly the case
for a minority of travellers who felt intrigued by the social linguistic differences
they encountered or by strange features of local speech. But for the majority,
especially in the heyday of the Grand Tour, language matters did not figure
among their prime interests, and first-hand remarks about social functions of
language were few. This is possibly why among the vast amount of research
literature available in English, until very recently not a single study can be
found on the linguistic experiences of travellers who undertook the tour.
Recently, John Gallagher has given two remarkable examples of how it is
possible to reconstruct the linguistic profiles of travellers on the Grand Tour.
For one of them, the young Protestant Sir Philip Perceval, who travelled to
France and Italy between 1676 and 1679, the historian integrated materials
from personal correspondence with the diary of Perceval's famous tutor, Jean
Gailhard, author of *The Compleat Gentleman*.[31] Gallagher's analysis brings to
light a wide range of interconnected experiences of language use and

---

[29] Stoye, *English Travellers,* considers problematic the attribution of the diary to Thomas Abdy,
and mentions also the travel writings of Cecil Williams (p. 28), John Harrington (p. 83), Francis
Windebank (p. 106), Thomas Rowlandson (p. 116) and Henry Neville (p. 137). The most famous
example is Michel de Montaigne who, in the middle of his journey through Italy, decided not to
deprive himself of this unique opportunity to fine-tune his written Italian. Far from being an
improvised text employing broken colloquial language, his narrative is written in a gentle prose
style, with the occasional idiom picked up on the road tastefully inserted with classical
eloquence. See Chapter 4.

[30] Peter Burke, *Languages and Communities in Early Modern Europe* (Cambridge, 2004), 11.

[31] On Jean Gailhard, 'gouverneur', a tutor specialising in foreign travel, see Jean Boutier,
'Compétence internationale, émergence d'une 'profession' et circulation des savoirs. Le tuteur
aristocratique dans l'Angleterre du XVIIe siècle', in Maria-Pia Paoli (ed.), *Saperi in Movimento*
(Pisa, 2009), 149–77.

acquisition involving the young aristocrat and his entourage: multilingual correspondence with polyglot relatives; use of guidebooks and histories of cities in the target languages; interactions with his tutor, servants and teachers enriched by instances of language-switching; the relationship between reading and language-learning.[32] The second traveller is John North, whose efforts to retain his language skills and cultivate bilingual competence while living in London after a tour of Italy reveals a singular interest in a hybrid identity by an Italianate Englishman.[33] North did not feel intimidated by the dominant anti-Italian atmosphere of the time; rather, proud of his newly acquired identity, he kept a diary in Italian, not merely as a means of practising the language, but also as a way of experiencing life in his native environment from this new cosmopolitan perspective.

Two quite different investigations into the language of the Grand Tour were published in Italy. One is the short but most valuable study *Lingua e dialetti d'Italia nella percezione dei viaggiatori sette-ottocenteschi* by Luca Serianni (2002).[34] The author discusses reflections on Italian linguistic diversity by many travellers and analyses their language attitudes, especially those expressed in the eighteenth and nineteenth centuries. The essay is rich in historical information and includes many vivid quotations accounting for different perceptions shaped by varying levels of language awareness. The second, *Ricordi di Italiano, Osservazioni intorno alla lingua e italianismi nelle relazioni di viaggio degli inglesi in Italia*, is an earlier study carried out by Gabriella Cartago (1990).[35] This book consists of a large corpus of Italian borrowings mentioned by English travellers in their writings from the sixteenth to the nineteenth centuries. The author examines events and situations that motivated travellers to memorise foreign words, local idioms, expressions and proverbs related to the habits and manners of Italians, many of which were later integrated into the English language. As this book includes a very impressive selection of data collected and classified with great accuracy from primary sources, it is the most valuable publication for anyone interested in language issues during the Grand Tour.

The monumental quantity of research literature on the Grand Tour means it is quite unrealistic to claim that all sources from other disciplines have been

---

[32] John Gallagher, 'The Italian London of John North: Cultural contact and linguistic encounter in Early Modern England', *Renaissance Quarterly* 70 (2017): 88–131.

[33] John Gallagher, '*Language and education on the grand tour of Sir Philip Perceval, 1676-9*', in Helmut Glück, Mark Häberlein and Andreas Flurschütz da Cruz (eds.), *Adel und Mehrsprachigkeit in der Frühen Neuzeit. Ziele, Formen und Praktiken des Erwerbs und Gebrauchs von Fremdsprachen* (Wolfenbüttel, 2019, pp. 113–34).

[34] Luca Serianni, 'Lingua e dialetti d'Italia nella percezione dei viaggiatori sette-ottocenteschi', *Italianistica*, 26 (1997), 471–90, rpt. in Luca Serianni, *Viaggiatori, Musicisti, Poeti, Saggi di Storia della Lingua italiana* (Milan, 2002), 55–88.

[35] Gabriella Cartago, *Ricordi di italiano. Osservazioni intorno alla lingua e italianismi nelle relazioni di viaggio degli inglesi in Italia* (Bassano del Grappa, 1990).

consulted for the present study. However, since a preliminary overview showed just how limited the available linguistic research was, publications relevant to other disciplines became a natural source for mine. The selection surveyed below gives an idea of how such references appeared in the secondary litera-ture, and how they were employed in this exploration of such a large terrain of sociolinguistic relevance.

Two classic and fundamental works on the French language that provide a wide range of data on early modern Europe, offering very useful insights on the Grand Tour, are *Histoire de la langue française des origines à 1900* by Ferdinand Brunot, and *The Teaching and Cultivation of the French Language in England during Tudor and Stuart Times* by Kathleen Lambley. Brunot's book is particularly useful for understanding the social inclinations and cultural ambitions of the British elite regarding the French language and culture, from Elizabethan times to the end of the Ancient Régime.[36] William Edward Mead's book *The Grand Tour in the Eighteenth Century* (1914) offers a valuable examination of the evolution of that cultural tradition, stressing that its original purpose was education and acquaintance with foreign languages. The author reports that the main hurdle to learning foreign languages was the inclination of travellers to associate with fellow countrymen: 'Not too communicative in his own tongue, he might well ask himself why he should go out of his way to exchange commonplaces in bad French or Italian with people he had never seen before and was unlikely ever to meet again for fear of committing some blunder in accent or grammar.'[37] In another classic study, *The Grand Tour* (1967), the popular historian Geoffry Trease surveys three centuries of travellers, from Philip Sidney to John Ruskin. He argues that changes in travellers' attitudes caused a loss of interest in language that set off the decline of that social institution.

Among the studies focusing on a particular historical phase, the book *The English Travellers of the Renaissance* by Clare Howard (1914) focuses on the attitudes of those young men who inaugurated the fashion of travelling abroad for the purpose of language learning.[38] John Lough's *France Observed in the Seventeenth Century by British Travellers* (1985) concentrates on a different historical period. The author analyses the observations and reflections of several generations of travellers, highlighting the daily experiences and educa-tional training of the community of young Englishmen hosted in the Loire valley.[39] Constantia Maxwell's 1932 work *The English Traveller in France 1698–1815* covers the era from the *Ancien Régime* until the Napoleonic wars.

---

[36] Ferdinand Brunot, *Histoire de la langue française des origines a 1900*, 13 vols. (Paris, 1934–5).
[37] Mead, *The Grand Tour*, 115.
[38] Clare Howard, *The English Travellers of the Renaissance* (New York, 1914).
[39] John Lough, *France Observed in the Seventeenth Century by British Travellers* (Stocksfield, 1985).

The book integrates social situations with personal memoirs about travelling, roads, inns, guidebooks and everyday conditions. The author laments the taciturnity of English travellers and reports some reactions to 'drawing-room life', with its celebrated polite conversation that often generated negative comments.[40] John Stoye's 1952 publication *English Travellers Abroad 1604–1667* analyses the influence of continental travel on English society and politics, drawing on a vast range of contemporary sources. The book describes the journeys both of important figures and obscure travellers: a discussion of particular interest deals with the different motives of moderately wealthy travellers, who were mainly townsmen, compared with the aristocratic elites. The author examines in great detail the habit of writing letters and diaries on subjects such as art, architecture and music, but also on education and politics.

The perils and adventures of travelling are the focus of *Travel in Early Modern Europe* (1978) by Antoni Mączak. This book deals with travellers from all over Europe, especially in the sixteenth and seventeenth centuries. It includes a comprehensive survey of various experiences of socialisation on the road, especially coping with practical problems such as crossing frontiers, dealing with foreign bureaucracies, accessing trustworthy guides, negotiating hospitality and seeking introductions to the local nobility. *The Grand Tour in the Eighteenth Century* by Jeremy Black (1992) is a seminal study on the attitudes of British tourists during the height of the Grand Tour. The historian presents unpublished material from library archives and public record offices and analyses a wide range of topics. These include travellers' educational background, their social status, routes and destinations, and practical issues such as costs and expenses, transport, accommodation, food and drink, politics, religion and the arts. Although there is no specific section on language, many linguistic references occur in quotations extracted from diaries and letters. The *Bibliography of British and American Travel in Italy to 1860* by Richard Geoffrey Pine-Coffin (1974) includes an introduction on the evolution of the Grand Tour, complete with evocative quotations. The author stresses the point that the majority of travellers had little contact with the local population: on the one hand, their interactions on the road were limited to innkeepers; and on the other, in the cities they socialised in the salons of the nobility, whose favours they constantly sought. Towards the end of the Grand Tour, a sense of cultural superiority replaced the modesty and curiosity of the early travellers, and many of the reported linguistic episodes illustrate this new tendency.

Many essays of various lengths found in the secondary literature have been most helpful for this study. One category consists of diaries, journals and correspondence from different phases of the Grand Tour, proceeded by an

---

[40] Constantia Maxwell, *The English Traveller in France, 1698–1815*, (London,1932), 40–1, n.2

editor's introduction to the social history of the country of origin or destination. Another category consists of a wide range of books and articles on specific aspects of the Grand Tour, many of which are rich in informative material on language. The latter includes monographs covering a great variety of themes, such as education and language training; conversations in teaching manuals and dialogues in pocket guidebooks; the use of spoken Latin as a lingua franca and elitist and popular taste in music, opera and theatre at home and abroad. Historical studies of the major cities situated along the standard tour itinerary are also rich with information about the presence of travellers and their life in these urban centres. The best account of the observations and emotions of English men and women in the great cities of Italy is by Rosemary Sweet, *Cities and the Grand Tour*. In this exemplary study, the author discusses not only English travellers' reactions to social life and the lessons of history, but also to their changing attitudes towards issues of national, cultural and gender identities. In addition to Sweet, who devotes a substantial amount of discussion to the issue of female domesticity and women's alternative perceptions abroad, the most useful monographs are *Fashioning Masculinity: National Identity and Language in the Eighteenth Century* by Michèle Cohen, and *Pleasure and Guilt on the Grand Tour* by Chloe Chard, both works in the field of cultural history, personal identity and the discovery of 'otherness', which also include important linguistic references.[41]

This Introduction is intended to place my investigations in the wider context of Grand Tour studies and to function as a preview of the main content. The book itself is organised into three parts as follows. Part I – Attitudes and Aptitudes – begins with an examination in Chapter 1 of the views and stereotypes about foreign cultures that travellers absorbed in their home country or developed at their destination. Chapter 2 assesses the positive and negative attitudes held by returning travellers, some of whom went so far as to adopt their favourite aspects of foreign behaviour. The linguistic training of several generations of travellers is discussed against the background of three centuries of social and cultural changes in Chapter 3. Part II – Encounters and Exchanges – focuses on travellers' command of foreign languages while abroad and how they used these to survive and socialise. In particular, Chapter 4 analyses opportunities for language acquisition and learning, while Chapter 5 concentrates on linguistic aids such as conversation manuals and the support of interpreters, mediators and informal teachers. The role of Latin and other lingua francas in communicating abroad is assessed in Chapter 6. Part III – Contrasts and Collisions – focuses on three fundamental sociolinguistic issues, such as standard vs. non-standard varieties (Chapter 7); attitudes to linguistic contact and language mixing (Chapter 8); and conflicting views of

---

[41] Chloe Chard, *Pleasure and Guilt on the Grand Tour* (Manchester, 1999).

language and society by male and female travellers (Chapter 9). Finally, the Conclusion returns to the issue of continuity and change in the tradition of the Grand Tour, with a view to highlighting the historic circumstances that helped motivate foreign language learning and the political changes that gradually corrupted this into the attitude of monolingual complacency.

Part I

Attitudes and Aptitudes

1 Images and Stereotypes

National Character

As it is widely believed that successful language learning depends on positive motivation, the first question we need to address is the relationship between motivation for language acquisition and attitudes to foreigners. It is therefore appropriate to begin with an overview of that vast terrain of stereotypical representations of foreign cultures that were in circulation in Europe at the time of the Grand Tour. A preliminary consideration is that travellers' attitudes differ from those of ordinary people who know their own communities but tend to generalise attributes of populations in countries they have never visited. Since gathering first-hand information was one of the main benefits of travel, young people who went on the road to see the world were in a good position to check preconceptions about foreign cultures against observable realities.[1]

Certainly most travellers, especially in the early days of the Grand Tour, based their opinions on information provided by classical authors, who were considered more authoritative than contemporary writers.[2] However, this changed later when travellers began to equip themselves with published materials containing descriptions of different nationalities. Indeed, many historians have pointed out that, throughout the Grand Tour, it is difficult to distinguish personal views from knowledge travellers had gleaned from books. Another reason for caution is that once the number of Grand

---

[1] Mączak explains that in most cases it is difficult to separate the ideas that travellers gleaned through reading works of other writers from the knowledge they themselves acquired abroad. He also explains that what was emphasised in travellers' descriptions of foreigners did not reflect what they saw, but rather what they were conditioned to expect, *Travel*, 282. From a more trivial viewpoint, the evolution of attitudes and perceptions must have been affected by the degree of comfort and distress they experienced during the journey. Goldsmith, travelling through Italy in 1755, made precisely this point: 'Countries wear very different appearances to travellers of different circumstances. A man who is whirled through Europe in a post-chaise, and the pilgrim who walks the grand tour on foot, will form very different conclusions.' Oliver Goldsmith, *The Miscellaneous Works of Oliver Goldsmith*, in James Prior (ed.), 4 vols. (London, 1837), I, 453.

[2] Classical languages, used by people who had different native languages and cultures, were felt to be lingua francas that functioned to channel shared beliefs and neutral opinions.

Tourists increased to include wealthy commoners, who were generally less open-minded and worldly-wise than their predecessors, perceptions became more dogmatic if not wholly inspired by stereotypes. This is not to say that the early phase of the Grand Tour encouraged more positive and less biased perceptions of others. Attitudes towards foreigners in the sixteenth and seventeenth centuries were exacerbated by religious antagonism far more than in the eighteenth and nineteenth centuries. But once the Catholic Church had ceased its campaign of harassing those who followed other religions, Protestant travellers became more open about stigmatising the character of inhabitants of Catholic lands.[3]

Another point to consider is the source of commonplaces about foreign people and the formation of national stereotypes. It is true that some prejudices had their roots in a pan-European tradition of making generalisations about foreigners but there were also nationally based preconceptions, shown for instance by the fact that Italians and the English did not share the same perceptions about the French. When Arthur Young travelled through Rouen, Montpellier, Nimes, Metz and Avignon in 1785, he found the company of French people everywhere very tedious and their conversation at a restaurant table extremely dull.[4] One year earlier, Marquis Malaspina also toured France and found the French superior and presumptuous, but sociable and good humoured. This Italian aristocrat was a well-travelled man who later became Chamberlain of the Holy Roman Empire and he hesitated at jumping to conclusions about the reputation of the French who, he heard from other travellers, were too

---

[3] Recent studies have demonstrated how the Catholic Church gradually changed its strict policies of persecution of Protestant heretics, both in Rome and other Italian cities, to adopt forms of dialogue and measures of persuasion. Irene Fosi, who based her research on the archives of Sant'Ufficio, has demonstrated that alongside the traditional oppressive system a climate of cultural suasion gradually emerged under Alexander VII. See *Papal Justice: Subjects and Courts in the Papal State, 1500–1750*. Trans. Thomas V. Cohen (Washington DC, 2011). Peter Mazur explains further that the new approach was extended to other Italian cities, where religious missionaries who were able to speak foreign languages were sent by Rome with a view to approaching scholars and young aristocrats, especially of Dutch, German and Scandinavian origin. See *Conversion to Catholicism in Early Modern Italy* (Abingdon, 2016).

[4] Young reports this often, for example in Montpellier, Nîmes, Rouen, Metz, and when in Avignon he writes:

I have often complained of the stupid ignorance I met with at table d'hôte. Here, if possible, it has been worse than common. The politeness of the French is proverbial, but it never could arise from the manners of the classes that frequent these tables. Not one time in forty will a foreigner, as such, receive the least mark of attention. The only political idea here is, that if the English should attack France, they have a million of men in arms to receive them; and their ignorance seems to know no distinction between men in arms in their towns and villages, or in action without the kingdom. Arthur Young, *Travels in France During the Years 1787, 1788, 1789* (London, 1892; rpt. 1906), 255–6.

vain. He wrote quite diplomatically that vanity is a common inclination in all nations, each having developed its own type: 'Germans, Italians and Spaniards are vain about their nobility, English and Dutch about their wealth, and the French about their intellect and esprit.'[5] A common view was that the French possessed a sparkling spirit, a quality which some nationalities appreciated, while others found it excessive and disapproved. Dr Ellis Veryhard, who travelled throughout Europe in the late seventeenth century, noted that 'The French are generally speaking, very curious, confident, inquisitive, credulous, facetious, rather witty than wise, eternal babblers – and in a word, they are at all times what an Englishman is when he's half drunk.'[6]

When Joseph Addison, the author of *Remarks on Several Parts of Italy* (1705), crossed the Channel for a Grand Tour, his main objective was to follow in the footsteps of the ancient poets but his diary soon became filled with observations about the people he encountered in France and Italy:

It is indeed very strange there should be such a diversity of manners, where there is so small a difference in the air and climate. The French are always open, familiar, and talkative: the Italians, on the contrary, are stiff, ceremonious, and reserved. In France every one aims at a gaiety and sprightliness of behaviour, and thinks it an accomplishment to be brisk and lively: the Italians, notwithstanding their natural fieriness of temper, affect always to appear sober and sedate … This difference of manners proceeds chiefly from difference of education: in France it is usual to bring their children into company, and to cherish in them, from their infancy, a kind of forwardness and assurance. … It may be here worth while to consider how it comes to pass, that the common people of Italy have in general so very great an aversion to the French, which every traveller cannot but be sensible of, that has passed through the country.[7]

Addison seems a careful and unbiased observer, but Dr Johnson, who knew him well, read his book with suspicion: 'As his stay in foreign countries was short, his observations are such as might be supplied by a hasty view, and consist chiefly in comparisons of the present face of the country with the descriptions left us by the Roman poets.' Johnson also commented: 'it is not a very severe censure to say that [many parts] might have been written at home'.[8] Horace Walpole, too, observed: 'Mr Addison travelled through the poets, and not

[5] See Alessandro D'Ancona, 'Francia e Italia nel 1786: Nella Relazione del viaggio di G.B. Malaspina', *Nova Antologia*, 16 December 1891, reprinted in Alessandro D'Ancona (ed.), *Viaggiatori e avventurieri* (Florence, 1974), 267.

[6] Ellis Veryard, *An Account of Divers Choice Remarks, etc. Taken in a Journey Through the Low-Countries, France, Italy, and Part of Spain; with the Isles of Sicily and Malta* (London, 1701), 107.

[7] Joseph Addison, *Remarks on Several Parts of Italy etc. in the Years 1701, 1702, 1703* (London, 1705) rpt. 2 vols. (1721), II, 37.

[8] Samuel Johnson, *The Lives of the Most Eminent English Poets with Critical Observations on Their Works*, 3 vols. (London 1801), II, 79–80.

through Italy; for all his ideas are borrowed from the descriptions, and not from the reality.'[9] However, some of the remarks made by Addison on Italian and French behaviour concentrated on the social life of the salon in the two countries, and do some justice to his curiosity:

> The most obvious reason is certainly the great difference that there is in the humours and manners of the two nations, which always works more in the meaner sort, who are notable to vanquish the prejudices of education, than with the nobility. Besides that, the French humour, in regard of the liberties they take in female conversations, and their great ambition to excel in all companies, is in a more particular manner very shocking to the Italians, who are naturally jealous and value themselves upon their great wisdom.[10]

If Addison was inspired by an admiration for classical knowledge, travellers of the following generations showed an interest in a more contemporary view of foreign people, sometimes related to an aesthetic rather than social vision of their cultures. The great painter Joshua Reynolds, founder and first president of the Royal Academy of Arts, having travelled on the Continent looking for philosophical explanations of the notion of 'beautiful', reached an original conclusion in his *Discourses* (1769–90) that counteracted theories of national taste: 'The *gusto grande* of the Italians; the *beau idéal* of the French and *the great style, genius,* and *taste* among the English, are but different appellations of the same thing.'[11]

Despite the constant transformations in the cultural and political circumstances at home and abroad, reflections on 'otherness' led most British travellers to believe that what was going on in their own country was the best, and that their own self-perceived moderation was superior to the excesses seen abroad. On the other hand, if tourists found that the natives abroad had not developed a positive image of their own nation, that was because foreign people were guilty either of ignorance or harbouring preconceptions. The English novelist Frances Trollope, having travelled through Europe and America before settling in Florence, held a strong view about the bad manners of the English abroad:

> I have long been convinced, that the cause why we bear, throughout France, Germany, and Italy, so many unpleasant observations on what are called our *national peculiarities,* arises from the fact, that the respectable class of travellers ... pass through these countries ..., so quietly as not to attract any notice whatever, and therefore the best amongst us cannot act as a balance weight against the worst, because the ordinary observers, who are precisely the people that raise the cry against us, know nothing whatever about them.[12]

---

[9] Letter to Richard West from Florence, 2 October 1740, I, quoted by Donald R. Johnson, 'Addison in Italy', *Modern Languages Studies*, 6 (Spring 1976), 32.

[10] Addison, *Remarks,* 2 vols. (1721), II, 17.

[11] Joshua Reynolds, Third Discourse, in Edward Gilpin Johnson (ed.), *Sir Joshua Reynolds's Discourses* (Chicago 1891), 83.

[12] Frances Milton Trollope, *A Visit to Italy* (London, 1842), 271.

The English reputation as described by Trollope, who was writing in 1842, was not new – it was recorded two and a half centuries earlier in the *Merchant of Venice* (1596), when the beautiful Portia, champion of good manners, mocks an Englishman who 'bought his doublet in Italy, his round in France, his bonnet in Germany, and his behaviour everywhere'. As the Irish journalist and novelist Lady Blessington wrote in *The Idler in Italy* (1823–8), 'The English, more than all other people, carry with them the habits and customs of their own country. It would appear that they travel not so much for the purpose of studying the manners of other lands as for that of establishing and displaying their own.'[13]

Remarks on specific national habits tended to be more reliable than those on national character, as they derived from observable behaviour rather than common stereotypes, which were more often shared by different nationalities. For example, a favourite *topos* of travel writers was to complain about Catholic practices and the excessively ceremonial forms of that religion. Three main points of criticism were the worldliness of the clergy, the predilection of Catholics for extravagant festivities, and widespread superstition about archaic rites and dubious miracles. In return, Italians and Spaniards, who enjoyed an international reputation for sobriety, associated heavy drinking with northern nationalities. On the one hand, table manners, which were readily observable in public places but varied considerably across frontiers, were the object of reproach by all nationalities; on the other, the domestic behaviour of ordinary people remained quite inaccessible to travellers.

Foreign sexual habits were also sources of astonishment for many travellers. Promiscuity and sodomy were often mentioned as being surprising or scandalous, but such comments were seldom considered in the light of their own national practices. Certainly the lure of prostitutes, with Parisian and Venetians courtesans having similar reputations, was a great attraction in both cities. Thomas Coryat proudly describes his *rendez-vous*; Richard Lassels confirms the presence of a high number of such women in Italy; and Boswell's letters and diary offer direct evidence of his vulnerability to the same custom. Criticism of libertine habits abroad must be assessed against the background of what has been pointed out by many Grand Tour historians: 'Some fathers preferred their sons to sow their wild oats abroad instead of at home, where they could not so easily escape the consequences.'[14] One can assume that the wide circulation of portable conversation manuals, including explicit dialogues for special purposes, confirmed that amatory adventures were an essential part of the agenda on continental expeditions.

It does not come as a surprise that John Gailhard's book *The Compleat Gentleman or Directions for the Education of Youth as to Their Breeding at*

---

[13] Countess of Blessington, *The Idler in Italy*, 3 vols. (London, 1839), III, 58.
[14] Pine-Coffin, *British and American Travel*, 50.

Table 1.1 *National character and gender relations in* The Complete Gentleman *by John Gailhard, 1678*

In behaviour	In conversation	In dancing	In speech	In making love
French courteous	The French jovial	The French danceth	The French sings	French diverts his mistress
Spaniard lordly	Spaniard troublesome	Spaniard walketh	Spaniard speaks	Spaniard adoreth her
Italian amorous	Italian complying	Italian vaults	Italian acts the comedy	Italian serveth her
German clownish	German unpleasant	German walloweth himself	German howls	German bestows gifts upon her

Home and Travelling Abroad, published in 1678 in London, included explicit references to men's and women's behaviour for the benefit of young Englishmen abroad. The manual included several entries of the type listed in Table 1.1 and was introduced by these words: 'And now I am upon this Subject, it will not be amiss for me here to insert a character of some Nations, out of which a Traveller may receive some Lights and Directions how to behave himself when he comes amongst them.'[15]

Today we can also look at the Grand Tourists' recollections of travel experiences as containing an immense repository of ideas about national identities and cultural differences. Such memories are also of great interest for literary studies since quite a number of them show evidence in many passages of the mutual feedback between fictional and non-fictional writing. For example, the code-switching in the passage below from Sterne's *A Sentimental Journey Through France and Italy* (1768) emphasises the cultural difference between the reserved nature of Englishmen abroad and the French open approach to the call of nature:

Madame de Rambouliet, after an acquaintance of about six weeks with her, had done me the honour to take me in her coach about two leagues out of town. Of all women, Madame de Rambouliet is the most correct; and I never wish to see one of more virtues and purity of heart. In our return back, Madame de Rambouliet desired me to pull the cord. I asked if she wanted any thing. *Rien que pisser*, said Madame de Rambouliet.[16]

---

[15] John Gailhard, *The Compleat Gentleman, or, Directions for the Education of Youth as to Their Breeding at Home and Travelling Abroad* (London, 1678), 183.

[16] Laurence Sterne, *A Sentimental Journey Through France and Italy by Mr Yorick*, ed. Gardner D. Stout Jr (Berkeley and Los Angeles, 1967), 181–2. Moderation, discretion and taciturnity were some of the attributes used by travellers to represent the English nature. In Sterne's vignette, the predominant attitude seems to be embarrassment. On the perception of the nature of Englishmen abroad, see also Brunot, *Histoire*, III, 243. The conceptualisation of Englishness

The French Art of Living

A visit to Paris was the chief attraction for European travellers in France. Indeed, most visitors were acquainted with only two itineraries in France: from the border to Paris, and from Paris to Italy. Many visitors had no knowledge of other areas in France except the Loire Valley, where it became fashionable for young travellers – especially the British – to attend French language classes. This limited experience of the country did not prevent them from voicing strong opinions about French customs, which persisted from the early days of the Grand Tour to the very end.

The Scottish travellers Archibald Alison and Patrick Fraser Tytler summarised their impressions of the French with these words:

What distinguishes the French from almost every other Nation is the *general diffusion* of the taste for the fine arts, and for elegant amusements, among all ranks of the people. Almost all Frenchmen take not only a pride but an interest in the public buildings of Paris, and in the collections of paintings and statues ... It is not in drinking clubs, or in sensual gratifications alone, that men of these ranks seek for relaxation, as is too often the case with us; but it is in the society of women, in conversation, in music and dancing, in theatres and operas, and cafés and promenades, in seeing and being seen.[17]

A positive perception of the French national character seems predominant throughout the evolution of the Grand Tour. For example, in the early seventeenth century, the Duke of Rohan, head of one of the oldest and most distinguished families in France and connected to many of the reigning houses of Europe, having travelled for a considerable time on the Continent, wrote: 'la nation française était tenue fort courageuse, fort clémente, fort courtoise en paix et en guerre, fort civile et fort spirituelle, vertues qui sont combattues de grand légèreté, inconstance, insolance, vanité et outrecuidance' ['The French nation was considered very brave, very merciful, very courteous in peace and in war, very civil and very spiritual, virtues which are contrasted with great lightness, inconstancy, insolence, vanity and overconfidence'].[18] Babeau, who quotes him, suggests that these are the qualities and defects that were later recognised by all visitors to France, and any emphasis on the latter depended on subjective preconceptions. One example of a critical evaluation

will be discussed in Chapter 9 in connection with the topic of foreignness popular with women travellers. In Sterne's story, another relevant detail is the name Madame de Rambouliet, which is almost homophonous with Madame de Rambouillet, who was Catherine de Vivonne, Marquise de Rambouillet (1588–1665), a literary figure famous in Paris for her fashionable salons, where she trained the *beau monde* in precious manners and ceremonious gallantry. Molière (1659) satirised her extravagant receptions in the play *Les Préciueses ridicules.*

[17] Archibald Alison and Patrick Fraser Tytler, *Travel in France, During the Years 1814–1815* (Edinburgh, 1815), I, 140.

[18] Albert Babeau, *Les Voyageurs en France: depuis la Renaissance jusqu'à la Révolution* (Tours, 1928), 35.

In the remise

Figure 1.1 *In the remise*, 1927. Illustration by Véra Willoughby (1870–1939) in Lawrence Sterne's *Sentimental Journey Through France and Italy,* Peter Davies, London

comes from the quarrelsome traveller Tobias Smollett, who attributed all the worse faults to the French. He considered them indolent, greedy, mean, ignorant, presumptuous, fat, impertinent, convoluted – and called them monkeys.

Another traveller with negative impressions was the Italian writer Vittorio Alfieri, mainly because he was a keen patriot with anti-French sentiments, and so he described his neighbours' nature as being a mixture of monkey and parrot.[19]

Against these two isolated expressions of prejudice, Babeau cites Arthur Young, who saw France as the most sociable country; Benjamin Franklin, who considered it the most pleasant to live in; Martin Sherlock, who was convinced that 'l'aimabilité is the typical character of the French'. John Moore agreed: 'cette politesse, cette urbanité a passé dans tous les rangs'; Laurence Sterne believed that even beggars were amiable; the Latvian-born German Heinrich Friederich von Storch remarked that French politeness was even superior to that of the ancient Athenians; the Italian Giovanni Francesco Gemelli-Careri felt that the French, more than any other nation, demonstrated such pleasant manners to foreigners; and the Russian Nikolay Mikhailovich Karamsine admitted that 'Je ne connais pas de nation plus ardente et plus éventée: J'ajout et plus aimable' ['I know of no more passionate nor more vibrant nation: and I must add more charming'].[20]

Evidence of this widespread appreciation of French manners is the fact that France had gained the highest reputation in Europe for the art of good living. Especially in the eighteenth century, travellers considered this accolade well deserved, at court as well as in private salons. Indeed, the courts of all European nations were inspired by that of Versailles, and all the salons of Europe imitated 'l'art de bien dire et de se parer avec grâce', while all the aristocracies of Europe took pride in being able to speak French. The most recurrent terms used to denote this French characteristic are 'grandeur' and 'seduction'. When comparisons with another great capital of Europe – London – emerged, that too was an acknowledgement of France's wealth and cultural achievements.

The traveller William Roots argued that, owing to its greater amount of business, London was regarded as 'rich, mercantile and independent', while Paris was 'gay, courtly, and aristocratic'. The historian John Andrews made the comment that the English rabble spend most of their money on drink, while the French poor save in order to keep up appearances.[21] Each capital has its own special features, and many travellers felt these reflected the respective national character. London was a typical capital city, whose people were absorbed in

[19] Ibid., 36. Vittorio Alfieri, a poet and playwright, often expressed anti-French attitudes, especially because of the tendency among the Italian aristocracy to use French instead of Tuscan (see also Chapter 6). An aristocrat himself, he benefited from exclusive introductions to the nobility, and had a lifelong liaison until his death with Princess Louise of Stolberg-Gedern, the former wife of Charles Stuart, the Young Pretender.
[20] Ibid., 36–7.
[21] William Roots quoted in Henry Asgill Ogle (ed.), *Paris in 1814* (Newcastle-Upon-Tyne, 1909). John Andrews, *A Comparative View of the French and English Nations* (London, 1785). Both quotes come from Maxwell, *English Traveller*, 8 n.2 and n.3.

a busy and hectic business routine; Paris was a very agreeable place to reside, more suited to a slow and pleasant existence, where people enjoyed leisure activities and had time to socialise and converse.

Certainly Paris became known as the capital of civilised behaviour and the *bon ton*, as shown by the passion for polite conversation and the profusion of compliments exchanged between a host and hostess and their guests. But some of the most perceptive travellers were unimpressed by the superficiality of conversation in the salons and remained quite critical of the artificiality of the formal attitudes displayed by that nation. 'The French', wrote Nugent, 'are the masters of complaisance and good breeding'.[22] Addison agreed that the French could be extremely graceful and delightful on social occasions, but he cast doubts on their substance, including their language – he thought English was superior for business as it was more clear and forceful, while French was 'eminently suited to "tattle in"', made up as it was of 'so much repetition and compliment'.[23]

However, one of the least contested arguments about the superiority of the French character involved their passion for intellectual entertainments, particularly theatre and literature. Travellers expressed great admiration for the French love for all kinds of spectacle, whether outdoor *petites comédies* or theatre and opera. There was also much appreciation for actors, and for the public's behaviour at the theatre. This was considered symptomatic of a national respect for intellectual work. Even more admired by travellers was French high society's deep regard for literary people, who were welcome in the salons of the top nobility more than in any other country. English travellers, in particular, admitted that the *literati* in London needed personal wealth or political contacts to be admitted to the houses of important people. Travellers also mentioned the Bibliothèque Royal in Paris and the great services provided by all libraries in France. They were most impressed by such national resources, including the fact that they were free to all, and that the public made much use of them.

As for the conditions of the French peasantry, reports by English travellers were inconsistent. Some who stopped in Paris but hastened on quickly to Italy, having never seen a true peasant, described the few people they observed in the countryside as looking quite prosperous; this is exemplified by Lady Mary Wortley Montagu's description of a 'fresh coloured lusty peasant in good cloth and clean linen'.[24] But many other writers were deeply unimpressed by the poor conditions of the peasantry. Adverse reports did not depend on

[22] Ibid., 41.

[23] Joseph Addison, Letter to Guardian, Blois, May 20 (1699), *The Works of Joseph Addison*, 3 vols. (New York, 1837), III, 117. At the end of the eighteenth century, John Andrews, in *A Comparative View of the French and English Nations in Their Manners, Politics and Literature*, was also critical: '[French] lost in strength what it had gained in politeness' (London, 1785), 185. Quoted in Cohen, *Fashioning Masculinity*, 3.

[24] Mary Wortley Montagu, Letter to Mr Wortley, Dijon 18 August 1739, in *Letters and Works of Lady Mary Wortley Montagu* in Lord Wharncliffe (ed.), 3 vols. (London, 1837), II, 310–11.

observations of different economic conditions in diverse rural districts: almost all English travellers acknowledged the utterly miserable state of peasants in France. The Abbé Le Blanc, a Parisian *literato* who travelled through England making interesting social observations, wrote that 'one must almost say that luxury reigns as much in the country in England as it does in the cities in France'.[25] The same comparison was made not only by the cantankerous Tobias Smollett, but also by the writer Arthur Young, who was an agricultural expert, and by Voltaire himself, who spoke with great distress about the miserable conditions of the peasants in his country.[26]

The French Revolution naturally changed Paris, and life in other towns as well as the conditions of peasants. The old ceremonious way of life was replaced by new republican ways. Most of the main streets and gathering places were deserted, and the fashionable cafés and restaurants were transformed and rearranged. The names of public spaces were altered. There were new fashions in dress, decoration and furniture. The nobility had been exiled, interned or executed. In the large and rich provincial towns, the wealth of France passed from the hands of privileged nobles into those of the new middle class, army officers, bureaucrats, tax collectors. The peasants bought land and were well-clothed and fed. Foreign visitors from distinguished families were divided in their observations: some felt that France no longer had reason to feel superior; others feared that the same disaster could soon befall their own country. All were curious to view the scene of the Revolution and were anxious to discover its consequences for Europe. Now that the old nobility had greatly declined, some felt little desire to linger in the country and, as many towns were falling into decay, Paris became the only French destination for travellers. But now it was a place for satisfying social curiosity more than stimulating the intellect.

Gradually it became clear that the damage done by the Revolution was not so serious as foreigners anticipated: it neither lasted very long, nor did it destroy the greatness of France. After Waterloo, the Bourbons restored good international relations, allowing the free circulation of travellers, which had been banned by Napoleon for more than a decade. And although writers suffered under the Terror and surveillance at the hands by Napoleon's police, the status of science and scientists, promoted so much after the Revolution, secured for post-Napoleonic France a new and honourable international position. Maxwell, commenting on the writings by visitors to Paris after the Treaty of Amiens, reports on the impressive public support shown to scientists, and the remarkable amount of scientific activity at the time.[27]

---

[25] Maxwell, *English Traveller*, 36 n.1.
[26] Ibid., 35, 36 and 36 n.1. It is noteworthy that in 1692–4 famine in France killed two million.
[27] Ibid., 44.

Italian Glory and Decadence

The major factor that European travellers perceived as being responsible for the national character of Italy was the submission of its people to the moral and cultural influence of the Catholic church. Many travellers ascribed the local habits and national customs of Italians, some of whom lived outside Italy after the Counter-Reformation, to their Catholic upbringing. While this view was shaped by anti-Catholic prejudice, especially among the most politically committed academics and diplomats, it is also true that Catholic militants from England, who saw it as their mission to reach Rome, were no less free from their own preconceptions. One of the most popular travel books of the seventeenth century was written by Richard Lassels who toured Italy five times as a governor to young aristocrats.[28] In his *Italian Voyage* (1670), he described Italian manners as 'most commendable': 'They have taught them in their bookes, they practise them in their actions, and they have spread them abroad over all Europe, which owes its civility unto the Italians, as well as its religion.'[29] This was, of course, the old perception of Italy, reflecting the culture of the Renaissance and the myth of the *Res Publica Litterarum*, which combined the ideal of a united Christendom with the memory of Roman civilisation, linking all European peoples.

The reality of Italy after the Reformation, and throughout the early modern era, was far more complex and multifaceted. While in the case of France it was difficult to apply the situation in Paris to the rest of France, in Italy it was impossible to make generalisations for two reasons. One was diachronic, since the perception of Italy and Italians evolved dramatically following changes in its international situation during the early modern period. Another was synchronic; the fact was that, although in France it was slightly presumptuous to generalise that Parisian manners were common to all French nationals, in Italy no city could appear to be representative of Italians living elsewhere. Indeed, at the time of the Grand Tour, Italy had been politically and culturally fragmented for ten centuries – since AD 560 precisely – when the new Lombard kingdom became separated from the Byzantine territories of the Peninsula. Thus, the sheer variety of governmental structures and local traditions became a source of attraction for interested travellers, some of whom set out to identify continuity of spirit and diversity of nature within that well-defined geographical entity which lacked a national identity.[30]

---

[28] One of them was, unusually, a young lady. See Richard Lassels, 'The Voyage of the Lady Catherine Whetenhall', Bibliotèque Royale de Belgique MS7119, fol. 40r (1650), in Edward Chaney (ed.), *The Grand Tour and the Great Rebellion: Richard Lassels and the 'Voyage of Italy' in the Seventeenth Century* (Geneva, 1985), 371.

[29] Lassels, *The Voyage*, 12.

[30] Particularly attractive to travellers were the old republics of the Peninsula, such as Genoa, Venice, Lucca and San Marino, whose governments, they thought, had a special strategy to preserve political freedom. See Introduction.

The international admiration for Italian Renaissance culture came to an end with the Counter-Reformation, when many well-educated sectors of society in non-Catholic countries began to develop ambiguous attitudes towards Italy. In England, where explicit anti-papal policies were issued by the crown, there was a growing tendency to demonise the Italians. It is well known that in the Elizabethan era, Italian culture enriched English society but engendered an equally impressive outpouring of social and moral criticism. The imitation of Italy's greatest intellectual traditions and literary forms was necessary for integrating an insular society like England into the mainstream European fold. But there was also a genuine fear of Italy's negative influence on the English way of life, which could lead to the importation of customs and habits that were considered typical of Italians' immoral tendencies. This anti-Italianism movement produced memorable quotations, such as the following from Roger Ascham, who explained a famous saying of the time (1570):

Inglese Italianato, è un diavolo incarnato, that is to say, you remain men in shape and fashion, but become devils in life and condition. . . . If some yet do not well understand, what is an Englishman Italianated, I will plainly tell him. He, that by living, & travelling in Italy, brings home into England out of Italy, the Religion, the learning, the policy, the experience, the manners of Italy. That is to say, for Religion, Papistry or worse: for learning, less commonly than they carried out with them; for policy, a factious heart, a discoursing head, a mind to meddle in all men's matters; for experience, plenty of new mischieves never known in England before; for manners, variety of vanities, and change of filthy living.[31]

William Harrison echoed this viewpoint in 1577: 'It is most true what Dr Tumer said: "Italy is not to be seen without a guide, that is, without special grace given from God because of the licentious and corrupt behaviour of the people."' William Moorecroft, a well-travelled, educated Protestant, tutor to the son of Sir William Cecil, who spent time in Italy in 1567, made the same point while recording his impressions of the country: 'None shall like Italy unless he be Italizate *[sic]*, and the proverb says *Anglus italizatus demon incarnatus* and so also say the French and Germans of their countrymen . . . The hills are woodless, the sea fishless, the women shameless and the men graceless.'[32] Thomas Nashe, in his picaresque novel *The Unfortunate Traveller* (1594), wrote of the visitor to Italy that: 'From thence he brings the art of atheism, the art of epicurising, the art of whoring, the art of poisoning, the art of sodomitry . . .

---

[31] Roger Ascham, *The Scholemaster* (1570) (London, New York, Toronto and Melbourne, 1909), 80–1. According to George Parks, *The English Traveler to Italy: First Volume, the Middle Ages (to 1525)* (Stanford, 1954), the first recorded use of the expression comes from a letter of Sir William Paget to the Privy Council dated 1546. See Edward Chaney, '*Quo Vadis?* in Chaney, *The Evolution of the Grand Tour*, 98 n.92.

[32] Quotes from Kenneth R. Bartlett, 'Travel and Translation: The English and Italy in the Sixteenth Century', in *BOLLETTINO DEL C.I.R.V.I* (Centro interuniversitario di Ricerche sul viaggio in Italia), 29–30, anno XV, I–II (gennaio–dicembre 1994), 55–6.

It is now a privy note amongst the better sort of men, when they would set a regular mark or brand on a notorious villain, to say that he hath been to Italy.'[33]

Despite such anti-Italian statements condemning all sorts of habits in that country, the Italophile movement was strong within some sectors of the intellectual world. One of its most respected supporters was Sir Thomas Hoby, a diplomat who visited France and Italy, and who translated Baldassare Castiglione's *Il Cortegiano*, one of the key books of the European Renaissance.[34] Regard for Italy in Europe from the Renaissance onwards was marred by suspicion about the credibility of its aesthetic values, especially on the part of populations who regarded themselves as solid, upright and straightforward. European religious wars and the Protestant denunciation of the Catholic church brought about a deterioration in the reputation of Italians in the eyes of many Europeans. The argument went that since Italians passively accepted corruption linked to Popery, they must have acquired the same vices but lost all the virtues once inspired by a beautiful and civilised country.

The first half of the seventeenth century was still permeated with positive attitudes towards Italy, and people like James Howell insisted upon the value of a visit to that country, because 'Italy hath beene always accounted the nurse of policy, learning, musique, architecture, and limning, with other perfections, which she disperseth to the rest of Europe.'[35] But increasingly from the middle of the century, an appreciation of the values of the country was combined with deprecation of various aspects of Italian life and the discreditable nature of its people. Pine-Coffin also recalls an anonymous pamphlet published in 1660, *The Character of Italy*, which accused Italian people of 'lust, idolatry, hypocrisy, lying and more besides, and the country was said to be strangled by the Inquisition and riddled with bandits and lice'.[36]

The rapid decline of Italy in terms of economic and cultural standards was investigated by one of the most authoritative voices of the time, the distinguished scholar Jean Mabillon, a Benedictine monk from St. Germain-des-Prés, Paris. While visiting Italy in 1684–5 to carry out research in ancient and medieval history, he and his companion Claude Estiennot were shocked to see the squalor and poverty of people in many cities, especially in the Papal State. Of Rome the latter wrote:

On n'y panse qu'à *campare*, c'est a dire qu'à ce qui peut servir à s'avancer et à se mettre à son aise, *panis et spectacula*. Peu de bien, si on ne peut en avoir beaucoup, mais jouir de ce bien et vivre sans s'encommoder et en prenant toutes ses aises, voilà le genie du

---

[33] Thomas Nashe, *The Unfortunate Traveller or the Life of Jack Wilton* (London, 1594), 54.
[34] Thomas Hoby, *The Book of the Courtier* (New York, 1906).   [35] Howell, *Instructions,* 42.
[36] Quotes by Pine-Coffin, *British and American Travel*, 5.

pays et un habile homme est celui qui, comme disait il y a quelque temps un cardinal, *sa camminare*.[37]

[They think only of *campare*, that is to say, what might be useful in order to get ahead and be comfortable, *panis et spectacula*. A little wealth, if you can't have a great deal, but enjoy this wealth and live without a care, enjoying all the pleasures it offers: this is the genius of the country and an able man is he who, as a cardinal said some time ago, knows how to *camminare*.]

The same impression of Italy was given by the Scotsman Gilbert Burnet, a theologian, historian and Bishop of Salisbury. He was in Italy in the same year as Mabillon, travelling through most cities with a view to understanding the origin of Italy's decay, and everywhere he went he was struck by the fact that 'the richest country in Europe' was full of beggars'. Lombardy with its lakes was most beautiful, but 'there is nothing, but poverty over all this rich country'. In Venice the landlords 'oppress their tenants so severely that the peasants live most miserably'. The countryside around Ferrara was totally neglected, though 'once one of the beautifullest spots of all Italy'. In the city of Ferrara, 'the grass grows in the streets and most of the houses are void'. The same could be seen in Pisa and Siena, 'formerly a very fine commonwealth'. 'The kingdom of Naples is the richest part of all Italy', but 'the commons here are so miserably oppress'd that in many places they die of hunger even amidst the great plenty of their best years'. Hence he concluded that the Italians are 'one of the poorest nations in Europe'.[38]

Burnet believed that responsibility for such decay lay at the door of the Catholic church and its clergy, whose authoritarianism was summarised by the Roman motto: 'Chi parla è mandato in galera; chi scrive è impiccato e chi sta quieto va al Sant'Officio' ('Those who speak are sent to jail; those who write are hanged; those who are quiet are sent to the Inquisition' – *quieto* 'quiet' is a play on *Quietism,* a movement condemned by the Pope as heresy in 1687). Bishop Burnet's *Travels: Or Letters Containing an Account of What Seemed Most Remarkable in Switzerland, Italy, France, and Germany* came out in English, French, Dutch and German, and its circulation throughout Europe spread the news about the misery of Italians under the Pope and their political oppression under the Spanish occupation.

This new assessment was confirmed in *Remarks* by Joseph Addison, who made quite explicit the contrast between the country and its people, who were reduced to a state of cowardice and deception by an oppressive church and

---

[37] *Correspondence inedited de Mabillon et de Montfaucon avec l'Italie*, in M. Valery (ed.) (Paris, 1846), I, 56, Letter by Claude Estiennot to Charles Bulteau, from Rome, 3 March 1685.

[38] Gilbert Burnet, *Travels: Or Letters Concerning an Account of What Seemed Most Remarkable in Switzerland, Italy, Some Parts of Germany etc. in the Years 1685 and 1686* (Rotterdam, 1686; reprint 1687). The references to Lombardy, Siena and Pisa are in I, 102, to Venice 64, to Ferrara 94 and to Naples in II, 9.

a corrupted clergy. Addison's book exerted much influence on new attitudes towards the national character of Italians. Reports about Italy by Samuel Sharp and Tobias Smollett were also exceptionally critical; their attitudes were so negative that the Italian-born Giuseppe Baretti, Secretary to the Royal Academy of Arts in London, was prompted to challenge their long list of distortions and slurs one by one. In his *Account of the Manners and Customs of Italy* (1768), Baretti argues 'with some indignation' that one must not confuse 'the peculiarities of character which remarkably distinguish the people of one Italian district from that of another', and adds that 'Superficial travellers are apt to speak of them in the mass; and they cannot fall into a greater mistake':

> There is very little difference comparatively speaking between the several provinces of England, because all their inhabitants live under the same laws, speak dialects of the same tongue much nearer each other than the dialects of Italy, and have a much greater intercourse between themselves than the Italians have had these many ages. No nations, distinguished by different names, vary more from each other in almost every respect than these which go under the common name of Italians.[39]

A more positive view of Italy gained ground in the second part of the eighteenth century, mainly because many tourists were looking for pleasant excursions in beautiful landscapes and ritual visits to the arts and antiquities. But the gap between travellers' perceptions and the reality of the country increased as they had little contact with the Italian population, with foreign visitors limiting themselves to sporadic gatherings with the members of the nobility and other distinguished residents. After the Napoleonic wars, tourists poured into Italy, and the new generation of visitors began to include middle-class citizens who had more time and interest in sightseeing than in observing people or under-standing the country's national character. By and large, it was taken for granted that Italians had become uncivilised if not degenerate but there was little interest in understanding why, except by a few extremely motivated women travellers.[40]

However, for a small section of the intellectual elite, these extreme contrasts were seen as the picturesque background of a romantic reality. The decadence of Italy became fascinating and included many attractive oppositions. One of them was between the past and the present, and this became a source of poetic inspiration to many artists and poets. Another contrast was between the beauty of Italy's arts and the oppressive nature of its society with its corrupted religious and political authorities. Another tension existed between the style of living within the colonies of foreign residents, completely detached from public life, and the miserable conditions of Italians living in the same cities.

---

[39] Joseph Baretti, *An Account of the Manners and Customs of Italy: With Observations on the Mistakes of Some Travellers with Regard to That Country* (London, 1768), II, 113.

[40] The contrasting views of male and female travellers will be considered in detail in Chapter 9.

Figure 1.2 *Dr John Bargrave between his nephew John Raymond and pupil Alexander Chapman, consulting a map of Italy,* 1647. Oil paint on copper by Mattia Bolognini (1605–67). ©Canterbury Dean and Chapter, Bargrave Collection

Giuseppe Baretti's insight had finally been acknowledged: Italy had no national character but shared a common paradox. In 1820, the poet Shelley summarised it as 'the paradise of exiles and the retreat of pariahs'. Two years earlier he had been less polite and more explicit:

There are two Italies; one composed of the green earth and transparent sea and the mighty ruins of ancient times, and aerial mountains, and the warm and radiant atmosphere which is interfused through all things. The other consists of the Italians of the present day, their works and ways. The one is the most sublime and lovely contemplation that can be conceived by the imagination of man; the other the most degrading, disgusting and odious. What do you think? Young women of rank actually eat – you will never guess what – garlick.[41]

Sound but Uninspiring Nations

Over the course of the Grand Tour, the British set off for the same continental destinations as most European travellers: Paris and Italy. This explains why the

---

[41] Percy Bysshe Shelley, Letter to Leigh Hunt, from Naples, 20 December 1818, in Thomas James Wise (ed.), *Letters from Percy Bysshe Shelley to J. H. Leigh Hunt* (London, 1894), II, 36.

debate over national characteristics centred on the French and the Italians more than other Europeans.

There were alternative itineraries to the route through France that joined Paris and the Italian cities, but these remained less popular. One ran through Holland, Paris being reachable from the Low Countries. A minority of motivated travellers visited Germany and Austria on their way back from Italy, choosing to journey through countries they had never previously seen. The Swiss cantons were not regarded as a very interesting region to visit, so Switzerland was just a stage in the journey to Italy. Spain and Portugal were not included in the Grand Tour for a number of reasons: travel in the Iberian Peninsula was difficult and hospitality was poor; the journeys were very long; and there were language barriers and health problems. Moreover, most Iberian cities were isolated and their social life reclusive. This was due to the provincial mentality of the local nobility, who were described as being more interested in opening up to the new world across the ocean than interacting with old Europe.

The Low Countries comprised two contrasting realities – the Protestant United Provinces (the Netherlands) and the Catholic Austrian Netherlands (western Belgium and Luxembourg). In the latter, public religiosity impressed some tourists such as Matthew Arnot, who wrote in 1742: 'The Roman Catholics cram every hole and corner with saints, whom the ignorant people worship with much devotion.'[42] By contrast, other tourists praised the liberal atmosphere of the United Provinces, where religious services of many faiths were held, particularly in Amsterdam. Travellers usually contrasted the two neighbouring countries with reference to the impact of their different religions on the population. According to Protestant visitors, the effect of Catholicism was quite striking, as noted by Thomas Shaw: 'as soon as he ... comes into a Popish country by any looser freer air and weakness of manners, running through all sort of people you meet, who are strangers to the wise and strict morality of the Dutch, and which contributed so much to their power and riches'.[43] The Reverend William Coxe, later Archdeacon Coxe, governor to Lord Herbert, writing to his mother Lady Pembroke in 1777 showed his appreciation of the religious atmosphere in Amsterdam: 'what pleases me most in these provinces is the universal toleration that is established. Calvinism is the reigning religion: but Luterans, Catholics, Jews, Greeks, Armenians, etc., have their separate Churches and are tolerated without reserve. I would that their liberal principal were more universal'.[44]

Amsterdam did not have the grandeur of Paris or the size of London but around 1700 it was the most commercial city in Europe, due to the remarkable

---

[42] Quoted in Black, *The British Abroad*, 57.   [43] Ibid., 244.

[44] This letter is quoted by Roger Hudson (ed.) with neither reference nor date, *The Grand Tour 1592–1796* (London, 1993), 255. Amsterdam had an international reputation for religious tolerance and was referred to as a model by some of the most liberal travellers.

industry of its people. It held around 300,000 inhabitants, and the Low Countries constituted the most highly urbanised area of Europe. But the Dutch had a reputation for being heavy drinkers and worse smokers, and Beckford called them "the most uncouth bipeds" in creation, and speaks of faces that would have dishonoured a flounder, and accents that would have confounded a hog'. It was also said that in the Low Countries 'the women were honest, if plain, but the men sucked up with their milk a desire and thirst for gain' due to the high taxes and the exorbitant cost of living and travelling.[45]

In the days of the Grand Tour, Germany (which was part of the Holy Roman Empire, a realm which once included Austria and Bohemia) was much less visited than France, Italy or even the Low Countries. The main problems connected with a journey there were practical, as the language, accommodation and transport were all less manageable than in France. The cultural and social rewards to be found in the cities along any itinerary through that area were also not quite as satisfying. There were some exceptions: Frankfurt's famous book fair; Heidelberg's international community of students; Hanover's royal court, which was very popular with British visitors after the accession of the Hanoverians to the British throne in 1714; and Vienna's imperial structure and appearance, which grew after the conflict with Spain that made it the dominant power in Italy. However, Prague was deemed quite inhospitable.

Frankfurt was a prosperous trading city, whose international fair was a literary as well as a commercial occasion from Gutenberg's time, when it became Europe's foremost printing centre. It attracted authors and scholars interested in doing business with publishers and booksellers. Lying at a crossroads of different cultures, it became a fashionable meeting place for academics and diplomats. Famous travellers who were eager to spend time in Frankfurt included Sir Philip Sidney, Sir Henry Wotton, Thomas Coryat, and James Boswell, but they all met up with distinguished intellectuals and aristo-crats, and not with common people. Heidelberg and Leipzig were well known to European visitors of all nationalities, and many international students went there to study German language and law. These cities were also famous for being among the cheapest places in Germany due to their large number of young residents. Visitors reported that the local students tended to be noisy and disorderly, spending evenings drinking, smoking and singing, but without being aggressive to strangers.

Vienna was not an especially impressive capital. Before it acquired its imperial splendours and gaieties, the Hapsburg capital was something of an outpost of Christendom, separated from the Turks only by the Hungarian

---

[45] The latter comment is from Malcom Letts, 'Cologne and the Journey to the Coast', in Lambert (ed.), *Grand Tour*, 137-52, who quotes Beckford's Letter of 26 June 1780 from Antwerp, *Italy with Sketches*, I, 21.

Empire. Foreigners were not always impressed by the hospitality of the Austrian aristocracy. Sir Robert Murray Keith, writing about his son and friends in 1786, said: 'I am afraid that from the stiffness of Austrian manners and the cold uninteresting style of conversation which prevails here, their staying in Vienna has, in point of amusement as well as of instruction, fallen short of their expectation, as well as my wishes.'[46] The Scottish surgeon Dr John Moore, who acted as governor to the young Duke of Hamilton for five years, and who assessed Vienna from the point of view of a responsible educator, wrote:

I imagine there is no city in Europe where a young gentleman, after his university education is finished, can pass a year with so great advantage; because, if properly recommended, he may mix on an equal footing with people of rank and have opportunities of improving by the conversation of sensible men and accomplished women. In no capital could he see fewer examples, or have fewer opportunities, of deep gambling, open profligacy, or gross debauch.[47]

Sometimes tourists came away from the cities they visited with the impressions they anticipated, but some did not find what they were told they would, and noted down their memories and experiences with an air of disappointment. Culturally, Germany lacked the excitement of Paris or Italy, but its appeal lay elsewhere – in its musical life, the distinction of its many courts, the cleanness of the country and the solidity of its people. A traveller who visited Vienna, Dresden, Berlin, Hanover, Kassel, Frankfurt, Mannheim and Stuttgart in 1753 wrote:

I have now finished my tour in Germany which I am very glad to have made but should not choose to begin it again. I have seen many things to admire some that have excited my displeasure, others contempt. The Germans in general are a good natured people, hospitable and generous, lovers of pomp and magnificence. I would not look for French vivacity, Italian cunning or English good sense amongst them. Take them as you find them and a traveller may pass his time very well amongst them. I speak of the German nation in general.[48]

Switzerland and the Alps did not become an attraction for tourists until the mid-eighteenth century. As Gibbon wrote later about his Grand Tour in 1755, 'the fashion of climbing the mountains and viewing the Glaciers had not yet been introduced by foreign travellers'.[49] When this happened, English tourists became about twice as numerous in Switzerland as those from all other nations. The fashion started after 1815, when reaching the Swiss cantons became easier

[46] Quoted in Black, *The British Abroad*, 66.
[47] John Moore, *A View of Society and Manners in France, Switzerland and Germany* (Paris, 1803), II, 272–3.
[48] Quoted in Black, *The British Abroad*, 64–5.
[49] Edward Gibbon, *Memoirs of My Life and Writings*, Henry Morley (ed.) (London, 1891).

using the fast roads built by Napoleon: but then travelling through the mountains became more of an exploration than a pleasure-tour. Before, the only reason to go near the Alps was to reach the other side. The mountains were the only obstacle on the way to Italy as very few travellers were willing to travel the longer distance to the south coast of France, to then face stormy waters and Algerian pirates during the crossing on a felucca from Marseille to Genoa. Lac Leman between Geneva and Lausanne was much admired, and one of the main attractions was the nearby village of Ferney, made internationally famous by Voltaire. Geneva was an oligarchic republic dominated by a few 'Lords of the Town', but with strict legislation to enforce social equality. In the mid-seventeenth century, the traveller Sir John Finch was most impressed by its local customs: 'It is not permitted to wear satin or silver, by reason there being a parity luxury in apparel would undo the meaner sort. At church, servants and others sit as they come, and no distinction of place or pews'.[50] Fifty years later, Addison wrote down his extensive observations on the Swiss national character:

It is the great endeavour of the several cantons of Switzerland, to banish from among them everything that looks like pomp or superfluity. To this end the ministers are always preaching, and the governors putting out edicts against dancing, gaming, entertainment, and fine clothes . . . Should dressing, feasting, and balls, once get among the cantons, their military roughness would be quickly lost, their tempers would grow too soft for their climate, and their expenses outrun their incomes . . . This is absolutely necessary in these little republics, where the rich merchants live very much within their estates, and by heaping up vast sums from year to year, might become formidable to the rest of their fellow-citizens, and break the equality.[51]

Municipal Identities

It was not unusual for Grand Tourists to say that what they found mostly impressive in foreign nations was the solidity of the country and the uniformity of society. However, looking at the standard routes of the Grand Tour and the personal agendas of travellers, the opposite seemed to be the case: cultural diversity and socio-political extremes appeared to be the most exciting features of the Continent. This is consistent with the fact that a continental tour without a visit to Italy could hardly be classified as a Grand Tour. Of course, one reason was that the Peninsula which stretched into the Mediterranean was the greatest repository of the glories of the past. But no less important was its modern reality since the historical divisions of Italy had developed such a mosaic of diverse customs and identities that nothing like it could be found in other parts of Europe.

---

[50] Quoted by Trease, *The Grand Tour*, 123.   [51] Addison, *Remarks* (1745), 285.

From the Middle Ages through to the Renaissance, Italy was well known for being a country of several hundred cities, all boasting a unique profile, a reputation which was well consolidated before the arrival of the Grand Tourists. If some travellers left home with certain ideas about the Italian national characteristics, what they all found in Italy was that each city had developed a distinctive character and its inhabitants a strong local identity. By the time Stendhal published his book *Rome, Naples et Florence* in 1819, the reasons for this peculiar situation had become very clear:

Italy has seven or eight centres of civilisation. The simplest action is performed in an entirely different way in Turin and Venice, Milan or Genoa, Bologna or Florence, Rome or Naples. Venice, notwithstanding the extraordinary misfortunes which must crash it, has a frank gaiety, while Turin is biliously aristocratic. Milanese good humour is as well known as Genoese avarice ... The Bolognese is full of fire, passion, generosity, and sometimes imprudence. The Florentines have a great deal of logic, prudence, and even wit, but I have never seen more passionless men: love in Florence is so little known that lust has usurped its name. As for the Neapolitan, he is the slave of the sensation of the moment.[52]

Most foreign visitors reported that they were truly mesmerised by the fragmentation of the country and the proliferation of different urban realities – so much so that when they came across a plethora of epithets and proverbs representing the singular features of Italian cities and the local character of the citizens, they were not caught by surprise. Throughout the era of the Grand Tour, travellers noted down such aphorisms in their letters and diaries as soon as they picked them up from other travellers on the road, or in the course of conversations with the locals.[53] What they invariably failed to say was that most such comments were also found in modern guidebooks and old travel literature. In any case, what they did not realise was that the custom of giving Italian cities nicknames actually came from a folk tradition passed down through generations. This habit was interpreted as a natural practice in a country with a visible sense of unity in diversity, as was clearly summed up by one of the first observers, Marco Antonio Sabellico, in his book *Enneades* (1504): 'nulla est civitas, nullus populous, qui non aliquid a finitimis differat' ['No city or people is similar to their neighbours in something'].[54]

Most of these proverbs and epithets were phrased in literary Italian, others in Latin, and only a few in the vernacular, as a high-status variety was deemed more appropriate for emphasising the singularity of places and the character of

[52] Stendhal, *Rome Naples et Florence en 1817* (Paris, 1817); English translation quoted in Maugham, *The Book of Italian Travel*, 69.
[53] These were not just specimens or momentos from new nations and cities; travellers were actually advised by language teachers to collect proverbs in foreign languages. See Lambely, *The Teaching of English*, 356.
[54] Marco Antonio Sabellico, *Enneadis*, XI, Lib. I, fo CCCXLVI (1504?).

the inhabitants. In the manuscript *Discours Viatique de Paris a Rome et de Rome à Naples et Sicile* (1588–9), written by an anonymous French traveller, a number of unique features of Italian cities are annotated in a language that reads like a mixture of popular Latin and literary Italian:

Quattro precipua castella in Italia, Fabriano nella Marca, Prato in Toscana, Crema in Lombardia, & Barletta in Puglia.	[Four main castles in Italy, Fabriano in Marches, Prato in Tuscany, Crema in Lombardy, & Barletta in Apulia.
Unus Petrus in Roma, unus portus in Ancona, una turris in Cremona.	One Peter in Rome, one port in Ancona, one tower in Cremona.
Sette colli di Roma. Palatino, Celio, Esquilino, Aventino, Celio *[sic]*, Viminale, et Quirinale.[55]	Seven hills in Rome, Palatino, Celio, Esquilino, Aventino, Celio *[sic]*, Viminale, and Quirinale.]

Compared with the wealth of proverbs and sayings about specific places in Italy, those collected by travellers in other countries were insignificant in number and substance.[56] Mączak quotes Fynes Moryson who reports that 'Among the cities of Netherland Haarlem is called great', Leyden is called 'faire', Delf 'rich', Torg 'Catholike'. He also says that 'people of Bruxelles are called devourers of Pullin, or Capo-eaters, the Hollanders in general hasen kopen, that is, Hare-heads'.[57] For the university town of Wittenberg in Germany, Ernest S. Bates reports the use of verses similar to those apparently also used by scholars in Angers, France:

Basse ville, hauts clochers, Riches putaines, pauvres escoliers.[58]	[Flat city, tall bell towers, Rich whores, poor students.]

---

[55] Luigi Monga, (ed.), *Discours viatiques de Paris à Rome et de Rome à Naples et Sicile (1588–1589)*, CIRVI (Centro Interuniversitario di Ricerche sul Viaggio in Italia) (Torino, 1983), 39; the quotation mentions Celio twice, whereas the seventh hill of Rome should be Capitolino.

[56] On his journey to the Low Countries, Germany, Italy and France, Skippon refers to quite a number of epithets collected in Italy, but not one from anywhere else. In addition to the three (about Vicenza, Genova, Messina) mentioned by other travellers in this chapter, one concerns Siena (*Siena si vanta di quattro cose, di Torre e di Campane; di Bardasse e di Putane*: 'Siena boasts four things, a tower, bells, buggers and whores'), four apply to the main Tuscan cities (*Fiorentini ciechi, Pisani traditori, Senesi pazzi, Lucchesi signori*: 'Florentins blind, Pisani traitors, Senesi mad, Lucchesi cavaliers'), and two concerning Rome are in Macaronic Latin (*Quod non fecerunt Barbari; fecerunt barbarini*: 'what the barbarians didn't do, the Barberini family did'), as is one describing the university town of Bologna (*Bononia docet mater Studiorum* is altered to *Mater furborum*: 'mother of scholarship' becomes 'mother of cheating'). Philip Skippon, 'An account of a journey', in Awnsley and John Churchill (eds.), *A Collection of Voyages*, 6 vols. (London, 1732), vol. vi.

[57] Mączak, *Travel*, 148. Mączak explains that 'by Torg (Torge), Moryson means Torgau in Upper Saxony', 313 n.52. Fynes Moryson, *Itinerary Written by Fynes Moryson Gent.* (London, 1617), 4 vols., rpt. Glasgow, 1907–8.

[58] Ernest Stuart Bates, *Touring in 1600. A Study in the Development of Travel as a Means of Education* (New York, 1911), 121.

The reason there are not many other traces of epithets in the writings of travellers is that most of them travelled quickly through Central Europe and did not know the languages there. Fynes Moryson provides a case in point: 'Bohemia I passed with speede, and was unskilfull in the language, so as I never observed any proverbial speech among them of this kind, neither hath it been my chance since that time to reade any such speeches in approved Authors.'[59] Certainly one traveller who picked up proverbs about cities from his travel guide without acknowledging the source was the Italian Sebastiano Locatelli, who wrote about Paris: 'intesi una volta questa bella sentenza: "Lutetia est infernus equorum, purgatorium hominum, et paradises mulierum"' ['once I heard this fine proverb: Lutetia is hell for horses, purgatory for men, and paradise for women'].[60]

Giovanni Ricci reconstructs the Italian tradition of nicknames and proverbs for places by looking at a number of publications issued during the Renaissance and explaining how most were designed to epitomise the distinctive profile of different cities. He points out that, whether in the original Latin, Italian or translated into other languages, all harked back to an old stock of commonplaces rooted in the Middle Ages, but which were still very much alive in the Renaissance. This is indicated by recurrent expressions such as 'Itali vocant' ['Italians say'] (Adorno, 1470); 'hominum praedictatione' ['people proudly claim'] (Sabellico, 1504); 'Venegia si dice' ['Venice is said'] (Münster, 1558); 'si danno ordinariamente questi titoli' ['such names are usually given'] (Ortelio, 1570); 'vulgare passimque notum ... dicterium' ['popular witty remarks'] (Reusner, 1585); 'vengono nominate comunemente con questi epiteti, che corrono cottidianamente tra le genti' ['are commonly described by these epithets that are of regular use among people'] (Magini, 1620).[61] If the original theme of that tradition was the architecture of remarkable cities, variations depended on a number of factors: from international reputations to local rivalries, from religious prejudice to sexual innuendo. Most travellers who trotted out the nicknames of cities or the stereotypical proverbs about the

---

[59] Moryson, *Itinerary*, III, 455. Moryson became a keen collector of local proverbs in Germany, once fluent in that language:

> Of the Cities in *Germany,* they say in the vulgar tongue: *Ulm die reichest, Augspurg**die hoffertigest, Trier die eltest, Nurnberg die Witzigest, Strasburg die edlest.* That is: *Vlms* the richest, *Augsburg* the proudest, *Trier* the eldest, *Nurnberg* the wittiest, *Strasburg* the noblest. That all *Germany* is blind, onely *Nurnberg* hath one eye. Of the Bishopricks vpon the *Rheine.* That *Chur* is the highest (because it is seated vpon the highest Alpes, neere the Spring head of the *Rheine), Costnetz* the amplest. *Itinerary*, III, 450–1.

[60] Sebastiano Locatelli, *Viaggio di Francia*, in Luigi Monga (ed.), CIRVI: Centro Interuniversitario di Ricerche sul Viaggio in Italia (Torino, 1991), 150 and 405 n.199 on the origin of the Latin proverb.
[61] Giovanni Ricci, 'Cataloghi di città, stereotipi etnici e gerarchie urbane nell'Italia di antico regime', *Storia Urbana* VI, 18 (1982), 6.

inhabitants were probably not aware of the complex ramifications of that folk tradition. The *Grand dictionnaire géographique et critique* by Antoine-Augustin Bruzen de la Martinière, printed between 1726 and 1768, reported that Italian cities:

ont une épithète qui marque leur qualité la plus remarquable. On dit par une espèce de proverb, Rome la sainte, Ravenne l'ancienne, Naples la noble, Padoue la docte, Florence la belle, Bologne la grasse, Venise la riche, Livourne la marchande, Gènes la superbe, Vérone la charmante, Milan la grande, Luques la jolie, et Casal la forte.[62]

[They have an epithet, a kind of proverb, which indicates their most remarkable quality. They call Rome the holy one, Ravenna the ancient one, Naples the noble one, Padua the learned one, Florence the beautiful, Bologna the fat one, Venice the rich one, Livorno the merchant, Genova the proud, Verona the charming one, Milan the great, Lucca the pretty one and Casal the strong one.]

This authoritative source includes almost the same entries as those collected by Fynes Moryson two centuries earlier, which he gave in their original form as well as in translation:

Touching the Cities of Italy, it is proverbially said among them: Roma la santa, Padoua la dotta, Venetia la ricca, Fiorenza la bella, Milano la grande, Bologna la grassa, Ravenna l'antica, Napoli gentile, Genuoa superba. That is: Rome the holy, Padoua the learned, Venice the rich, Florence the beautifull, Milan the great, Bologna the fat, Ravenna the ancient, Naples the Gentile, Genuoa the proud.[63]

Ricci contrasts the reputation of Italy's capital and non-capital cities, indicating that the profile of the former was not necessarily more consistent, since characterisations of towns such as Bologna, Genoa and Ravenna dated back to as early as the thirteenth and fourteenth centuries.[64] There was actually more diversity in descriptions of the capital cities. For example, Naples was sometimes described as 'noble' and other times as 'gentile'. But apart from the beauty of its location, life in Naples was deemed so chaotic both night and day that the situation justified another motto: 'mai si mangia, né si beve: mai si dorme: mai si muore', meaning that the city was always awake. While that might have been exciting for locals, it must have been disorienting for travellers, as suggested by another saying: 'vedi Napoli, e poi mori' ['See Naples and die'], reported by the Italian Giuseppe De Conti.[65] Venice was internationally known for its wealth and unique oriental style ('Venetia, Venetia, chi non ti vede non ti pretia' ['Venice, Venice one needs to see you

---

[62] Antoine Augustin Bruzen de La Martinière, *Le grand dictionnaire géographique: historique et critique* (Amsterdam and Rotterdam, 1732), IV/2, 266.
[63] Moryson, *Itinerary*, III, 455.   [64] Ricci, 'Cataloghi di città, etc., 15.
[65] Giuseppe De Conti, *Viaggio d'Italia. Un manoscritto del Settecento*, in Barbara Corino (ed.) (Novara, 2007). The first quote about Naples is on p. 167, the second quote on p. 183.

to appreciate you']⁶⁶). But it was also a famous destination for amatory adventures. A saying that survived for a long time among natives, functioning as a warning to tourists and other adventurers, pointed out the hazards epitomised by the 'four Ps' – the *pietra bianca*, the *prete, the pantaleone, the putana,* referring to the dangers of Venice's 450 slippery bridges, the intrigues of priests, the tricks of merchants and seductiveness of prostitutes.[67]

Many such aphorisms left quite an impression on travellers: not only did they help in remembering city nicknames, but some also functioned as useful reminders about safety measures for comfortable travelling. Unsurprisingly, a number of proverbs were targeted specifically at Protestant visitors to Rome, traditionally called 'the Holy City', but also known as the 'Mistress of the World' or 'the Metropolis of Popery' – in other words, a place where priests and Inquisition spies were far more enterprising than in Venice. One local motto was used famously by Sir Henry Wotton, later English Ambassador to Venice, as a warning to Milton on his journey to Rome: 'I pensieri stretti e il viso sciolto' ['Your thoughts close and your countenance loose', meaning 'keep your thoughts to yourself and your face unconstrained'].[68] Moryson, too, reported similar proverbs collected in Italy:

The Italians say in their tongue: *Queste cose si richiedono nel viandante, l'occhio di Falcone (per veder' lontany), l'orecchie d' Asino (per udir' bene), il viso di simia (per essere pronto al riso), la bocca di porcello (per mangiar'd' ogni cosa), le Spalle di Camelo (per portar' some con patienza) le gambe di Cervo (per fuggir' pericolo) e un' sacchone pien' pieno di danari (perche chi ha danari, signore e chiamato).* That is in English; These things are required in a Traveller, the eye of a Hawke (to see farre off), the eares of an Asse (to heare the least whispering), the face of an Ape (to bee ready to laugh in soothing), the mouth of a Hogge (to eate whatsoever is set before him), the backe of a Camell (to beare burdens patiently), the legge of a Hart (to flie from danger), a huge great purse top full of gold (because he that hath mony, is called Lord.) We in *England* vulgarly say, that a Traveller to *Rome* must have the backe of an Asse, the belly of a Hogge, and a conscience as broad as the Kings high way.[69]

Rome was usually called *la santa* as a religious centre, but was also the capital of an ancient civilisation, 'Capo e Compendio del Mondo a cui non è cosa simile ne seconda' ('Rome of the World Compendium and Head, Admits no like nor can be seconded'), as reported by Raymond in his *Itinerary* (1648).[70]

---

[66] Ernest Giddey, 'Le condizioni materiali e spirituali del viaggio in Italia alla fine del XVI e all'inizio del XVII secolo, in Giorgio Botta (ed.), *Cultura del viaggio. Ricostruzione storico-geografica del territorio* (Milan, 1989), 78.

[67] John Georg Keysler, *Travels Through Germany, Bohemia, Hungary, Switzerland, Italy and Lorrain* (London, 1756; reprint 1760), IV, 7.

[68] *The Life and Letters of Sir Henry Wotton*, Logan Pearsall Smith (ed.) (Oxford, 1907), I, 22.

[69] Moryson, *Itinerary*, III, 452.

[70] John Raymond, *An Itinerary Containing a Voyage Made Through Italy, in the Year 1646 and 1647* (London, 1648), 173.

But the risks of living in the 'holy city' were nicely summarised by another proverb, which said: 'Roma la Santa, popolo cornuto; Roma paradiso de' preti, purgatorio de' frati, inferno de' cavalli' ['Rome, the Holy City, where the people are cuckolds; Rome, a paradise for priests, purgatory for monks, hell for horses']. The attribute *cornuto* meaning 'cuckold' suggests that the motto did not express an insider's viewpoint, but rather that of visitors from outside; it is consistent with another proverb: 'In Roma vale più la Putana che la moglie romana' ['In Rome a slut is worth more than a Roman wife'], mentioned by William Thomas in 1544.[71] Even on this topic Moryson produced a relevant example: 'The Italian Travellers say, *Da l'hoste nuouo, & da la putana vecchia Dio ci guarda:* From a new host, and an old Harlot, God deliver us.'[72]

Ricci explained that the classic tradition of describing the singular features of Italian cities merged with the popular practice of satirising local customs, making allusions not only to citizens' behaviour ('in vestitu, in oratione, in consiliis, in persequendis iniuriis, erga hospites, in literis, in mercatura, in re bellica' ['in the manner of dressing, speaking, making decisions, pursuing crimes, managing hospitality, education, business, wars']) but also to more trivial matters, such as feminine willingness and masculine qualities.[73] Of course, passing witty remarks about neighbours was not just an Italian tendency, but in the Peninsula their intensity was exacerbated by the so-called *campanilismo* (a term derived from *campanile* 'bell tower', an enduring symbol of the superiority of one's city, village or even urban district). One case of self-celebration is the folk etymology of the name of Verona, which consists of the first letters of the three main cities of Italy – VEnetia, ROma and NApoli – recollected by Raymond, who explained: 'whatsoever is contained in those three Cities may be found in *Verona*. Her wealth may be compared to that of *Venice*; Her Monuments of Antiquity equall even those of *Rome*, neither is the delightfull situation inferiour to that of *Naples*'.[74]

However, most aphorisms reflecting 'campanilistic' rivalries usually expressed niceties about others rather than promoting one's own attributes. Some sayings about rival cities were quite innocent, like *Bolonia la grassa, Padova la passa* ['Bologna is opulent, Padua surpasses it'].[75] But others tended to be harsher, like *Reggio la reale, Modena la porcile* ['Reggio is royal, Modena is a pigsty'].[76] Of course, Italian travellers were more familiar than their foreign counterparts with this regional repertoire, as shown by Canon De

[71] William Thomas, *The Historie of Italy* (London, 1549), in George B. Parks (ed.), *The History of Italy* (Ithaca, NY, 1963).
[72] Moryson, *Itinerary*, III, 453.
[73] Ricci, 'Cataloghi di città, stereotipi etnici e gerarchie urbane nell'Italia di antico regime', 4-7.
[74] Raymond, *An Itinerary Containing a Voyage Made Through Italy, in the Year 1646 and 1647*, 226.
[75] Ibid., 208.   [76] De Conti, *Viaggio d'Italia*, 50.

Conti from Casale in Piedemont, who wrote of his regrets at not having drawn the appropriate conclusions about his *vetturale* (coachman), whose birthplace was the nearby city of Alessandria (30 km away): 'Il perfido vetturale che ci aveva piantati era moro di nome, alessandrino di patria, e bresciano di domicilio, qualità tutte, che dovevano insospettirci' ['The evil coachman who had abandoned us was called Moro, was originally from Alessandria, and was resident in Brescia, all of which should have raised our suspicions'].[77]

It is noteworthy that in the repertoire of mottos and proverbs collected by travellers in Italy, quite a few contain references to women, including *putane* and *cortezans*. From Turin and Genoa down to Sicily, foreign visitors collected a plethora of such linguistic souvenirs. This should not be surprising given the age of the travellers – most were in their twenties or even younger – who were often embarking on their first continental, and possibly amorous, expedition. What might be surprising is that, if one gives credit to those stereotypes, the standard itinerary of the Grand Tour seems to have been designed around key destinations for sexual tourism.

Boswell, having arrived in Turin, wrote: 'the ladies in Turin were very beautiful, and I thought that I might allow myself one intrigue in Italy, in order to increase my knowledge of the world and give me a contempt for shameless women'.[78] Most British tourists found Genoa to be the city with the most beautiful women and the meanest men, and perhaps that was not too surprising, given that it was the capital of cicibeism (see Chapter 2).[79] James Howell reported in his *Instructions* (1618) that 'it is proverbially said, there are in Genoa, Montaines without wood, Sea without fish, Women without shame, and Men without conscience'.[80] The French traveller Raby d'Amerique wrote that 'les Milanaises sont grandes, bien faites, [ayant] en apparence beaucoup de gorge' ['Milanese women are big and well-formed, and they reveal a lot of throat (they are shameless because they bare the neck, i.e. they are *decolleteés*, a word first attested in 1821)'], while another adds that in Lombardy 'les paysannes [sont] svelte et jolies filant sur les pas de leur portes' ['countrywomen look slim and pretty on their doorsteps'] and the Venetians definitely demonstrate 'façons lascives et attrayantes' ['lascivious and attractive ways'].[81] A catchy summary of the subject was that Italy is 'A paradise inhabited by devils', an expression used by Wotton in Florence and

[77] Ibid., 283.

[78] James Boswell's Letter to Rousseau, from Lucca, 3 October 1765, in Frank Brady and Frederick. A. Pottle (eds.), *Boswell on the Grand Tour, Italy Corsica, and France 1765–1766* (New York, Toronto, London, 1955), 3.

[79] Pine-Coffin, *British and American Travel*, 47. On the connection between cicisbeism and the town of Genoa, see Chapter 2.

[80] Howell, *Instructions*, 41.

[81] Gilles Bertrand, *Le Grand Tour revisité: pour une archéologie du tourisme: le voyage des français en Italie, milieu XVIIIe siècle-début XIXe siècle* (Rome, 2008), 244–5 n.99 and n.101.

by Misson in Naples.[82] Ellis Veryard in his *Account* published in 1701 recalls
a saying from Sicily: 'a Messina assai polvere, pulce e Putane' ['in Messina
they have Dust, Fleas, and Whores enough'].[83] While the Frenchman
Nicholas Audebert found the most beautiful women in Modena, the Italian
Sebastano Locatelli reported that Mantua was the city with a nationwide
reputation for male sexual exuberance.[84]

Thomas Coryat in his book *Crudities* recollects a proverb heard on his way to
Venice in 1608, 'Quanti ha Venetia ponti e Gondolieri, Tanti ha Vicenza Conti
e Cavallieri', and explains 'That is, looke how many bridges and Gondoleers
Venice doth yeeld, so many Counts, and Knights doth Vicenza'. This was not
a kind remark about Venice, nor was the other famous motto:

Vin Vicentin,	[The Wine of Vicenza,
Pan Paduan,	The Bread of Padua,
Tripe Trevizan,	The Tripe of Treviza,
Putana Venetian.	The Cortezans of Venice.][85]

Many travellers did not miss the opportunity to pass comment on or indeed to
challenge the truth of the proverbs they collected. Thomas Coryat was
obviously not the first to enjoy this special attraction of Venice, but he was
alone in claiming that the travel literature did not include adequate information
to assist travellers on this matter. With his typical enthusiasm, he carried out
a quality test of this last item on the list of the Veneto's regional delicacies. His
conclusion was that in a city with at least twenty thousand such women,
a gentleman could easily find one to his liking but he also issued the warning
that many 'are esteemed so loose, that they are said to open their quivers to
every arrow'.

---

[82] Henry Wotton, *The Life and Letters of Sir Henry Wotton*, in Logan Pearsall Smith (ed.), 2 vols.
(Oxford, 1907), I, 21; François Maximilien Misson, *A New Voyage to Italy*, 2 vols. (London,
1695), I, 308.

[83] Veryard, *An Account,* 225.

[84] The first quote is from Nicolas Audebert, in Adalberto Olivero (ed.), *Voyage d'Italie* (Rome,
1981), II, 67; the second is from Locatelli, *Viaggio*, 284, who comments: '*Questi benedetti
mantovani hanno una gran proclività verso le donne*' ['These blessed men from Mantua have
a great proclivity for women']. See also n.50, p. 436.

[85] Coryat, *Crudities*, II, 14.

2   Attractions, Affectations, Aberrations

Linguistic Benefits of Travel

A key point about the evolution of the Grand Tour is that, once it ceased to be the culmination of a young gentleman's education, travel assumed the less ambitious objective of offering an opportunity to see the world. For the most motivated travellers, there was also a change in the vocational content of learning: while training in classical studies was more typical of the first phase of the Grand Tour, the study of arts and architecture became dominant in the second phase. Despite such changes, for the best part of three hundred years language learning never completely ceased to be a focal point of the foreign experience, although the role attributed to it did change from being a medium of classical scholarship to serving as a vehicle of modern civilisation.

In Renaissance England, it was political need that marked a change from the days of solitary academic travellers who expended individual effort and resources on learning languages during their studies abroad, to those of young men whose foreign travel was subsidised through ad hoc schemes introduced by the crown and universities, and who thus ceased to be travelling as private individuals. At that time the English court had become conscious that Latin was no longer sufficient for communication between the intellectual elites of Europe, and this awareness increased with the Reformation movement against the Roman Catholic Church. Peter Burke remarked how much Elizabethan England was concerned about its linguistic isolation, recounting a relevant quotation of the time: 'Nobody in the sixteenth century except an Englishman was expected to speak English, not even the perfect ambassador.'[1] More or less at the same time, in a language manual that appeared in London in 1578 for teaching conversational Italian – the lingua franca of the time – one of the dialogues made the same point:

---

[1] The reference in Burke, *Languages and Communities* is to 'a distinguished historian of the Renaissance', 115.

What thinke you of this English tongue, tel me, I pray you? It is a language that wyl do you good in England, but passé Douer, it is worth nothing. It is not then vsed in other coutreyes? No sir, with whom wyl you that they speake? With English marchants.	Che vi pare di questa lingua Inglese, ditemi di gratia. È un[a]lingua che vi farà bene In Inghilterra, ma passate Douer, la non val niente. Dunque non è praticata fori in altri paesi? Signor no, con chi volete che parlino? Con i mercanti Inglesi.[2]

Even more telling than the point made about the 'English marchants' – a precursor to the monetarist approach to foreign language education – is the reference to the linguistic profile of the 'perfect ambassador'. Indeed, English diplomats resident in France and in many courts of the Italian peninsula were expected by their sponsors in the English court to write notes home about foreign languages and social customs.[3] But this was not only an English preoccupation as it was a matter of national interest to make sure that young members of the nobility could use the appropriate language not only to establish contacts but also to promote their knowledge abroad, while observing and appraising foreign cultures.

One example was Sir Philip Sidney, whose official travel licence shows that he was allowed to journey abroad to gain experience in international diplomacy. A specific condition written into his licence was that he could travel specifically 'for his attaining to the knowledge of foreign languages' but he was ordered to avoid 'territories or countries of any prince or potentate not being with us in amity or league', certainly an allusion to Italy.[4] Sidney reached Paris at the age of eighteen and was welcomed to the city by Francis Walsingham, a radical Protestant, formerly head of Elizabeth's secret service. The secret agent was officially asked to take this Oxford graduate under his protection, and in no time Philip became a successful young man at the French court. This was by virtue of his extraordinary command of the French language: according to many reports, everyone was astonished at the fluent conversations of the 'Baron de Sidenay'.[5] When Queen Elizabeth heard about the Saint Bartholomew's Day Massacre in Paris (1572) carried out by Roman Catholics against the Huguenots, she instructed Walsingham to procure her most valuable apprentice diplomat a licence to return home. Interestingly, the

---

[2] Brian Richardson, 'Varie maniere di parlare': aspects of learning Italian in Renaissance Italy and Britain', in Vilma de Gasperin (ed.), *Ciò che potea la lingua nostra: Lectures and Essays in Memory of Clara Florio Cooper*, special supplement of *The Italianist*, 30 (2010), 91.

[3] Stoye, in his *English Travellers,* refers in particular to the periodical reports of English diplomats who were resident in Italian courts, 91.

[4] Quoted in Trease, *The Grand Tour*, 17.   [5] Ibid.

young Philip felt he had just begun his tour so he disobeyed the Queen, travelled to Frankfurt, Vienna, Buda(pest) and eventually reached Venice and Padua.

The Queen and the Privy Council were happy to issue royal licences to all reliable applicants even though quite a number of the young noblemen, once on the Continent, changed their itineraries. Some were willing to act as secret agents when it was deemed necessary to obtain sensitive information useful to the court. One of these was Sir Henry Wotton, another remarkable young man who soon earned respect for his diplomatic interests and linguistic flexibility. Born into a family with close ties to the royal court, he attended Oxford to study diplomacy under Alberico Gentili, a distinguished Italian academic of the Protestant faith who had fled the Peninsula to escape the Roman Inquisition. Wotton, who already had a good command of Italian when he obtained his royal licence to leave England, headed for Germany where he planned to study German and law. He was allowed to visit Frankfurt for the book fair but then he continued on to Geneva, Vienna and Prague. At that point he decided to aim for Venice, but to be safe, he chose to disguise himself as a German Catholic. According to a travel companion, his command of German was good enough to deceive a native. Initially Wotton did not like Venice and decided to move south into the Papal States. He stayed in Rome for five weeks, with occasional visits to Naples, retaining his German disguise while travelling around. But he had to leave Rome suddenly as he was introduced to an Englishman whom he had identified as a dangerous spy for the local Catholic English College. Before returning home after five years abroad, Wotton decided to spend time in Geneva to improve his command of French. With his diplomatic training at Oxford, his practical experience serving the secret service, and his near-native mastery of French, German and Italian, he was offered the post of ambassador in Venice at the age of only twenty-six. His knowledge of Italian in particular must have been quite extraordinary as he did not resist yet another temptation to don foreign disguise, this time as an Italian going under the assumed name Ottavio Baldi while he was in residence at the Scottish court.

Fynes Moryson was another Englishman who was so fascinated with travel and foreign languages that he visited almost every country in Europe before reaching the Middle East. He was in Italy in 1593–5 and after returning home he wrote an *Itinerary*. The book contains valuable information about cities, monuments, practical advice and cost details but his narrative stands out for his descriptions of proudly eluding the Inquisition authorities through his multi-lingual skills. Moryson was another keen polyglot who could pass himself off as a Frenchman or a German according to circumstances. Like Wotton, he reported being suspicious of a person sitting next to him at the public supper table who described himself as a German merchant on his way to Milan. Moryson decided to address him in his excellent German but was immediately aware of the poor quality of his interlocutor's language. The embarrassed merchant explained that he came from a francophone region of Germany. Moryson, growing more mistrustful, decided to switch into his equally excellent French, only to quickly realise that the dubious character had an even worse command of that language. After reverting to Italian, they finally admitted that they were both English and were unhappy about revealing their nationality to strangers. Many such incidents of pretence are reported in travel diaries from Elizabethan and Jacobean England. At that time, if there were good reasons for travelling on the Continent in disguise, a fake foreign identity certainly provided an incentive for language learning.[6]

A traveller who was adventurous, eccentric and witty but somewhat unrepresentative of his time, though quite conventionally attracted by the prospect of a prestigious career, was Thomas Coryat. However, Coryat's travel book is still typical of this time in two ways. One way is the fulsome display of his classical knowledge when reporting on cultural and artistic matters he came across on his journey to Venice. Another is his eccentric manipulation of language, showing evidence of a taste for baroque narrative decorated with witty experiments in multilingual blendings of modern languages, Latin and Greek. The great Ben Jonson, who met Coryat at the Mermaid Club, referred to him using epithets such as 'Tongue-Major of the company' and 'Bold carpenter of words'.[7] Thomas Coryat deserved them as he was quite a formidable linguist. He spoke Greek and Latin regularly on his journey whenever he could not communicate in French or Italian. Apparently, while travelling in the Levant and India, he learned Turkish, Persian, Hindustani and Arabic, once using the latter to shout at a mullah who was praying too loudly in a minaret in Agra. In Persia, confirming his passion for making speeches, he delivered an oration in the local language in the presence of Jahangir, the Mughal Emperor.[8]

The adventures of Thomas Coryat were many and disparate as he travelled alone and on foot. In Germany he was confronted by a number of hungry peasants after stealing from their vineyard: 'I being not able to speake Dutch asked them whether any of the company could speake Latin ... Then he like a very sociable companion interposed himselfe betwixt us as a mediator.'[9]

---

[6] The story is mentioned during the journey recorded in *Itinerary* vol. I, p. 363. Moryson was obviously proud of his linguistic performance as he reports the same episode again in connection with the advantages of learning foreign languages in vol. III, p. 381.

[7] Quotations taken from Trease, *The Grand Tour*, 52.

[8] For Coryat's encounters on the road, see R. E. Pritchard, *Odd Tom Coryate, The English Marco Polo* (Stroud, 2004), and for his linguistic experiences while travelling to India, especially 243–8. The multilingual skills of Coryat are probably exaggerated in the report by Edward Terry, chaplain of the English Embassy to the Great Mughal, in *The Travels of Mr Thomas Coryat,* printed in *The English Acquisition in Guinea & East India,* by R. B. *[sic]* (London, 1700), 170–6.

[9] Coryat, *Crudities*, II, 254.

When stopped by bandits in Germany near Baden, he pretended to be a beggar: 'I put off my hat very courteously unto them ... and very humbly (like a Mendicant Frier) begged some money of them ... expressing my minde unto them by such gestures and signes, that they well knew what I craved of them.'[10] On another occasion he became lost and needed to ask for directions:

> It was my hap in this journey betwixt Oppenheim and Mentz to have such a notable companion as I never had before in all my life. For he was both learned and unlearned. Learned because being but a wood-cleaver (for he told me that he was the Jesuits wood-cleaver of Mentz) he was able to speake Latine. ... he was unlearned, because the Latin which he did speake was such incongruall and disjointed stuffe, such antipriscianisticall eloquence.[11]

Coryat was also impressed by polyglots, whose hyperbolic performances he described in great detail. He met one such man in France: 'The other Turk was a notable companion and a great scholler in his kinde; for he spake sixe or seven languages besides the Latin, which he spake very well: he was borne in Constantinople.'[12] He encountered another in Switzerland: 'a singular linguist ... For he spake seven languages, being very skilful in Hebrew and Greek tongue, and a famous traveler';[13] and a third in Italy: 'Truly I perceived him to be an excellent Scholler, a very eloquent discourser in the Latin, a fine Grecian, ... he studied the Hebrew tongue very diligently ... to discourse with the learned Rabbins of the Jewes, ... and he doth often so earnestly dispute with them, that he hath converted some of them to Christianity.'[14]

Fascinated by language absurdities and excesses, Coryat was mesmerised by the local Bergamo dialect, reputed to be the most brutish in Italy: 'The language of this City is esteemed the rudest and grossest of all Italy as the Boeotian dialect was the basest of all Greece.'[15] Cities known for having the best or worst language were a favorite *topos* among the vast repertory of mirabilia found on the Grand Tour, such as encounters with bandits, public executions and urban Jewish ghettos. In Coryat's case, the inclination to adorn his narrative with a myriad of linguistic details was in tune with the cultural climate of the late Elizabethan age.[16]

---

[10] Ibid., II, 198–9.   [11] Ibid., II, 269.   [12] Ibid., I, 211–12.   [13] Ibid., II, 100.

[14] Ibid., I, 272.

[15] A commonplace in sixteenth-century England was that the more distant a variety was from the purest form of the language, the more barbarous and morally degenerate were its speech communities; see Joseph M. Williams, '"O! When Degree is Shak'd": sixteenth-century anticipations of some modern attitudes towards usage', in Tim William Machan and Charles T. Scott (eds.), *English in Its Social Context: Essays in Historical Sociolinguistics* (Oxford, 1992), 73. It is interesting that for both French and Italian, travellers' references to their purest versions were supported by information about the gentle manners of their speakers (see Chapter 7). One exception was, of course, Smollett (see the section, 'The Art of Conversation').

[16] Franco Marenco, 'Introduzione', in Franco Marenco and Antonio Meo (eds.), *Thomas Coryat, Crudezze, 1608* (Milan, 1975), 1–38.

Another quite extraordinary traveller at the beginning of the Grand Tour was Philip Skippon. Having graduated from Cambridge and studied law at Gray's Inn, he travelled between 1663 and 1666 with his tutor John Ray, a botanist and linguist, to Germany, Italy, Switzerland, France and the Netherlands. Not only was he quite relaxed about speaking a number of foreign languages, he was actually excited, like Moryson and Coryat, whenever he managed to pass himself off as a native speaker, either for fun or in an emergency.[17] With a strong interest in language, and keen to follow the practice of reporting on cultural diversity, his approach was both enthusiastic and accurate. For example, he made reference to polyglots whenever he met them and also kept careful records about the rare speakers of English on the Continent.[18] He enjoyed language games in the company of fellow travellers and missed no chance to collect epithets describing the qualities (mainly sexual) of rival cities.[19] He drew unusual mechanisms in his sketchbooks with great precision and classified in his diary every possible situation where language functioned as a barrier or a bridge to a new culture: for example, bilingual bills of health; cities renowned for the best language or the worst accent; survival terms for use on the road; Latin inscriptions and epitaphs; specimens of unusual languages (Maltese and Romansh); multilingual customs of linguistic, frontier and religious minorities; and speech habits of the upper and lower classes, e.g. in church or at the theatre.[20] As a traveller who believed that language was a key *topos* for explaining human diversity, Skippon described in detail all the circumstances that could improve one's understanding of the dissimilarities between different lands and peoples.

The outbreak of the English Civil War in the second half of the seventeenth century led many young gentlemen of various ages to leave the country, sometimes while still very young, for their own personal safety and for that of their family estates. By that time, preparing for a diplomatic career or a court appointment was no longer the only reason for travelling, but government licences and passports were still needed to do so and they bore the standard phrase 'to get languages in good perfection' as one of the most frequent motivations for travelling abroad. Robert Montagu (Lord de Mandeville) was fifteen when he left England. Robert Devereux third Earl of Essex was seventeen. John Raymond was a little older and for that generation long periods of residence abroad were a good political solution. It was even more advantageous if their absence from England included a long stay in one of the favoured continental centres for language learning – the Loire towns in France, and Siena

[17] Skippon, 'An account', 383.
[18] Ibid., for polyglots: 503, 440; for English speakers: 365, 377, 400.
[19] Ibid., for language games: 481; for epithets: 536, 563, 587, 615, 641, 646, 647.
[20] Ibid., respectively, 483 and 590; 644–5 and 563; 642 and 648; 378, 529, 550; 624–5; 697–9, 695–6, 509–10; 534; 502.

in Italy. Unlike Coryat, who was in his early thirties when he left home – an unusually late age to do so during the first century of the Grand Tour – the sons of the aristocracy who ventured abroad from England at this time tended to be even younger than Skippon, who was twenty-one. Their comments about language learning were very often included in correspondence with families back home, especially in connection with the parental investment in the experience abroad, as we see in a letter by this young man on his way back to England in 1717:

> I have done what has been in my power towards perfecting myself in French, and have learnt as much Italian as the small share of conversation, which strangers can have with the people of the country would admit of. As for German language it is so extremely difficult, my staying has been so short in any one place, and the accents and manner of speaking so different all over Germany, that I could not propose to myself to make any progress in it.[21]

In the eighteenth century, the golden age of the Grand Tour, France and Italy became attractive to a wider variety of Grand Tourists as there was a strong inclination among all the aristocracies of northern Europe to see themselves as rough nations with crude attitudes that could benefit from immersion in the gracious manners of modern France or in the artistic style of glorious Italy. The transformation of the Grand Tour from an educational experience into one of entertainment was reflected by an increase in negative comments as the social fashion spread. At the end of the century, a comment by Lady Knight in Rome summarised this decline: 'I am very apt to think that the present mode of travelling is turned rather to amusement than to improvement.'[22] But even in the early part of the century, when the social fashion for travel started and Italy was still renowned for its classical traditions, travelling for educational purposes was regarded with suspicion with some comments aimed at the dubious linguistic benefits of a tour. Alexander Pope was one of these sceptics, as shown in the satirical verses of *Dunciad* (first published in 1723):

> Led by my hand, he saunter'd Europe round,
> And gather'd ev'ry Vice on Christian ground;
> Saw ev'ry Court, heard ev'ry King declare
> His royal Sense, of Op'ra's or the Fair;
> The Stews and Palace equally explor'd,
> Intrigu'd with glory, and with spirit whor'd;
> Try'd all *hors-d'oeuvres*, all *liqueurs* defin'd,
> Judicious drank, and greatly-daring din'd;
> Dropt the dull lumber of the Latin store,
> Spoil'd his own language, and acquir'd no more;

[21] Quoted by Black, *The British Abroad*, 291.
[22] Lady Phillipina Knight, *Lady Knight's Letters from France and Italy 1776–1795*, Lady Elliott-Drake (ed.) (London, 1905). Quoted by Black, *The British Abroad*, 300.

> All Classic learning lost on Classic ground;
> And last turn'd Air; the Echo of a Sound!
> See now, half-cur'd, and perfectly well-bred,
> With nothing but a Sola in his head.[23]

Another critic was William Cowper, who gave voice to his opinion in the moralistic poem *The Progress of Error*, published in 1782:

> From school to Cam or Isis, and thence home;
> And thence with all convenient speed to Rome.
> With reverend tutor clad in habit lay,
> To tease for cash, and quarreled with all day;
> With memorandum-book for every town,
> And every post, and where the chaise broke down;
> His stock a few French phrases got by heart,
> With much to learn, but nothing to impart;
> The youth, obedient to his sire's commands,
> Sets off a wanderer into foreign lands,
> Surprised at all they meet, the gosling pair,
> With awkward gait, stretch'd neck, and silly stare,
> Discover huge cathedrals built in stone,
> And steeples towering high much like our own;
> But show peculiar light by many a grin
> At popish practices observed within.[24]

On the other hand, a few years before that Adam Smith, in his work *The Wealth of Nations* (1776), defended what he regarded as the only enduring advantage of travel: providing a young man with the opportunity for language learning. He himself had first-hand experience as a travelling tutor, having left a successful academic career to take his charge abroad. But the outcome of such a journey was far from favourable; he remarked of the young Englishman that 'in other respects he commonly returns home more conceited, more unprincipled, more dissipated, and more incapable of any serious application either to study or to do business than he could well have become in so short a time had he lived at home'.[25]

Aping the Foreigners

Most public and private remarks about the linguistic implications of travel, and the inclinations of the young men after settling in back home, pointed in the same direction. Philosophers and educationists feared that a positive tour

---

[23] Alexander Pope, *The Dunciad*, Book IV, in John Butt (ed.), *The Poems of Alexander Pope* (London, 1963).
[24] William Cowper, *The Progress of Errors* (1782), rpt. in *The Poems* (Boston, 1860), 39–40.
[25] Adam Smith, *The Wealth of Nations* (London, 1776), in Dugald Stewart (ed.), *The Works of Adam Smith*, 5 vols. (London, 1811), IV, 171.

experience could have a negative outcome if the young man had not taken advantage of language learning opportunities. Parents and instructors were concerned that language immersion abroad should not take place in a cultural void. None, however, mentioned the possibility that early exposure to foreign languages interfered with the natural development and mastery of a young person's native language.[26] Moreover – as pointed out by Bacon – the risk of acquiring a modern tongue, rather than using a dead language like Latin as a lingua franca, presented new hazards that worried families more than institutions. The risk was that the experience of full immersion in a modern language abroad in order to 'perfect its knowledge' could tempt the young mind to adopt foreign habits.

However, if the risk of going native was too remote, the risk of acquiring foreign manners was quite real. There was plenty of evidence of such a tendency throughout Europe, from the Renaissance to the rise of nationalism. Virtually every generation had been confronted with a lifestyle which had originated abroad, much admired by most but usually imitated by few; this social trend was often combined with an interest in the most fashionable modern language of the time. But when foreign behaviour began to be granted more respect than native manners, not everyone was impressed by the French *bon ton* or, the Italian *gentilezza* or *sprezzatura* (gracious nonchalance). In most countries, criticism arose especially from the common people and men of letters. The aristocracies were more exposed to foreign customs, as they were used to encouraging their sons to become one of the locals, and many ended up adopting foreign manners as well as their dress. There were, of course, different degrees of visibility and national tolerance. While Italian style and French fashion were commonly seen as far away as Russia and Poland – where German etiquette was also very influential[27] – they were more visible and certainly were considered more scandalous across the Channel.

The earliest adaptation of foreign manners was the Italianisation that took place in the sixteenth century in Elizabethan England, but also in other European countries.[28] The emphasis of that movement, however, was academic and literary rather than social and frivolous. Once Italy became known to Europeans for its principal role in promoting a cosmopolitan Renaissance, its gracious sophistication was studied and admired by the intellectual elites, who deemed its culture, language and style to be supranational, almost a revived version of classical Latin. The Englishmen who gained a reputation as Italophiles were diplomats like Thomas Hoby, the translator

---

[26] Alexander Pope was a rare exception, see the reference to 'Spoil'd his own language, and acquir'd no more' in *The Dunciad*.

[27] See Mączak, *Travel*, 157.

[28] See Charles G. Nauert Jr, *Humanism and the Culture of Renaissance Europe* (Cambridge, 1995).

of Castiglione's *Courtier*, one of the most influential texts of the Renaissance; scholars like William Thomas, author of the first *Italian Grammar* and *The History of Italy*; and politicians like Thomas Cromwell, chief minister of King Henry VIII at a time when the term *Italianate* did not have a pejorative meaning. It was when England entered a period of isolation from the Catholic Continent, due to the excommunication of Queen Elizabeth, that hostility towards Italy and Italians took on the flavour of a religious war.[29]

However, in Elizabethan England, it wasn't only Italian fashion that was being criticised, as all travellers who returned home from foreign lands were ridiculed by popular satirists for their new manners. There is evidence that dowdy Englishmen were offended by their compatriots wearing extravagant clothing, displaying foreign manners and modifying their native language after years spent abroad. Howard quoted the following comment: 'You shall see a dapper Jacke, that hath beene but over at Deepe, wring his face round about, as a man would stir up a mustard-pot, and talke English through the teeth, like ... Mingo de Moustrapas.' Thomas Nash, in his fictional diary *The Unfortunate Traveller* (1594), also satirised Frenchified Englishmen who returned from France after some years: 'and when they come hom, they have hyd a littlewéerish leane face under a broad French hat, kept a terrible coyle with the dust in the street in their long cloaks of gray paper, and spoke English strangely'.[30]

The imitation of foreign manners at home also included manifestations of language use, as reported by many travellers, but a few, like Horace Walpole, carefully attempted to escape that social convention: 'I have not brought over a word of French or Italian for common use; I have so taken pains to avoid affectation in this point, that I have failed only now and then in a *chi è là?* to the servants, who I can scarce persuade myself yet are English.'[31] Walpole had a special eye for social conformism and soon realised that, as the century advanced, Anglomania was growing in France just as French manners had spread in England. The local aristocracy imported race horses, private clubs and tea parties, but did not acknowledge these as a foreign fashion: 'If something foreign arrives at Paris, they either think they invented it, or that it has always been there.'[32] The same was happening in other European countries, such as Italy, where tea drinking had

[29] See Sara Warneke, *Images of the Educational Travellers in Early Modern England* (Leiden, 1995), especially chapter 4, 'The devil incarnate: The Italianated Traveller'. Most reports from the time scorn the hybrid identity of returning travellers. However, one recent study emphasises the cultural enrichment demonstrated by a young traveller, John North, on his return from Italy, who was proud of his new cosmopolitan mentality. See Gallagher, 'The Italian London'.

[30] Howard, *The English Travelers*, 26–7.

[31] Horace Walpole, Letter from Sittinburn, 13 September 1741, in *Letters of Horace Walpole*, 4 vols. (Philadelphia, 1842), I, 173. Cohen in *Fashioning Masculinity* remarks that, despite the widespread ostentatiousness of many who had been on a Grand Tour, 'The true gentleman ... displayed neither his foreign clothes nor his foreign tongue', 59.

[32] Horace Walpole, Letter CXLVI from Arlington St 30 November 1769, *Letters of Horace Walpole Earl of Orford to Sir Horace Mann*, 4 vols. (London, 1843), vol. I, 173.

become fashionable, imported from France as indicated by the expression 'à l'Angloise'. The tea ritual was certainly to be found in the home of the famous castrato singer Senesino, who picked up the habit during his sixteen years in London, and once back home made a point of inviting all distinguished English visitors who passed through Siena to take tea with him.

Dr John Moore, the Scottish surgeon who became a governor out of his sheer passion for travelling, admitted disliking the insular prejudices of Englishmen abroad, but also their absurd affectations after returning home:

There are instances of Englishmen who, while on their travels, shock foreigners by an ostentatious preference of England to all the rest of the world, and ridicule the manners, customs and opinions of every other nation; yet on their return to their own country, immediately assume foreign manners, and continue during the remainder of their lives to express the highest contempt for everything that is English. I hope he will entirely avoid such perverse and ridiculous affectation.[33]

While this scoffing at Frenchified compatriots was quite tame compared with the darker comments about Italianised Englishmen, both attitudes were unrepresentative and short-lived compared with the madness of adopting 'fine cloths', 'foreign airs' and 'new phrases' from France in the eighteenth century. Many visits to that country were reported as having the sole purpose of training young men to become citizens of the world simply by crossing the Channel. The art of conversation and the art of pleasing women were the two main skills of the Frenchified fop.[34] While the final destination of the Grand Tour was still elsewhere (as Nugent pointed out in his book *The Grand Tour,* published in 1749, 'Italy for fine cities surpasses the rest of Europe'),[35] tourists began to linger longer in France as its society and etiquette came to set the new European cultural standard. Dr Veryard wrote in 1701:

Our English seem of late to be strangely infatuated with, and fond of, whatever bears the name of *French.* My Lord's perruque fits not well till *Monsieur* has had a hand in it, and my Lady relishes not her victuals, unless they are served in with a *French* sauce. The Exchange Woman would have a poor trade, had they not the knack of *Frenchifying* their wares; and a Courtier could hardly pretend to the quality of Huff and Beau unless he's spent some time at a *French* academy and entertained Masters of Sciences of that Nation.[36]

A visit to Paris was a must for every Englishman claiming to be an *homme du monde,* as the art of living was best learned in situ, and those who were attracted by the sites and opportunities in the French capital were not just students of

---

[33] Moore, *A View of Society and Manners*, Letter XCVI, II, 381.

[34] Cohen, *Fashioning Masculinity*, 39.

[35] Nugent, *The Grand Tour*, III, 19. However, one should note that Nugent is one of those travel writers who possibly never visited Italy in person, as pointed out by Sweet in *Cities and the Grand Tour*, 15, n.45.

[36] Veryard, *An Account*, 108.

Figure 2.1 *What is this my son Tom*, 1774. Mezzotint with some etching. Published by R. Sayer & J. Bennett, London. ©The Trustees of the British Museum

manners but also men of letters. They all felt the obligation to pay homage to French society and French fashions. Even Dr Johnson, certainly one of the least conformist men of the time, when in Paris on his only visit to the Continent in the autumn of 1775 is said to have purchased a pair of new stockings, a new wig, and a more suitable hat to conform with French fashion.[37] Two years

---

[37] Maxwell, *English Traveller*. The author reminds us that Dr Johnson was in Paris with the Thrales in 1775, and this was his only visit to the Continent, 7, n.2.

earlier, while touring Scotland, Dr Johnson was mocked by his Scottish friend James Boswell: 'You can't ride. You are a delicate Londoner; you are a - macaroni.'[38] It was a hyperbolic comment, a trendy expression among Londoners, undeserved but certainly funny.

The term 'macaroni' described a French style of high fashion, very popular with dandies, which included wearing a tall powdered wig with a *chapeau bras* on top, as portrayed in many satirical caricatures published in London in the early 1770s. Despite the fact that the term related to French not Italian habits, an association with the latter must have been in the air since the character Marlow in the play *She Stoops to Conquer* (1773) by Oliver Goldsmith, when reprimanding himself in Act IV for his own stupidity, cries out: 'O, confound my stupid head, I shall be laughed at over the whole town. I shall be stuck up in caricatura in all the print-shops. The Dullissimo Maccaroni.' Certainly, this vogue grew out of the tradition of the Grand Tour and did not wear out quickly: throughout the 1770s, the expression 'English Maccaroni' denoted someone who went on the Grand Tour only to acquire a fashionable look.

The Art of Conversation

By the eighteenth century, the Grand Tourists' normal way of socialising abroad was through taking advantage of introductions to distinguished residents and attending social gatherings in their salons. Some visitors first undertook lessons in French or Italian conversation in their respective countries. The success of such language training, which also served as instruction in how to interact politely, is not difficult to imagine, given the different cultural traditions and lack of correspondence between English gentility, French gallantry and Italian *cavalier servitude* (a term used by Byron, see 'Shocking Foreign Customs'). Saint-Evremond is reported to have stated: 'Generally no Conversation would be more agreeable than that of the French, if they could talk a little less, and that of the English, if they could speak a little more than they do.' But Dr Johnson, writing in the middle of the eighteenth century, harboured a more critical view and distinguished between what he called 'genuine' politeness and the practice of the 'exterior and unessential part of civility', explaining that 'the former aimed at putting the other before the self, and curbing one's vanity; the latter consisting of the minutiae of visiting and talking "frippery and slight silks" with the ladies.'[39] By Dr Johnson's time, *la conversation parisienne* had developed as a form of social entertainment that

---

[38] James Boswell, in Frederick A. Pottle and Charles H. Bennett (eds.), *Boswell's Journal of the Tour of the Hebrides with Samuel Johnson, LL.D.*, 58.

[39] Both quotations are found in Cohen, *Fashioning Masculinity*, the one by St Evremond on page 149, n.47, and that by Johnson on page 132, n.46. The author refers to these comments in the context of the relationship between conversational style and national character, where she

required, among other features, an obsessive repetition of compliments and use of the most elaborate politeness formulae. This was also known as 'polite conversation', a custom perceived by foreign visitors who were little inclined to submit themselves to the fashion, as superficial social occasions burdened with the exchange of unnecessary compliments and frivolous formalities. Smollett did not see any value in these '*dialogues gallants*', a sort of ridiculous flirtation performed by men with women, which he put down to the typical nature of French men:

He piques himself upon being polished above the natives of any other country by his conversation with – the fair sex. In the course of this communication, with which he is indulged from his tender years, he learns like a parrot, by rote, the whole circle of French compliments, which you know are a set of phrases, ridiculous even to a proverb; and these he throws out indiscriminately to all women, without distinction, in the exercise of that kind of address, which is here distinguished by the name of gallantry: it is no more than his making love to every woman who will give him the hearing.[40]

If some visitors found the conversation of the French nobility superficial, others appraised it as being witty and graceful, part of the delightful manners with which they were welcomed into local 'drawing-room life'. But most observers who went abroad with a serious intent could not help disliking this artificiality. Dr Moore was extremely unimpressed with *la vie des salons* in Paris, which he reported as being obsessed with conversational trivialities such as what the king ate and wore, which horse he rode, and so on.[41] Polite conversation was a broad term that included different types of social occasion, as well as diverse types of performances and social skills. Indeed, when reporting on their soirées in France and Italy, many English visitors stressed the different nature of their interactions. Usually they distinguish French *conversations* from what Italians called *conversazioni*, and indeed the latter then assumed the meaning of social gatherings, in contrast with the gallant French version.

However, Italian *conversazioni,* especially in the salons of the highest nobility where travellers expected to become involved in discussions on literature and the arts, were also tedious affairs. In the absence of a stimulating exchange of ideas, a buffet orchestra with singers and games of cards compensated for the disappointment. But this was not enough to meet the expectations of scholars and men of letters like Horace Walpole, who commented: 'Roman conversations are dreadful things! Such untoward mawkins as the princesses! And the princes are worse.'[42] In other Italian cities, apparently there was not much more in the way of entertainment. John Moore felt most disappointed by

---

concludes that 'by the end of the eighteenth century, the monosyllabic English tongue and the taciturnity of its native speakers were fused into a common national trait, manliness', 107.

[40] Smollett, *Travels*, 104.   [41] Moore, *A View of Society etc.* Letter VI, I, 34.

[42] Walpole, Letter from Rome, 23 April 1740, in *Letters of Horace Walpole* (1842), I, 151.

his evening *conversazioni* in Florence: 'a great deal of bustle, and a continual change of place', but 'scarcely any change of company, or any variation of amusement'.[43] Samuel Sharp related a similar opinion about the upper-classes in Naples:

They are . . . so unaccustomed to entertain one another . . . But upon these occasions they are very pompous, and, what is extraordinary, the lying-in Ladies receive company in great crowds, the day after their delivery, which, however, as soon as the compliments are paid, retire immediately into the adjacent chambers, where they form themselves into card parties, or *converzationi*.[44]

William Patoun, the secretary of Lord Brownlow who was asked to plan his journey to Italy, gives a good flavour of Roman conversations in his impressionistic but most instructive report, *Advice on Travel in Italy* (1766):

Upon the whole the Resources at Rome for an English man are to be derived more from the Place than the inhabitants. The Conversationi are the dullest things in the World. You go in, you make your Bow to the Lady of the House, you Stare at the Company playing at Games for Sixpences which you never are at the pains to learn and then you huddle with the groups of English into a Corner, talk loud, often at the Expence of the Company, grow tired & go home. Such often is the Case with travelers.[45]

Of course, the dynamics of the social discourse involved in conversations in an Italian boudoir or in a French salon were not easily detectable even by foreigners who were proficient in the language. Compliments were quite likely to involve subtle double entendres more than superficial trivialities, especially when dialogues involved Italian *cavalier serventi* or French *petit-maîtres* and their respective ladies, all of whom were experienced in the language of the salons.[46] Clearly such polite conversations involved a type of sociability which was difficult to interpret and join in with, even for native speakers who were outsiders with respect to that particular social group.

As the eighteenth century was drawing to a close, the social art of conversation in Europe was also dying out. The French aristocracy had never seen why they should learn English, while the Italian nobility was increasingly confronted with new colonies of English residents who had emigrated to the

---

[43] John Moore, *A View of Society etc.* Letter XXXVI, I, 381. The poet Thomas Gray confirmed this: 'Lent in Florence comprised of a sermon in the morning, full of hell and devil; a dinner at noon, full of fish and meagre diet; and, in the evening, a sort of assembly at the principal people's house, full of what I cannot tell' (19 March 1740); quoted in John Ingamells (ed.), *A Dictionary of British and Irish Travellers in Italy, 1701–1800* (New Haven and London, 1997), 426.

[44] Samuel Sharp, *Letters from Italy: Describing the Customs and Manners of That Country, in the Years 1765, and 1766 etc.* (*London*, 1766), 109.

[45] William, Patoun, 'Advice on Travel in Italy', in Ingamells (ed.), *British and Irish Travellers*, xlvi.

[46] The special role of these male aristocrats within French and Italian societies will be discussed more fully at the end of this chapter.

romantic cities of the Peninsula.[47] Travellers reported that in a city like Rome, Italian soon ceased to be the language of conversation. In addition, its nobility, who never felt sympathy towards the patriotic unification of the country, began to regard themselves as being closer in manners and distinction to the foreign residents. French and English quickly became the languages of their salons, while Italian, the native language in Florence, offered no threat either to the international status of French or to the language loyalty of the large community of English émigrés. The same state of affairs was witnessed in other cities, such as Turin, Genoa and Naples, where Byron was often invited by Lady Blessington, the glamorous Irish writer, who portrayed him in *The Conversations of Lord Byron* (1834) as 'a lively, brilliant conversationist' but certainly not a *poseur*.[48]

Language Performers Extraordinaire

A type of linguistic entertainment that came as a surprise to most visitors in Italy was the performances by *improvvisatori*. These were men or women who recited impromptu verses to the accompaniment of a stringed musical instrument, which in some cases they themselves played. Many travellers described their ecstasy at witnessing wonderful recitals by these solitary language artists, and expressed more respect for their skills than for the social game of polite conversation. Montaigne reported that during his visit to Italy in 1580–1, he was struck by the presence of *improvvisatori* at most inns: 'Il se trouve quasi à toutes les hostelleries des rimeurs qui font sur le champ des rimes accomodées aus assistants' ['At almost all inns there are poets who spontaneously make up rhymes appropriate for their listeners'].[49]

Later travellers could come across an *improvvisatore* or *improvvisatrice* in most Italian cities, but Tuscany had the reputation of being the birthplace of the most talented of them. Italians usually referred to such language performers as *poeti* and *poetesse*, as they could sing or recite verses, usually in *ottava rima*, on virtually any subject suggested by the audience. The Scottish novelist Tobias Smollett, someone who was not easy to please, praised the techniques of their art using the highest compliments:

One of the greatest curiosities you meet with in Italy, is the Improvisatore; such is the name given to certain individuals, who have the surprising talent of reciting verses extempore, on any subject you propose. Mr Corvesi, my landlord, has a son,

---

[47] See Hamilton, *Paradise of Exiles,* especially 62–97.
[48] From Ernest J. Lovell Jr, *Lady Blessington's Conversations of Lord Byron* (Princeton, 1969), 53.
[49] Michel de Montaigne, *Journal de voyage en Italie par la Suisse et l'Allemagne en 1580–1581* (Paris, 1774), rpt. in François Rigolot (ed.) (Paris, 1992), trans., *The Journal of Montaigne's Travels in Italy by Way of Switzerland and Germany in 1580 and 1581*, William George Waters (ed. and trans.), 3 vols. (London, 1903), 145–6.

a Franciscan friar, who is a great genius in this way. When the subject is given, his brother tunes his violin to accompany him, and he begins to rehearse in recitative, with wonderful fluency and precision. Thus he will, at a minute's warning, recite two or three hundred verses, well turned, and well adapted, and generally mingled with an elegant compliment to the company. The Italians are so fond of poetry, that many of them, have the best part of Ariosto, Tasso, and Petrarch, by heart; and these are the great sources from which the Improvisatori draw their rhimes, cadence, and turns of expression.[50]

Sometime two *improvvisatori* performed in pairs, in which case it was customary to refer to the duo using the Virgilian expression *Arcades ambo*, and to their performance with the saying *et cantare pares, et respondere parati* ('Arcadians both, and both equally skilled in the song, and ready in the response'). The true celebrities among them, however, were the solo performers, many of whom were ladies of passionate emotions, and who were not always blessed with good health or appearance. William Patoun, a secretary keen to deliver to his master Lord Brownlow the most faithful account of his Italian exploratory visit, reported:

A Certain Poetess who used to live at Bologna, called the Corilla, Middle aged & ugly, is an extraordinary Person – to see her at any body's House, would be worth while not so convenient at her own, as she sometimes is troublesome to Strangers, in wanting to make parties into the Country, and has often proved very expensive without any meaning or interested Motive. She is the most celebrated Improvisatrice in Italy – and can sing in Verse and Rhime upon any Subject you please to give her, for an hour together.[51]

The Scottish painter Allan Ramsey told Dr Moore that he himself heard Signora Corilla sing for an entire hour, powerfully inspired and taking only few pauses of about five minutes each during which she recovered her breath and voice: 'At her first setting out, her manner was sedate, or rather cold; but gradually becoming animated, her voice rose, her eyes sparkled, and the rapidity and beauty of her expression and ideas seemed supernatural.'[52] The Scottish writer Joseph Forsyth, who was in Italy in 1802 and 1803, just missed Signora Corilla's performances but heard about her reputation: 'The crowned and pensioned Corilla drew lately the admiration of all Italy, and Signora Fantastici is now the Improvvisatrice of the day.'[53] He had the opportunity to observe carefully Fantastici's artistry, concluding that 'her sentiment and imagery flowing in rich diction, in measure, in rhyme, and in music, without interruption, and on subject unforeseen'. He was so impressed by her impromptu performance that he was himself tempted to put to test the spontaneous skill of the performer:

[50] Smollett, *Travels*, 237–8.   [51] Patoun, 'Advice on Travel', xliii.
[52] Moore, *A View of Society and Manners in Italy*, II, 196–7.
[53] Joseph Forsyth, *Remarks on Antiquities, Arts and Letters, During an Excursion in Italy in the Years 1802 and 1803* (4th ed., London, 1835), 48.

She went round her circle and called on each person for a theme. Seeing her with her fan, I proposed the fan as a subject; and this little weapon she painted as she promised, '*col pennel divino di fantasia felice*' ['with the divine brush of happy fantasy']. In tracing its origin she followed *Pignotti,* and in describing its use she acted and analysed to us all the coquetry of the thing. She allowed herself no pause, as the moment she cooled, her *estro* [inspiration] would escape.[54]

Forsyth, who wrote one of the best books on Italy, was so impressed with the Italian art of improvisation that he stated that its simplicity of construction, combined with its repetitions and inspired digressions, reminded him of Homer's poetry ('I once thought of Homer in the streets of Florence').[55] He discovered that the oral tradition of improvising rhymes had existed in Florence as early as the fifteenth century, when the two blind Brandolini brothers excelled in singing Latin verses extempore. At the same time, the poet Serafino dell'Aquila was deemed to be 'the first Improvvisatore that appeared in the language', but he 'was gazed at in Italian courts as a divine and inspired being, till he published his verses and dispelled the illusion'.[56] Forsyth drew the conclusion that such powers of imagination did not suit the depth and quality expected of compositions in the written language. He thought that this also applied to the outstanding Signora Fantastici, whose verses 'are dull enough, [thus] I should suspect that this impromptu-exercise seldom leads to poetical excellence'.[57]

The other custom, of singing memorised stanzas of poems, especially those of the famous poet Tasso, was encountered especially among the less-educated people. While in Venice in 1701, Joseph Addison came across this practice among the gondoliers performing in the narrow *calles* of the city: 'when one begins in any part of the poet, it is odds but he will be answered by somebody else that overhears him; so that sometimes you have ten or dozen in the neighborhood of one another, taking verse after verse, and running on with the poem as far as their memories will carry them'.[58] More than a century later, in 1816, John Hobhouse, commenting on Lord Byron's line in *Childe Harold* referring to Venice, which read 'Tasso's echoes are no more', explained: 'The well-known song of the gondoliers, of alternate stanzas, from Tasso's *Jerusalem* (1581) has died with the independence of Venice. Editions of the poem, with the original on one column, and the Venetian variations on the other, as sung by boatmen, were once common, and are still to be found.'[59] One day Byron and Hobhouse were taken to the Lido by a gondolier and his companion who sang not the Venetian but the Tuscan version of the poem. He

[54] Ibid., 48–9.   [55] Ibid., 51.   [56] Ibid., 50.   [57] Ibid.   [58] Addison, *Remarks* (1745), 69.
[59] John Cam Hobhouse, Letter of Saturday 29 November 1817, quoted by Philip W. Martin in *Byron: A Poet before His Public* (Cambridge, 1982), 176. The author recalls similar accounts by Goethe, Stendhal, D'Israeli and Rogers, suggesting that such performances were extremely rare and payment was also involved.

said that that he was a carpenter and knew at least three hundred stanzas from the poem, explaining also that not only gondoliers but 'several among the lower classes ... are acquainted with a few stanzas'.[60]

Many travel books confirmed that Italians had a genius not just for reciting and singing but for acting as well. In the early modern period, Italian theatre performances also included a great deal of improvisation. In Italy, the theatre was one of the most favourite evening entertainments. But foreign visitors usually complained about the superficiality of the scripts and the obscenity of the plays, and drew little satisfaction from them. Addison's report is representative:

The comedies that I saw at Venice, or indeed in any other part of Italy, are very indifferent, and more lewd than those of other countries. Their poets have no notion of genteel comedy, and fall into the most filthy double meanings imaginable, when they have a mind to make their audience merry. There is no part generally so wretched as that of the fine gentleman, especially when he converses with his mistress; for then the whole dialogue is an insipid mixture of pedantry and romance. But 'tis no wonder that the poets of so jealous and reserved a nation fail in such conversations on the stage, as they have no patterns of in nature.[61]

These were the actors of the *Commedia dell'Arte*, highly skilled professionals, originally closer to the *buffoni di piazza* rather than the *attori del teatro erudito*. But with time they developed into virtuoso performers, nomadic specialists who were well-trained particularly in the art of manipulating language and adapting the content of a play to different cities. Not only were they able to engage with linguistically diverse audiences, but they also managed to capture the mood of each theatre in order to respond to different social tastes.[62] Rarely, if ever, did audiences realise the extent to which the dialogues were prepared in advance, the way in which the performance was put together, and the manner in which the texts were adapted for linguistically different destinations. We do know from various contemporary accounts that performances were not wholly impromptu, and that the improvised lines were meant to give the impression of being more spontaneous than premeditated.

But we can work out why Addison, like most foreign visitors, did not understand what was happening on the stage. In Venice, the character of Pantalone would mock the dialect of the upper classes, and that of Arlecchino or Zanni would ironically overemphasise the features of the rural language of the servants from Bergamo. If they were performing in Lombardy, in order to please local audiences they needed to exaggerate the stereotypical

---

[60] Ibid.   [61] Addison, *Remarks* (1745), 67.

[62] See my own observations on the art of impromptu performers of the past, 'Histrionic transgressions: the Dario Fo-*Commedia dell'arte* relationship revisited', in Michael Caesar and Marina Spunta (eds.), *Orality and Literacy in Italian Culture* (London, 2006), especially 26–7.

features of the Venetian language, which was a foreign tongue in that region. At the same time, they were able to manipulate the sounds and expressions of the local dialects as markers of social distance. For example, the language used to portray a pedantic Doctor from the university of Bologna would be full of distorted Latinisms, while that of a Spaniard Captain was a mixture of Italian and Spanish.

This required a level of multilingual awareness and abilities which had no precedent in any theatrical tradition. The early term *commedia all'improvviso* reflects performances that were adapted to the taste of specific audiences. Indeed, the ability of such linguistically gifted actors to reinvent the text for different audiences was recognised by some late admirers of the Italian *Commedia*. Diderot spoke of the Italian *ivresse* (euphoric excitement, literally 'drunkenness') in his *Discours sur l'art dramatique* (1758). Goethe was also better informed about the tailored content of the comic performance he saw in the Teatro San Luca in Venice in 1786.

It seems that two important points about the tradition of the *Commedia dell'Arte* were not entirely appreciated by the Grand Tourists who had the opportunity to view those performances. One was that, unlike most by the other nations, Italy had no common language. The other was that the language that even well-educated Italians spoke among themselves was not the language of writing, and the language of writing was not commonly spoken, except with foreigners. This was quite a challenge for any comic theatre which, being the most oral and least literary form of theatre, required a community of native speakers of the national language. But if this was a limitation for the *Commedia dell'Arte*, it also accounted for the international success of the troupes of *improvvisatori*. They were able to perform in France or Bavaria, Spain or Poland as successfully as on their Italian stomping ground. But this, too, could not be appreciated by a Grand Tourist who was taken to a comic play in Venice or Naples, with no understanding of dialect, a poor command of Italian, and companions who were unwilling or unable to explain its uniqueness. Indeed, the great linguist and critic Gianfranco Folena defined the *Commedia dell'Arte* as the 'greatest legacy of Italian theatre to Europe'.[63]

Shocking Foreign Customs

Many British travellers stated that they were quite open to foreign customs but found some of them ridiculous and not easy to commend. Surely top of the list was the continental habit of kissing as a gesture of friendship, in Coryat's words 'a custome that I never saw before, nor heard of, nor read of in any history'. He

[63] Gianfranco Folena, *Il Linguaggio del caos. Studi sul plurilinguismo rinascimentale* (Torino, 1991), 122.

noticed this practice in Venice and commented: 'I observed an extraordinary custome amongst them, that when two acquaintances meete and talke together at the walking times of the day, . . . they give a mutuall kisse when they depart from each other, by kissing Saluations, one anothers cheeke.'[64] The same habit was reported later by travellers in France, like Robert Wharton: 'I had the honour to kiss him on each cheek, a ceremony that we should think rather ridiculous in England; but I have mentioned before, that is quite the *Ton* here.'[65] More problematic than a kiss on the cheek between two men was a kiss exchanged between a man and a woman. In France, this normally involved a kiss on the forehead, something that was unknown elsewhere in Europe. In Molière's play *Le Sicilien*, one of his characters observes with great indignation a Frenchmen kissing an Italian lady and remarks: 'la manière de France est bonne pour vos femmes; mais pour les nôtres elle est un peu trop familière' ['the French custom might be fine for your women; but for ours it is rather overly familiar'].[66] However, during the best part of the Grand Tour there were far more shocking foreign habits to be discovered abroad.

Venice and Paris alone had in common the use of forks at the dining table and umbrellas for rain, and they also shared a licentious *joie de vivre* which applied to both sexes, something that reached its peak in the eighteenth century. Indeed, the Catholic priest Richard Lassels lamented that many travellers 'desire to go into Italy only because they hear there are fine courtesans in Venice',[67] since for most of them, amatory adventures were not a scandalous matter. After the French Revolution, the traveller and diarist Catherine Wilmot admitted 'amazement at beholding the women from 15 to 70 almost in a state of nature because . . . after all the revolutions of this magic Lantern Country, a drawing Room is the same to-day that it was in the courteous age of Louis 14th'.[68]

It was just at the turn of the eighteenth century that a new Italian custom broke down the last barriers of morality in an already corrupt society. This was the phenomenon of the *cicisbei*, which involved husbands entrusting young men to escort their wives to public functions. But once women began to choose their own escorts, the fashion turned into a recognised system of adultery which, as explained by Mary Wortley Montagu writing to the Countess of Mar in 1718, allowed a married lady to reward her attendant *cavaliere* 'according to her inclination . . . but the husband is not to have the impudence to suppose this any other than pure Platonic friendship'.[69]

---

[64] Coryat, *Crudities*, I, 398–9.   [65] Black, *The British Abroad*, 233.
[66] Quoted in Luigi Monga (ed.), *Sebastiano Locatelli*, 401 n.177.
[67] Lassels, *The Voyage of Italy*, preface section 2.
[68] Catherine Wilmot, *An Irish Peer on the Continent (1801–1803), Being a Narrative of the Tour of Stephen, 2nd Earl Mount Cashell, Through France, Italy, etc.*, in Thomas U. Sadler (ed.) (London, 1920), 22–3.
[69] Mary Wortley Montagu, *Letters and Works*, II, 76.

French visitors like Montesquieu were more surprised than indignant about this social custom: 'C'est la chose la plus ridicule qu'un sot peuple ait pu inventer' ['It is the most ridiculous thing that a stupid people could invent'],[70] while some Britons like Dr John Moore were quite philosophical about it: 'there are no such amusements in the country as hunting and drinking'.[71] But the vast majority of observers followed the example of the ferocious Samuel Sharp, who used strong words to argue that *cicisbeism* was evidence of the degradation and debauchery to which priests and politicians had reduced Italy. Quite unlike the extreme gallantry of the French, it was seen as a custom reflecting the sexual repression promoted by the Catholic religion. This view reinforced a national stereotype which had emerged during the Reformation/Counter-Reformation conflicts, painting 'the Italian character as cynical (or indeed "Machiavellian") and immoral'.[72] Some tourists, who were surprised by such liberties between married women and the cicisbei, showed concern that they could set a bad example for British women travellers.[73] But the enlightened jurist Charles Dupaty, who visited Italy in 1785, rather than resorting to that stereotype, raised some interesting questions:

Cicisbeismo merits close attention. It is said that in no place is it as in vogue as in Genoa. What is a *cicisbeo* in appearance? What is he in reality? In what manner does a woman take a *cicisbeo*? In what manner does a man wish to *be a cicisbeo*? What do the husbands think? Is the *cicisbeo* the lieutenant of a husband? To what extent is he so? What is the origin of this usage? For what reason does it persist or change? What influence does it have on customs? Can traces or similarities be found in the customs of other peoples?[74]

Bizzocchi quotes this passage, commenting that, unfortunately, Dupaty never completed his research; but Bizzocchi himself provided a useful insight to support the view of the French jurist who was interested in spelling out the complexity of the phenomenon.

The trend apparently originated in Genoa, a city close to France where a similar role existed in the local tradition – the *petit-maître*, a frivolous and libertine type of dandy.[75] In Spain, two synonymous terms described the same ambiguous position of a 'friend of the house': *chichisveo*, from Italian, and *petimetre*, from French. Bizzocchi also cites a connection with the old folk

---

[70] Charles de Montesquieu, *Lettre sur Gênes*, 1728, in *Voyages de Montesquieu*, 2 vols. (Paris, 1774; Bordeaux 1894), II, 293.

[71] Moore, *A View of Society and Manners in Italy*, II, 416.

[72] Roberto Bizzocchi, 'Italian Morality and European Values in the Eighteenth Century' in Paula Findlen, Wendy Wassyng Roworth, Catherine M. Sama (eds.), *Italy's Eighteenth Century: Gender and Culture in the Age of the Grand Tour* (Stanford, 2009), 52.

[73] Reported by Black, *The British Abroad*, 43.

[74] Quoted in Bizzocchi, 'Italian morality and European values in the eighteenth century', 42.

[75] For a discussion of the *petit-maîtres* in France and their caricatures in London theatres, where they were obviously well known, see Brunot, *Histoire*, VIII, 240–2.

tradition of *valentinage* – one day a year when a wife could take a lover, from St Valentine, which was a variation of *cicisbeism*. Being a godparent also provided alternative roles to those of the natural mother and father, and was legitimised through the Christian rite of holding someone else's child at its baptism. Such popular customs and their variations spread all over Europe among the large masses who became urbanised in the sixteenth century after leaving rural communities where popular beliefs based on obscure rituals had survived for centuries. One such ritual is the *charivari*: a rural custom to expose an old poseur guilty of choosing much too young a wife. Bizzocchi concludes that 'other people of Europe, including Protestant peoples, knew or had known a practice of married life which allowed the open existence of a third figure, the woman's male companion'.[76]

Indeed, the expression *cavalier servente*, preferred by the Italians, was free of the negative connotation of *cicisbeo*, which was more popular with disapproving foreign visitors. As for the etymology of the term, Pine-Coffin suggests that its origin was 'from a Hebrew word transliterated *shoshebhin* that in Rabbinic literature describes the guardian or patron who protected the right of women after marriage'.[77] This would explain why the term, if not the habit, originated in the city Genoa, with its conspicuous Jewish community. Unsurprisingly, when foreign visitors decided to take part in this social game, they referred to themselves more often as a *cavaliere servente* rather than *cicisbeo*, as Horace Mann did during his sojourn in his official position as British envoy in Florence.[78] But others who were more interested in the role than in its stereotype made no mystery of their willingness to conform with the local customs. Onc such man was Auguste Frédéric Louis Viesse de Marmont, who wrote about it quite frankly in the memoirs of his stay in Rome:

> The freedom of the women passes all belief and their husbands permit it, speaking cheerfully and without embarrassment of their wives' lovers. I have heard M. Falconniere talk of his wife in a quite incredible way ... In my role of young man and foreigner I was only too glad to benefit by the consequences.[79]

Women travellers held quite a different view of this much-criticised Italian custom. Their perspective, which will be discussed in Chapter 9, derived from

[76] Bizzocchi, 'Italian morality ... etc., 53.
[77] Pine-Coffin, *British and American Travel,* 46 n.13. For an alternative etymology, see page 141.
[78] His lady friend was Elisabetta Capponi, Marchesa Grifoni, one of the most beautiful women in Florence; see R. W. Ketton-Cremer, *Thomas Gray, A Biography* (Cambridge, 1955), 43. Horace Mann was the British envoy in Florence for fifty years. He received British travellers and treated them most hospitably but some visitors did not comment positively on his services. Gibbon thought that Mann's 'most serious business was that of entertaining the English at his hospitable table', and William Fitzwilliam wrote that 'he has been so long out of England, that he has lost the manliness of an Englishman, and has borrowed the effeminacy of Italy', Ingamells, *British and Irish Travellers*, 636.
[79] Quoted by Hibbert, *Rome, The Biography of a City*, 219.

a deeper perception of the social phenomenon rather than a moral preconception against it. The decline of this practice began with the Napoleonic occupation of Italy, but for political rather than ethical reasons. Lord Byron was able to observe this fashion's last days and he made no secret of his view about the *cavalier serventi* in a way that was neither moralistic nor paternalistic:

Perhaps I am in the case to know more of them than most Englishmen, because I have lived among the natives, and in parts of the country where Englishmen never resided before . . . I have lived in their houses and in the hearts of their families, sometimes merely as 'amico di casa', and sometimes as 'amico di cuore' of the Dama, . . . I should know something of the matter, having had a pretty general experience among their women, from the fisherman's wife up to the Nobil Dama, whom I serve. . . . In short they transfer marriage to adultery . . . The reason is that they marry for their parents, and love for themselves . . . It is to be observed that while they do all this, the greatest outward respect is to be paid to the husbands, not only by the ladies, but by their Serventi – particularly if the husband serves no one himself (which is not often the case, however).[80]

Another shocking custom that travellers came across in Italy, worsening even further this Catholic country's reputation for moral degradation, was the phenomenon of *castrati*. This practice originated within the Catholic church in the sixteenth century, when young boys who had been emasculated after an accident were trained to sing high notes. It is uncertain whether these boys were natural altos, or eunuchs emasculated for medical reasons or for a musical purpose.[81] The fact is that the first *castrati* were admitted into the Papal choir in Rome in 1599, and the fashion grew over the seventeenth and eighteenth centuries. During all this time, the church adopted an ambiguous policy whereby it condemned the practice of castration and yet welcomed the best *castrati* in performances of religious music.

The practice developed very quickly once boys from poor families and orphans (called euphemistically *figliuoli* or *figliuoli angelini*: 'little angel-sons' or 'angel children') were admitted into conservatories that functioned as 'seminars for children who were destined never to produce any', to use the piteous words of Mme du Bocage in her *Letters* of 1757–8.[82] The main reason for international indignation was that the Catholic religion prohibited female performances on the stage. The Protestant movement objected, claiming that by allowing castratos, Popery justified acts of physical violence that contradicted human nature. The Scottish physician John Moore castigated the Catholic custom using the strongest words:

---

[80] Byron, Letter to Mr. Murray, Ravenna, 21 February 1820, in Thomas Moore (ed.), *Letters and Journals of Lord Byron* (Frankfurt, 1830), 413.
[81] Patrick Barbier, *The World of the Castrati. The History of an Extraordinary Operatic Phenomenon* (Paris, 1989), Eng. trans. (London, 1996, reprinted 2001), 19–23.
[82] Quoted by Barbier, ibid. 37.

The natural sweetness of the female voice is ill supplied by the artificial trills of wretched castratos and the awkward sinewy fellows dressed in women's clothes, is a most deplorable substitution for the graceful movements of elegant female dancers. Is not the horrid practice which is encouraged by this manner of supplying the place of female singers a greater outrage on religion and morality, than can be produced by the evils which their prohibition is intended to prevent?[83]

Other travellers, such as Montesquieu, were shocked by this custom, and also referred to the natural depravity of Italians, epitomised by the saying – which apparently originated in France – that sodomitic love with people of the 'third-sex' was practised 'in Spain by knights, in France by nobles and pedants, in Germany by very few people and in Italy by everyone'.[84] Two remarkable men joined the choir of condemnations. One was Giacomo Casanova, once in love with a 'false castrato', a young girl disguised as a boy; another was the Marquis De Sade, who referred to them as 'espèces de monstres'. Given the delicate palate of the latter, his words are surprising: 'J'en fut révolté. On ne se fait point à entendre sortir d'un gros corps d'homme bien massif et bien informe, une petite voix claire et beaucoup plus haute que celles de femmes' ['I felt disgusted. One cannot believe that a massive and shapeless male body can produce a fine clear voice, much higher than those of women'].[85] The tendency to refer to *castrati* as 'monsters', 'circus animals' or 'biological curiosities' was quite common among foreign visitors. They all favoured the use of the derogative term *castrato,* which according to some derived from the Sanskrit *sasrtram* (meaning 'knife'). The term, in parallel with *cicisbei,* was more common outside Italy, and in some languages it was paired up with the words for eunuch, cripple and capon. In Italy, the term eunuch was reserved mainly for young boys after this operation, but without a pejorative connotation; professional usage preferred to associate it with *musico* or *virtuoso,* showing more social respect for the musicians.[86]

We know that many famous travellers were put off by this unnatural phenomenon, such as Maximilien Misson, Abbé Labat, Jean Pierre Grosley and Joseph Addison, but public respect for *virtuosi* in Italy was very high. Eventually, *castrati* began to attract the admiration of foreigners too, including English audiences, who had initially been more disapproving than the French. One admirer was Francis Mortoft, an uncompromising Protestant who attended Mass at St Peter's primarily to hear the castrati sing.[87] Others included William

---

[83] Moore, *A View of Society and Manners in Italy,* II, 89.
[84] Quoted by Barbier, *The World of the Castrati,* 154.
[85] Donatien Alphonse François de Sade, *Voyage d'Italie or a Critical, Historical and Philosophical Dissertation on the Cities of Florence, Rome and Naples, 1775–1776* (Paris, 1995), 68.
[86] Barbier, *The World of the Castrati,* 2.
[87] Francis Mortoft, *Francis Mortoft: His Book. Being His Travels Through France and Italy 1658–1659,* in Malcom Letts (ed.) (London, 1925), 104.

Beckford, who was fascinated by the castrato singer Luigi Marchesi in Naples who performed at the San Carlo theatre with 'a voice that was possibly the clearest and most triumphant in the world', and by 'the artistry of the world's finest singer who makes me more than ever effeminate'.[88] In addition to these more liberal minds, there were music specialists such as Dr Charles Burney and concert lovers such as Dr John Swinton who asked to be received by Farinelli, the greatest *castrato* of all times. Apparently they waited patiently to meet him, as did other European celebrities, including Mozart, Gluck and the Holy Roman Emperor Joseph II.[89]

Castrati ended up being admired and well paid not just in Italy; they were actually booked to perform in great numbers by foreign impresarios. In most countries to which they were invited, such as Spain, France, England, Germany and Russia, they were welcomed by the most distinguished audiences, and even received the official protection of royal and imperial patrons. In London, they were sometimes idolised and sometimes parodied by people like Samuel Pepys and John Evelyn, who went as far as listening to them sing in private gatherings because the public performance of a feminised voice in a masculine body at first was too shocking on the musical scene. But once top *castrati* opera artists like Farinelli and Senesino travelled abroad to sing, the aristocracy and the general public alike gave them a triumphal welcome. The passion for hearing a soprano voice performed by a virtuoso male ended at the start of the nineteenth century, overlapping with the decline of cicibeism and with the final days of the Grand Tour.

[88] Beckford, Letter XXII, *Italy with Sketches*, I, 251.
[89] Barbier, *The World of the Castrati*, 220.

3   Linguistic Training at Home

Classical and Modern Languages

One cannot expect to find much consistency over the three centuries of the Grand Tour in the linguistic training of several generations of travellers who harboured different aims and aspirations. Moreover, language education during that long period was inspired by different philosophies, diverse methodologies and a considerable variety of disparate teaching materials. However, some trends can be discerned in connection with key issues in language teaching, such as written vs. spoken language, or a literary focus vs. conversational ability. The discussion below deals with travellers from England, a country where language education was particularly contentious due to religious tensions and its geographical position. Within the English context, the range of educational institutions was very wide, and included grammar schools, boarding colleges, academies and universities, in addition to private lessons given by hired tutors and foreign governors who worked as language instructors in private homes. The main point here is that the trends identified in this chapter are indicative of the general climate of language education since the standard of instruction, as always, varied from teacher to teacher, and the level of attainment from pupil to pupil.

Throughout the Renaissance, the common denominator in all educational enterprises was the commitment to equip pupils with a good knowledge of Latin and Greek, deemed necessary for their university studies. For many centuries, Latin had been the dominant language of education, commerce, religion and government; knowledge of modern languages, especially Italian and French, began to compete with Latin only at the end of the sixteenth century. This change was based on a new concept: the mastery of any language developed intellectual abilities, but the study of Latin grammar, which was an end in itself, could also function as an instrument for learning modern languages.[1]

---

[1] This approach lasted throughout the best part of the early modern period and became known as the 'grammar-translation' method. All Grand Tourists had been taught Classical Latin at school,

Throughout the best part of the Grand Tour, the leitmotif in language education was the superiority of classical studies over modern languages, and a major point of contention was whether the latter could be taught without recourse to Latin grammar. Even in the Elizabethan period, the educational value of modern vernaculars – English, French and Italian – had already begun to attract the attention of famous scholars. One was Philip Sidney, the poet and courtier; another was Thomas Hoby, the translator of Castiglione's *Cortegiano*, who gained the admiration of Roger Ascham, also a supporter of the vernacular, as expressed in the *Scholemaster* (1570): 'so well translated into English by a worthie ientleman Syr Th. Hobbie, who was many ways well furnished with learning, and very expert in knowledge of divers tongues'.[2] The rivalry between the classical and the vernacular languages was revisited by the schoolmaster and educator Richard Mulcaster, who stated: 'I do not think that anie language, ... is better able to utter all arguments, either with more pith, or greater planesse, than our English tung is.' He argued that a schoolchild should be taught his own language properly before Latin grammar, and strongly condemned the situation whereby 'the childe consumeth the flowre of his learning youth' in learning to write a Latin epistle, 'though well he can not write half a pistle in Englishe'.[3]

Italian was the first foreign vernacular that stimulated the interest of elites throughout Europe, overtaking its closest competitors, French and Spanish, in popularity.[4] There were manifold reasons for this: throughout the Renaissance, Italian was the international language of European courts; it was also the lingua franca of diplomacy; the language was used in political and commercial exchanges between Europe and the Levant; it was a vehicle for education in many renowned Italian universities, and it was regarded as the language of civilised behaviour and polite conversation in the most exclusive circles in Europe. This last reason was much promoted by Stefano Guazzo in *La civil conversazione* (1574), a famous book which was translated into several languages, and which placed Italian in a privileged position, especially in those countries – like England – whose language was little known abroad.

In the seventeenth century, the supremacy of the Italian language began to be challenged due to changes in political and cultural circumstances in Europe. One factor was the consolidation of national cultures which, unlike in Italy, led to more educational value being placed on the vernaculars and a more

and those who learned modern languages were instructed using a methodology based on Latin grammar.
[2] Ascham, *The Scholemaster*, 65. Ascham's comments include the observation that 'Castiglione's book, advisedly read, and diligently followed, but one year at home in England, would do a young gentleman more good ... than three years travel abroad spent in Italy'.
[3] Richard Mulcaster, *The First Part of the Elementarie* (1582: facsimile reprint, Menston, 1970).
[4] During the Stuart period, Spanish was learned only in exceptional cases. See Lambley, *The Teaching and Cultivation of French*, 263.

utilitarian emphasis in foreign language teaching. Italian retained its reputation as a beautiful language but French acquired greater currency as an international lingua franca. The position of modern languages in education was still not as strong as that of Greek and Latin, which continued to be considered the pillars of logic and eloquence for anyone interested in arts and humanities. Accordingly, grammar was still perceived as the supporting structure for competence in any language. Giovanni Torriano, a prolific author of textbooks, made this point forcefully: 'As it is impossible to saile the ocean without a compasse, unless at randome; so likewise to attaine a language without rules.'[5] In a similar vein, the linguist J. Smith explained in 1674 how wrong it was to think that grammar was necessary only for the study of classical languages:

Although it be generally granted, that grammar is necessary for the obtaining of those tongues called linguae mortuae, viz. Latine, Greek and Hebrew, and because they are no where nationally spoken: yet, perhaps, some will question its necessity in the modern european languages, and be apt to say, converse with the natives is the best tutor. But 'tis easie to demonstrate, that grammatical principles are great helps to these, seeing without them, no man can be an exact critick or translatour. For he would learns a tongue (par routine) by rote, will never be able, either to write it, or speak it perfectly.[6]

In 1693, Locke voiced the strong criticism that young gentlemen, who were forced to learn the grammars of foreign and dead languages, were 'never once told of the Grammar of their own Tongues'.[7] He held strong views about language education, not only assigning precedence to formal training in one's own native tongue, but also giving full support to learning French as a second language – to be taught as soon as young men of rank could 'speak English' – in addition to Latin, a language 'absolutely necessary to a Gentleman'.[8] The philosopher also made innovative suggestions, including proposing a conversational method for teaching Latin. He was not the only one to expose some absurd practices that were common in language teaching. The classical scholar John Clarke, headmaster of several grammar schools, also criticised teaching modern languages through Latin grammar, as well as teaching Latin grammar through the medium of Latin.[9]

---

[5] Giovanni Torriano, *New and Easie Directions for Attaining the Thuscan Italian Tongue* (Cambridge, 1639), 1.
[6] J. Smith, *Grammatica quadrilinguis, or Brief Instructions for the French, Italian, Spanish, and English Tongues* (London, 1674), preface, 65.
[7] John Locke, *Some Thoughts Concerning Education* (1693) in R. H. Quick (ed.) (Cambridge, 1892), 147.
[8] Ibid., 138.
[9] Quoted in Cohen, *Fashioning Masculinity*, 125 n.7. For an insight into the practice of using Latin to teach French, see Lambley, *The Teaching and Cultivation of French*, 342 and 354. It was not unusual to teach a foreign language through the medium of another non-native language, for

In the first half of the eighteenth century, the French language had become fashionable all over Europe, like most manners and trends from France. Apart from the language's connection with a flourishing literature and its role as the new diplomatic lingua franca, speaking French was a sign of distinction in private social milieus. Throughout Europe, boys were learning it at school, or at home from a private tutor; girls also learned French, preferably from a governess. There is evidence that in England some parents' aspiration was for their daughters in particular to acquire French as a first language, and from a young age a number of girls were forced to speak nothing but French. Cohen explains that this practice was partly rooted in social convention, partly in a common prejudice that females could only learn a language by imitation because they lacked the disposition to study grammar.[10]

Italian, whose decline in popularity started during the previous century, began to gain new ground because of the success of Italian music and the new taste for opera which was spreading throughout Europe. Indeed, Italian was regarded as the only language appropriate for singing, and opera-goers felt that without the ability to read the libretti and follow the action on stage, an operatic performance could not be fully appreciated (unlike today). From the 1760s onwards, Italian became fashionable again, which attracted more teachers from Italy and resulted in the publication of a large number of textbooks, dictionaries and new editions of Italian classics. This was also linked to a revival of interest in the art, archaeology and literature of the Peninsula, and it gained further impetus via the widening popularity of the Grand Tour with the wealthy middle classes. But the language's appeal still centred on its aesthetic rather than utilitarian value, as noted by some authors of famous textbooks. For example, in the translator's preface to the Italian version of the Port-Royale *Grammar of French* (1750), we find: 'For we observe that 'tis become, in some measure, a greater subject of reproach to persons of distinction, not to know Italian, than to be ignorant of Greek or Latin.'[11] In Evangelista Palermo's grammar book (1755), the author states:

It is needless to enlarge upon the sweetnes and delicacy of the Italian language, it being well known in all the courts of Europe, and is at present the regning taste of the English nation; the knowledge whereof, besides being useful to all travellers, lovers of music, merchants, and to those who are desirous of reading the classics in Italian, is reputed as a fine qualification for both sexes, and no small part of polite education.

Likewise, we find in the preface to Masson's textbook of Italian (1771):

---

example using French as a mediating language to learn Italian. See Gallagher, 'Language and Education', 5.

[10] Ibid., 84–5. For a discussion of this point and the consequences of this common view, see Chapter 9.

[11] [Port Royal] *A New Method of Learning the Italian Tongue* (London, 1750), II.

Languages are the keys to knowledge, and to intellectual amusement. The Italian, amongst the modern, bears no inconsiderable rank. It is not less estimable for the beauty and harmony of its pronunciation, than for the many elegant and masterly works which have appeared in it, as well in prose and in verse. And it is now become a fashionable, and necessary part of polite education.[12]

The Italian scholar E. H. Thorne reported that by the end of the eighteenth century, nearly all educated Englishmen and women had studied at least some Italian.[13] Once the pool of language learners expanded to include boys and girls with little or no Latin at all, some textbooks began to include small sections on basic grammar as a tool to support their more practical guided learning approach. A path was being prepared for the point John Stuart Mill made in his inaugural address at St Andrews (1867) more than half a century later. His argument gave a blessing to the new vision of the difference between learning classical languages and modern languages. He said the fact that a modern language can be learned by imitation, like infants acquiring their native language, does not involve rational thought. Learning Latin grammar, on the other hand, trains the student not in a language for communication purposes but in the use of the mind's faculties.[14]

Literary and Non-Literary Focus

The belief that Latin grammar should be studied specifically to train the mind was reinforced by the arguments put forth by John Stuart Mill. But the idea that the grammar of a classical language could provide a sort of linguistic template for describing and learning other tongues survived the impetus for education in modern languages. The debate proved to be controversial in another way, as instructors dealing with *langues vivantes* rather than dead languages increasingly needed to prioritise the scope of their teaching and indulge the tastes of their learners. This was a new problem as the main objective of humanistic education had been to teach dead languages principally for the purpose of reading great classical literature.

The late Renaissance in England, as elsewhere, proved to be a time of theoretical discussions and pedagogic experiments on whether language learning should be literary or non-literary in scope. While the upper classes were dedicated to reading literary texts in Italian and French, and learning to write

---

[12] Both quotations from Lucilla Pizzoli, *Le grammatiche di italiano per inglesi (1550–1776), Un'analisi linguistica* (Florence, 2004), 58 n.79.

[13] E. H. Thorne, 'Italian teachers and teaching in eighteenth century England', *English Miscellany*, 9 (1958), 145. The best account of interest in learning Italian in eighteenth-century Europe remains Folena, *L'italiano in Europa*.

[14] For a detailed discussion of learning Latin for mental training as a masculine pursuit, see Cohen, *Fashioning Masculinity*, especially 82–8 and 99–103.

according to these models, there was an increasing desire to learn to speak modern languages for use in polite conversations within European courts, with foreign visitors at home and when travelling abroad. The integration of oral language skills with written language abilities, however, presented problems which are unknown today, as it was most unusual to come across authentic sources of spoken language at that time. This explains why so much emphasis was devoted to teaching pronunciation. But it also accounts for the fact that many teachers, who were normally native speakers of the language, decided to publish their own teaching materials. On the one hand, this suited their own preferences in terms of pronunciation of the language; on the other, it helped meet specific priorities in terms of scope (literary vs. non-literary) and special purposes (scholars vs. merchants; travellers vs. singers, etc.).

One of the earliest approaches to teaching spoken language was based on the innovative but controversial idea of teaching Latin through dialogues, which was introduced by the Spaniard Juan Vivès in Basel in 1539 and soon spread throughout Europe.[15] Claudius Hollyband adapted the same model and constructed parallel dialogues for teaching French (1573) and Italian (1578), which he published in London. The idea was that English-speaking pupils could learn to speak a non-native language for use either in everyday situations or polite conversation through comparing the foreign structures and vocabulary with those in their native language. The approach was developed further by John Florio, one of the most active intellectuals in Elizabethan England. His famous *Firste Fruites* (1578) included forty-four parallel texts in English and Italian, followed by a grammatical section (*Necessarie Rules*). His whole concept was much richer than Hollyband's: it included an outline of the grammar, and a selection of parallel dialogues containing extracts from classical Italian writers in prose and verse. The latter was designed to help English pupils who wished to become fluent in the spoken language while working their way through Italian literature.

While the strong interest in language teaching was linked to the appreciation and enjoyment of the country's literature and cultural refinements, the market for a more utilitarian approach to learning modern languages was expanding too. This new taste involved in particular the wealthy middle classes, townsmen rather than gentry, who were in search of social and cultural emancipation. Practical manuals emerged on the market offering not only a more communicative approach to language learning, but also models that could be used for exhibition in polite conversations and self-promotion within the appropriate circles.[16] The language teaching materials adopted by prestigious schools and

---

[15] Jean Luis Vivès, *Exercitatio Linguae Latinae* (Venice, 1539).

[16] For a full discussion of the sixteenth-century market for language manuals that offered speedy results, see George Arthur P. Padley, *Grammatical Theory in Western Europe (1500–1700): Trends in Vernacular Grammar* (Cambridge, 1988), 134. An exceptional insight into language-

the universities of Oxford and Cambridge were quite a different case. These were still designed to train students for academic studies of literature rather than conversation.[17] John Sandford, a classicist and scholar of modern languages, educated at Balliol College, Oxford and later Chaplain at Magdalen College, published a Latin grammar and a grammar for each of the most important European languages: French, Italian and Spanish. The type of pupil he had in mind was a young university academic, mainly interested in acquiring linguistic competence in order to interpret texts and enjoy literature – certainly not someone concerned with conversation and practical language use.[18]

As the seventeenth century progressed and England became more conscious of its own cultural identity and economic power, learning modern languages tended to become more practical and utilitarian. Classical studies and literary training still occupied a prominent role in education but the study of modern languages was gradually fine-tuned to fit an instrumental vocation.[19] During the late seventeenth and early eighteenth centuries, the new growth in interest in the French language and its literature marked a waning in the study of Italian, as mentioned earlier. This was due partly to the decline of Italian as an international language, and partly to criticism of contemporary Italian poetry and prose: the former was considered too superficial and the latter over-elaborate.[20] It is interesting that the publishing industry reflected this crisis not by an outright cessation in producing Italian textbooks, but by integrating previously separate teaching approaches in one manual. Two important text-book editions explained this deliberately mixed approach, with a view to meeting a variety of interests and being more commercially viable. One was written by Thomas Uvedale (1711), who explained that his manual 'is one of

---

learning in early modern London can be found in Gallagher, 'The Italian London': 'Foreign-language teachers were clear on one point: a language could not be satisfactorily learned in isolation or solely from the pages of a book', 95.

[17] Early in the seventeenth century, both Oxford and Cambridge began to offer tuition in modern languages on request. John Florio was the first teacher of Italian and French at Oxford (in 1613–14), while Giacomo Castelvetro was probably the first to do so at Cambridge. External instructors were usually attached to the Chair of Modern History, whose professors bore the cost of this teaching from their own salaries. It was not until 1724 that the British government decided to finance a programme for teaching modern languages at the two universities.

[18] Travellers with a solid university education, like Dallington and Moryson, who believed foreign languages should be learned both at home and abroad, insisted that serious preliminary studies of grammar and literature were a prerequisite. Of all language learners abroad who picked up a language just by mixing with its speakers, Moryson criticised in particular merchants, women and children who neglected any serious study of the language. See Lambley, *The Teaching and Cultivation of French*, 225 and 239.

[19] Torriano, the most influential author of language manuals for much of the seventeenth century, in the preface to his book *The Italian Tutor* (1640), made it clear that his dialogues contained 'italianisms and neiceties of the language', and that his textbook was 'now published for the speede and ease of such a desire to attain perfection of the said language'.

[20] See Thorne, 'Italian teachers', 143.

the best books I have compos'd, you may be able, in a short time, to speak Italian, and understand any author, as well in verse as prose'. The other was by Arrigo Pleunus (1715): 'I hope this book will please you, since without the help of any other you may learn to speak Italian in a very short time, and understand all authors as well in verse, as in prose.'[21]

The next Italian grammar, which appeared a few years later (1723), was published by Angelo Maria Cori, someone with strong connections with the music world. He presented himself not only as 'a Roman: master of the Latin, Spanish and Italian languages etc . . .' but also as being active in adapting *melodrammi* at a time when Italian opera was beginning to gain many followers in London theatres. Cori also signed the translations of many Italian libretti, and it cannot be a coincidence that his textbook aimed to meet the demand of pupils who were interested 'a intendere e comprendere libri o discorsi italiani' ['in appreciating and understanding Italian books or conversations'] while also helping them 'a conversare ed esprimere i loro concetti sì in voce che in carta' ['to converse and express their ideas whether orally or on paper'].[22] Italian music and opera in London was to flourish for a number of years, Italian being regarded as the perfect language for singing. It is significant that although there was a profusion of bilingual libretti produced so that the public could enjoy the performances fully, the Italian texts eventually appeared without English translations.[23] The fashion for Italian opera attracted new interest in learning the language but while some were able to speak it based on their memory of libretti dialogues, apparently not many practised writing Italian.

By the middle of the 1730s, interest in Italian opera had declined in England, and the study of Italian lost popularity over the next three decades. But from about the 1760s, what turned the tide again was the indispensable contribution of Giuseppe Baretti, the distinguished scholar appointed Secretary to the *Royal Academy of Arts*, who was actively involved in promoting Italian arts and literature. He arrived in London in 1751, became a close friend of Samuel Johnson, and gained a much respected social and academic position in literary circles. His publications span his thirty-two years of residency in England, and were highly influential in making Italian language and literature attractive again. Oxford and Cambridge were now recruiting modern language teachers, and one of them, Agostino Isola, was responsible for publishing new editions of *Orlando Furioso* and *Gerusalemme Liberata*, the two most popular Italian works.[24]

---

[21] Thomas Uvedale, *The New Italian Grammar: Or, the Easiest and Best Method for Attaining That Language* (London, 1711), and Arrigo Pleunus, *A New, Plain, Methodical and Compleat Italian Grammar, Whereby You May Very Soon Attain to the Perfection of the Italian Tongue* (Livorno, 1715). Both works quoted in Pizzoli, *Le grammatiche di italiano*, 76–77.

[22] Ibid., 45.   [23] Thorne, 'Italian teachers', 144.

[24] This must have contributed to the popularity of these two heroic poems among many travellers, who often referred to them in their writings, particularly those who recognised the rhythm of their stanzas in the verses performed by the *improvvisatori*. See Chapter 2.

The revival in interest was literary this time but the new positive image of Italy, which owed much to the activities of Baretti, made knowledge of Italy and its language fashionable again, both intellectually and socially. The climate was again favourable for acquiring some knowledge of Italian suitable for light conversations, which was complemented by the revived popularity of opera all over Europe. Italian was felt to have more gentle sounds than any other language, which made its study popular with ladies of the aristocracy. An active promoter of this new trend was Annibale Antonini, an instructor who lived in Paris for thirty years (1726–55) and specialised in teaching the language and editing Italian classics, Ariosto and Tasso in particular, specifically *à l'usage des Dames*.[25]

As the Romantic era was about to begin, interest in Italian classics merged with the passion for music as well as scholarship in art, architecture and archaeology. For the less motivated, a journey to Italy in order to indulge in beholding the picturesque countryside was the ultimate adventure for young men and increasingly for women too. The famous statesman Charles James Fox, who was a lover of classical literature as much as he was a *bon viveur* in Parisian salons, wrote to a friend in 1767: 'For God's sake learn Italian as fast as you can, if it be only to read Ariosto. There is more good poetry in Italian than in all other languages that I understand put together. In prose too it is a very fine language. Make haste and read all these things that you may be fit to talk to Christians.'[26]

Memory and Imitation

If the conversational vs. literary approaches represent the two opposite tendencies in language teaching, the use of dialogues vs. the grammar-translation method informed their respective practices. But this clear-cut distinction is mainly illustrative as the methodology used for one generation of learners was modified by other circumstances, such as the books that publishers marketed, and the teachers' availability, reputation and connections. For example, Latin grammars were usually adapted for teaching other languages, and the Medieval

---

[25] Gianfranco, Folena, 'Divagazioni sull' italiano di Voltaire' in *L'italiano in Europa,* 396–432, quotes from pp. 405 and 427. First published in *Studi in onore di Vittorio Lugli e Diego Valeri* (Venice, 1961), 391–424.

[26] Charles James Fox to Richard Fitzpatrick, from Florence, 22 September 1767, in *Memorials and Correspondence of Charles James Fox*, 2 vols. (Philadelphia, 1853) I, 44. Charles James Fox, who was instructed in French during his late teens in France (see 'Literary and Non-Literary Focus'), learned Italian later. He always believed in formal instruction and reading classical literature: 'I read nothing but Italian, which I am immensely fond of, particularly the poetry'; he later wrote to his nephew: 'I advise you to have a master and to read Dante and other difficult books.' Letter from Florence, 6 August 1767, *Memorials and Correspondence of Charles James Fox*, I, 55.

passion for dialogues re-emerged everywhere as a strategy for language learning. Both approaches generated a vast amount of language teaching material over the centuries and never ceased to inspire teachers engaged with diverse types of learners.

The best instructors were usually the authors of textbooks, and most of them never hesitated to draw on new ideas from across linguistic frontiers. Some merely plagiarised foreign textbooks, with a view to taking advantage of methods which were successful abroad and which could be promoted as novel at home. This encouraged authors to stress the innovative qualities of their textbooks, although the emphasis was more often on dismissing old materials rather than applying new ideas. If the teacher claimed to be adopting a totally innovative approach, a new textbook was the prerequisite for publicising it but producing a book was also instrumental in acquiring the right connections. This was normal practice as authors needed to secure protection and sponsorship from within the higher circles of society, the milieu which usually supplied the keenest learners of foreign languages.

Such complex dynamics explain why authors were concerned to explain how their approach would meet the needs of their pupils, either in the book's preface or the dedication. Native competence was highly valued, and many authors advanced this as the main requirement for effective teaching. But many non-native writers presented themselves as experienced instructors able to teach several languages.[27] More problematic than the lack of native competence was the linguistic isolation some teachers suffered through being cut off from their original language community. In some cases, this was reported as affecting their familiarity with colloquialisms, especially for Italian, a language whose spoken usage was strongly marked by regional traits. But it could also affect writing style in languages other than Italian, whose written code was strictly regulated by the *Accademia della Crusca*, especially for literary usages.[28]

---

[27] For example, the author Francesco Colsoni called himself a 'Teacher of languages' in the frontispiece to his textbook (1688), and in one of his dialogues (*Fra due Giovani che voglion imparare il Francese insieme*), a young man who wants to learn French suggests Colsoni as an experienced teacher. When his friend asks: *sarà egli francese di nascita?* ['will he be a French native?'] he replies: *Non só s'egli sia Francese, basta ch'ei parla benissimo* ['I do not know if he is French, it suffices that he speaks very well']. Francesco Colsoni, *The new trismagister or the new teacher of three languages etc* . . . (London,1688). In the highly competitive sector of foreign language teaching in the eighteenth century, many teachers gave instruction in more than one language. In London, René Milleran and Vairasse d'Allais taught French as a foreign language as well as English to speakers of other languages. See Lambley, *The Teaching and Cultivation of French*, 354. Pleunus taught French, Italian and German, as well as Latin, and Baretti taught Italian, French and Spanish. See Alessandra Vicentini, 'English language and cultural stereotypes in the eighteenth century: the first grammars of English for Italian learners', *Quaderni del CISRIL*, 8–9 (2009–10), 2–18, esp. 2 n.4.

[28] It is important to point out the different aims of the first two language academies in Europe. The Italian academy, inspired by purism, favoured the literary models of the past. See Arturo Tosi, 'The *Accademia della Crusca* in Italy: past and present', in Bernard Spolsky (ed.), *Language*

In Elizabethan England, the most influential work on language teaching was *The Schoolmaster* by Roger Asham, a classical scholar and tutor to Elizabeth before she became queen, published posthumously in 1570. The book was not only influential in establishing the principles of humanistic education; it also elaborated pedagogical practices whereby a young gentleman's knowledge of Greek and Latin literary texts would help to shape his language use and conversational style. A specific type of exercise suggested by Asham was double translation: from the original Latin to the pupil's English, to be used in turn to recreate the Latin text. This practice was believed to have the dual advantage of building linguistic consciousness while teaching language skills.[29] Another of Asham's methods was imitation, whereby pupils were trained to create original texts in the target language while practising their personal style and correct pronunciation. Such exercises were based on the presupposition that language consciousness was a mental discipline that needed to be trained. Thus, the cross-fertilisation of skills was thought to be the best procedure for learning a modern language.[30]

In the second half of the sixteenth century, teachers exploited a mnemonic technique based on switching from language to language, as it was assumed that modern language learning could benefit from the model of practising various types of dialogues. This was a method of medieval origins, used to teach readers to deal with practical situations as well as academic debates: once applied to modern language teaching, the focus switched from learned disputations to everyday conversations. As mentioned earlier, the language scholar who first shifted from stressing knowledge about a language to learning how to use the language was John Florio, born to Michelangelo Florio, a Protestant refugee from Tuscany who arrived in London in 1550.[31]

John Florio, the best-known linguist of the time and Queen Elizabeth's personal language tutor, was active both in Oxford and London, mixing with the cream of Elizabethan aristocracy, among whom he promoted a strong interest in Italian language and literature. His extensive output of linguistic and literary works spanned more than thirty years, reflecting his attempts both

---

Academies and Other Language Management Agencies, Special Issue of *Language Policy*, 10, 4 (2011), 289–303.

[29] Linguistic consciousness is used here in the sense of sensitivity to the mother tongue and transfer of its functions to a non-native language, rather than in the sense of social awareness of linguistic issues.

[30] The same theory was implemented in Hollyband's book *The French Schoolmaster*, which appeared in England in 1580; the same year, *The English Schoolmaster* was published in France by the same author, who was also an advocate of practical language teaching and a keen believer in the direct method.

[31] Catholic–Protestant tensions in England had the advantageous outcome of bringing a large number of Protestants from Italy to non-Catholic countries. Many were active intellectuals with an academic or literary background, and some took advantage of their native linguistic competence to become language tutors and authors of language textbooks.

to educate the English aristocracy about Italy and to equip Elizabethan travellers for living and communicating abroad. John Florio always regarded himself as an Italian, but having been born in London and never having been to Italy, a large number of the dialogues in his teaching materials were set in England. These were complemented by a substantial collection of Italian proverbs, which served not only as an homage to the art of memory – the so-called *ars memorativa* of the Renaissance – but also provided evidence that a colloquial approach to language teaching should take precedence over written composition. Indeed, a dominant principle in Elizabethan England was that the aim of modern language education was 'to get the student speaking as soon and as proverbially as possible'.[32]

Florio was an admirer of Montaigne and a translator of his *Essays*, and in all his textbooks he dismissed an emphasis on language composition in favour of exercises linked to everyday usage. Florio's *Second Fruites* (1591) included a *Giardino de Recreatione*, with a collection of several thousand proverbs that the author described as follows:

Giardino di recreatione, nel quale crescono fronde, fiori, e frutti, vaghi, leggiadri, & soavi; sotto nome di sei mila prouerbij, et piaceuoli riboboli, italiani, colte, scelti da Giovanni Florio, non solo utili, ma dilettuoli per ogni spirito vago della nobil lingua Italiana.[33]

[A leisure garden where fronds, flowers and fruit grow and meander gracefully; under the name of six thousand proverbs, and wonderfully colourful expressions, all Italian, gathered and chosen by Giovanni Florio, not only useful but a delight to any free spirit who speaks the noble Italian language.]

It is interesting that among these proverbs we find a number of maxims that some travellers later reported to have collected during their Italian journey (see Chapter 2). Another set of handy phrases, also similar to those previously discussed, warns travellers against common risks: *Dio ci guardi da sette cose, da puttana di bordello, da frate di mantello, da barcaruolo da traghetto, da prete da grossetto, da barbiere salariato, da vescovo senza entrata, et da giuoco da tre dadi* ['God protect us from seven things: from the whorehouse slut, from the friar in his habit, from the ferryman, from a Grosseto priest, from the salaried barber, from the bishop with no income, and from the game of three dice'].[34]

---

[32] William Edward Engel, 'Knowledge that counted: Italian Phrase Books and Dictionaries in Elizabethan England', *Bollettino del CIRVI*, 31–2, Gennaio–Dicembre 1995, XVI, Fascicolo I–II, 117.

[33] John Florio, *Second Fruites* (London, 1591). This was an expanded version of *First Fruites* (1578) which included the *Giardino di Ricreatione*.

[34] Quoted in Spartaco Gamberini, *Lo studio dell'italiano in Inghilterra nel '500 e nel '600* (Messina-Florence, 1970), 122–4.

After these publications, Florio devoted himself to the compilation of a massive bilingual dictionary, which appeared in two editions (1598, 1611). The original edition, *A Worlde of Wordes*, was a textbook designed to include 'the words of twenty good Italian auctors', which in fact drew from a much wider selection of contemporary writers. The second edition, *Queen Anna's New World of Words*, included a grammatical appendix, *Necessary Rules and Short Observations for the True Pronouncing of the Italian Tongue*. The main feature of this vast undertaking was the comprehensive range of language skills Florio aimed to incorporate in this work. Another innovative feature was the choice of dialogues: none was conceived as a commonplace situation involving anonymous characters but rather took the form of mini-narratives, inspiring intellectual curiosity about the foreign country and respect for its people.

Another milestone in language textbooks was the work of Hollyband or Claude de Sainliens, the French Huguenot who came to England as a refugee in 1564, and who enjoyed a brilliant career as a French language teacher to the London aristocracy over some forty years. He was the first to produce a textbook for teaching French to English pupils, and ten years later he adapted the same approach for Italian, concentrating on the direct method: 'to get the pupil [to] read and pronounce the foreign language accurately and as soon as possible'.[35] There were other textbooks on the market that still treated spoken language as being subsidiary to written language, and in these cases some of the challenging aspects of oral competence, like pronunciation, were minimised, revealing some naïve stratagems to overcome the problem of conversation. This is from Uvedale (1611):

> To get the true Italian accent, 'twill be sufficient to read over the lines of the following page, wherein all the difficulty of the Italian pronunciation is in the syllables mark'd with a star: when we know how to pronounce them we can pronounce all the Italian language.[36]

The project that dominated the international scene of language teaching in the seventeenth century was that of the famous Czech educationist Jan Amos Komenský, known as Comenius, whose first edition of *Ianua Linguarum* appeared in 1631. His work revolved around the relationship between native and non-native language, and he suggested that the early years were the optimum age for natural language learning. His theory, giving precedence to language use over linguistic norms, recalls that of John Florio, but his work was rooted in a more comprehensive vision of language pedagogy, based on enjoyment/ engagement rather than discipline.

---

[35] Rinaldo Charles S. Simonini Jr, 'The Italian pedagogy of Claudius Hollyband', *Studies in Philology*, XLIX (1952), 144–54.

[36] Quoted in Pizzoli, *Le grammatiche di italiano*, 117 and n.208.

Another remarkable 'linguist', as he called himself, was Giovanni Torriano, who was active in teaching English to Italians, and later Italian to the English in London in the middle of the seventeenth century. He was also involved in the Italian book trade in London, and boasted a number of distinguished sponsors, to whom he dedicated his works. But most of his later self-published textbooks were burned in the Great Fire of London in 1666. A noticeable feature of his approach was his stress on spoken language, with attention to pronunciation. Torriano compiled a dictionary and published a textbook, *The Italian Tutor,* in 1640. This was followed by *Della Lingua Toscana Romana* (1657) which included an appendix of dialogues specifically targeted to travellers in Italy. He constructed dialogues with an enhanced colloquial rather than formal character, bringing them closer to real-life situations and thereby rendering the language more authentic: he also applied this rule in his *Selected Italian Proverbs,* which were carefully chosen to be 'very useful for travellers'. In a century dominated by the theories of Florio and Comenius, another breakthrough was the principle that speaking should be practised even before other skills, such as reading or listening, were properly mastered. This is what Torriano wrote in 1639:

But if for want of practice you should fall short of speaking it, strive for the understanding of it: for diverse Englishmen have translated good Italian authors both verse and prose, which have had no pregnant expression. Againe if you would be perfect in speaking it, let no opportunity passe, nor the feare of erring withdraw you purpouses; for I have dayly experience of many that will not attempt speech, because they mistrust they shall not utter it perfectly; but such in my opinion would faine swim before they goe imo the water.[37]

In a subsequent textbook, the *Italian reviv'd or the Introduction to the Italian Tongue*, published in 1673, Torriano spelled out how innovative the book was compared with his previous publication: it included 'a new store-house of proper and choice dialogues, most useful for such as desire the speaking part'. He also qualified in surprising detail the practical use of this linguistic repertoire for travellers who 'intend to travel into Italy, or the Levant. Together with the modern way of addressing letters, and stiling of persons, as well as in actual discourse, as in writing'.[38]

More Motives, Less Motivation

In the second part of the seventeenth century, the language teaching scene in Europe was dominated by a flourishing production of grammar books. This

[37] Giovanni, Torriano, 'To the corteous reader', in *New and Easie Directions*, quoted in Pizzoli, *Le grammatiche di italiano*, 83 n.115.
[38] Giovanni Torriano, *Italian Reviv'd or the Introduction to the Italian Tongue* (London, 1673).

new trend followed the famous 1643 grammar of Benedetto Buonmattei, a scholar from Tuscany also known as *il principe dei grammatici* ('the prince of grammarians'). Another equally successful grammar, *Maître Italien*, was written by Jean Vigneron, who lived in Paris under the Italianised name Giovanni Veneroni and passed himself off as a Florentine. Ferdinando Altieri published a popular grammar book in the first decade of the eighteenth century which included a dictionary and ran to many editions. In the preface he called himself 'professor of the Italian tongue in London', but later he resettled in Italy, where he worked as a teacher of English, publishing an English grammar *'che contiene un esatto e facil metodo per apprendere questa lingua'* ['containing an exact and easy way to learn this language'].

The eighteenth century saw also the revival of an emphasis on literature and, accordingly, the skills that were given priority were reading literary texts and writing, with composition exercises based on previously analysed texts. The idea was to train good translators of the literary language, and the most frequent exercises resorted to translation into and from the target language. The following dialogue between a tutor and his pupil, from Veneroni's book *Short specimen* (1760), summarises well the revival of the grammar-translation approach:

Avrei gran piacere di poterla parlar con franchezza. – Perchè non legge qualche libro d'istoria, o di lettere familiari? – Adesso non ne ho alcuno; ma per l'avvenire voglio comprarne. – Se ella vuole imparar bene la lingua, è necessario perfezionarsi nelle regole della grammatica. – Dice benissimo; ed io credo che tradurre da una lingua in un'altra sia il vero mezzo per imparare. – Se cosi pensa perchè non lo pratica? – Mi manca un buon dizionario, e senza questo è difficile poter fare una buona traduzione.[39]

[It would please me greatly to speak it fluently. – Why don't you read a history book or family letters? – At present I have none; but I want to buy some in the future. – If you want to learn the language well, you need to study the grammar rules. – It is true what you say and I believe that translating from one language to another is the right way to learn. – If that's what you think, why do you not do it? – I don't have a good dictionary and without that it's not easy to make a good translation.]

As the role of literature in building the necessary platform for language studies was promoted again, some teachers felt they needed to restore learners' confidence in their speaking skills, since an expanding audience of more demanding pupils was required, by an increasing number of textbooks, to spend too much time reading. This is how the author Laurentio Casotti made the point in his dialogue *Frà due gentilhuomini* in 1709:

– Intende quel che legge? – Intendo meglio dì quel che parlo. – V.S. mi perdoni, parla Italiano bene, non li manca ch'un poco d'essercitio, ò pratica. – La ringrazio del coraggio che mi fa. Pronuncio jo bene? – Assai bene: se lei s'applicherà, parlerà in

---

[39] Giovanni Veneroni, *Short Specimen* (London, 1760), 84.

poco tempo perfettamente la lingua Italiana. ... – Che Libri legge V.S. – L'historia dell'Avila. Le Commedie del Moliere. L'Historia del Guicciardini. Il Pastor Fido, &c.[40]

[– Do you understand what you read? – I understand better than I speak. – My lord, forgive me, you speak Italian well, all you need is a bit of practice. – Thank you for your encouragement. Is my pronunciation good? – Very good: if you apply yourself you will speak Italian perfectly in a short time. . . . – What books are you reading my lord? – The History of Avila. Moliere's Plays. The History of Guicciardini. Il Pastor Fido, &c.]

The stress on grammar and translation remained dominant in the eighteenth and early nineteenth centuries, something that is reflected in the large number of grammars, dictionaries, and anthologies that included foreign language prose and verse, as well as 'readers' which contained lower level passages for oral practice. These usually constituted the materials adopted by teachers in schools and universities. Despite the popularity of these new grammars and the revival of the grammatical approach to language teaching, paradoxically the eighteenth century was dominated in Europe by a popular passion for French, which meant mainly language used for polite conversation in salons, while the desire to learn Italian was becoming restricted to the circle of music lovers.[41]

The spreading taste for opera, combined with the perception that Italian was the language which sounded the most beautiful, meant that learners were drawn from a wider public, and it followed that a greater choice of teachers and textbooks became available. However, this popularisation led to superficial learning and casual application. The people who reacted against this new climate and made serious attempts to increase respect for Italy and its language included Giuseppe Baretti, Vincenzio Martinelli and Francesco Sastres, all linguists and friends of Dr Johnson.

With such rapidly changing trends, it was easy for language teachers to rail against the inadequacy of previous educational methods and materials in meeting the needs of a public who showed diverse interests in learning foreign languages but who were increasingly less motivated to apply themselves to serious study. Unsurprisingly, an increasingly common criticism was that those instructors who started with teaching grammar began where they should end, and many linguists and the general public alike seemed to prefer more user-friendly methods and materials. Vincenzio Martinelli was someone who caught

---

[40] L. Casotti, *A New Method of Teaching the Italian Tongue to Ladies and Gentlemen* (London, 1709), 84. 'Avila' must be Enrico Caterino Davila, whose *Historia delle guerre civili di Francia* (Venice, 1630) was widely read in the seventeenth and eighteenth centuries.

[41] The method that combined reading aloud under supervision in order to learn the correct pronunciation with studying the principal grammatical rules and memorising vocabulary from short dialogues was called 'grammar and rota'. However, the number of instructors who taught 'by rota' alone, in other words purely through conversation without teaching any grammatical rules, was apparently quite significant in the eighteenth century. See Lambley, *The Teaching and Cultivation of French*, 331.

the new spirit of the time vis-à-vis the increasing demand from the new sectors of foreign language consumers. In an essay (*Lettere Familiari e Critiche*, 7, 1751), he drew the distinction between *scolari letterati* and *scolari non letterati,* differentiating between pupils who were trained in classical studies and/or English grammar and those who were not. According to him, a common mistake among language teachers was not taking this distinction into account and losing their pupils' interest.

As time moved on most practitioners mitigated their overly structured methods by producing materials that relied on simplified approaches. Gasparo Grimani produced an innovative textbook in 1788, *Ladies's New Italian Grammar*, whose title and approach are justified in the preface: 'as ladies in general have not learned Latin or Greek, when they attempt the study of any language, grammatical terms terrify and discourage them, and they look upon grammar as a monstrous production'. This problem must have been widely acknowledged, as new textbooks appeared with titles such as *The Complete French Master for Ladies and Gentlemen* (1767). Indeed, grammar was taught only to boys, and usually using Latin-based terminology which girls did not normally learn, as illustrated in the initial dialogue '*Entre une Dame et le Maître des Langues*' in Claude Mauger's *French Grammar* (1688):

> Monsieur, je n'ai pas appris la langue Latine, je ne sais pas
> que c'est que Grammaire, qu'un Nom, qu'un Verbe ... et je
> voudrais pourtant bien apprendre par Règles, et non par
> Routine. Je vous prie de m'en informer.
> Il est très raisonnable ... La Grammaire est l'Art de bien Parler.[42]

> [Sir, I have not learned Latin, and do not know what is meant
> by grammar, noun, verb ... and I would prefer to learn by rule
> rather than rote. Please let me know what they are.
> It is very reasonable ... Grammar is the art of speaking.]

There is no doubt that the cosmopolitan atmosphere of the eighteenth century, with the accompanying interest in modern languages, increased the quantity of learners even if not the quality of their achievement. The capricious mood of the new elites is best represented by two cases of extreme approaches. One is mentioned by the novelist Fanny Burney, who admitted enjoying the textbook *Easy Phraseology for the Use of Young Ladies Who Intend to Learn the Colloquial Part of Italian Language*, which was constructed around dialogues between a dog and a cat. There was a distinct generational change in attitudes towards language learning, which can be seen by contrasting her casual approach with the commitment of her father, Dr Charles Burney, who learned Italian as a musical historian. When he needed to give music lessons in

---

[42] Claude, Mauger, *French Grammar* (London, 1688), 45–51.

Figure 3.1 *A tour to foreign parts*, 1778. Etching by Henry William Bunbury (1750–1811). ©The Trustees of the British Museum

preparation for his journey to Italy, he taught himself Italian while travelling on horseback between jobs.[43]

Another textbook which demonstrated the mixing of modern language studies with less honourable motives was *Italian Exercises*, published in 1800 by Cesare Mussolini, who explained in the subtitle that it was 'a collection of Italian and English dialogues, entirely new; containing a short history of the most distinguished personages in Great Britain'. Indeed, an unusual feature of the book was the author's apology for his English translations of the Italian conversations. But his innovative content consisted of bilingual dialogues which included gossip and scurrilous remarks attributed to London celebrities of the time, all identified by first name, surname and title.

The argument about the correct sequence for teaching the various elements of a language carried on for much of the eighteenth century, when the

---

[43] The episode is reported by his daughter Madame D'Arblay [Fanny Burney] in *Memoirs of Dr Burney* 3 vols. (London, 1832), I, 108–9.

popularity of Italian opera and the success of the Grand Tour ushered in a less academic though more positive attitude towards foreign tongues. But as ambition grew while motivation did not, the warnings about false expectations became more explicit. The traveller Henry Coxe, in his book *Picture of Italy*, warned strongly against departing for Italy without some rudiments of the language, making certain that one's repertoire was drawn from the authentic spoken tongue, not the literary language or, even worse, from opera libretti: 'as for learning *Italian* merely as a dead language, or that of books, the traveler in so doing would but lose his time'.[44]

Age and Achievement

A traveller's age before departure and the length of education at school or university are useful clues for interpreting their linguistic attitudes and motivation, while a more equivocal factor is whether a learner was educated in classical studies, with or without modern languages. In the seventeenth and eighteenth centuries, school leavers and university undergraduates tended to be very young, as demonstrated by the age of most young men who embarked on a journey abroad as an extension of their education, usually between fourteen and seventeen. For a boy in his late teens who had completed several years of classical language studies at school and/or university, the prospect of becoming fluent abroad with near-native pronunciation was practically the same whether or not he had also received training in a foreign language before departure. Of course, some young men and women were fortunate to come from families who believed in investing in private language tuition if the opportunity to achieve good levels of fluency was not available at their school or university.

Within the flourishing sector of foreign language learners – the cosmopolitan nobility and wealthy bourgeoisie – a new custom was to hire private tutors, either full-time or part-time. The fashion spread rapidly throughout Europe, so we know that quite a number of young men who were sent on the Grand Tour from England learned the rudiments of a foreign language in this way. It became increasingly common for young ladies too, who were trained by their governesses, some of whom were briefed to speak nothing but French.[45] Lessons for adults were usually given in the client's house. But when the pupils were small children, it was not unusual for a tutor to be required to spend all day with them, often for several years, while speaking nothing but the foreign

---

[44] Henry Coxe [pseudonym of John Millard], *Picture of Italy* (London, 1815), x.

[45] Having a foreign governess in an aristocratic home was not uncommon in early modern Europe, but this subject has been investigated only recently. See Susan N. Bayley, 'The English Miss, German Fräulein and French Mademoiselle: foreign governesses and national stereotyping in nineteenth- and early twentieth-century Europe', *Journal of the History of Education Society*, 43, 2 (2014), 160–86.

language. The resulting level of competence in children was quite different depending on whether parents hired a visiting tutor for occasional language sessions or chose to keep a governor or governess in full-time residence.[46] When the foreign language was used all the time, children grew up speaking it as a native language but the service of a part-time tutor was the best option to assure both fluency in the foreign language and normal development of the native tongue. Clearly, such a high level of language mastery was a privilege for the few who were educated at home, and near-native competence in a foreign language was unlikely to be achieved by effective but occasional instruction such as that received in boarding schools and universities.

Some travellers recorded positive comments about their private tutors or teachers at their school but no level of language attainment can be inferred from the comments of grateful pupils, whose main intent was to praise their instructors. Moreover, claims about their personal level of linguistic achievement before departure had not been tested in real-life situations. Throughout their journeys, language-related comments by most travellers, if any, remained vague and subjective, and they relied on expressions such as 'passable pronunciation', 'reasonable knowledge', 'perfect language' or 'speaking very prettily' that recall the same wording used by teachers and authors.

According to many travellers who journeyed abroad after the Grand Tour had become fashionable, several years of education before departure had left them with just a smattering of French or Italian. Even worse was the evidence of their negative attitudes towards foreign countries, which undermined the motivation and self-confidence necessary for learning a language in a natural setting. Although during the eighteenth and nineteenth centuries it was not rare for schools to include foreign languages in the curriculum, these subjects were seen as having low academic status for boys, and as being much more appropriate for the education of girls. Of course, there were young men who applied themselves keenly to the study of modern languages but they belonged to a small elite who were passionate about the arts and humanities, which were becoming more attractive to the upper classes than to the wealthy bourgeoisie.[47]

It is difficult to draw generalisations regarding the outcome of travellers' linguistic training during the early modern period. One limitation is that, although much has been written about the principles and practices of language teaching in diverse contexts, the focus tends to be teacher-centred (methods and materials) rather than learner-centred (age and achievement). Another relevant

---

[46] Nicholas Hans recalls that 'almost every exiled aristocrat . . . resorted to giving private lessons as a living'; *New Trends in Education in the Eighteenth Century* (London, 1966), 188.

[47] The turning point was in the middle of the eighteenth century, when methods and materials for teaching modern languages became less conditioned by the knowledge of Latin grammar. See 'Memory and Imitation'.

point is that some of the attitudes and aspirations of the language learners in our period sound almost naïve today, at a time when we have lost faith in the role of linguistic authorities and have much less confidence in the power of memory and imitation as instruments of learning.

A quick exploration of some individual experiences shows how a supportive family background and good training in classical studies could maximise the travel experience as an ideal foreign language learning opportunity. The most striking case is that of the French philosopher Michel de Montaigne whose father, following the advice of some humanist friends, instructed his son's German tutor to speak to him only in Latin as a *langue vivante*. Apparently Montaigne did not speak French until the age of seven, when he began to study ancient Greek. But by the age of 13, when he started studying law, he had already developed a formidable language awareness, which he later used to teach himself to speak and write Italian while travelling in Italy for fourteen months.

Philip Sidney, the scholar and diplomat, was only 18 when he embarked on his first diplomatic visit to France, where it was reported that he performed not only with a fluent command of the language but also with 'ready and witty answers [which] were good testimonial to the grammar school where French had been included in the curriculum'.[48] It might not have been unusual for English boys from such a privileged background to start their education already fluent in French, which at the time was a language widely spoken among the English nobility.[49] We know that Henry Wotton had a similar upbringing, receiving some instruction at home from his mother and a tutor. At Oxford, he wrote a play based on Tasso's recently published *Gerusalemme Liberata* and became a close conversant with Alberico Gentili, the famous Italian professor of civil law. By the age of twenty, Wotton had gained a good command of Italian and left England to further his academic studies abroad, where he diligently and intensively studied German and French. Fynes Moryson was a Fellow at Cambridge when he decided to travel around continental Europe in 1591. He had a solid background in classical studies, but apparently only a smattering of modern languages before his departure. Certainly, he applied himself most conscientiously to language studies in the countries where he resided – Germany, France and Italy – achieving such a high level of competence that he could pass himself off as a native.

Governors, whether engaged at home or abroad, made an important contribution to the success of a tour for some travellers, though not necessarily a positive one on the language-learning front. When Lord Harrington's sixteen-year-old

---

[48] Trease, *The Grand Tour*, 17.
[49] Charles-Pierre Bouton, *Les Grammaires Françaises de Claude Mauger à l'usage des Anglais* (Paris, 1972), quoted in Cohen, *Fashioning Masculinity*, 142.

son John left Cambridge for Florence and Siena, he kept up regular Greek and Latin lessons with his tutor Mr Tovey, and learned Italian as he went along. The philosopher Thomas Hobbes, already a tutor at the age of twenty-two when he accompanied the son of William Cavendish on his Continental travels, became very interested in cultural debates at foreign universities and learned to speak French and Italian (in his words 'mediocretly'), but apparently some tutors 'while accompanying these blue-blooded lads derived more profit than their pupils'.[50]

Richard Lassels built up a reputation as a governor and travel-writer, as well as for his recommendation that all 'young lords' ought to make the Grand Tour, but not before the age of fifteen or sixteen. Possibly his advice was justified but not in the case of James Bovey, a London merchant's son who was only fourteen when he left home: by the time he returned at the age of nineteen, he had mastered several languages and had become an authority on trade and commerce. An even more impressive example was Robert Boyle, the future chemist, who was sent abroad with his brother when he was only eleven; after two years in France he was fluent in French, and then travelled to Italy, where he learned Italian while studying Galileo's theories. The poet John Milton, son of a humble scrivener, studied Latin, Greek and Hebrew at St Paul's School in London, taking additional private lessons in French and Italian. When he left Cambridge for Italy with an MA in 1632, he could read and write six languages and compose verses in at least three. On the other hand, John Evelyn, who studied at Balliol College, Oxford, did not learn any modern foreign languages before travelling to France and Italy, but soon became fluent in them while studying art and architecture abroad.

Joseph Addison, who left England in 1699, marks the transition to the new century and new attitudes towards language learning. Although a classical scholar in Oxford and a Latin poet out of time, he was ignorant of modern languages, and while in France and Italy, by his own admission, he had to work very hard to overcome his lack of aptitude for languages. This tendency was becoming the norm as the majority of travellers were not great linguists when they left home. But there were some notable exceptions. One was Thomas Coke, who lost both parents at the age of ten and, as the heir to an immense fortune, decided to go abroad at fifteen, accompanied by an academic tutor from Cambridge and a cohort of servants, with a view to learning French and Italian in the appropriate centres of excellence. He did so while enjoying himself and spending fortunes in acquiring ancient books and antiquities, as well as having a good time in wild Sicily and in Parisian salons, before returning home and starting a political career at the age of only twenty-one.[51]

---

[50] Trease, *The Grand Tour*, 51.
[51] Writing from Rome at the age of sixteen, he said he had already 'become a perfect virtuoso, and a great lover of pictures'. One year later, after travelling in Switzerland, Germany and France, he

Two other prominent representatives of the eighteenth century are Thomas Gray and Horace Walpole; they met at Cambridge, where they studied Greek and Latin, and both took Italian lessons but apparently neither had much command of the spoken language. While in Italy, Gray translated Dante, Giovanni Battista Guarini, and Tasso, but he confessed: 'Eleven months, at different times, have I passed at Florence; and yet (God help me) know not either people or language.'[52] On Horace Walpole's return to London, the future statesman and son of the first British Prime Minister admitted: 'I talk no French, but to my footman; nor Italian, but to myself.'[53] Oliver Goldsmith also studied at university, although not with any dedication, and graduated at Trinity College, Dublin, but was totally incapable of speaking any modern language. James Boswell was also a graduate from Edinburgh, with a strong background in law and Latin, a language which, amusingly, he spoke abroad before he was fluent in French and while he was trying to learn Italian in Italy. Edward Gibbon, too, was not much of a linguist, leaving England without having developed fluency in any modern language at school or Oxford. However, he became practically bilingual in French while in Lausanne, where he lived for five years, even publishing a book in French. But by his own admission his Italian remained poor, although he had studied in Turin and Siena ('the shortness of my time, and the use of the French language, prevented my acquiring the facility of speaking').[54]

During the century of Enlightenment, with its cosmopolitan atmosphere and significant cultural exchanges between the European elites in the fields of the arts and architecture, history and music, it is notable that the most prominent young Englishmen had solid training in classical studies but not in modern languages. However, there were some young people from eccentric backgrounds who counterbalanced this dearth of good linguists. One was the novelist and art patron William Beckford, heir to an immense fortune who demonstrated great literary ability as a youth. His mother wanted to have him educated not at school and university, but by a private tutor, John Lettice; he took Beckford at the age of seventeen to Lausanne, where he learned to write French as correctly and eloquently as his own language. Another was the politician Charles James Fox, mentioned earlier, who came from an even more unusual family. He owed to his liberal father the privilege of interrupting his education at Eton College at the age of fourteen; he was taken by his father to Paris to learn to gamble, to lose his virginity to a certain Madame de Quallens, and to learn the language. It is no surprise that when he returned to

---

wrote that he 'wished to spend one more winter in Italy, to confirm myself in the language and virtuosoship of that Country'. Quoted in Ingamells, *British and Irish Travellers*, 225.

[52] Thomas Gray, Letters of Thomas Gray to Richard West, London 21 April 1741, in John Mitford (ed.), *The Works of Gray*, 2 vols. (London, 1835), II, 142.

[53] Horace Walpole, *Letters* (1842), I, 175.   [54] Gibbon, *Memoirs*, 149.

Eton after a year of immersion in that environment, he had been aesthetically as well as linguistically transformed: as his headmaster put it, he was 'attired in red-heeled shoes and Paris cut-velvet, adorned with a pigeon-wing hair style tinted with blue powder, and a newly acquired French accent'.[55] It is not clear whether the schoolmaster's reference to young Charles's noticeable French accent was meant as a positive comment about evidence of his mastery of the foreign language, or a negative remark about him speaking English with a French accent.

[55] Loren Reid, *Charles James Fox: A Man for the People* (Columbia, 1969), 16.

Part II

Encounters and Exchanges

4   Language Acquisition and Learning Abroad

Interactions on the Road

While few travellers disclosed information about their education in their writings, even fewer were willing to put on paper details about their personal achievements and failures on the road. Rarely were comments in their diaries and correspondence negative or self-critical, possibly because the audience these were aimed at – families, private sponsors or government institutions – were the very people who had financially supported their education before departure and subsidised their foreign travel as a language-learning experience.

However, most of these reports explicitly refer to how more or less inclined travellers felt about involving themselves in the typical challenges of the journey, such as making everyday enquiries about directions or engaging in negotiations regarding the schedule. For most young noblemen, who had been brought up in luxury at home, it was not easy to enter into impromptu conversations with strangers, or to cope graciously with the basic conditions en route and the modest lifestyle at their destinations. Of course, some chose to travel economically and that meant, above all, journeying alone. This certainly presented them with better chances to learn languages through daily practice. One adventurous solo traveller was Thomas Coryat (1608); another was William Lithgow (1609), a young man full of mental and physical energy who traversed Europe mostly on foot; yet another was the academic Fynes Moryson, who also travelled alone (1593), and much of the time incognito through personal choice. What we constantly read in travel accounts of solo travellers is that they made a point of mingling with local people wherever they were, and invariably boasted about their progress in the language they spoke with the locals.

Travelling incognito served many different purposes. Some early travellers were attracted to certain destinations, such as Rome or other Italian cities, during the years of the Inquisition. They knew they would enjoy more freedom of movement in a Catholic country if they were able to hide their nationality and religion. But there were also noblemen who preferred not to disclose their identities for a variety of reasons: some in order to speed up procedures with municipal authorities, others in order to escape the inevitable social ceremonies with royal families and local aristocracies. The choice of solo or incognito travel was quite exceptional and was mostly confined to the early years of touring.

What one finds at the other extreme is that many sons of the aristocracy were accompanied on their journey by a considerable train of staff and servants, especially during the seventeenth and the eighteenth centuries. It was quite unlikely that those who chose to travel in such a grand style would become directly involved in the nitty-gritty negotiations and problem solving connected with the daily routine. Particularly at the height of the Grand Tour, when the opportunity to travel on the Continent became more widely accessible, some noblemen made history for the grandeur of their processions and the ostentation of their train of attendants.[1]

But lone adventurers and extravagant convoys of travellers were the exception; the majority of young men decided to tour the Continent with just one friend, or in the company of a secretary, tutor or servant, or a combination of these. Often, they ended up joining another traveller's party for convenience and safety. Since the most frequently encountered travellers on the road were from England, they had plenty of opportunities to come across other Englishmen, and ended up gravitating to their compatriots more or less all the time. For most small parties or solo travellers who were ignorant of the local languages, the risk of losing their way was very high as there were no signposts or border demarcations and linguistic boundaries rarely if ever coincided with political frontiers. Along most routes, enquiring about the direction of the next city, or even the name of a river, proved to be a difficult and frustrating endeavour. An anecdote shared among English travellers was reported by the poet John Taylor in 1630 as an example of the stupidity to be found in rural communities, but it actually gives a fairly good idea of how isolation could render enquiries hopeless and journeys adventurous: 'A Country man being demanded how such a River was called, that ranne through their Country: hee answered, that they never had the need to call the River, for it always came without calling.'[2]

The change in languages spoken along the route must have been noticeable, but not necessarily striking to most ears. Those following the standard itinerary

---

[1] Many authors discuss the issues of the high cost and grandeur of some Grand Tours. See for example Trease, *The Grand Tour*; Mączak, *Travel* and Black, *The British Abroad*. Two episodes are reported by Trease, 136 and 218. One concerns William Beckford, the art connoisseur who was reputed to be the richest commoner in England due to an inherited fortune, who departed for Italy with a convoy that was mistaken for that of the Russian Emperor. Another famous example towards the end of the Grand Tour was provided by Lord and Lady Blessington, who travelled from Paris to Italy in 1822 surrounded by such a grandiose display of wealth that their procession became infamously known along the route as the 'Blessington Circus'.
[2] John Taylor, who called himself 'The Water Poet', is quoted here by Mączak, *Travel*, 18–9.

to Paris from Calais, and from there south into the depths of Italy, could not fail to hear strong variations in accent and intonation in what, on the impression, sounded like different languages. But those travelling from the north to the south of Europe along a different route further to the east would encounter just on the relatively short stretch between Vienna and Venice at least five different local languages spoken by the indigenous communities: German, Slovenian, Friulian, Venetian and Italian. Edward Browne, a future president of the College of Physicians, mentioned this issue when relating his experiences:[3]

This my return from Venice to Vienna, about three hundred and fifty Italian miles, was the most quiet journey I ever made, for not meeting with good Company I performed it alone, and upon one Horse; and although there are several Nations, and no less than four Languages spoken upon this road, yet I met with no disturbance from any, nor did any one ask from whence I came, or whither I would go, no trouble as to Bills of health, and good accommodation in the Inns at an easie rate.

When crossing the Alps, the more popular western route from the Savoy in France to the Piedmont in Italy would not leave a traveller with the impression of entering a different linguistic world every fifty miles. But those going from Switzerland into Italy passed from German-speaking communities to French

Figure 4.1 *The Paris diligence*, not dated. Watercolour by Thomas Rowlandson (1756–1827). ©The Paul Mellon Collection, Yale Center for Studies in British Art, USA

---

[3] Browne, *A Brief Account,* 88.

and Italian, or vice versa, so that it was not possible to enquire the name of the next village in the same language.

In the eighteenth century, many travellers were inclined to use large, fast public coaches in France, which in the last quarter of the century travelled up to 60 miles a day and held up to ten people. After an initial acclimatisation to the other passengers, conversation was usually good for filling the time, especially if the company was stimulating. Alison and Tytler describe the feeling of familiarity that fortunately grew between travel companions during a journey from Paris to Lyon, which included two English friends – one of whom was Joseph Palmer, nephew of Sir Joshua Reynolds – a surgeon, a Paris textile merchant, a young lady and a Knight of Malta who amused the company with an account of the coronation of Louis XVI, at which he was present:[4]

> In an instant, every tongue is at work, and every individual bent upon making themselves happy for the moment, and contributing to the happiness of their fellow travelers. Talking, joking, laughing, singing, reciting – every enjoyment which is light and pleasurable is instantly adopted.

But not everyone was able to appreciate uninhibited socialising in the small confines of a coach. Vehicles which were full, slow and noisy often were disconcerting to travellers who were unwilling to lower their defences caused by shyness or overcome the handicap of using their schoolboy French with strangers. Robert Wharton, a strong supporter of travel by public diligence, appreciated the interactions it entailed, commenting that it provided a 'way of seeing the French People as much as possible and being sure not to be imposed on'.[5] Many tourists using hired carriages reported endless quarrels over delays, accidents and costs with the coach drivers – whether postilions in Germany, *voiturins* in France or *vetturini* in Italy. William Smith, later a Member of Parliament, illustrated the type of problem that occurred when travellers could not communicate well with such people:

> He was near 40 minutes before he produced the horses with a postilion as slow as the last. Threats, entreaties, signs were as ineffectual as with the other. We still moved on, our accustomed funeral pace ... between one and two the carriage stopped at the gates of Dusseldorf ... We found, as we knew we should, the gates of the city shut, and had therefore the pleasure of sitting in the carriage till five o'clock when they were opened.[6]

Mączak reports the observations made by the Polish poet Zygmunt Krasiñskion a long-distance coach journey in 1845, who was most impressed by the extraordinary relationship between the two postilions and their horses:

---

[4] Alison and Tytler, *Travels in France*, II, 254.   [5] Quoted in Black, *The British Abroad*, 130.
[6] Ibid., 133.

The eight horses galloped on and on whilst all the time, day and night, I could hear the postillions talking to them, in Polish at first, but the further we drove the more I could hear Ruthenian, that incessant kind of speech, no longer heard in other lands, with which a man tries to inject strength and life into his beasts with words, entreaties, complaints. Every other minute the coachman yelled from his box, or the post-boy groaned and squealed – now they urged the horses onward, now they struck them with their whips.[7]

Some travellers who were able to hire a carriage and choose their own drivers expressed their gratitude for the willingness and flexibility of such key characters which contributed to the success of their journey. The most helpful of them provided the horses, assumed responsibility for the journey at an agreed rate, and saved the travellers from disputes with unscrupulous innkeepers. Many, like the Italian Sebastiano Locatelli and his party, were so impressed with their *vetturino* that they called him 'our first language teacher'[8]. But that was a fortunate state of affairs as drivers were often hired under pressure of time, and those who spoke the language of the country did not speak that of the passengers, or vice versa. Whenever travellers and drivers did not share a language, the party was at the mercy of the latter for sorting out business arrangements with the hostel keepers and formalities with the custom officers. When they could communicate with each other, the traveller had better control over the decisions of the driver but they were all still at the mercy of the custom officers' intrusions and the inn-keepers' greed.

When the roads were very bad, accidents and overturned carriages were frequent, so requests for help were part of the routine. This provided another source of linguistic adventure with unpredictable consequences. A traveller whose carriage broke down between Orléans and Toulouse in 1783 during a night of heavy rain reported that, after sending the postilion to the next town for a new carriage, his party approached a peasant house for help:

In this cottage we saw a great deal of poverty but to make amends for it there was as much chearfulness. The Pere de Famille was a fine old hardfac'd fellow who could speak nothing but patois. His wife who had lived in Montauban spoke French such as it was. The daughter and sons spoke it still worse but I could understand their Provençal or Languedocian or whatever it is pretty well from its great affinity to the Italian. I never met anywhere with sincerer hospitality. It is almost worth while to break a wheel to experience it.[9]

Once travellers reached the Alps and completed the ascent of Mont Cenis, which was the normal route from France into Italy, the French public diligence was left behind or the traveller's private carriage disassembled to be transported by mules in a convoy with the passengers. For the descent through the

[7] Mączak, *Travel in Early Modern Europe*, 5.   [8] Locatelli, *Viaggio di Francia*, 129.
[9] Quoted in Black, *The British Abroad*, 173.

Figure 4.2 *The manner of passing Mount Cenis*, 1755. Grey wash, with pen and black ink by George Keate (1729–97). ©The Trustees of the British Museum

valley, two strong porters carried each passenger in a chair supported by long poles. Such porters were reported to be almost legendary characters, incredibly strong but agile, who would whisk the passengers down steep stony roads. Travellers were 'for the first five or six minutes . . . under some fright', but then they were encouraged by the porters to converse with them, as Thomas Brand reported.[10]

A different means of transport most travellers would have used, especially in flat countries such as Holland and Germany, consisted of a covered boat drawn by horses on a towpath. The only trouble was that most foreign travellers would not have been accustomed to winter travel on boats skidding over the ice or being pushed at incredibly fast speeds by the wind. The Anglo-Irish poet Oliver Goldsmith reported: 'when they spread all their sails, they go more than a mile and a half a minute, and their motion is so rapid that the eye can scarcely accompany them . . . and in these you are sure to meet people of all nations. Here the Dutch slumber, the French chatter, and the English play at cards'.[11]

[10] Ibid., 33.
[11] Oliver Goldsmith, Letter to his uncle Contarine from Leiden, in James Prior (ed.), *The Life of Oliver Goldsmith, from a Variety of Original Sources* (London, 1837), I, 163.

Passport and custom inspections provided the least appreciated opportunities for language practice as frontier officers everywhere made a point of not speaking foreign languages. All travellers indicated that they were often annoyed, and some even intimidated, by these officials; but those who felt they had suffered abuse at their hands did not know what course of action to pursue. Since legal action was slow and expensive, the remedy for distinguished travellers was to go straight to the nearby authorities. George C. Carpenter reported on an incident after he disembarked in Dunkirk in 1717, which was fortunately solved through quick negotiations between peers: 'The next day we sent to the Count de Rouville, Governor of the town, to complain of the insults we had received from the officers. All he did was to order our things to be restored to us and that the fellows should beg our pardon. He also invited us to dine with him the next day.[12] In September 1785, the future historian Edward Nares, travelling with his elder brother George, arrived in the port of Calais and recorded his first impression of the foreign country:[13]

nothing could exceed my astonishment to be awakened out of my first sleep, by three armed men at my bedside, enquiring in French tongue, who I was, whence I came, whither I was going, and what my business might be in France ... The moment we disembarked ... we seemed to be in the New World ... Monks were to be seen in all the streets, in the habits of their order, with their feet bare in sandals ... The carriages, carts, horses and even dogs were different ... my brother ... declared ... that considering all things, ... he was much more struck with the difference in manners, persons, customs ... than upon his first interview with American Indians.

At Calais, all travellers described a typical frontier situation, with a crowd of hangers-on offering help with the language for a small fee. But there were also curious individuals and beggars milling around – like the monk famously described by Sterne in his *Sentimental Journey*. Another story goes that a Capuchin lay brother who approached the 'Milords and Ladies from England' with a leaflet written in English explained that the Capuchin fathers lived on charity. But the charity of a certain Reverend William Jones took the form of improving the English of the leaflet![14]

Tipping was, of course, one of the main headaches of being exposed to the locals while en route, especially considering that when one did not know the local customs regarding such payments, even knowledge of the language was of little assistance. After negotiating a good start at Calais, the same issue cropped up at each inn, posthouse or auberge along the journey. Oliver Goldsmith, writing about his rough crossing from Dover to Calais that took only three hours and twenty minutes – a record time before the age of the

---

[12] Quoted in Black, *The British Abroad*, 172.   [13] Ibid., 17–18.
[14] Quoted in Douglas Woodruff, 'From London to Paris', in Richard Stanton Lambert (ed.), *Grand Tour: A Journey in the Tracks of the Age of Aristocracy* (London, 1935), 42.

steamboat, but with 'all of us extremely seasick' – reported that once they disembarked in France, every creature who approached them and touched their trunks expected sixpence. Goldsmith and his party were also the target of a man who specialised in English travellers:

We were directed to the Hotel d'Angleterre, where a valet-de-place came to offer his service, and spoke to me ten minutes before I once found out that he was speaking English. We had no occasion for his services, so we gave him a little money because he spoke English, and because he wanted it.[15]

Alexander Leslie, Earl of Leven, was unhappy about aspects of his journey between Lille and Paris and strongly complained to the postilion, who came out with a very typical remark to vent his frustration with the travellers: 'One of them had the impudence this day to tell us, after we had given him sixpence to drink, that we paid like Frenchmen and not like Englishmen, and gave us names, upon which Sandie thrashed him.'[16]

Italy was even more infamous than France for persecuting foreigners by staff asking for tips on every occasion. The writer and linguist Jacques Cambry reported in his *Voyage Pittoresque en Suisse et en Italie* (1801) that while in Italy in 1788: 'Cette emplette donna le temps au charron, au sellier, au maréchal, au diable d'accourir en criant *bona mancia, bona mancia. Cazzo, bona mancia*, sont les seules mots jusq'à present que j'aie entendu dans l'Italie' ['This transaction provided a chance to the wheelwright, to the saddler, to the marshal, to the devil to rush around crying *bona mancia, Cazzo* (good tip, Fuck! – literally 'prick') ..., which are the only words I've heard up till now in Italy'].[17]

Quarrels involving bargaining were even more frequent than quibbles about tipping. Even in sober and proper Switzerland, travellers could be disappointed with the standard of accommodation at an inn:

Mr Rolle whose apartment was hardly better, was charged 10s 6 for his. There is no redress, and we were forced to submit to the injury, which was attended indeed with no small degree of insult. Rolle could only revenge himself by swearing heartily at the man in English, who did not understand a word he said.[18]

Once travellers arrived at a posthouse or inn, the exact price of the accommodation needed to be agreed with the landlord on the spot, either through the services of the coach driver if the cost of the journey was all-inclusive, or by one of the convoy if the party was travelling with its own coaches. Then all the distinguished travellers were served a meal at one table, and their servants were seated at another. If the inn hosted locals as well as foreigners, this provided an

---

[15] Oliver Goldsmith, Letter to Sir Joshua Reynolds, dated June 1770, in James Prior (ed.), *The life of Oliver Goldsmith,* II, 289.
[16] Quoted in Black, *The British Abroad*, 132–3.
[17] Jacques Cambry, *Voyage Pittoresque en Swisse et en Italie*, 2 vols. (Paris, 1801), I, 339.
[18] Quoted in Black, *The British Abroad*, 92.

excellent opportunity for language practice. However, some travellers chose to retire to their bedchambers rather than eat at the table d'hôte. This happened for a variety of reasons, ranging from individual taciturnity to an attitude of social superiority – or even in the expectation of being undressed and put to bed by one of *les filles de la maison*. And who could predict whether a young gentleman found a better opportunity for language learning at the table d'hôte or in the bedroom (as discussed later in Chapter 5)? According to evidence uncovered by Mączak, a number of travellers drew attention to the fact that French innkeepers would deliberately employ maidservants in order to attract clients.[19] This is corroborated by John Evelyn's observations that an elegant inn situated off the beaten track in France often suggested that guests could expect to find interesting company within.[20]

Most young travellers had a fairly good sense of their priorities once on the road and, whether alone or in the company of a competent tutor or an attractive *jeune fille*, survived the linguistic challenge of dining with foreigners at the common table. However, this was a privilege associated with stopping at inns situated at the crossroads along the major routes through France and Italy. Once the party diverted from the main roads or chose to follow unusual itineraries, especially in isolated mountain areas, they might encounter hospitality that was not disappointing, but the conversation usually suffered. This proved to be the experience of Norton Nicholls, a friend of the poet Thomas Gray, who crossed Switzerland with two companions, having chosen an uncommon route from Paris to Milan. Nearing Berne, a German-speaking area between francophone Lausanne and the Italian-speaking region of Valchiavenna, he reported:

You may judge whether luxury has much to do here when I tell you that a bailiff or governor of a district kept the inn at which I lodged madame his lady cooked my supper and served it afterwards, and all the family kept me company to do me honour though we did not understand a syllable of each others language.[21]

The improvised hospitality offered by the Swiss officer confirms the infrequent traffic and the lack of accommodation on that mountain route. Indeed, the most experienced innkeepers, usually well-travelled people themselves, would open their businesses in popular locations after careful consideration of the distances between cities and posthouses. Foreign innkeepers in particular were aware of the habit of travellers sticking with their compatriots. This tendency, which became quite noticeable among the English in the seventeenth century, was reflected by the increasing number of hotels, auberges and pensions targeted at the English from Calais all the way down to Rome.

---

[19] See on this point Mączak, *Travel*, 144.
[20] *The Diary of John Evelyn*, E. S. de Beer (ed.), 5 vols. (Oxford, 1955), II, 108.
[21] Quoted by Black, *The British Abroad*, 36.

Segregation and Socialisation

Mączak reports that over the course of the seventeenth century, in addition to well-known inns located at international destinations, new lodgings appeared bearing names that indicated the country of origin of travellers and pilgrims. In Rome, for example, new inns included *The Crown of France*, *The King of Demark*, *Fortune of Vienna*, *The Florence*, *Posta di Genova*. There were at least two inns displaying signs written in French – *Petit Paris* and *Petit Louvre* – while another going under the Italian name *Il Tedesco* ('the German') was obviously trying to attract guests from Germany.[22] According to the historian, this reflected more than just a preference for travelling with compatriots for convenience and security; it showed the tendency for foreigners to settle in close proximity to one another after arrival. Apparently, the *Hotel d'Angleterre* soon became one of the most popular inn names in France and Italy. A small sample of names in Rome aimed at English travellers – the most numerous nationality abroad – includes *Villa di Londra*, *Pensione di Londra*, *Albergo di Londra*, *Albergo alle Isole Britanniche*, *Albergo di Inghilterra*. Milan had the *Gran Brettagna*; in Verona there was the *Torre di Londra*; in Vicenza the *Regina d'Inghilterra* and in Venice the *Regina d'Inghilterra* and the *Caffè di Londra*. Naples also had a *Gran Brettagna* and a *Villa di Londra* as well as an *Isole Britanniche*. In Sicily, there was even a rest station near the summit of Mount Etna named *Casa degli Inglesi*.

For the best part of three hundred years, the cities found along the standard itinerary of the Grand Tour were known to be swarming with English people, especially young men, most of whom stayed in close proximity to each other.[23] One of the classic circuits ran from Paris to the Loire Valley, then either south to Lyon or east to Leipzig or Frankfurt, carrying on to Geneva and Lausanne; then to Milan, Padua, Venice, Bologna, Florence, and finally Siena and Rome. In all these favoured cities, variously sized colonies of English merchants, bankers and other businessmen mingled with semi-permanent scholars and highly mobile travellers and adventurers.

The following is a description of the life of *les Milords Anglais* in Paris, from a letter sent by a concerned Earl of Chesterfield, who intended to warn his son about the danger of associating with his own countrymen:

As soon as they rise, which is very late, they breakfast together to the utter loss of two good morning hours. Then they go by coachfuls to the Palais, the Invalides, and Notre-Dame; from thence to the English coffee-house where they make up their tavern party for dinner. From dinner, where they drink quick, they adjourn in clusters to the play, where they crowd up the stage, drest up in very fine clothes, very ill made by a Scotch or

---

[22] For a detailed discussion of inn signs and names, see Mączak, *Travel*, 67–8 and his select bibliography on the subject, 304 n.107.

[23] This pattern of self-segregation is discussed in Luca Serianni, 'Lingua e dialetti', 55–88.

Figure 4.3 *The arrival of a young traveller and his suite during the Carnival, in Piazza de' Spagna, Rome, c.*1775. Pen and brown wash over pencil by David Allan (1744–96). ©Windsor Castle Royal Collection Trust

Irish tailor. From the play to the tavern again, where they get very drunk, and where they either quarrel among themselves, or sally forth, commit some riot in the streets, and are taken up by the watch.[24]

From the seventeenth century, the city of Paris was full of Englishmen and their company was apparently inescapable. In the eighteenth century, the social convention of the Grand Tour brought an increase in their numbers but not in the quality of their linguistic skills. For the more blasé travellers of the time, speaking with the locals in their own languages was felt not to be necessary.

Quite a number of young Englishmen chose to journey down the Loire Valley, 'another favoured by English tourists for perfecting their French accent and the pursuit of other studies in quiet and healthy surroundings'.[25] Those who wanted to include Germany in their tour stopped at Frankfurt or Leipzig, both centres of the international book trade, the latter with a famous university. The motivation for passing time in those cities was literary as well as commercial since scholars and students were attracted by the prospect of doing business with the publishers and booksellers. In Lausanne one would find 'quite a little

---

[24] Philip Dormer Stanhope Chesterfield (Earl of), *Letters to His Son, 1737–1768* (1774) (Philadelphia, 1874), Letter CCXXII, 318.
[25] Trease, *The Grand Tour*, 118.

colony of English', as it was another city favoured by scholars for its libraries, and by parents who wanted their children to be educated abroad but far away from the Catholic institutions of France and Italy.

Milan was an obligatory stop, as it sat at the crossroads between the east–west and north–south itineraries, but it was also an attraction in itself, with its fortifications and cathedral, and above all its opera house La Scala. The famous university city of Padua, with its unique botanic gardens, was linked to Venice by a comfortable river-trip of only twenty-five miles. As early as 1617, Henry Wotton noted that 'our English swarm at Padua', with fifteen hundred English students lodged there. Siena, another university town, was a very popular city in Tuscany 'for perfecting one's Italian, but was overfull of Germans and Englishmen'.[26] For the most motivated travellers, common sense suggested that, in order to improve their proficiency in a language, it was more useful to mingle with local contemporaries: this is what Fynes Moryson did, withdrawing to the little hill town of San Casciano between Siena and Florence, where there were no other foreigners. His behaviour was typical of a determined personality and was not uncommon in the early days of the Grand Tour, when most travellers felt they were under pressure to fulfil the main purpose of their journey – gaining linguistic competence. But not many were happy to avoid places crowded with compatriots and social occasions where not a word of the local language would be heard.

In Leghorn there was a large colony of British businessmen as the town was a compulsory destination for all Englishmen who needed to dispatch baggage, souvenirs, books and art collections before returning home. But despite the frequent boat sailings to England from its port, 'no tourist worth his salt would have used the Atlantic route as a passenger', yet it was a place 'where one shall hardly meet with any but English men'.[27] Rome, the Holy City, constantly hosted a large number of itinerant visitors and semi-permanent residents, who had the most varied justifications and excuses for a long stay there, especially the young travellers. The two most well-known meeting points in Rome for the English community were the *Caffè degli Inglesi* and the famous hotel *Ville de Londres* in Piazza di Spagna, both included in a drawing by the Scottish artist David Allan, who lived in Rome in 1767–77.[28]

In the eighteenth century, most British tourists were known to have developed a sense of superiority about being monolingual, which quickly became very infectious at a time 'when the contrast between prosperity at home and decline in Italy had become marked'.[29] Increasingly, travellers were happy to

[26] Ibid., 41.   [27] Ibid., 83 and 124.

[28] David Allan's drawings are now in the Royal Collection of Windsor Castle Library.

[29] The growing tendency towards monolingual complacency is discussed in detail in Chapter 5. For the evolution of attitudes of the British touring Italy, see Pine-Coffin's introduction in *British and American Travel*, especially 45–54.

spend time abroad, but after obtaining a licence and resources from their families, then taking up residency in the cities of their choice, they no longer sought contact or friendships with the local inhabitants for the linguistic benefits it might bring. Rather, 'they avoided them at mixed receptions, preferred to exclude them from their own parties, and even disdained to learn the language'[30]. The new ethnocentrism avant la lettre must have worried their parents and tutors, who felt that they were not getting a return from their educational investment. The crisis in language learning must have been quite noticeable since some of the young lads felt it necessary to overtly reject parental criticism about this issue. Thomas Pelham, a future Whig politician, attempted to justify his behaviour to his parents (1777):

> it is a general complaint that the English do not mix with the people of the country, they are in; which in France or Germany I should grant to be a fault, but in Italy I believe to be rather a fortunate circumstance, for the Italians I have seen are either the most ignorant, or the most artful men that can be seen and from whose conversation you cannot gain any new idea or improvement. Italy is certainly worth the notice of every man of reading as the seat of so many interesting transactions but in every other respect, it is the worst country, that a young man can go to.[31]

As late as the early nineteenth century, a disconcerted Heinrich Heine confirmed the persisting habit of self-segregation by most Englishmen: 'They are too numerous in Italy not to be mentioned; they sweep over the land in swarms, they lodge in every inn, crowd everywhere to see everything, and it is impossible to imagine . . . a picture gallery without a mob of Englishmen.'[32] The tourists led the life of the leisured class of the country, often dining in the private houses of English noblemen, diplomats or businessmen who had settled within the secluded cloisters of the émigré community. By the end of the eighteenth century, French and English had become the languages of the salons, which fortified the English determination to speak no language other than their own while dining, entertaining or dancing. *Conversazioni* at tea-parties *à l'Angloise* were the most fashionable social events in the century of the Enlightenment throughout Europe. But most British travellers refused to attend them, either because they felt uninspired by that particular social game, or because they lacked the appropriate company.

Most travellers remarked on the widespread appetite for the theatre, which they could enjoy in French and Italian cities along the Grand Tour. In Italy, wherever there were English tourists, there were operas to attend; and some Englishmen could speak knowledgably about the performances as they had developed a taste for opera during the regular Italian seasons staged in London.

---

[30] Ibid.   [31] Thomas Pelham, Naples, 3 May 1777, quoted in Black, *The British Abroad*, 51.
[32] Heinrich Heine, *Heine's Pictures of Travel*, Charles Godfrey Leland (ed.) (Philadelphia, 1879), 285.

This passion was inspired by the international fashion for music and drama, but going to the theatre also provided a unique occasion for intensive socialisation, as well as holding out promising prospects for acquiring the local language. For much of the eighteenth century, the Italian opera employed a new kind of recitative, and the operas ran for five hours, including lengthy intervals: unsurprisingly, this created ideal opportunities for elaborate negotiations and transactions between the gentlemen and ladies in the boxes.

Opera houses in France and Austria did not seem to provide as entertaining an evening out as the Italian theatres. According to John Petty, Earl Wycombe's father, he and his companion Major Green did not enjoy the theatre soirées in Austria because of 'the stiffness of Austrian manners and the cold and uninteresting style of conversation which prevails here'.[33] In France it was different, and indeed many English tourists informed others that there was no better way of improving their French than to visit a theatre with a French text in their hands.[34] According to Joseph Palmer, nephew of Sir Joshua Reynolds and author of *A Four Months' Tour of France* (1776), who was much impressed by the great attentiveness of French audiences when he was in Paris in 1775, this was due to their love of the pleasures of the intellect: 'During the representations here the attention of the house is remarkable; there is no whistling between the fingers, no bawling for roast beef, no pelting the parterre with oranges, but the public behaviour is such, as becomes those who lay claim to the title of a polished people.'[35]

If this comparison did not reflect well on some sectors of theatre-goers in England, Italian audiences were deemed even worse. Beckford was very impressed by the San Carlo opera house in Naples, with its seven tiers of boxes that he thought made it one of the most magnificent theatres in Italy. But the sensitive young Beckford was astonished that occupants of the boxes held parties, with much eating, drinking and talking during the performances.[36] This was not uncommon at Italian opera houses and explains the extraordinary success of a theatre soirée as a superior form of socialisation. Naples hosted not only the famous San Carlo theatre but also another three or four, as did Florence. Most historical cities, such as Milan, Turin, Bologna, Siena, Vicenza, Parma and Padua, had one or two theatres, while Rome and Venice led with eight theatres each. The atmosphere during a theatrical evening performance was unique. Music played an important role, but it was far from being the main attraction. Apart from eating and drinking, there was much movement in and

---

[33] Quoted in Black, *The British Abroad*, 66.
[34] Reported in Woodruff, 'From London to Paris', 52.
[35] Joseph Palmer, *A Four Months' Tour*, 2 vols. (London, 1776), I, 109.
[36] Beckford's exact words are: 'The court being present, a tolerable silence was maintained, but the moment his Majesty withdrew ... every tongue broke loose, and nothing but buzz and hubbub filled up the rest of the entertainment,' *Italy with Sketches*, 251.

out of the boxes for amorous intrigues, and the curtains or shutters of boxes could be closed off on the side facing the auditorium. In eighteenth-century Italy, many travellers became aware of the decadent but fascinating atmosphere created by this unique form of entertainment. William Beckford was soon able to appreciate the relationship between the theatre and the *joie de vivre* of the Italian nobility, which he captured so well in this description:

In the fashionable world, the morning is spent in a slovenly deshabillé, that prevents their going out, or receiving frequent visits at home. Reading, or work takes up a very small portion of this part of the day, so that it passes away in a yawning sort of nonchalance. People are scarcely wide awake, till about dinner-time. But, a few hours after, the important business of the toilette puts them gently into motion; and, at length, the opera calls them completely into existence. But it must be understood, that the drama, or the music, do not form a principal object of theatrical amusement. Every lady's box is the scene of tea, cards, cavaliers; servants, lap-dogs, abbés, scandal, and assignations: attention to the action of the scenes, or even to the actors, male, or female, is but a secondary affair.[37]

While some observers of Italian customs and manners were able to appreciate the peculiarities of Italian theatre soirées, many travellers failed to understand the reasons for the audience's inattentiveness. One such bemused tourist was the French scholar and future politician Charles de Brosses: 'The pleasure these people take in spectacle and music seems much more obvious through their presence than through the attention they pay to them. Apart from the front rows, where there is a degree of silence, even in the pit, it is not good form to listen, except at interesting moments'.[38] Another French observer, the Abbé Gabriel-François Coyer, a keen Italian opera lover himself, explained: 'In France we go to the opera to follow the work, there they go for conversation or to visit each other in the boxes. They only listen and go into ecstasies when arias are sung.'[39] Barbier cites both of these clear-sighted observers in order to focus on an important national difference in taste:

This pinpoints the great divide between the two nations, French opera attached prime importance to recitative, that unique art of declamation in music that often made the dramatic quality of the recitative equal to that of the aria … In Italian opera, by contrast, the recitative … was of little interest and the Italian opera depended most of all on the innumerable arias which displayed the rich vocal range of the castrato or the woman singer.[40]

[37] This section on the San Carlo theatre in Naples does not come from the London edition of 1834, but from the collection *Dreams, Waking Thoughts, and Incidents in a Series of Letters from Various Parts of Europe* (Cambridge, 1928), I, 251–3, also available at www. biblioteca virtual universal.
[38] Charles de Brosses, *Lettres familières écrites d'Italie en 1739 et 1740*, 2 vols. (Paris, 1869), II, 313.
[39] M. [Abbé] Coyer, *Voyages d'Italie et de Hollande* (Paris, 1775), II, 207, quoted in Barbier (ibid.), 78–9.
[40] Ibid.

Language Classes and Other Lessons

Interest in learning a particular language was a sensitive indicator of the attraction a foreign country held for travellers, of the social value attributed to the foreign culture back home, and of the material value of linguistic competence in the job market in the tourist's home country. This is why so much of the capital invested in a journey by parental or institutional sponsors was used to pay for language classes. Travellers themselves knew first-hand, and sponsors had acquired enough experience to realise that of the three main types of opportunity for acquiring linguistic knowledge abroad – language classes, academic studies through the medium of a non-native language and everyday interactions – the former was not necessarily the most important. Fynes Moryson epitomises someone who journeyed abroad with clear priorities in mind. He left Cambridge, uninspired by his academic prospects there; he decided to study various academic subjects at different universities on the Continent and succeeded in becoming fully competent in German, French and Italian. His extraordinary multilingual profile has already been mentioned; his near-native skills made him both proud and linguistically ostentatious but he was someone who never needed additional language classes during the course of his studies abroad.[41]

Throughout the first half of the seventeenth century, a number of highly motivated young academics chose Italian universities for their academic excellence, and Padua for its more liberal policies, which was ensured by the independence of Venice in a Catholic-dominated Peninsula. German universities were growing in number and reputation – such as Leipzig, which was Moryson's favourite city, and Heidelberg, preferred by Henry Wotton – but soon studying in Germany became impossible because of the Thirty Years' War. France appeared to be an attractive country, and once sponsors identified a few respectable places of learning there, studying abroad was no longer confined to Italian universities. The idea of gaining a privileged education alongside gallant manners began to exert a powerful influence over the families of the English ruling classes.[42]

William Hammond's correspondence with his father, who sent him to study medicine in Paris and Padua, expressed his gratitude: 'there is no greater Advantage towards the Study of Physick than Travelling', although he himself had doubted the wisdom of trying to acquire medical training abroad.[43] This is possibly because he felt he had no solid basis for studying through the medium

---

[41] For Moryson's polyglottic skills, see Mączak, *Travel*, especially 78.
[42] Howard suggests that this was a reaction to the Tudor enthusiasm for letters; see *The English Travelers*, 45.
[43] William Hammond to his father, Paris, 2 February 1656; quoted in Brennan, *The Origins of the Grand Tour*, 153.

of a non-native tongue, certainly in France where he felt no special affinity for the language. Although not a great linguist, Hammond was certainly a good and honest assessor of his limitations regarding language learning:

> it cost me above ten Year's time, before I cou'd obtain so much Mastery in the Latine, as I have done in Eight Months of the French: Yet the much greater Proficiency I see others have made in as little time (by having the Advantage over me in Loquacity & in Totally abandoning themselves to French Conversation) ... be pleas'd to Consider that two years spent in France with an English Companion, is but Equivalent to one year, spent entirely amongst none but French.[44]

Once in Italy, young William fared better in Florence (which he called the 'Asylum of all Virtuosos'), where he felt he was acquiring a working knowledge of Italian: 'At my first coming to Florence, the Inticement of an Opera made me loyter away so much time ... I have since made an end of the Summer in this Town, my most Visible Improvement is in the Language, of which I have enough to carry me thorowout Italy.'[45] But he did not hide his change of interest from his parents: 'I have been far from losing my time this Summer in matter of Physick; having at times been Student, Doctor & Patient, & really, Sir, the last is worst, and most Cargeable Condition.'[46] When William's family accepted that medical training stopped being a priority for him, he enrolled in one of the best riding academies before returning home.

Many members of the English ruling classes began to consider that, together with the various fields of academic knowledge – medical, legal, economic, military – which were better acquired abroad, other skills were also instrumental in contributing to a gentlemanly profile, such as riding, fencing and dancing.[47] They sought lessons in these civilised pursuits for their sons so that they could become proficient in the essential arts of courtiers. But in the second half of the seventeenth century, with the increasing importance of the French language and the decline of Italian as the European lingua franca, more young Englishmen endeavoured to acquire the rudiments of the language across the Channel, especially those who were planning an educational journey and had not studied modern languages at school or university.

Mr Hainhofer, the governor of Robert Montagu Lord Mandeville, took his young charge to Saumur in the Loire Valley, where he engaged the services of

---

[44] Ibid. 163.   [45] William Hammond to his father, Florence, 22 August 1658. Ibid., 218.
[46] Ibid. 219.
[47] Some travel tutors, such as Jean Gailhard, considered these classes excellent opportunities to improve the foreign language. He wrote in *The Compleat Gentleman* that 'I would have every other master of Exercise to be a kind of a Language-Master', their job being 'to put [the traveller] upon discourse'. Quoted in John Gallagher, '*Language and Education on the Grand Tour of Sir Philip Perceval, 1676-9*', in Helmut Glück, Mark Häberlein and Andreas Flurschütz da Cruz (eds.), *Adel und Mehrsprachigkeit in der Frühen Neuzeit. Ziele, Formen und Praktiken des Erwerbs und Gebrauchs von Fremdsprachen* (Wolfenbüttel, 2019), 113–34.

tutors in fencing, singing, the guitar, dancing and Latin. Thomas Abdy wintered in the same area, at Blois, having chosen it for the benefit of learning the language but he also had lessons in mathematics, music, and dance as well as the native tongue.[48] He intended to show evidence of his progress by writing half of his diary in English and then completing it in French.[49] But not all young Englishmen were equally motivated, and some honest reports indicated little success in academic disciplines, apart from learning the language of everyday life. William Trumbull, later Chief Secretary of State, made no secret of this in his autobiography, written in his old age: 'I went abroad and spent about 2 years in France and Italy [1665–6] where I learnt little besides the Languages, partly from my youth and the warmth of my temper, partly from lazynesse and debauchery.'[50]

If the travellers were accompanied by a governor, he himself taught the local language or hired additional tutors to instruct the boys in languages, academic subjects, arts and social skills from music to horsemanship. Unsurprisingly, those who were not brilliant academically, or who did not possess any scholarly motivation, longed to escape to the pleasures of the French capital or the excitement of an Italian city they had heard so much about. We have evidence that tutors had difficulty keeping their pupils away from local entertainments as suggested in a note by the governor of Thomas Cecil, a future politician and brave soldier, 'who was spending time at dog-fights, horses and worse amusements in the company of the young Edward Seymour Earl of Hertford, who was a great hindrance to Thomas's progress in the language'.[51]

When foreign sojourns disguised as educational experience became common, they ended up being much criticised. But even in the early days, when the training was genuinely academic, some sceptics expressed bemusement at this endeavour. For example, the Earl of Chesterfield did not believe in the segregated nature of language immersion programmes for young boys living abroad:[52]

They are commonly twenty years old before they have spoken to anybody above their schoolmaster, and the Fellows of their college. If they happen to have learning, it is only Greek and Latin; but not one word of modem history, or modem languages. Thus prepared, they go abroad as they call it; but in truth, they stay at home all that while; for being very awkward, confoundedly ashamed, and not speaking the languages, they go into no foreign company, at least none good, but dine and sup with one another only, at the tavern.

[48] William Hammond to his father, Florence, 22 August 1658, 31.
[49] Brennan considers problematic the attribution of the diary to Thomas Abdy.
[50] The Travels of the Honourable Banaster Maynard, in Brennan, 'The Origins of the Grand Tour', 231.
[51] Quoted in Howard, The English Travelers, 40–1.   [52] Chesterfield, Letters, CLIV, 167.

From a broader educational perspective, men who had been educated at Oxford and Cambridge, and who believed in more conventional academic training, were even more critical of the standards of the French academies, some of which lacked balance in the amount of physical versus intellectual exercises they provided. Edward Hyde Earl of Clarendon, who believed that it was 'pernicious for a boy to be sent abroad at an early age, and there was no necessity for their getting the French accent at an early age', was another critic of the education supplied by French academies:[53]

All that is to be learned in these Academie, is Riding, Dancing, and Fencing, besides some Wickednesses they do not profess to teach. It is true they have men there who teach Arithmetick, which they call Philosophy, and the Art of Fortification, which they call the Mathematicks; but what Learning they had there, I might easily imagine, when he assured me, that in Three years which he had spent in the Academy, he never saw a Latin book nor any Master that taught anything there, who would not have taken it very ill to be suspected to speake or understand Latin.

Of course, many young gentlemen left England for France at the prompting of their families, who were trying to shield them from the turmoil of the Civil War. In the Loire Valley, they were safe and not too distant from home should there be relevant political developments. But there were also travellers inspired by the study of the humanities and antiquities who continued to look to Italy for better fulfilment of their educational aspirations in those fields. Thomas Howard Earl of Arundel, who died in Padua, was one such student, and Sir Roger Pratt, the classical architect, also matriculated from that university. The most famous Grand Tourist of that generation was John Evelyn who, after passing through France, lived in the most important cities of Italy while studying languages, gardening, architecture and antiquities.

In the eighteenth century, engagement with the arts increasingly became a favourite pleasure during an Italian journey, and many of the next generation of travellers developed a serious interest in them, some becoming dilettanti and others true cognoscenti.[54] Thomas Coke, the future politician and patron of the arts, was a boy of fifteen when he embarked on his Grand Tour with a Cambridge tutor. He undertook Italian lessons at the Turin academy before studying painting as well as ancient and modern architecture in Rome for ten years, from the age of twenty-four to thirty-four. There was a growth in travellers with a keen interest in acquiring skills in the modern arts, music and painting in particular, which were internationally recognised as the greatest achievements of eighteenth-century Italy. It is likely that many dilettanti,

---

[53] Quoted in Howard, *The English Travelers*, 128–9.

[54] Black comments that 'the terms of cognoscente and connoisseur became terms of abuse' and quotes the future politician Philip Francis: 'To a man really curious in the polite arts, Rome alone must be an inexhaustible fund of entertainment; but what can be more disgustful, than to see our young people give themselves the airs of cognoscenti'. *The British Abroad*, 266.

virtuosi and cognoscenti used the local language quite adequately in *conversazioni* about their artistic and social aspirations.

The generation that travelled on the Continent around the middle of the eighteenth century also included some of the most brilliant writers and adventurous socialites – for instance Horace Walpole, Thomas Gray and James Boswell. But, by their own admission, they understood that language competence was not the top priority in the social salons of cosmopolitan Europe, and possibly not even an intellectual achievement to be appreciated privately. Indeed, whenever they sought language lessons, this was more as an excuse to engage in social intercourse rather than to prepare for academic studies or to better understand the foreign country and communicate with its people. Certainly they would have not challenged the superior multilingual competence of the previous generations of travellers, many of whom were able to study difficult disciplines through the medium of a non-native language at foreign universities.

The next two sections discuss travellers' familiarisation with the notion of the 'best' or 'pure' versions of the two main languages they encountered along the standard itinerary of the Grand Tour. Many travellers remarked that the speech communities in these areas exhibited the most polite manners and gentle behaviour, which they interpreted as evidence of a connection between a speaker's nature and the quality of their language.

The 'Best' French

Today, the Val du Loire in France is famous for its wine and chateaux but in early modern Europe it owed its international reputation to its language.[55] Throughout the era of the Grand Tour the region attracted many travellers, acting on the common belief that the 'best' French was spoken there, thus making the cities of the valley an ideal place for language learning. However, in many European countries there was no lack of competent French teachers, and good quality teaching materials were available everywhere. In particular, countries close to France had a tradition of teaching French at schools and universities, so many cities in the Low Countries were an educational option for the Englishmen who would have found France unsafe due to its religious tensions. Fynes Moryson was someone who learned French fluently while studying in Leyden through the medium of that language.

Switzerland was another much sought-after location for studying French when parents were worried about the wars between France and England or felt it inappropriate to send their sons to be educated in a Catholic country. The young Edward Gibbon was dispatched to Lausanne by his family 'to cure him

---

[55] Brunot, *Histoire, 'Le français hors de France au 18. siècle'* (Paris, 1934–5), VIII, 253.

of an adolescent attack of Roman Catholicism'.[56] He wrote home in 1763 that 'We have some English here, most of them raw boys just escaped from Eaton.'[57] The city was a favoured destination for many British families, and as late as 1784 William Blackett found 'quite a little colony of English' there.[58] While many tourists preferred Lausanne, a good number of others chose Geneva, which was outside the Swiss confederation; there, English parents could secure their offspring's education in 'French language without the pitfalls of Catholicism'.[59] Robert Boyle, the author of *Skeptical Chymist*, lived as a young boy in Geneva for two years. Apparently he learned French like a native while engaging in physical exercise and reading romances before heading over the Alps to Italy[60]. Dr John Moore sent his son, the future Corunna hero, to Geneva while he himself was busy travelling as governor to the boy Duke of Hamilton on a Grand Tour of Italy.[61] Another student there was William Beckford who, after the premature death of his father, was deliberately taken by his tutor to stay with some distant relatives in Geneva so that he could learn 'to write French as correctly and elegantly as his own language'.[62]

However, from the middle of the seventeenth century, when the international status of French began to overtake that of Italian, Paris became the most obvious place to study the language in spite of all the difficulties there; alternatively, students could begin their French language training in Paris before embarking on an academic programme somewhere else. Most young Englishmen who had studied Latin and Italian arrived in France with little or no knowledge of the language; and unless they remained there some length of time, they did not greatly increase their proficiency in it. Those who were sent to be educated at French universities, hoping to pick up the language quickly during their course of study, were often disappointed as they found that the language could not be absorbed easily, and thus lessons were not understood.

In Paris, Edward Browne, a few days after his arrival, wrote: 'I bought the Gazette for 5 Solz, which though I could not understand it all, I hammered out the meaning of a great part of it.' After less than a fortnight he managed to write an entire French sentence to his family, though not very correctly: 'Je commence parie un peu Frangois et j'esper que je parlerai mieux dan un Mois.' And ten days later, describing the second service which he attended at the Protestant temple in Charenton, he noted: 'I begin to understand the Minister.' By the time he left Paris after a stay of nearly four months and had made his way to Montpellier, he was able to tell his father that, despite the great distance he

[56] Trease, *The Grand Tour*, 180.
[57] Edward Gibbon, Letter to his stepmother, Lausanne, 7 December 1763; *Private Letters of Edward Gibbon (1753–1794)*, Rowland E. Prothero (ed.), 2 vols. (London, 1895), I, 50.
[58] Quoted in Black, *The British Abroad*, 95.   [59] Ibid., 37.
[60] Reported by Stoye, *English Travellers*, 293.   [61] Trease, *The Grand Tour*, 187.
[62] Ibid., 195.

had travelled, 'haveing somewhat of the language, I could entertain my self with the French, who are good companions in a journey'.[63]

John Lauder was another young man sent over to France, as his father put it, 'to studying french tongue and the Laws'. While he was trying to acquire French through language lessons, he used his knowledge of Latin to communicate. But when he arrived in Orléans after two months in Paris, his French was still quite inadequate, as he put himself:

> In our returning amongst the best merriments we had was my French, which moved us severall tymes to laughter; for I stood not on steeping stones to have assurance that it was right what I was to say, for if a man seek that, he shall never speak right, since he cannot get assurance at the wery first but must acquire it by use.[64]

For most young Englishmen in France, the Grand Tour began with ten months' residence in Paris studying French. Some decided to stop even before Paris, in Amiens on the Somme, where certain monks would teach travellers the rudiments of French for ten and sixpence a month.[65] The excellent plan of residing in Paris long enough to learn French, enjoy the delights of the capital and then proceed to Italy had some justifications but also held some dangers. The latter became quite obvious even in the early days of the Grand Tour: while the attraction of the metropolis was enormous, exposure to political intrigues and scandalous vices suggested an alternative itinerary. Many families began to think that it was best to initiate their young boys into a foreign lifestyle outside the capital, and once they mastered the language and developed the appropriate cultural defences they would be better able to cope with life in Paris. Certain provinces of France were better known to the English than others. Aix-en-Provence was much admired for its elegant provincial society. Montpellier was famous for its medical tradition, and the air there was considered particularly healthy.[66] The Riviera was not yet developed, and Avignon was where many Jacobites had found refuge. But such cities were much too close to the final destination of the journey – Italy.

A diversion to the Loire Valley after residency in Paris permitted an easy return to the capital due to the short journey, and the Loire towns – Orléans, Blois, Tours, Saumur, Angers – were described as the most pleasant cities in

---

[63] Browne, *A Brief Account of Some Travels in Divers Parts of Europe* etc. (London, 1673), Letter to his father, rpt. by Simon Wilkin (ed.), *Sir Thomas Browne's Works, Including His Life and Correspondence*, 4 vols. (London, 1836), I, 70.

[64] John Lauder, *Journals of Sir John Lauder, Lord Fountainhall, with His Observations on Public Affairs and Other Memoranda, 1665–1676*, in Donald Crawford (ed.) (Edinburgh, 1900), 16.

[65] Reported in Woodruff, 'From London to Paris', 44.

[66] Apart from Paris, other favourite universities were Bordeaux, Poitiers and Montpellier. Lambley points out that Montpellier was a popular destination and a desirable city for university education at the beginning of the seventeenth century, when it was a Protestant town. *The Teaching and Cultivation of French*, 233.

France. Orléans was famous for its school of law at the university. Tours was a large and handsome town described as 'the garden of France'. Saumur had a long tradition of English connections, as it was a stronghold of the Huguenots. Blois, more than the other towns of the district, carried a reputation for the purity of its dialect. In 1644 Evelyn reported: 'Bloys is a towne where the Language is exactly spoken, the Inhabitants very courteous, the [ayre] so good that it is for the cause to ordinary nursery of the Kings Children; & the People so ingenious, that for Goldsmiths Worke, & Watches no place in France affords the like.'[67] On his arrival in Paris in 1643, he 'tooke a Master of the French Tongue', and once he moved to the Loire he wrote; 'Here I tooke a Master of the Language, and studyed the tongue very diligently.'[68] Many travellers followed that same path. The fact that many French Huguenots lived in the area and that the cities of the Loire, especially Blois, had plenty of Protestant residents was an asset, as that sector of the population was judged safe and friendly by the English.

Some cities in the Loire collected a larger number of nationalities than others. Addison, who was in Blois in 1700, reported that 'all the languages of Europe are spoken except English, which is not to be heard, I believe, within fifty miles of the place'.[69] But that was certainly a convenient exaggeration since more or less at the same time Thomas Coke and his Cambridge tutor Thomas Hobart found Angers 'full of young bloods of English society'.[70] Robert Montagu Lord Mandeville, who arrived in Saumur in 1699, also found a concentration of foreign students of French:

I forgott to speake first something of the situation of the towne, the which I found very pleasant being seated at the foote of a little montaigne and having the fine river of Loire running by it, with also a curious pleane and medowes. As for the place of it selfe, it is very little but always full of strangers of all kind of Nations, because of the cheapness of the pensions and exercises of the body, the goodnes of the Language, as also because the Protestans have a church and colledge in the towne the which is something rare in France.[71]

Young men were eventually sent to the cities of the Loire Valley, rather than to other French cities equally known back home, because of a combination of factors: the pleasant landscapes and favourable climatic conditions; the

---

[67] John Evelyn, *Memoirs Illustrative of the Life and Writings of John Evelyn, Comprising His Diary from 1641 to 1705/6, and a Selection of His Familiar Letters*, William Bray (ed.), 2 vols. (London, 1818), I, 60.

[68] Ibid. I, 62.

[69] Addison's letter to Mr Congreve from Blois can be found in Lucy Akin, *The Life of Joseph Addison*, 2 vols. (London, 1843), I, 77.

[70] Trease reports on some of Thomas Coke's language and artistic training while in France and Italy in *The Grand Tour*, 136–42.

[71] The travels of Robert Montagu, Lord Mandeville (April 1649–April 1654), f. 27, in Brennan, *The Origins of the Grand Tour*, 109.

quietness of these cities compared with the turbulent environment of the capital, and the reputation of the schools, with their accredited language teachers. One of these teachers, Charles Maupas of Blois, published a famous grammar in 1618, which included a dedication to George Villiers Earl of Buckingham, something which no doubt contributed to the good reputation of the city among the English. Many generations of travellers were aware that in England the 'best language' was recognised as the speech of educated speakers from a broad area in the south of the country, while France could draw on a centre of natural linguistic purity. Blois, '[a city] lying in the very middle of France', was considered by the unanimous consent of all Frenchmen, Parisians included, to be the best 'for the true pronunciation of the language'. At some point a clique of French teachers in London, a sort of 'Little Blois', decided to take advantage of the English obsession with accent and, priding themselves on being the sole repositories of the pure French language, 'tried to persuade everyone that Bretons and Normans cannot speak correct French'.[72]

The self-segregation of the English in the Loire Valley was mentioned in diaries and letters at least as often as the quality of the French language there. However, foreign travellers and residents did not seem interested in elaborating on the historical or cultural background which contributed to the impression that the local language of the Loire represented the best French. It is true that some made occasional comments on the French spoken in other cities, perhaps for the purpose of justifying their choice of residence. For example, Robert Montagu wrote in his diary that 'Fontenay la batu a little towne which stands in a plaine and I was told that the inhabitants thereof speake the worse Frence in all France'.[73] The city, now called Frontenay-Rohan-Rohan, lies in the district of Poitou, not too far from the Loire. Even closer are Angers and Nantes where, according to Thomas Wentworth – a future politician with a keen interest in languages – local communities were rude and spoke bad French.[74] Quite apart from consisting of second-hand information, such statements were often expressions of local prejudice, and it is plausible, as Stoye suggests, that what most travellers usually sought in Blois or Saumur would have been equally available in Normandy.

---

[72] French teachers from the Low Countries were criticised for the same reason. Lambley, *The Teaching and Cultivation of French*, 223, 230, 326. The international fame was particularly acknowledged in London, when concern for the right accent produced such admonitions as 'better no teacher at all than one with a provincial accent'. Even Alexander Pope satirises this obsession for a pure French accent in his *Imitations of Horace*: 'This lad, sir, is of Blois . . . His French is pure.' 2 vols. (Edinburgh, 1764), II, 235.

[73] Brennan, 'The Travels of Robert Montagu', *The Origins of the Grand Tour*, 114.

[74] The passage is quoted in Stoye, *English Travellers*, 44. Of course, rudeness and bad (in the sense of corrupt and crude) language are attributes that always went hand in hand in the description of linguistic landscapes (see also Chapter 7).

The 'Purest' Italian

Tuscany in Italy was the equivalent of the Loire Valley in France, and of all its cities, Siena was the one with an international reputation for the purest language. Yet, if we read the diary of Tobias Smollett, published as *Travels Through France and Italy* (1766), when he stopped in the city on his way from Florence to Rome, he did not get a favourable impression:

Of Sienna I can say nothing from my own observation, but that we were indifferently lodged in a house that stunk like a privy, and fared wretchedly at supper. The city is large and well built: the inhabitants pique themselves upon their politeness, and the purity of their dialect. Certain it is, some strangers reside in this place on purpose to learn the best pronunciation of the Italian tongue.[75]

Smollett stopped in Siena at the height of the Grand Tour in 1764, in the company of his friend Samuel Sharp, both characters famous for not saying anything positive about the cities they visited in their journey; as Sterne spelt out, they 'made a whole tour ... without one generous connection or pleasurable anecdote to tell of'.[76] It is more of a surprise that ten years later, even harsher comments about Siena were issued by the Marquis de Sade, another traveller who used ungenerous words towards the city, its inhabitants, and their language:

J'arrivai à Sienne à midi et demi, aux Tris-Rois; le chemin beau, mais montueux. Je ne conçois pas comment il se peut que le langage soit, comme on le dit, si épuré à Sienne. En 1321, celle ville était plongée dans l'ignorance, et il n'y a pas dix-huit ans qu'ils ont une bibliothèque publique. . . . Comment se peut-il que ce ne soit pas dans la capitale que le langage soit le plus agréable, et que cette pureté se soit reléguée dans une ville presque deserte?[77]

[I arrived in Siena at half past twelve, at the Three Kings; the road was beautiful but hilly. I cannot believe how it can be the case that the language in Siena is the purest. In 1321, that city was immersed in ignorance, and it is only eighteen years since it acquired a public library. . . . How can it be that it is not the capital city that has the most pleasant language, and its purity is confined instead to an almost deserted city?]

It is quite likely that the author of *120 Days of Sodom* was either unequipped with appropriate guidebooks or misunderstood some of their historical references. It cannot be a coincidence that the year 1321 mentioned in his diary entry is famous in the history of the University of Siena (founded in 1240). This was the year when the city authorities welcomed a large group of students and professors from the University of Bologna, establishing its reputation as a centre of intellectual freedom. As for his misinterpretation about the purity of the Italian language, it seems that de Sade expected the same process of

[75] Smollett, *Travels*, 245.   [76] Sterne, *A Sentimental Journey*, I, 88.
[77] de Sade, *Voyage d'Italie*, 78.

standardisation, which in France focused on Paris, to apply to the much more diverse Italian situation. As previously discussed, there had not been such a process in Italy for two reasons: the country was politically fragmented; and no linguistic homogeneity was possible, as different dialects had evolved in a totally decentralised context. It is interesting, however, that the notion of linguistic 'purity' with reference to Siena was mentioned by these two well-read travellers of different nationalities. This suggests that this notion was widely associated with Siena, and indeed it was remarked on in most of the travel literature available in both France and England.

As in France, where foreign students and tourists sought language classes and other lessons in a number of historical cities, eventually concentrating in the Loire, a similar pattern saw young foreigners scattered around the many universities of the Italian peninsula. Padua was the main destination, where many competent teachers could be found; one traveller who acknowledged benefitting from their services towards the end of the sixteenth century was Henry Wotton. Soon after that, in the early seventeenth century, William Lithgow was also pleased with his time there: 'In Padua I stayed three moneths learning the Italian tongue, and found there a Country Gentleman of mine, Doctor John Wedderburnea learned Mathematician, but now dwelling in Moravia, who taught me well in the language, and in all other respects exceeding friendly to me.'[78] Rome was another favourite city, being the essential destination of all travellers in Italy, and various distinguished gentlemen decided to settle there; Robert Southwell, a future diplomat and president of the Royal Society, did so in 1660–1. Turin had the advantage of being the first major city after crossing the French frontier, and some travellers decided to stay there for some time. Florence was an ideal city for the studious tourist wishing to combine sightseeing with language classes, and it had the additional advantage of being located in Tuscany, the birthplace of Dante, Petrarch and Boccaccio. These three great Italian classical authors wrote in their mother tongue, which later became the literary language adopted by all eminent writers from the Peninsula, such as Ludovico Ariosto and Torquato Tasso, the best-known Renaissance authors who were not themselves native speakers of the language. In the magical atmosphere of Florence, which Wotton called 'a paradise inhabited by devils',[79] several generations of travellers studied Italian, fascinated by 'the beauty and security of the place, and the purity of the language'.[80] The native fluency of the local teachers in a vernacular which

---

[78] William Lithgow, *A Most Delectable and True Discourse etc.* (1609); and enlarged version in *Rare Adventures and Painful Peregrinations by W. Lithgow* (London, 1632; rpt. London, 1906), 38.

[79] Henry Wotton, Letter to Lord Zouche written at Florence this 25th of June, 1592, in Smith, Logan Pearsall (ed.), *The Life and Letters*, 2 vols. (Oxford, 1907), I, 281.

[80] Ibid., Letter to the Earl of Salisbury, At Venice the first of August 1608, I, 439.

was close to the phonetic system represented by the written language was an inspiring factor when reading Italian classical literature, as was stressed by an anonymous traveller to Florence in 1778: 'The Abbé Pelori who comes to me every day for two hours is the best Italian master I have ever met with and the circumstance of having so good an interpreter of this difficulty has made me undertake to read the Inferno of Dante.'[81] The same teacher is mentioned by other English residents, including Edward Gibbon; he was in Florence two years previously and felt that his teacher was good but too demanding:

Nous nous sommes remis à l'Italien très serieusement. L'Abbé Pilori [sic] maître general à la nation Angloise depuis vint ans est venû pour la premiere fois. Il me donne l'heure de cinq du soir où l'on est tout à fait disoeuire ici. Je le crois tres bon mais il voudroit mener ses Ecoliers un peu vite. Si vous ne l'arretez pas il vous met d'abord à la poesie et à la traduction.[82]

[We have applied ourselves to the study of Italian very seriously. The Abbé Pilori, the teacher of the English community over the last twenty years, came to us for the first time. He gave me an appointment at five in the evening, when everybody here is lazing about. I think he is a good teacher, but he wants to push his learners a little too fast. If you don't slow him down, he takes you straight to poetry and translation.]

In the previous century, the poet John Milton spent time in Florence improving his Italian and he was fascinated by what the Tuscans had done to promote their language throughout the Peninsula. Milton was also most impressed by the number of academies in Italy, many of which were grouped into societies of virtuosi which focused on linguistic discussions and literary compositions in Italian and Latin, and he was also acquainted with a number of Italian poets and academicians. Other English scholars and writers before him had gravitated to such learned societies. One was John Evelyn, who accepted an invitation to the academy of *Umoristi* in Rome, whose members debated the best ways to defend the purity of the Italian language. Apparently many men of letters, including John Evelyn, the founder member of the Royal Society, deplored the fact that there was no academy in London for the improvement of the English language.[83]

At the end of the sixteenth century, Siena was a small city that had lost its economic supremacy of the Middle Ages, but being located between Florence and Rome on the famous Via Francigena meant that it was still

---

[81] Quoted by Black, *The British Abroad*, 290.

[82] Edward Gibbon, *Gibbon's Journey from Geneva to Rome: His Journal from 20 April to 2 October 1764*, Georges Alfred Bonnard (ed.) (London, 1961), 120.

[83] Others supporting the establishment of an academy to regulate the use of English were John Dryden (1664), Daniel Defoe (1697) and Joseph Addison (1711). See a discussion on the standardisation of English and language attitudes in Edward Finegan, 'Style and Standardisation in England: 1700–1900', in Tim William Machan and Charles T. Schott (eds.), *English in Its Social Contexts* (Oxford, 1992), 118–20.

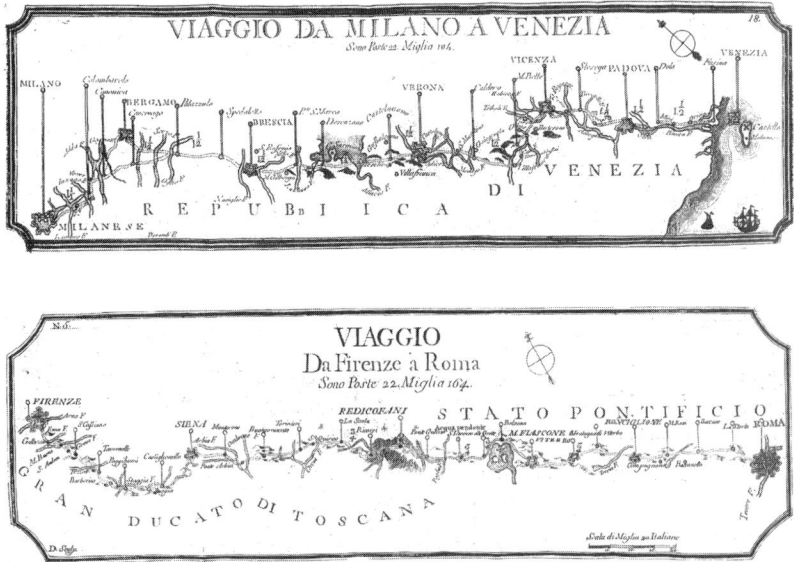

Figure 4.4 *Viaggio da Milano a Venezia*, and *Viaggio da Firenze a Roma*, not dated. Collezione Simeom (B272). ©Archivio Storico della Città di Torino

an ideal stopover for bankers and merchants. Its geographical position and the prestige of its university helped increase the flow of foreign students between the fifteenth and seventeenth centuries, when it became one of the favourite destinations of young German noblemen attracted by the *Kavalierstour*. Siena also boasted several learned academies, such as *Gli Intronati,* as well as many famous linguists with an interest in classical languages, including Orazio Lombardelli. He was active at the end of the sixteenth century as a professor of *Umanità* (Greek and Latin languages and literatures) and dedicated two of his works to two of his most distinguished English students, Henry Wotton and Robert Peckham. Another famous student who based himself in Siena some fifty years earlier was Thomas Hoby. While studying at Padua in 1554 he developed the habit of recording the names of English noblemen he encountered, and after moving to Siena he noted down no fewer than nine or ten he had met at evening dinners given by the Imperial Ambassador, the Spanish scholar and writer Don Diego de Mendoza. Hoby's objective after leaving Padua was to 'travaile into the middes of Italye, as well as to have a better knowledge in the tung, as to see the country of Tuscane, so much renowmed *[sic]* in all places'.[84] At that time Siena had already increased its international reputation with students and travellers from all nations but for someone with a strong motivation to pick up the language in a natural setting, the concentration of compatriots there was not an advantage.

Over the course of the seventeenth century, the number of foreign students and travellers in Italy from all over Europe increased. There were still a large number of Germans, but also many Englishmen and even students from Poland. Reports by many visitors described their amazed impressions of the main piazza in the centre of Siena, as can be seen in this entry from a Polish traveller:

having entered the market-place you will see a beautiful and large fountain higher up in the square, from where you can look around you at the whole square laid out before you like an enormous scallop, paved all over in level bricks and interspersed with stripes of white marble so that it looks like a real shell.[85]

The town also inspired great admiration for its peaceful environment, pleasant community and pure language, as noted by three famous English travellers around the middle of the seventeenth century:[86]

The people here are very civil, and even sociable too; which together with the good ayre, the good exercises for gentleman, the good language, and the great priviledges, make many strangers drawbridle here, and sommer it at Siena, the Orléans of Italy. (Richard Lassels, 1635)

The ayre is very wholsome, much agreeing with the constitution of strangers, the Inhabitants very curteous, a great deale suiting to the humours of forreigners, and besides the purity of the Italian Language, is here profest and spoken; these and the like conveniences make it much frequented by travellers, and indeed mov'd us to settle our selves there, for some Moneths. Here we stayd not to see the rarities of the Place, which are not many in number; but to get some knowledge and practise in the Vulgar Tongue. (John Raymond, 1646)

This city is counted a very good place to sojourn in for a stranger that would learn Italian, as well because the citizens here speak the purest language, as for that they are very civil and courteous to strangers. Besides, by reason of its situation, the air is temperate in summer-time; provisions also are reasonable. (Rev. John Ray, 1663)

These three quotations are interesting for what they have in common but also for their differences. The first mentions the parallel role Siena played to one of the Loire towns; in the second, 'Italian Language' is used interchangeably with 'Vulgar Tongue'; and in the third, the local language is referred to as Italian. Indeed, in the seventeenth and eighteenth century, *Tuscan* was still the normal

---

[84] Thomas Hoby, *The Travels and Life of Sir Thomas Hoby, 1547–1564*, in Edgar Powell (ed.) (London, 1902), 17.
[85] See Mączak, *Travel*, 211.
[86] Lassels, *The Voyage of Italy*, 236. Raymond, *An Itinerary*, 50. John Ray, *Observations Topographical, Moral, & Physiological: Made in a Journey Through Part of the Low-Countries, Germany, Italy, and France* (London, 1673), 342.

term used on the Italian peninsula to refer to (a) the common literary language; (b) the vernacular spoken in Tuscany; (c) the second/foreign language occasionally used by cultural elites throughout Italy and (d) the lingua franca of cosmopolitan Rome, a city whose international community of residents was multilingual. The term *Tuscan* emphasised the vernacular origin of the literary language, while *Italian* stressed its geographical circulation, but both notions were used interchangeably by most specialists. Indeed, playwrights, poets and men of letters such as Carlo Goldoni, Vittorio Alfieri and Giuseppe Baretti often preferred the former to emphasise the origin of the language, and occasionally the social affectations of its speakers. They also employed elaborate derivations of the term, such as *toscaneggiare* ('to Tuscanise'), *toscaneggio* and *toscaneggiatura*, and a number of variants showing various degrees of ostentation (e.g. 'Il conte è altrettanto nimico d'ogni toscanesmo, d'ogni toscaneria, d'ogni toscaneggiatura, e d'ogni toscaneggiamento'[87]). Tuscany was also commonly referenced for the purity of its language by professionals from different fields, like the great music teacher Pier Francesco Tosi. In his *Opinioni de' cantori antichi, e moderni* (Bologna 1723), Tosi, a castrato singer himself, advised opera students to perfect their study of Latin grammar in order to understand what they were singing in church, and learn how to read and pronounce Italian perfectly, 'not having been born in Tuscany being no excuse for ignorance'.[88]

Despite the prestige of Tuscany in general and Florence in particular, thanks to the fame of masters such as Dante Alighieri, Francesco Petrarca, Giovanni Boccaccio, Niccolò Machiavelli and many others, the reputation of Siena as the city where 'citizens ... speak the purest language' is due to some differences between the vernaculars, above all in the area of pronunciation. The most noticeable phonetic trait which made Sienese seem more pleasant and more understandable to foreigners was that, unlike Florentine, the local accent was not affected by a peculiarity of the voice referred to as *gorgia toscana* (literally 'Tuscan throat').[89]

---

[87] Giuseppe Baretti, in Luigi Piccioni (ed.), *La scelta delle lettere familiari* (Bari, 1912), 269. The sense is: 'The count is against all shades of Tuscan affectation whether big or small.' Some English travellers became aware of this tendency, like Lady Sidney Morgan, who commented: 'To speak with the Tuscan accent is supreme mauvais ton, and savours of vulgar affectation. The young lady, who, fresh from her visit to Florence, indulges in the Italian accent, is technically said to speak in punto [sic] di forchetta' (*Italy*, I, 294). The translation of the idiom 'in punta di forchetta' ['to speak with too much affectation'] is given in the *Dizionario Italiano, ed Inglese* compiled by Giuseppe Baretti himself (Livorno, 1828). See also Chapter 9.

[88] Quoted by Barbier, *The World of the Castrati*, 61.

[89] This phonetic peculiarity was already noted by Dallington: 'the Florentine hath the best words, but his pronunciation is somewhat too gutturall'. See Robert Dallington, *A Survey of the Great Dukes State of Tuscany: In the Yeare of Our Lord 1596* (London, 1605), 63. For a full discussion on language diversity in Italy, see Chapter 7.

When touring through the Italian peninsula, several travellers mentioned the problem of trying to understand not only the local dialects but also regional variations of the literary language, which was used by the literate sector of the social elites as a lingua franca. With the exception of Siena, whose variety enjoyed the reputation of being pure, Tuscan itself as spoken in some of its local communities could present comprehension problems. Indeed, many travellers recalled the saying about the best Italian: *lingua toscana in bocca romana* ('The Tuscan language in a Roman mouth'), which they found memorable and fully justified. It was true that in multilingual Rome, the extreme features of the Tuscan vernacular were minimised by the local residents, even though they were speakers of diverse regional or even national backgrounds. Even Samuel Sharp, the companion of Smollett during their journey through France and Italy, and famous for not finding many good things to say about any place, seemed to agree with other travellers about the 'best' Italian:

I should therefore suppose, as Florence is exceptionable, that Rome (if it were possible to avoid countrymen) is the place where a foreigner should go for Italian. It is a well known proverb *Lingua Toscana in Bocca Romana*, that is to say The Tuscans write pure Italian, the Romans pronounce it purely.[90]

---

[90] Sharp, Letter XLVII, Florence, May 2, 1766, *Letters from Italy*, 243.

5   Aids, Strategies and Facilitators

Interpreters and Mediators

Apart from those Grand Tourists who were exorbitantly wealthy, and thus were accompanied by a large number of servants, attendants, instructors, cooks and even artists to draw sketches of the landscapes and ruins, the majority of travellers went abroad in the company of only one person, whose role is variously described in the literature as a tutor, a governor or a 'bear-leader'.[1] This key figure was chosen to provide vital assistance in terms of practical, educational and moral supervision, and his key role was to act as an interpreter in order to minimise the time wasted in everyday communications and maximise language practice with selected audiences. Mączak distinguishes between two categories of guardian. One was the tutor or governor, usually a clergyman or an academic with knowledge of the relevant languages, who made decisions while on the road and functioned as academic advisor during residence abroad. The other was more like an assistant or a secretary who had been assigned the responsibility of looking after his charge *in loco parentis* but who usually had no experience of travelling abroad nor knowledge of foreign languages.[2]

The first category of guardian typically consisted of high-profile individuals who either had just started or had interrupted an academic life to become governor to a young member of the nobility for a limited period of time before returning to pursue their own university career. They were expected to act as a director of studies, plan cultural visits and academic courses, select teachers, guides and ciceroni, and report on the pupil's progress to the family. Luminaries from various academic disciplines, such as Thomas Hobbes, John Locke, Ben Jonson, Joseph Addison and Adam Smith, travelled through Europe with their charges. But there were also others who learned the profession of tutor on the ground and, having chosen to continue in that role,

---

[1] Francis Bacon stated that young men ought to travel with some 'tutor or grave servant who hath the language and hath been in the country before', *Of Travel*, 87.
[2] Mączak, *Travel*, 124–8.

eventually built up a considerable reputation in that capacity. James Hay was such a person, and he was in great demand among the aristocracy in England. Hay travelled abroad as a governor as many as eight times in thirty years, and was able to draw on the personal introductions and reliable contacts he had developed in various countries.[3]

Another remarkable governor, although little is known about him, was Robert Moody, who accompanied Banaster Maynard to France and Italy. On his return, he compiled a very informative diary of their travels, writing in the first person and including a dedication to his charge's father, Lord Maynard. Brennan suggests that the meticulously written records of their three-year journey abroad reflected Moody's attempt to utilise the manuscript either as a means of becoming integrated into his employer's social circle, or of consolidating his position if he was already employed by the family.[4] He appeared to be a well-travelled, widely experienced and reliable escort, certainly someone who prided himself on his language competence: 'We enter'd in the Porta del Popola the 23 of December in the year of our Lord God 1660, and tooke up our Lodgin at the signe of the Gambery in Strada Corso, I having liv'd thre years in Rome before, I knew the language and the Citty as well as if I had been borne in it.'[5]

Guardians of either type who were not able to speak the necessary languages were at as much a loss in foreign environments as their charges. Certainly, quite a number of them did not miss the opportunity to take language lessons alongside their pupils. The following letter was sent from Tours by a certain David Stevenson, the tutor of George Legge of Lewisham, to his father, the Earl of Dartmouth:

> At seven the fencing begins, which lasts usually till half eight, when we breakfast. At nine the dancing master and Lord Lewisham open the ball, which seldom closes before eleven; from that time to one French is the only employment; from one to two, hour of dinner, the Abbé reviews our compositions. At half after three we begin reading to the Abbé; this exercise usually lasts two hours, when we walk.[6]

However, there is evidence that some guardians who had some knowledge of the foreign country of destination and its language were sent abroad in advance to build up personal experience and expertise in both. William Patoun was the author of an interesting report entitled *Advice on Travel in Italy,* written in 1766 for his employer, whom he referred to as 'my Lordship ... who has already

---

[3] María Dolores Sánchez-Jáuregui, 'Educating the traveller: the tutors', in María Dolores Sánchez-Jáuregui and Scott Wilcox (eds.), *The English Prize: The Capture of the 'Westmorland', an Episode of the Grand Tour* (New Haven, 2012), 92. A caricature of James Hay as a bear-leader was drawn by the Italian Pier Leone Ghezzi in *c.*1725 (now in the British Museum). Dr Hay is portrayed accompanying a British lad, who has the face of a small bear, around the ruins of ancient Rome. For the role of a tutor specialising in foreign travel, see Boutier, 'Compétence international'.
[4] Brennan, *The Origins of the Grand Tour*, 230.   [5] Ibid., 255.
[6] Letter by David Stevenson to the Earl of Darmouth, 20 September 1775, D (W) 1778/V/885, SRO. Quoted by María Dolores Sánchez-Jáuregui, 'Educating the traveller: the tutors', 88–97.

Figure 5.1 *Dr James Hay as a bear-leader*, undated. Drawing by Pier Leone Ghezzi (1674–1755). ©The Trustees of the British Museum

travelled in France' so that 'it is unnecessary to suggest any thing previous to your arrival at Lyons'.[7] The short but entertaining report includes information

---

[7] Patoun, 'Advice on Travel', xxxix. William Patoun was a connoisseur of Italian paintings and a fine artist himself. In 1768, he accompanied Sir Gregory Turner and Richard Jodrell to Italy along the same itinerary he recommended. See Ingamells, *British and Irish Travellers*, 747.

and tips about the Italian cities where the gentleman was planning to stop on his way to Rome. The text is linguistically interesting, suggesting that the envoy understood the local language well, although he proudly admitted that the task was not easy: 'even to Me who spoke their Language easily, and knew the Custom of the Country, it was the most disagreeable task imaginable'.[8]

Travellers were probably well advised not to use the linguistic services of guardians such as Moody, Stevenson or Patoun to perform one of the most important tasks abroad: writing letters of introduction. Such correspondence required an elaborate style, which could not be improvised by foreign tutors but was easily accomplished by local ciceroni or professional scriveners available everywhere. The importance of such correspondence should not be overlooked as receptions and invitations from local people of distinction were essential. So was access to courts and salons, which provided opportunities to meet politically powerful individuals and members of the local elite. James Boswell, who often pursued important men as well as willing women during his travels, captured the essence of the problem of relying on linguistically competent guides with his typical sense of humour. Having engaged a bilingual Swiss guide from Berne, a certain Jacob Hänni, he would tell people he met on the road that 'one of my servants is German and the other is French'.[9]

The world of the arts was a domain where linguistic inadequacy could cause not just unpleasant embarrassment but serious loss. For a long time, travellers had brought back various curiosities as a memento of their adventures. But as the Grand Tour became fashionable, many who visited Italy and admired the masterpieces in Venice, Bologna, Florence and Rome wanted to acquire a sample of art or a good copy to take home.[10] Young travellers and tutors who lacked knowledge of fine art needed to rely on agents and ciceroni when making such purchases. If the tutor had some knowledge of the foreign language, he could monitor agents' competence during these transactions. But in many cases, when neither the tutor nor the tourist was confident about their own judgments, the only solution was to find somebody trustworthy. Experienced ciceroni were the main linguistic intermediaries between travellers and the local community. They were characters one could not do without, always present in every city with an international reputation, often well equipped with valuable artistic and social

[8] Ibid., xl.
[9] James Boswell, Letter of Wednesday 6 June 1764, in Frederick A. Pottle (ed.), *Boswell in Holland 1763–1764* (New York-London, 1928), 273. For the language mediation of servants recruited locally, their hiring and dismissal, see Gallagher, 'Language and Education', especially 10–13.
[10] Many Grand Tourists sought the work of Rosalba Carriera in Venice, and of Pompeo Batoni in Rome, who alone painted portraits of more than 150 British visitors.

skills. Their multifarious expertise was known to most foreign visitors as much as the skills of persistence and manipulation attributed to them by some travellers.

It should not be surprising to read in most travellers' reports that Italian ciceroni always attempted to defraud travellers, so a reliable recommendation was essential. William Patoun, a painter himself, who as mentioned earlier organised his employer's journey to Italy to purchase fine art, was quite helpful on this point:

After you are settled in your Lodging, ... a Cicerone is the Next Necessary Meuble. There are two young Men at Rome at present who act in that Capacity. Messrs Morison & Byres, both Scotch men [*see* Colin Morison, *and* James Byres – editor's note] – and both very worthy, tho the last circumstance is by no means a consequence of the other. Morisson is esteemed the best Medallist & Classic Scholar, Byres the most agreable & communicative. Having a regard for both, I cannot recommend one in preference to the other. The gratuity given them, by any private Gentleman is twenty sequins for the Course, and thirty if two Companions. I need not hint to your Lordship that they are treated on a genteel footing, and have the honour of dining often with All the Young Men of Rank that travail. They are both Originally Painters, and of course know the Pictures as well as the Antiquities.[11]

Since not only a guided tour of a city but also the purchase of artwork depended on the linguistic abilities of the ciceroni, their fees varied considerably as did their moral standing. Indeed, one needs to distinguish between the two quite different types of cicerone that travellers referred to in their diaries and letters without qualifying their role and status.

One category of cicerone refers to artists and/or antiquarians whose academic expertise was also sought for guided tours or for commissioning works of art. As many art historians explained, this professional figure was a cicerone-cum-agent. The first use of the term comes from Addison in 1719: 'It surprised me to see my *Ciceroni* so well-acquainted with the busts and statues of all the great people of antiquity.'[12] Another important attestation is offered in a witty remark made by Edward Wright in 1720:

The *Cicero* of ours, I think, might have been reckon'd among the Antiquities and Rarities of the Place; he disdain'd to speak any thing but Latin to us; and though he rode an Ass, he was learned as if his Ass had been a Pegasus. I know not whether the Titles of Cicerones for those sort of Antiquaries be more ancient than this old Gentleman, else he might possibly have been the Occasion of others being so called; for he seems to be an Original.[13]

[11] Patoun, 'Advice on Travel', xlv.
[12] Addison, *The Works of Joseph Addison*, 'Dialogues on medals' (1721), I. i. 443. The OED defines cicerone as: 'A guide who shows and explains the antiquities or curiosities of a place to strangers. (Apparently originally given to learned Italian antiquarians, whose services were sought by visitors seeking information about the antiquities of a place; subsequently usurped by the ordinary professional "guide")'.
[13] Edward Wright, *Some Observations Made in Travelling Through France, Italy &c. in the Years 1720, 1721 and 1722* (London, 1730), 177–8.

Both Addison and Wright were reporting on their experiences in Rome at the time when the Prince of Wales (James Francis Edward, the so-called Old Pretender) established the Stuart Court-in-exile in Rome, around which a large number of Grand Tourists and Jacobite followers alike gravitated. In order to follow the hectic social life of the Prince, Catholic émigrés required diplomatic protection and passports, and British tourists asked for introductions to English-speaking guides. Within the large circle of art dealers and art connoisseurs active in Rome, there were also young artists and architects offering art instruction, copies of paintings and drawings of classical sculptures while seeking patronage and employment. Many called themselves artists, copyists or even professors of painting and architecture; others were quite happy with the label 'ciceroni'.[14]

Thomas Jones, a Welsh landscape painter in Rome, defined a cicerone as: 'a Person who attended Strangers to show and explain the Various Buildings both Modern and Ancient, Statues and Pictures and other Curiosities in this City and its Environs'[15]. The label was also embraced by the most prominent of such professionals, artists such as Thomas Jenkins and the antiquarian and art dealer James Byres. The latter spent over thirty years in Rome, where he became familiar with many British travellers and was chosen as a personal guide by Edward Gibbon in 1764.[16] In the following year, another prominent scholar living in Rome, Colin Morison, a pupil of Mengs, offered the same service to James Boswell (see Chapter 6). Even the great archaeologist Johann Joachim Winckelmannat at some point acted as a cicerone to the 4th Duke of Gordon.[17]

While hiring such fashionable artists and antiquarians was a privilege of the British who enjoyed the salon life in Rome, this did not prevent the term 'cicerone' from being used to refer to the occasional guides who were active

[14] The English plural is often spelt *cicerones*. It is noteworthy that the term 'cicerone' in this sense was chosen for the title of the essential book on the Italian arts, *Der Cicerone: Eine Anleitung zum Genuss der Kunstwerke Italiens* (1855) by the distinguished Swiss historian Jacob Burckhardt, who was very interested in the experiences and aspirations of the Grand Tourists.

[15] Quoted in Brinsley Ford, 'James Byres: Principal antiquarian for the English visitors in Rome', *Apollo* 99, June 1974, 446–61. Another famous cicerone was Francesco (de') Ficoroni (1664–1747), an Italian scholar, art connoisseur and antiquarian who became so famous among Grand Tourists in Rome that he was made Fellow of the Royal Society in London.

[16] Gibbon reported: 'My guide was Mr Byres, a Scotch antiquary of experience and taste; but in the daily labour of eighteen weeks, the powers of attention were sometimes fatigued till I was myself qualified, in a last review, to select and study the capital works of ancient and modern art'; *Memoirs*, 151. Many commentators observe that Gibbon probably meant eight weeks, as six weeks was the usual time allocated for a tour of Rome.

[17] In view of the distinguished status of some artists and dealers who did not mind the appellation 'cicerone', Smollett's comment that 'No Englishman above the degree of a painter or cicerone frequents any coffee-house' seems an exaggeration; Letter XXX, 2 February 1765, *Travels*, 253. It is hard to believe that the use of such establishments in a cosmopolitan city like Rome changed so much from what George Berkeley observed fifty years before that: 'British Jacobites and Hannoverians frequented different coffee-houses'; *Letters*, 103, 6 April 1717, quoted in Ingamells, *British and Irish Travellers*, 82.

La uera Guida de' gl' Oltramontani   Moftra l' antiche, e le moderne piante,
Ho qui retratto al natural fembiante: E le fabriche eccelfe de Romani.
                    Al' Mag.co Andrea Vachario.

Vi ho dedicato il ritratto di Giouanni Groffo da Lucerna Soldato della guardia di N.Sre fi per l' amicitia
ch' e tra uoi dúa come anco per le molte ftampe che hauete dell' antiche e moderne fabriche de Roma.
Riceuetela dunq, come cofa da bono amico, et Dio ui conferui. In Roma lanno 1613. Franc. Villauena.
                    Con priuilegio del fommo pontefice et licenza de fuperiori.

Figure 5.2 *Johann Hoch (Giovanni Grosso) Swiss guard and cicerone in front of Trajan's column*, 1613. Engraving by Francisco Villamena (1565–1624). ©Istituto Nazionale per la Grafica (Gabinetto dei Disegni e delle Stampe), Rome

in all the historic cities of Italy. These were normally called 'ciceroni da piazza' in Italian, and made themselves available to visitors of less ambition and more modest means[18]. The Holy City in particular was known to be populated by a crowd of occasional ciceroni, many of whom were *abbati*, other soldiers of the Vatican Swiss Guard, keen to make a bit of money on the side; having some knowledge of foreign languages, whether through their own efforts or through life's chances, they acted as guides to the city. A well-known guide was Giovanni Grosso da Lucerna, whose portrait in his Swiss Guard uniform was engraved by Francesco Villamena in 1613 with the following caption:

La uera Guida degl' Oltramontani	[The true Guide of those over the mountains
Ho qui retratto al natural fembiante:	I have depicted it as it is:
Moftra l'antiche e le moderne piante.	Showing ancient and modern districts
E le fabriche eccelfe de Romani.	And the sublime architecture of the Romans.]

From the passing comments and occasional remarks about these guides that many travellers hired locally, it is impossible to generalise with regard to the language of cicerones at the peak of the Grand Tour. Certainly all of them played an important role in the artistic and tourist scene of eighteenth-century Rome, but their very diverse social and linguistic backgrounds must have allowed them to deliver their explications in quite a range and different varieties of languages: from academic English to Church Latin, from French as a lingua franca to a Swiss dialect of German, from literary Italian to the Roman version of Tuscan.[19]

Throughout the Grand Tour, most tourists returned with at least one story or joke about their experience with amateurish ciceroni. The following is an exquisite example from Charles Dickens's *Pictures from Italy*, written while he was passing through Mantua after the city had been despoiled by Napoleon's troupes:

I put up at the Hotel of Golden Lion, and I was in my own room arranging plans with the brave Courier, when there came a modest little tap at the door ... and an intensely shabby little man looked in, to inquire if the gentleman would have a Cicerone to show the town. His face was so very wishful and anxious ... and there was so much poverty

---

[18] The definition given by Niccolò Tommaseo in *Dizionario della Lingua Italiana* (1861–74) is: '"Cicerone da piazza", o semplicemente "cicerone", chi mostra ai forestieri le cose rare, o quelle ch'egli reputa rare, della città' ['"Cicerone da piazza", or simply "cicerone", who shows strangers the rare things, or rather what he deems to be rare, of the city']. The entry specifies that the role can be performed by a friend and not necessarily by a professional: 'Fa da cicerone ad un amico, a una signora, anco chi cicerone non è per mestiere'. In the same vein, the French language historian Brunot, describing Dr Johnson's journey to Paris, explained: 'Barretti *[sic]*, qui faisait office de cicerone, lui épargna sans doute la peine et l'humiliation de parler (mal) français' ['Barretti *[sic]*, who acted as cicerone, saves him, without a doubt, the trouble and humiliation of speaking (bad) French']. *Histoire*, VIII, 277. On Samuel Johnson's disinclination to speak French, see further below in Chapter 6, note 34.
[19] For a distinction between the Tuscan language and the Roman variety of Tuscan, see Chapter 4.

expressed in his faded suit and little pinched hat . . . I engaged him on the instant . . . We were now in the street . . .

I inquired if there were much to see in Mantua.

'Well! Truly, no. Not much! . . . So, so', he said, shrugging his shoulders apologetically.

'Many churches?'

'No. Nearly all suppressed by the French' . . .

'What shall we do next?' said I

He looked up the street, and down the street, and rubbed his chin timidly; and then said, glancing in my face as if a light had broken on his mind, yet with a humble appeal to my forbearance that was perfectly irresistible:

'We can take a little turn about the town, Signore!' (Si può far un piccolo giro della città).[20]

It is quite interesting that, while terms like *ciceroni* often recur in travel writing, the same cannot be said about *interpreters*, although we know that many individuals did perform translation duties. It is in the context of the few stories where the term 'interpreter' comes up that one understands why it was worth mentioning someone acting in that role. Here is the great Scottish architect Robert Adam reporting how a conversational difficulty was resolved in a theatre through unsolicited help: 'we passed the evening very agreeably as I found an abbé who interpreted for me and I made a language of my own, half English, half French and a little sprinkling of Italian'.[21] Another instance concerns Lord Cranborne, whose French was so fluent (he wrote his diary in that language) that he was invited by the King to act as an 'interpreter' when other Englishmen came to the court.[22] The first anecdote was an example of an unplanned initiative, while the second reflected positively on the author himself. But in the many cases, when neither the traveller nor his tutor could get by without the help of an interpreter, mention of his services would have reflected negatively on their own linguistic confidence and competence.

Guides and Conversation Manuals

There had never been a shortage of guides written in the main European languages or in translation. Pilgrims heading for the Holy Land had relied on manuscript guides in Latin but then Rome became the new destination for pilgrimages, and the first publishers to be active there at the end of the sixteenth century were German. At first, pilgrims and visitors to Rome could not acquire

[20] Charles Dickens, *Pictures from Italy* (London, 1846) rpt. (Mineola, New York, 2016), 76–7. Of course, Dickens knew Italian well, which was shown by his sensitive use of local idioms (see Chapter 8).
[21] Robert Adam from Pisa, in John Fleming (ed.), *Robert Adam and His Circle, in Edinburgh & Rome* (Cambridge, MA, 1962), 128.
[22] Reported by Stoye, *English Travellers*, 30.

city guides written in their own languages but soon a number of travel books in the vernaculars were published in the major centres of Europe. Clare Howard states that 'they became necessary to men of moderate education who could not read the local guidebooks written in the language of the country they visited'.[23] The guidebook *Theatro delle città d'Italia* (1629), by the author and publisher Francesco Bertelli from Padua, was one of the most famous. It ostentatiously declared its own excellence for foreign readers (*'corre per le mani di curiosi e forestieri con applauso grande'*) but its most innovative feature was a set of illustrations offering bird's-eye views of 65 Italian cities, so that travellers looking from an elevated position could check the accuracy of their maps.[24]

In the second half of the seventeenth century, the production of guide-books expanded. One sector of the genre specialised in practical manuals listing objects and sights to be viewed, and they included, for the first time, trivial information about the price of meals, transportation details and currency conversion rates (see Chapter 3). Indeed, travel books and guide books were not easy to use as tools for language practice, and anyone embarking on such an important tour would not want their planning, once at a foreign destination, complicated by unnecessary linguistic difficulties.[25] Ordinary conversation manuals focused on everyday situa-tions encountered on the road, listing the most frequently needed expres-sions in a bilingual format. There were also more specialised materials that included parallel texts presenting the most useful niceties for achieving the right tone in polite conversations. As early as the sixteenth century, multi-lingual conversation manuals were available on the market, enabling pil-grims, merchants and travellers to refer to a single volume when learning and practising a number of languages.

Mączak analyses various dialogues from that period from the point of view of someone interested in the life and hospitality at an Elizabethan inn, and comments that one of the aims of these authors was to amuse their readers. As for rather private matters relevant to the needs of travellers, the historian states that in the manuals, 'the subject of defecating itself introduced an element of ribald humour', as shown in this sample of conversation:

---

[23] Howard, *The English Travelers*, 193.

[24] Francesco, Bertelli, *Theatro delle città d'Italia* (Padova, 1629). Standing on the top of a hill looking down at a city was such a common thing to do abroad that it become a *topos* in the paintings of the Grand Tour. Naturally, this was mentioned by many Grand Tourists, as discussed in Sweet, *Cities and the Grand Tour*, 105 and 29. See also *Introduction* and Chapter 9.

[25] In addition, the guidebooks and descriptions of these countries which were available in London were in English, and many of those published in France which were in French had been adapted for foreigners. See Lambley, *The Teaching and Cultivation of French*, 348.

L̃ateinisch.	Frantzösisch.	Spanisch.	Welsch.	Englisch.	Teütsch.
Prosit	bon prou vous face	buena pro vos haga	buon pro vi faccia	moch good do it you	es bekumme euch wol
Volo	ie vueil	yo quiero	io voglio	i will	ich wil
Tu voluisti	tu as voulu	tu quezifte	tu volefti	thou woldest	du hast gewollen
Ille vult	iceluy veult	aquel quiere	colui vuole	he will	der wil
Volo facere	ie vueil faire	quiero hazer	io voglio fare	i will do it	ich wils thün
Ego feci	i'ay faict	yo hize	io ho fatto	i haue done it	ich habs gethon
Vade	va ten	ve	va	go	gang
Stes	demeure	esta	sta	ftonde	ftand
Tu neminem finis dormire	tu ne laisse perfone dormir	tu ne dexas dormir ninguno	tu non lassi dormir nessuno	thou fateft no body flepe	du laffeft niemant fchlaaffen
Quare?	pourquoy	porque?	perche?	why fo	warumb?
Quid tota nocte nihil aliud facis quam ftertere	pource que ne fais toute la nuyct autre chofe que ronfler	pour que toda la noche no hazes fino roncar	per che tu non fai altro che ronfare tuta la notte	for thou doft nothunge all the nyght but fnorke	darumb das du die ganze nacht nichts thüft dann fchnarchlen
I dormitum	va coucher	ve a dormir	va a dormire	go flepe	gang fchlaaffen
Nondum	non point encore	aun non	non ancora	not yet	noch nit
Eas, nam necesse eft vt cras bene mane furgas	va, car il te fault demain le uer bien matin	ve, que es necessario que te leuantes mañana en buena hora	va, perche domane bifogna che tu ti leui abuon hora	go for then muft rpfe to mo rowe by tyme	gang/ dann es ift not das du mer= gens zytlich auf ftendeft
Quid faceret?	a quoy faire?	a que hazer?	a che fare?	what tho do	was zü thün?
Oportet te ferre literas Mediolanum verfus	il te fault porter les letres a Milan	es necessidad que lleuar las letras a Milan	bifogna che tu porti lettere a Milano	thou muft beare fettres to Mylan	du müft brieff gen Meyland tragen
					R̃ iij

Figure 5.3 *Sex linguarum latinae, gallicae, hispanicae, italicae, anglicae et teutonicae dilucidissimum dictionarium* ('Easy dictionary in six languages, Latin, French, Spanish, Italian, English and German'), 1579. Christoph Froschauer, Zürich. (In early new German the term 'Welsch' corresponded to 'Italienisch' in modern German).

I would faine go to sleepe. Let us go.
Shew me the privies.
They be at your chamber: smell it.
Oh! how he stincketh, marke.
It passeth a gilly-flower in sent.
Let us goe hence, oh mischiefe.[26]

Throughout the period of the Grand Tour, conversation manuals remained very popular, with new editions offering revised content, such as the cost of accommodation, the choice of menus and dishes, and the service facilities; also, increased attention to authentic language use was combined with better information about social customs. Another feature that reflected the expanding market was a flexibility that ensured the parallel texts of dialogues were appropriate for as many speakers as possible in various situations. The segment below comes from the 11th edition (1733) of *The Compleat French-Master for Ladies and Gentlemen* by Abel Boyer:

[26] Mączak, *Travel*, 37.

Draw the curtain.
Give me a Night cup.
Undress yourself, *or* pull off your Clothes.
Pull off your Shoes and Stockings.
Help me to pull off my Coat.

Shall we lie together?
I love to lie alone.
I love to have a bed-fellow, *or* to lie double.[27]

Mączak comments that such dialogues are so adaptable that it is not at all clear 'to whom is this remark supposed to be addressed'. And he goes on to state: 'If . . . a traveller got a room on his own, then – if we are to believe the phrase-books and manuals – it was inevitable he would have to tease a kiss out of the chambermaid.'[28] Almost the same refrain appears in a dialogue rendered in seven languages, taken from a manual for travellers printed in the Low Countries and quoted by the historian Ernest S. Bates:

My she-friend, is the bed made? Is it good?
Yea, sir; it is a good feather-bed; the sheets be very clean.
Pull off my hosen and warm my bed; draw the curtains and pin them with a pin.
My she-friend, kiss me once and I shall sleep the better . . . I thank you, fair
    maiden.[29]

Looking at similar materials that were also very popular in the eighteenth century, Blunden draws attention to the *Gentleman's Pocket Companion for Travelling in Foreign Parts* by Thomas Taylor (1722), which contains useful descriptions of the roads, distances, maps, and dialogues in English, French, Italian, German and Spanish. Blunden comments that 'it was intended rather for the many than "the Wise and Great"', and adds, 'as for the dialogues, the following from a discourse on rising may serve':

What maiden is that?
She is not a maid. She is marry'd.[30]

The taste for such 'male matters' suitable for a gentlemen's club was not entirely innovative in eighteenth-century conversation aids aimed at travellers. Already in the sixteenth century, some manuals were full of double entendres such as the one above, suggesting that a repertoire of explicit language concerning intercourse and useful expressions for courting was a competitive

[27] Abel Boyer, *The Complete French Master for Ladies and Gentlemen* (London, 1761) quoted in Mączak, *Travel*, 38.
[28] Ibid.
[29] Bates, *Touring in 1600*, 245. The author reports quotations from William Brenchley Rye, *England as Seen by Foreigners in the Days of Elizabeth & James the First: Comprising Translations of the Journals of the Two Dukes of Wirtemberg in 1592 and 1610* (London, 1865).
[30] Edmund Blunden, 'From Paris to Geneva', in Lambert (ed.), *Grand Tour*, 60.

feature in guidebooks for travellers who were not pilgrims, bankers, merchants or even soldiers.[31] Indeed, soldiers had their own conversation manuals, such as *Dialogues en françois et latine, pour server de guide aux militaires et aux personnes qui voyagent* by P. A. Alletz (1760).[32] A concern with guiding consumers to making the right choice among such a vast array of more or less permissible publications can be found in 'The preface to the reader' in Torriano's last conversation manual, where he stressed that 'These dialogues, as my former, consist of general phrases, familiar but not vulgar.'[33] On the other hand, the great sexual freedom revealed through the contents of these books presupposed spontaneous behaviour and less language censorship than one is used to in printed material today. Certainly, during the best part of the Grand Tour, unrestricted sexual desire was typical of the upper echelons of society from which travellers came.[34]

Today we may wonder whether, in early modern Europe, travel abroad presented young men with opportunities they had not experienced at home. The answer is possibly not so arcane, as even today there is a widespread expectation that in another country different norms of moral behaviour apply. Reading these diaries and memoirs, one realises that the transitory nature of a traveller's daily life provided temptations both to the young men and to the females they encountered. Some Grand Tourists made this quite plain: a gallant encounter offered a chance to test whether women made themselves more easily available than at home. This attitude was captured well in a comment made by someone in an Italian theatre who overheard the incorrigible James Boswell making explicit proposals to a married woman sitting in the next box: 'A traveller expects to accomplish in ten days as much as another will do in a year.'[35]

Extempore Teachers

There is plenty of evidence from the research literature that *cherchez la femme* was part of the Grand Tour experience. Most historians of the Grand Tour stress that fathers encouraged their sons to seek early sexual experiences abroad in

---

[31] Gamberini, *Lo studio dell'italiano*, 50.   [32] Bertrand, *Le Grand Tour revisité*, 230 n.41.

[33] Torriano, *The Italian Tutor*, from 'The preface to the reader' (Cambridge, 1640); quoted in Pizzoli, *Le grammatiche di italiano*, 70 n.99.

[34] Mączak points out the large amount of material in multilingual manuals and dictionaries that concerns sexual vocabulary. He explains that throughout the best part of the Grand Tour, it was 'abundantly clear that people were free to talk about specific parts of the anatomy'. At the same time, authors of language manuals were fully aware of what readers were likely to expect from them. The historian concludes that conversation manuals and pocket dictionaries have 'never been fully exploited before' as historic sources, and 'both their contents, and their omissions, give us some idea of the moral censorship'.

[35] Boswell, Letter from Turin, 12 January 1765, *Boswell on the Grand Tour, Italy etc.*, 31.

order to avoid surprises and escape consequences more easily. Women historians like Cohen and Chard explain further that while young travellers viewed
the tour as an exotic adventure, their families recognised the educational benefit
of fashioning their masculinity with foreign women.[36]

Black quotes two documents about the maturing of young noblemen abroad.
One is by the Earl of Chesterfield, writing of his illegitimate son Philip
Stanhope's time in Rome: 'The Princess Borghese was so kind as to put him
a little upon his haunches, by putting him frequently upon her own. Nothing
dresses a young fellow more than having been between such pillars, with an
experienced mistress of that kind of manége.'[37]

The second concerns Sir Brooke Boothby, about whom the British envoy in
Turin wrote when Boothby was sixteen: 'He attached himself while here to
a very clever woman, who was of great service to him; she brushed him up
greatly.'[38] There can be no doubt that the opportunity for male travellers to be
together with female company, unconstrained by pressure from their family,
was also advantageous for language learning. This point requires further
research, but a letter cited by Black to a London newspaper dated 1725 does
not sound like a minority report. It was written by someone using the pseudonym Tibullus who had been sent on his travels when seventeen, 'and [I] spent
betwixt three or four years abroad, during which time I worshipped the merry
deities, and only acquired the languages necessary for entertaining the fair'.[39]

Because of parental concern about the educational benefits of travel, young
tourists were conscious that they needed to employ their time in the best
possible way. This meant not missing any opportunities, especially if the
journey lasted months rather than years, and making the most of their transient
situation away from the eyes of their families. However, there were quite
striking differences in the ease of getting to know local women, depending
on the foreign country and the woman's social status. While ordinary women
were apparently well hidden in Italy, rich and elegant ladies were not at all
inhibited about inviting foreign noblemen to their palaces. In France the atmosphere was even more licentious, not only within the upper echelons of society
but also among peasants and maidservants at the inns. This was a pleasant
surprise for the young men, whether they came from the north or south of
Europe.[40]

Many travellers drew attention to the fact that French innkeepers would
deliberately employ gorgeous chambermaids in order to attract clients. Mączak

---

[36] Cohen, *Fashioning Masculinity*, especially 57–63; Chard, *Pleasure and Guilt*, 34–9.
[37] Black, *The British Abroad*, especially 196.   [38] Ibid., 197.   [39] Ibid., 190.
[40] It is certainly the case that the majority of women that young Britons met during the Grand Tour
came from either the higher social echelons or the lowest strata. There are almost no reports of
encounters with ordinary women of the same age and some refinement with whom the travellers
could have developed a companionable relationship.

Figure 5.4 *Seduction in a tavern*, not dated. Etching and roulette in brown ink. Print made by Jacobus Buys (?). ©The Trustees of the British Museum

mentions cases of innkeepers and their daughters working in full cooperation.[41] One such case is reported by the young priest Sebastiano Locatelli, who travelled from Bologna to Paris in 1664–5. He found that the unexpected hospitality in many taverns in France was a system introduced by the innkeeper to 'assassinate' his clients more gently:

[41] Mączak, *Travel*, 241.

Trovassimo l'osteria ben proveduta di belle figlie, ma così rustiche e diverse dalle altre, che il solo aver dato cenno un de' compagni di baciarne una, secondo il costume di Francia, non le rivedessimo più. (Può essere andassero a nascondersi in luoghi dove avrebbero forse avuto gusto d'esser trovate, ma noi, stanchi dal viaggio montuoso e sassoso, ci buttassimo co'stivali sui letti, in quel mentre si preparava la cena) ... Io fui de' primi che mi addormentai perchè vennero tutte quante quelle signore vergognose a tirarci i stivali, assai meglio ornate et abellite di prima, essendosi mostrate forse cosi alla prima vergognose per esser trovate così scapigliate. Parlavano qualche poco lontane dal buon francese, mescolando co' savoiardi la dicitura, ma a noi riuscivano di con-solatione nel parlare, ma più nelvederle. Seppero così bene prenderci con gli occhi all'amo e dilettarci soavemente l'udito che ci buscarono prima di cena 15 baiocchi per testa ... e quelle che a prima vista facean le schizignose credo (s'avessimo voluto ci avrian servito anco da spose).[42]

[We found the inn full of lovely young ladies who were so very bashful and different from the others that when a companion, in accordance with French custom, made as if to kiss one, that was very nearly the last we saw of them. (Perhaps they went to hide in places where they would have enjoyed being found, but we, tired from our mountainous, rocky journey, threw ourselves, boots and all, onto our beds while dinner was being prepared) ... I was one of the first to fall asleep but then all these shy ladies came to pull off our boots, much better dressed and done up than before, since perhaps they had been embarrassed at being found in such a dishevelled state. Their French was fairly good, though mixed with some Savoyard words, but we delighted in listening to them, and looking at them even more. They knew well how to catch our eyes and delight our ears and they earned 15 *baiocchi* per head from us before dinner ... and they who had seemed so fussy at first would, I'm sure, (if we'd wanted) have gone on to serve us in bed.]

How much French was practised during such encounters with peasant girls speaking rustic dialects is not known. But while the episode ended up inno-cently for the usually exuberant Italian priest, for most members of the gentry, interacting with foreign females of low rank was usually no less an exotic and instructive experience than with ladies of high social status.[43] Lord Dalrymple found the former type of partner more exciting than the aristocratic women he met in Paris in 1715: 'The people here are more gay, the ladies less handsome, and much more painted, love gallantry, more than pleasure, and coquetry more

[42] Locatelli, *Viaggio di Francia*, 283.
[43] There were quite different views on the matter. The French teacher Wodroeph commented that Paris was a good place 'pour hanter la cour et baiser les Dames and Damoiselles' ['to hang around the court and pick up married and unmarried women'], but to learn French one should go to Orléans a better location for the purpose of study. A quite different opinion was that of Francis Lockier (1667–1740), Dean of Peterborough and friend of Dryden and Pope, and a good linguist himself, who argued: 'you go and get French, and it would be best if you could avoid making an acquaintance with any Englishmen there. To converse with their learned men will be beside your purpose too, if you go for so short time: they talk the worst for conversation and you had rather be with the ladies'. From Spense's *Anecdotes*, 1820, quoted in Lambley, *The Teaching and Cultivation of French*, 349–50.

than solid love ... I believe I shall only make love as I used to do to some chambermaid. I have already had some adventures of that kind.'[44]

Throughout the Grand Tour, Venice always attracted a large number of foreign visitors through its reputation for the memorable amatory adventures on offer amid its magical palaces. Richard Lassels, who combined the role of Catholic priest with that of a governor for young travellers, strongly condemned the fact that so many young men 'desire to go into Italy only because they hear there are fine courtesans in Venice', and 'travel a whole month together, for a nights lodgeing with an impudent woman'.[45] For such brief encounters, one of the conversation manuals mentioned in the previous section would have been adequate. Indeed, Venetian brothels became popular with clients from all nations, and experienced customers warned their juniors before the journey that 'Venice is the most calculated for luxurious idleness of any place I know and therefore very dangerous to you'.[46]

Coffee houses, gaming rooms and especially theatres were the ideal location for meeting all categories of women and engaging them in conversation, with the view to reaching some arrangement. William Beckford, observing such interactions within a *ridotto* (a living room inside a theatre) in Venice in 1780, wrote that before the play began, 'there were a great many lights and a great many ladies elegantly dressed, their hair falling very freely about them, and innumerable adventures written in their eyes'.[47] Theatre attendance was greatly approved of by tutors and families because they believed that there was no better way of improving command of a foreign language than to go to a play with the text in one's hands.

Within a theatre, boxes, *ridotti* and casinos were not just the natural habitat of gentlemen, married women and their cicisbei; they were also places where many courtesans operated in disguise. Parisian theatres were also meeting places for actors, singers and dancers. They thus held a wide appeal for a variety of social reasons and provided travellers with plenty of opportunities to meet women from all social echelons: not only theatre-goers, but also the so-called *filles de l'opéra*. In 1785 William Bennet wrote about an actress called Mme de Gazon in Paris, 'a lively little opera singer well known to many young Englishmen who have shared her favours, and as Gazon signifies turf, are said by the wits of Paris to have been on the *turf*'.[48] The following quotation shows

[44] Black, *The British Abroad*, 196.   [45] Lassels, *The Voyage of Italy*, Part I unpaginated preface.
[46] Letter by the Marquis of Tavistock to the Earl of Upper Ossory, quoted by Black, *The British Abroad*, 196.
[47] Beckford, *Italy with Sketches* (Philadelphia, 1834), I, 87–8.
[48] The traveller was William Bennet (1746–1820), Fellow of Emmanuel College Cambridge and later Bishop of Cloyne, who went to the Continent as a travelling tutor. Quoted by Black, *The British Abroad*, 9 and 256.

how the press back home reported the adventures of young British tourists who fully immersed themselves in sexual adventures abroad:

Our Gentry will make themselves as famous in making conquests among the French women, as their brave ancestors have been heretofore in subduing the French men . . . We hear from Paris that one of the dancers at the opera, called La Salle, so remarkable for her chastity, as to have obtained the name of Vestal, has at last surrendered to a young English nobleman, who was introduced to her at an assembly in woman's apparel, and so far insinuated himself into her favour, as to be permitted to take part of her bed.[49]

Several British visitors recorded their disgust at the perverse habits and immorality they encountered in Venice, which they thought exceeded even that in Paris. The ineffable Thomas Coryat noted with surprise that the same system of state control applied to the commerce of sex in Venice; he was the first tourist to comment on this. Apparently, a century later Thomas Nugent was disoriented by the confusion between courtesans who could be mistaken for *zentildonne* (ladies of quality) and *zentildonne* who could be taken for prostitutes. It was difficult to believe that the linguistic and conversational skills of these two types of women were so similar.[50]

Coryat was one of the few visitors to Venice who made no secret of his liaisons with one of those professional ladies, which was in keeping with his exuberant personality and his inclination to record the local habits meticulously: 'So did I visit the palace of a noble courtesan, view her own amorous person, hear her talk, observe her fashion of life, and yet was nothing contaminated therewith, nor corrupted in manner.'[51] During most of the Grand Tour period, there must have been astonishing differences in the lifestyles of such ladies of pleasure, if we are to believe Coryat that many were 'esteemed so loose, that they are said to open their quivers to every arrow', whilst others were extremely well-educated and skilled in both polite and intellectual conversation: 'Also thou will finde the Venetian Cortezan (if she be a selected woman indeede) a good Rhetorician, and a most elegant discourser, so that if she cannot move thee with all these foresaid delights, shee will assay thy constancy with her Rhetoricall tongue.'[52]

Coryat's emphasis on the two extremes of this profession was not an exaggeration. Mannered and educated women who aspired to become involved in salon life used their conversational bravura as an entry to the world of the nobility. They were called *cortigiane oneste* ('honest courtisans'), to be distinguished from ordinary working prostitutes. Such *entreneuses* were skilful in a boudoir but also brilliant conversationalists and could recite fine poetry or

---

[49] Ibid., 194.
[50] Nugent, *The Grand Tour*, III, 88–92. As already suggested, Nugent's comment could be based on passages from other travel books. See Chapter 2, note 35.
[51] Coryat, *Crudities*, I, 409.   [52] Ibid., 405.

Figure 5.5 *Coryat meets the Venetian courtesan Margarita Emiliana*. From *Coryat's Crudities*, 1611

hold forth like orators on literary topics in the salons. Their language ability was described as most deceptive in public places and seductive in private sessions: this was another shocking experience for most Englishmen, who considered silence to be the best quality in a woman.

Since Venice was one of the most cosmopolitan cities of Europe as well as a busy port serving many foreign destinations, Venetian courtesans must have specialised in speaking a number of languages. Two languages were a requirement above all others: Venetian, used with the local nobility, and Tuscan for men of distinction from elsewhere in the Italian peninsula. The eloquence of Venetian courtesans was a tourist attraction, and the following monologue by the legendary Veronica Franco leaves no doubt as to her outstanding verbal dexterity – in this case responding to an insult – or to her confident bilingualism:

The sword that strikes and stabs in your hand – the common language spoken in Venice – if that's what you want to use, then so do I: and if you want to enter into Tuscan, I leave you the choice of high or comic strain, for one's as easy and clear for me as the other . . . Whichever of these you wish to use, as you do elsewhere, to speed on your arrows in a contest of insults exchanged between us, choose the language that you prefer, for I am equally happy with them all, because I have learned them for exactly this purpose.[53]

Venice was a cosmopolitan centre even during its centuries of decadence and economic stagnation. For example, the numerous Germans in Venice had a trading post – the Fondaco dei Tedeschi – which attracted a large number of German-speaking prostitutes into town. Unsurprisingly, when the Council of Ten introduced stricter measures against foreign prostitutes as early as 1572, a witness at the trial of Sofia Solarin called her 'a ruffiana che allogia tutte le meretrici thodesche che vengono qua a venetia e sempre ne ha tre o quattro' ['a pimp who lets rooms to German whores here in Venice, and she always has three or four'].[54]

The city of Rome was another international centre of sexual encounters, where foreign prostitutes could not be passed unnoticed. Mączak cites a story told by one of the companions of von Aschhausen, Prince-Bishop of Bamberg. A Swiss courtesan called Annette operated a process of natural selection which had a linguistic basis:

---

[53] The passage comes from Veronica Franco, *Poems and Selected Letters*, edited by Ann Rosalind James and Margaret F. Rosenthal (Chicago, 1998). Franco was a *cortigiana onesta* who learned the profession from her mother but she was also a distinguished literary figure who wrote two volumes of poetry. The literature on Renaissance courtesans in Venice is vast and can be found in Elizabeth Horodowich, who also refers to the monograph *The Honest Courtesan: Veronica Franco, Citizen and Writer in Sixteenth-Century Venice* by Margaret Rosenthal (Chicago, 1992).
[54] Ibid., 187.

This Annette was also approached by a German who . . . addressed her in Italian. She answered him: *Signore, sono accompagnata ista sera* [Sir, I have company tonight]. When it transpired, however, that he was German and asked her whom she was entertaining, she replied that she had not realised he was German and invited him to come; it would be a good opportunity for him.[55]

A great variety of such experiences were recounted by James Boswell, who was keen to explore all social landscapes and their diverse female inhabitants. He frequently visited prostitutes in Venice and Rome, and when he arrived in Turin, a certain Captain Billon procured various willing girls for him, for whom his rudimentary Italian language was more than adequate. He said that he spoke German 'with unusual ease' with a chambermaid at the Court of Brunswick, the 'sweetest girl of eighteen' who entered his bedroom as a *blanchisseuse* (laundress) and 'came back from time to time'.[56] But he advanced his knowledge of the German language further in Dresden with 'petites adventures' and 'flammes passegères'. Back in Rome, his diary was filled with details of the sums spent on 'des filles', including 'une fille charmante' and even a 'monster'; he rigorously annotated these items in his expenses.[57] 'Appétissante' was the term Boswell used for a friend of Lady Mary Wortley Montagu with whom he had another flirtation, as he did with many other rather sober ladies, including two simultaneously in Siena, who 'enabled him to pass several happy weeks in that quiet city' with daily lessons in Italian and flute-playing.[58]

A very entertaining language lesson under the supervision of a female companion was recorded by a thirty-year-old Italian man after he arrived in the city of Gorizia, north of Venice, in 1779; at that time Gorizia was in a German-speaking area. He made such an impression on the innkeeper that she took a fancy to him. She wished to give him a special welcome with a glass of wine, but she could not speak Italian nor could her guest understand German. This is how the traveller recalled the experience:[59]

Bevve un bicchierino di vino con me, e m'insegnò a dir *Gesundheìt*; e da' movimenti del bicchiero intesi che volea dirmi ch'io beessi alla sua salute, com'ella beeva alla mia. Come io non avea proferito bene questa parola, me la fece ripetere due o tre volte, e sempre empiendo e vuotando il bicchieretto di nuovo vino.

---

[55] Mączak, *Travel,* 250.

[56] James Boswell, Letter of Monday 13 August 1764, in Frederick. A. Pottle (ed.), *Boswell on the Grand Tour, Germany and Switzerland, 1764* (New York, Toronto and London, 1928), 60.

[57] James Boswell, 'Introduction', in Brady and Pottle (eds.), *Boswell on the Grand Tour, Italy etc.*, xi.

[58] Boswell, *Boswell on the Grand Tour, Italy etc.*, Letter to Porzia Sansedoni [Original in French], 13–14.

[59] Lorenzo Da Ponte, *Memorie di Lorenzo Da Ponte da Ceneda Scritte da Esso* (Nuova Yorca [New York], 1829), I part II, 5–8.

[We drank a glass of wine together, and she taught me to say *Gesundheit*; and from the movement of the glass I guessed that she wanted me to drink to her health, as she was doing to my health. As I did not pronounce the word correctly, she asked me to repeat it two or three times, always filling up and drinking our glasses of wine.]

Since the conversation could not advance very far, the enterprising hostess asked her servant to fetch a book from next door, and when alone again with the visitor she looked up a number of pages and inserted bookmarks there. His recollection continued: 'Era quel libro un dizionario tedesco e italiano: ai lochi indicati lessi queste tre parole *Ich liebe sie*; e trovai che significavano *Io amo voi*. Come la seconda parte di quello era il dizionario italiano, così cercai la congiunzione e, e le feci rileggere le stesse parole *und ich liebe sie*'. ('The book was a German-Italian dictionary: at the places indicated I read these three words *Ich liebe sie* and found that they meant *I love you*. Since the second part was an Italian dictionary I looked up the conjunction *and*, and let her read these same words *und ich liebe sie*.) The following morning the young man practised at breakfast the little German he had learned: 'Io aveva imparato ormai tutti i principali complimenti. Per esempio, *buon giorno; come state? avete dormito bene?* Ma nessun complimento a quella donna piaceva fuor che *Ich liebe sie*.' ('By now I had learnt all the main compliments. For example, *good morning, how are you? Did you sleep well?* But no compliment pleased that woman other than *Ich liebe sie*.') Eventually he had to leave this hospitable inn, and drew some conclusions:

Passai dieci, o dodici giorni nell'albergo di questa donna, ed ora col dizionario, ora colla grammatica alla mano, facemmo quattro o cinque ore di conversazione ogni giorno, e quasi sempre sull'argomento medesimo, e che sempre finivano con un *Ich liebe sie*. A capo di questi giorni m'accorsi di aver fatto un vocabolarietto, quasi tutto composto di parole e di frasi d'amore, e questo mi servì poi moltissimo nel corso delle mie giovenili conquiste, in quella città ed altrove.

[I spent ten or twelve days in this lady's inn, and at times with a dictionary, at others with a grammar book, we did four or five hours of conversation a day, nearly always on the same subject, and always ending with an *Ich liebe sie*. At the end of this period I noticed I had acquired a small vocabulary almost wholly composed of words and phrases of love, and this was extremely helpful in my youthful conquests in that city and elsewhere.]

This is how the young man was introduced to German, a language he later used for many years when he became the official poet to the court of Emperor Joseph II in Vienna. His name was Lorenzo Da Ponte, the great author who wrote the libretti of some of the most famous operas, including Mozart's three masterpieces *Don Giovanni*, *The Marriage of Figaro* and *Così fan tutte*.

Gestures and Body Language

Many travellers reported their incomprehension or disapproval when watching natives communicate using gestures. But when verbal communication was not an option, they themselves resorted to signs and gesticulations, like actors and mimes on a stage, in order to get their message across. An early confirmation that the habit of gesticulating was common in Italy came from Fynes Moryson (1593), a traveller who was a keen observer of foreign habits. Being an English Protestant, he could only be admitted into the College of Jesuits in Rome by disguising himself as a native. He reported that he went 'attired like an Italian', and when he encountered the guards, was most careful to avoid 'strange gestures' that could betray his true identity as an Englishman rather than an Italian.[60]

Italians had a long-standing reputation as a nation of communicators who always resorted to complex gestures, 'especially with the head, fingers, or both, and more particularly when they are disputing and quarrelling'.[61] Writing in 1846, Dickens was fascinated by the art of gesticulation amongst the inhabitants of Naples, whose expressiveness he reported with some puzzling details:

Everything is done in pantomime in Naples [. . .] A man who is quarrelling with another, yonder, lays the palm of his right hand on the back of his left, and shakes the two thumb – expressive of a donkey's ears – whereat his adversary is goaded to desperation. Two people bargaining for fish, the buyer empties an imaginary waistcoat pocket when he is told the price, and walks away without a word: having thoroughly conveyed to the seller that he considers it too dear. Two people in carriages, meeting, one touches his lips, twice or thrice, holding up the five fingers of his right hand, and gives a horizontal cut in the air with the palm. The other nods briskly, and goes his way. He has been invited to a friendly dinner at half-past five o'clock, and will certainly come. [. . .] in Naples, those five fingers are a copious language.[62]

Some travelers drew a distinction between different social uses of hand signs, suggesting that many gestures were restricted to informal situations: 'the motion of the fingers, indicative of a familiar salute in Italy'.[63] Others, like

---

[60] Moryson, *Itinerary*, 303.
[61] Brian Hill, *Observations and Remarks in a Journey Through Sicily and Calabria, in the Year 1791* (London, 1792), 34.
[62] Dickens, *Pictures from Italy*, 142–3. Lady Morgan, among others, gave a description of the habit of gesturing in the poorest quarters of Naples. But in her often passionate representation of Italians, one does not feel the same empathy as in the passage above: 'Here too we first saw the professional Neapolitan beggars, a curious class, all filth, dirt, gesticulation, and pantomime. Even the little children go through all the contortions and grimaces of their elders to obtain charity, which none here are ashamed to crave, not even one who appeared to us to be a subaltern officer of the guard, and who begged a carline'. Lady (Sidney) Morgan, *Italy* (London, 1821), III, 140.
[63] William Stewart Rose, Letter VII from Abano, August 1807, *Letters from the North of Italy* (London, 1819), 71.

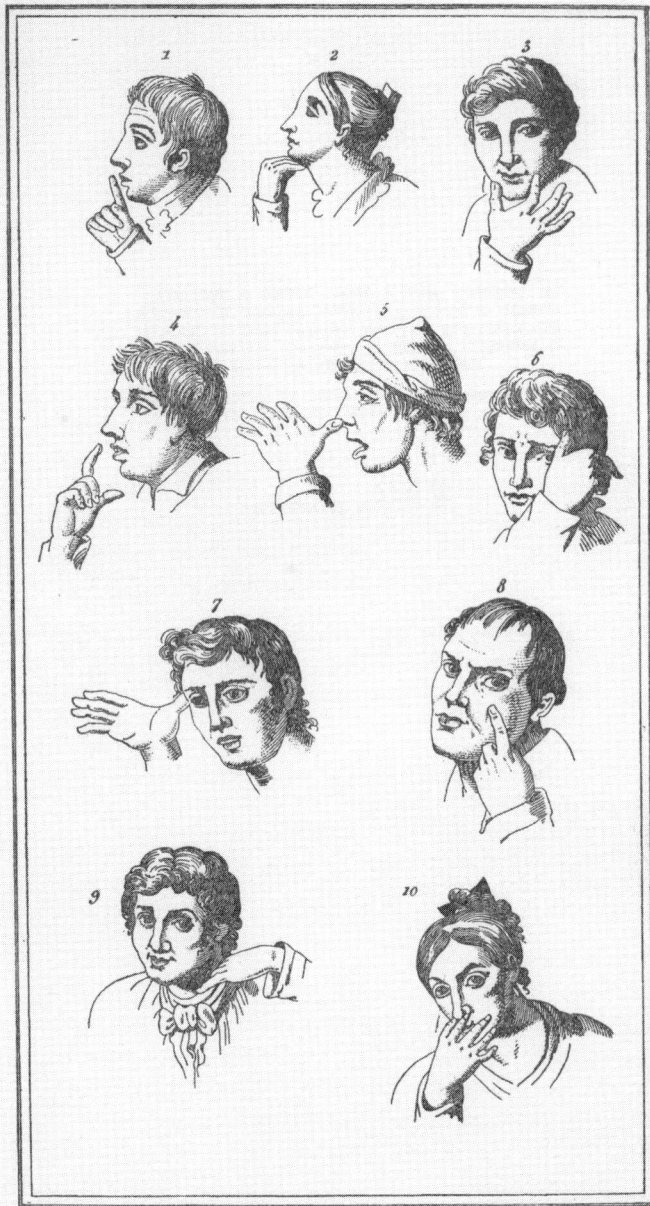

Figure 5.6 *Neapolitan gestures*, 1832. From *La mimica degli antichi investigata nel gestire napoletano (Ancient mimicry investigated in Neapolitan gestures)* by Andrea de Jorio. Stamperia del Fibreno, Naples, rpt. in 1964

Henry Coxe (a pseudonym used by John Millard), began to distinguish between the different meanings of the same gesture in different countries:

Beckoning with the hand in England and Germany, signifies 'Come hither;' but in Italy, it means only 'I salute you.' A motion with the hand backwards too, signifies with us, 'Go away'; but in Italy means 'I shall come directly'. To beckon with the inverted hand over the shoulder, means 'Go; I do not believe you'. To pull the corner of the eye down with the forefinger towards the nose, means 'That man who will not be played with'. Sometimes they represent an interlude or farce at Rome, where these signs are introduced, which must therefore prove very interesting to strangers.[64]

Certainly, signs and gestures showed significant variation not only across nations but also between different classes within the same country. Sebastiano Locatelli was secretly able to watch the Queen of France in Paris, who was very particular about keeping others at a respectful distance. For example, when she was giving instructions to chambermaids engaged in dressing her, she did so using gestures, never with words ('Mai parlò, facendosi servire co' cenni').[65] In Italy, women of high rank had their own language of gestures, and although it was cryptic in origin, in the eighteenth century this had come into the public domain. In Coxe's guidebook *Picture of Italy* (1815), he alternated his conversational dialogues with detailed descriptions of the gestures used by ladies of quality:

A lover will seldom approach his mistress at church, but addresses her by signs; and they may be saying the tenderest things imaginable, without it being possible for the uninitiated to understand a single syllable, or entertain any suspicion that they are conversing together. To lay the open hand on the chin, and then cross the lips with two fingers, signifies, 'You are beautiful; I should be happy to speak with you'. If the lady only repeats the latter part of the sign, it is understood that consents; but if she adds a motion of the hand, as if fanning herself, it means 'Be gone! I do not wish to speak to you'. Raising the point of the fan almost imperceptibly, and then gently lowering it, means 'Yes, I have no objection'. Ladies of quality, when giving this answer, slowly incline the upper part the body, and then resume their former attitude. In general, they avoid looking at the man, any more than by a quick glance of the eye after they have made the sign.[66]

If body language was employed even in churches in Italy, it was used in more sociable environments such as casinos, coffee houses or theatres, if not more explicitly then certainly more often and more daringly. The meaning of gestures was not always clear to outsiders, and those employed by Italian ladies in public places must have disoriented quite a few foreign gentlemen.[67] Even the perspicacious James Boswell felt confused at first by the hesitation and then the open audacity of a distinguished Italian lady:

---

[64] Coxe, *Picture of Italy* (London, 1815), 260–1.   [65] Locatelli, *Viaggio di Francia*, 237.
[66] Coxe, *Picture of Italy*, 260.
[67] Cartago reports a number of observations of British travellers of this phenomenon of non-verbal flirting which she calls 'pantomima galante'. Cartago, *Ricordi di italiano*, 44 n.3.

At night I sat a long time in the box of Mme B., of whom I was now violently enamoured. I made my declarations and she ... told me, 'It is impossible. I have a lover' (showing him), 'and I do not wish to deceive him'. Her lover was the Neapolitan Minister, Comte Pignatelli, in whose box she sat. He was a genteel, amiable man. He went away, and then I pursued my purpose. Never did I see such dissimulation, for she talked aloud that I should think no more of my passion, ... I was quite gone. She then said to me, 'Whisper in my ear,' and told me, 'We must make arrangements', ... She bid me call upon her next day at three.[68]

Hans Ottokar Reichard's *Guide de l'Italie*, published by 1793, included in the section about Venice the exact meaning of *parler à l'oreille* ('to whisper in one's ear', meaning make an assignation).[69] He stated that this was a typical idiom used by a lady speaking to her cicisbeo, and added the etymological information that it was derived from the archaic Italian word *cicisbeare*, in French *chuchoter*, meaning 'to whisper'.

While ignorance of social protocols caused surprise and embarrassment, the personal pride of Grand Tourists was more at stake when they had to resort to body language in order to communicate crucial information. Reports about using gestures are not found in the memoirs of travellers of high rank, as these men were accompanied by tutors or attendants who were able to communicate with the locals. Conveying an urgent message to a foreigner through body language was more typically experienced by lone travellers or small groups where no one had knowledge of the foreign language.

The young priest Sebastiano Locatelli left us some memorable recollections of his miming skills in much trickier situations. He always managed to achieve good communication, while leaving his audience in hysterics. For example, in France again, he and his party, still lacking experience in either the customs or the language, stopped for supper. Locatelli, being the most enterprising in the group, asked the innkeeper for a chicken by miming the gesture of wringing its neck. Unfortunately it was Rogation Monday, a day marked in France with full abstinence from eating meat and since Locatelli was dressed in his priest's robes, the local crowd regarded him with great incredulity and disapproval. On another occasion, this time while travelling back to Italy, Locatelli and his group crossed into the region of Brig in Switzerland and stopped to eat at an inn. Unlike earlier, they were now all fluent in French, but in this German-speaking area between France and Italy no one in the inn spoke either of those languages. It was Friday, a fasting day, and the group did not wish to eat meat, so Locatelli volunteered to convey with gestures their preference. The recollection of the story is a little gem for any scholar of kinesics:

---

[68] Boswell, Letter from Turin, 12 January 1765, *Boswell on the Grand Tour*, 31.
[69] Hans Ottokar de Reichard, *Guide de l'Italie, 1793* (reprinted Paris, 1971), section X5 unpaginated.

To have nothing but dry bread to eat after having looked at a meal fit for a king was really too much. As for fruit, it would be a miracle to find any in this country, and even if one succeeded it would cost the earth. At last, having commended myself fervently to God ... a bright idea suddenly struck me. Before they lay, I said to myself, hens in this country must cackle just as ours do. I beckoned to our hostess and then, squatting in the middle of the room where we were, just as though I wanted to lay an egg and catch it in my hands to prevent it falling on the ground, I began to cry, as hens do, 'co co a i hò feda co co a i hò feda', holding in my hands a ball of paper the size of an egg. I was immediately understood, and our hostess went off and fetched a large basket full of eggs.[70]

Monolingual Complacency

Complacency is often associated with a reluctance to speak foreign languages, an aversion that can be so deeply rooted in monolinguals that they believe their inability is not an individual disposition but a national characteristic. An answer to the question of whether the Grand Tour provided an opportunity for all travellers to value the knowledge of foreign languages and a convenient means for learning them must take into account such individual attitudes. At one end of the spectrum, many travellers did develop a positive aptitude for foreign languages and a conspicuous sense of curiosity for alterity in foreign countries. At times this inspired such an extreme sense of conformism that some generations were infected with an obsession for 'going native' or 'aping the foreigner'. But at the other end of the spectrum, especially after the Grand Tour became a wider social convention, a large number of travellers displayed an ingrained aversion to learning foreign languages.

The transition from the one attitude to the other cannot be clearly traced, as travellers reported in their accounts what they thought readers would want to read: references to interactions with foreign people reflected the cosmopolitan spirit of the time, and the linguistic achievement was an expected educational benefit of travel. Still, in the late eighteenth century, at the climax of Encyclopedism, the French Abbé de Binos preached that: 'La connessaince de la langue du pays où l'on va est essentielle, que rien ne la peut suppléer, ni l'expression des signes, ni meme le secours des interprètes' ['The knowledge of the language of the country where one is going is essential, so that nothing can replace it, neither sign language nor even the assistance of interpreters'].[71] This was the stated aim in many travel accounts, but what actually occurred abroad often failed to match the best declarations of intent. As the number of Grand Tourists increased during the eighteenth century, contact with the natives

---

[70] Locatelli, *Viaggio di Francia*, 314.
[71] Abbé de Binos, *Voyage par l'Italie en Egypte, au Mont-Liban et en Palestine ou Terre-Sainte* (Paris, 1787), 66–7. Quoted in Bertrand, *Le Grand Tour*, 230.

declined, and communication with locals almost disappeared. While the least-motivated travellers stopped seeking out social interactions, and a small number felt happy with survival communication skills, the majority relied on gestures, phrasebooks and interpreters.

In order to better understand such complacency as a form of cultural superiority, one needs to appreciate monolingualism as a defensive frame of mind. Persistent monolinguals often state that they wish to avoid the babble of a language they do not understand and in this way refrain from any act of infantilisation.[72] One may ask whether in the last stage of the Grand Tour this was an act of defence against a language they could not comprehend or against speakers they did not wish to communicate with. Travel was originally pursued for the multiple experiences enjoyed through interacting with different people; but when travellers no longer desired to communicate with foreigners, the language barrier was deemed insuperable, and this was used as an excuse to protect one's own otherness.

There is little doubt that an unwillingness to unlock one's alterity and the reluctance to learn foreign languages originate in an individual's temperament. But a special political and cultural environment is required in order for this attitude to spread within a national group. One should remember people like Michel de Montaigne and Fynes Moryson, two of the best linguists in the community of travellers, whose language skills developed from different motivations but the same disposition: the Frenchman expressed the cosmopolitan spirit of the Renaissance, while the pragmatic Englishman believed that appropriating another language obliterates traces of one's origins.[73] As the centuries went by, the attitudes of travellers from France and Britain changed, as the result of some fundamental changes in their national communities. As long as the intellectual elites of their nations felt part of the same *Res Publica Litterarum*, they went prepared to submit to the foreign languages and alien habits of other nationalities. But when France and Britain took the lead in Europe, intellectual curiosity and cultural participation gave away to indifference and feelings of superiority.

At that point, the French aristocracy as well as the English nobility and gentry began to resent the suggestion they should learn foreign languages. This coincided with an era when even ordinary people began to feel that other nations should learn their language, rather than them learning the languages

---

[72] Apparently, this was a common tendency among the English in the eighteenth century. Quoting a source from that time, Brunot remarks that many Englishmen in France had some knowledge of the language, but chose to remain silent unless they could master it completely. *Histoire*, VIII, 272.

[73] Mączak discusses the widespread distrust among travellers at the time of acute religious tensions in revealing one's identity for fear of troubles or discrimination. Moryson was a typical example. See *Travel*, especially 134–6 and 312 n.21.

of others. It is not surprising that by the end of the eighteenth century, it was quite obvious to an Italian traveller in Paris that Frenchmen dismissed foreign languages and had never heard anyone speak a single word of them.[74] Likewise, Lord North and his party of friends were surprised that at a dinner party in Leipzig in 1752 'a very few of them could talk anything but German'; they excused their own monolingualism but found that of other nations 'disagreeable enough'.[75] Despite increasing manifestations of cultural complacency among the cosmopolitan elites of the two countries, waves of Anglomania in France and Gallomania in Britain spread in the eighteenth century. But the main attraction was striking national clichés rather than encounters with these foreigners, something that became very visible when the French began to ridicule the British/foreigners, and when continental customs came under attack in Britain. At that point, most tourists travelling from either place remained convinced that their own country was the best in the world.

It was this growing conviction about national superiority that helped to bring about the decline in travel as a means of advancing one's education. For many travellers during the heyday of the Grand Tour, a continental trip consisted of taking in superficial curiosities, having lost its original purpose of shaping 'a complete person'. In Britain, the few who still believed in the original objectives of a tour began to express disappointment and regret about this change. The novelist Frances Trollope pointed out that 'the people that raise the cry against us [English travellers] are those . . . who every year scramble abroad for a few weeks, instead of spending their money at Margate or Brighton'.[76] A totally new class of tourists began to be spotted abroad, and the most serious and motivated travellers began to make fun of their compatriots 'whose knowledge of foreign tongues was restricted to *mangez* and *changez*', and for whom either a local courier or a multilingual *valet de place* had become indispensable.[77] Some of this new type of traveller displayed smugness and arrogance in their correspondence by happily referring to their inability to speak foreign languages. The great William Hazlitt, reporting on his crossing from Brighton to Dieppe, mentioned that among the passengers was 'an English General, proud of his bad French'.[78] Richard Dreyer, having arrived on the Continent in 1791, wrote without shame that 'my spleen was soon moved by the imposition practised on us the moment we set feet on land. Our trunks were given to porters . . . telling us (or at least the waiter who understood

---

[74] The traveller was Marchese G. B. Malaspina, who observed in 1786 that: 'i francesi fanno poco conto delle nazioni estere' ['the French do not have much consideration for foreign nations'], and while in Paris said that he never heard a single foreign word being used by anyone. Quoted by D'Ancona (ed.), *Viaggiatori e avventurieri*, 254.

[75] Quoted in Black, *The British Abroad*, 63.   [76] Trollope, *A Visit to Italy*, II, 272.

[77] Wilson, 'The Decline of the Grand Tour', 164.   [78] Ibid., 161.

their tongue) that they would return and carry them the remainder of the way, when we had breakfasted'.[79]

With Britain's growing wealth and the expansion of the means for fast travel abroad, this change became more noticeable. Letts explains: 'The travellers' conviction that all foreigners were fools, their determination to speak no language but their own, . . . their habit of exclaiming "No! No! No!" to every enquiry must have tried the patience of fellow-travellers, inn-keepers, post-ilions and officials alike'.[80]

While some commentators on the Grand Tour became disenchanted with the new attitude towards travel which resulted in an experience that hardly enriched the human intellect, a large proportion of new tourists did not see the ridiculousness of their own attitude of superiority. Some evidence of this change in linguistic behaviour came from the press, as expressed by the unambiguous humour of the satirical magazine *Punch*. Below is a selection of key pieces of advice for travellers which was published in an 1845 edition under the heading SMALL CHANGE *for Persons Going on the Continent*:

5. Recollect very few people talk English on the Continent, so you may be perfectly at your ease in abusing foreigners before their faces, and talking any modest nonsense you like, in the presence of ladies, at a *table d'hôte*. Do not care what you say about the government of any particular state you may be visiting, and show your national spirit by boasting, on every possible occasion, of the superiority of England and everything English.

7. If you go to a theatre and do not know a word of the language of the pieces, do not hesitate to talk as loudly as you can, or to laugh preposterously at the gibberish, which it is a marvel to you anybody can understand.

11. Be sure to take English servants with you. They are useful in speaking the language, settling the bills, and taking you to see the most remarkable sights of the country.

13. Buy a dialogue-book, and, if you study it attentively all the way up the Rhine, and at all the places you visit, you will be able, by the time you reach London, to ask 'Which is the nearest way to Cologne?' in no less than eight different languages.

14. Attend most scrupulously to the above golden rules, and you will . . . impress foreigners with the belief that England is without a doubt . . . the most civilised country in the world.[81]

---

[79] Quoted in Black, *The British Abroad*, 171.   [80] Letts, 'Germany and the Rhineland', 132.
[81] Quoted in Alan Wykes, *Abroad, A Miscellany of English Travel Writing 1700–1914* (London, 1973), 83–5.

6   Latin and Other Lingua Francas

A Multipurpose Language

The fact that Latin was a language without a speech community, *Eine Sprache ohne Sprachgemeinschaft* – a notion defined by L. Bieler and used by Burke[1] – was not the only factor that helped Latin attain the position of a supranational lingua franca. In addition, it gained prestige from being the parent language of an entire family of modern idioms. Moreover, Latin was consistently perceived as superior, a classical language expressing the perfection of the common civilisation that formed the roots of all European nations. By contrast, the modern vernaculars were perceived as having been corrupted by interference from languages spoken by non-European populations. Indeed, the position of Latin as the universal language was reinforced after the Renaissance as both a way of accessing classical knowledge and as a vehicle for academic learning. The two related networks of religion and scholarship shared this common legacy before the Reformation, but once the religious community began to disintegrate, Latin lost ground in favour of the vernaculars. This change did not dramatically affect religious networks, but it did gradually insinuate itself into the academic community and spread to other domains: the courts, diplomacy, the judiciary and the everyday life of social elites.[2] The experiences reported by travellers during the Grand Tour shed light on this major language shift, during which Latin's hegemonic role in European relations finally gave way to the dominance of the vernaculars.

During the early phase of the Grand Tour, when the nobility and the gentry were the only classes that employed travel as a means of completing a privileged education, the elite were very keen for their sons not to miss an opportunity to show their competence in Latin.[3] This was the best way of

---

[1] Burke, *Languages and Communities*, 44.
[2] Françoise Waquet, *Le latin ou l'empire d'un signe, XVIe–XXe siècle* (Paris, 1998).
[3] Tóth stresses the fact that in Hungary, Latin also served as a secret language to prevent women and inferiors from understanding discussions, and it is easy to imagine that the same happened elsewhere. István G. Tóth, *Literacy and Written Culture in Early Modern Europe* (1996; Engl. trans., Budapest, 2000), 139–40.

presenting their own credentials to other members of the European aristocracy, and the use of Latin as the language of courtesy in salons was also more accessible to them than the language of everyday communication in foreign countries. For as long as the social elites admired Latin without reservation, they wished to be educated to speak it, and lack of knowledge of Latin meant semi-literacy, which made ordinary folk feel a deep sense of inferiority. Indeed, poorly educated people such as notaries and schoolmasters showed off by using bombastic but inaccurate forms of Latin in order to appear to be educated.

Unsurprisingly, from the second half of the seventeenth century, young scholars who went abroad to study at famous foreign universities with a view to specialising in classics, law or medical studies were not at all pleased with the switch from Latin to a vernacular. John Lauder was sent from Scotland to France to study French and law and he expected to use his knowledge of Latin on most official occasions. For example, in Orléans he visited the Jesuits' college, where he reported that 'I discoursed with the praefectus Jesuitarum, who earnestly enquired of what religion I was, for a long time I would give him no other answer but that I was religion christianus.'[4] But his contemporary, Edward Browne, who was fortunate while in Paris to attend medical lectures given by the famous scientist Guy Patin, wrote that 'I was much disappointed in my expectations of understanding all hee said by reason hee used French tongue so much.'[5] Ellis Veryard was another student who noted that French academics preferred to use their native tongue in lectures and publications: 'not only publish the greatest part of their Books therein, but even in explicating their Dictates in the Schools use as much French as Latin, tho' they are very expert in both'.[6] The English doctor Martin Lister discussed the decline of Latin as international language at the end of the seventeenth century when visiting the great Benedictine scholar Mabillon, author of *De Re Diplomatica,* who stated that he was afraid 'it might be with us, as it was with them [the English], since they cultivated their own Language so much, they began to neglect the Ancient Tongues, the Greek and the Latin'.[7]

Even in the early days of the Grand Tour, some young travellers' correspondence with their families started to include comments about the time and money spent on acquiring what they called 'this difficult dead language', though they still recognised Latin as a worthwhile instrument to gain personal introductions abroad. In a letter to his anxious father in 1656, William Hammond included some caustic remarks about the difference between learning a dead language and a modern one through the same method. He was in France, where he felt that in a short time he had achieved a much higher level of

[4] Lauder, *Journals*, 12.
[5] Edward Browne, *A Brief Account of Some Travels ... etc.* Quoted by Peter Burke, *The Art of Conversation* (Cambridge, 1993).
[6] Veryard, *An Account*, 109.   [7] Quoted in Lough, *France Observed*, 320.

competence in the language than after several years of training in England: 'they [previous letters in French] might at worst shew you my Proficiency in this Crabbed Tongue, which is so contrary both in Syntaxe & Pronunciation to our English, that it may well goe hand in hand with Latine for matter of difficulty'.[8] Indeed, the Grand Tour is a mirror of the ascent and decline of Latin as a lingua franca, and its progressive retreat from use in ordinary spheres to the more institutional domains marked the steps of its gradual descent into obscurity.

Written and Spoken Latin

The vitality of Latin in the sixteenth and seventeenth centuries continued to rest on the fact that scholars from different countries could correspond in the language, and even many laypeople could speak and understand it. Latin's role as both a written and spoken language maintained their sense of belonging to an international community, for which a supranational medium of communication was necessary. However, many historians state that knowledge of Latin was not any greater in Catholic countries at that time. This was because competence in Latin was weaker in regions with low literacy, and standards of education were usually higher in the Protestant world. For example, in Spain knowledge of Latin was rare even at university. During the first quarter of the sixteenth century, lectures were delivered in Latin only at the university of Alcalá and a century later, a doctorate could be obtained from Salamanca without any knowledge of Latin at all.[9] In Italy, it was brought to the attention of the Pope as early as 1513 that a substantial proportion of the clergy did not know Latin, and this led to the foundation of seminaries from the late sixteenth century onwards to remedy the situation.[10] In the Catholic world, seminaries trained priests to use simple Latin for baptisms, weddings, funerals and other orations but in Protestant countries, Latin instruction was still synonymous with learning grammar and training the intellect.

In clear contrast with southern Europe, Latin had long been taught in western and central Europe in order to cultivate literacy, but also with strong emphasis on oral skills. Spoken as well as written Latin were thought to be of practical importance for making speeches and delivering sermons, both at university and in one's professional life. With the humanistic emphasis on classical Latin, new teaching methods spread which allowed for more flexible approaches: less rigid norms, simplified structure and more tolerance for neologisms. Such changes were a response to the increasingly dominant role of Latin as a lingua franca in

---

[8] Letter of William Hammond to his father, Paris, 13 January 1656, in Brennan, *The Origins of the Grand Tour*, 163.

[9] Bates, *Touring in 1600*, 48.   [10] Burke, *Languages and Communities*, 50.

secular rather than religious spheres. The practice of speaking and writing Latin was also common in the north of Europe, the Baltic countries and Russia, having already established itself in the eastern regions, particularly Poland and Hungary.

This lack of a clear-cut geographical division between knowledge of spoken Latin and its use as the language of liturgy is confirmed in the writings of many travellers. For example, in Catholic Poland and Ireland, knowledge of Latin was widespread. The Polish historian Mączak explains that 'in the general opinion of all Europe "any" Pole, even a servant or blacksmith, was able to make himself understood in Latin'.[11] Tóth confirms that Poland and Hungary were frequently described as places where some knowledge of Latin was surprisingly common. He recounts the experience of travellers who found that not only did customs men, coach drivers and traders actively use the language but also 'peasants and shepherds'.[12] Burke stresses the fact that lower-class Hungarians used to speak Latin more fluently than many priests did elsewhere.[13] According to Tóth, the main reason for this was the fact that 'in areas where several languages were spoken, Latin survived as a language of communication'.[14] In Germany too, until the early part of the seventeenth century Latin was spoken fluently by people from diverse backgrounds – some claim in a less corrupted form than in Poland. However, an Englishman passing through Germany in 1655 found only one innkeeper who could speak Latin. Apparently this decline was due to the Thirty Years' War, and the civil wars in the previous half-century made the use of Latin in France less common than in Germany.[15]

Throughout the sixteenth century, Latin was ordinarily spoken by the English upper classes with ease and correctness, and this was reinforced by the language becoming fashionable under Queen Elizabeth.[16] In England, a knowledge of Latin was essential for all careers, and its study occupied most of a student's day. For a long time, Oxford and Cambridge required students to speak Latin not only with their teachers but also 'at meals, ... or in the college hall or chapel'. In order to achieve the expected level of fluency, not only were Latin grammars written in Latin, adhering to the direct method, but in the so-called grammar schools 'the boys were supposed to speak Latin in class and even in the playground'.[17]

In the first half of the seventeenth century, English travellers to France sensed that Latin was beginning to suffer something of a crisis as an international academic language. Many of them reported how inadequate they felt at the prevalence of French over Latin in domains where they did not expect it.

---

[11] Mączak, *Travel*, 140.   [12] Tóth, *Literacy and Written Culture*, 144–5.
[13] Burke, *Languages and Communities*, 46.   [14] Tóth, *Literacy and Written Culture*, 142.
[15] Bates, *Touring in 1600*, 47.   [16] Ibid.   [17] Both quotations from ibid., 54.

James Howell explained in his *Instructions* in 1642 that 'it is all very behoof-full, that he [the English traveller] have a passable understanding of the Latine tongue', but he regretted that 'in France they presently fall from the Latine, to dispute in the vulgar tongue'. He also offered a political explanation for this turn of events: 'So that it were not amisse for him to spend some time in the New Academy, erected lastly by the French Cardinal in Richelieu, where all Sciences are read in the French tongue, which is done of purpose to refine, and enrich the Language [as well as to encourage the Gentry to the Arts].'[18] The mobility of students and teachers, made possible by the use of Latin as the academic lingua franca, was beginning to be challenged by the use of verna-culars. But this new policy was not uniformly implemented, nor did it dis-courage the use of Latin, which most of the elite had acquired in their youth. Even in Italy, where the use of Latin in some disciplines lasted until the eighteenth century, some universities, including Siena, employed the vernacu-lar as early as the late sixteenth century to teach subjects such as the Tuscan language, mathematics and even anatomy.[19]

Quite apart from the problem of reactivating their ability to speak and understand spoken Latin, many travellers reported that they had to use the language to communicate with people they met on the road who were neither members of the clergy nor from the educated elite. Coachmen and ostlers are often mentioned as being able to reply to their queries using a sort of "travel-lers' Latin" which was adequate enough to convey survival information to their customers. Soldiers, who led a nomadic existence, were occasionally reported as being able to do the same. Burke calls the Latin spoken by such people a 'pidgin' and explains that it was most likely a jargon 'without frills and indeed without most of the resources of the language' – i.e. without inflections, and with verbs reduced to infinitives. The historian gives as an example the expression *vinum bibere,* which would have been sufficiently understandable to get served in a tavern.[20] Mączak also mentions peasants who, in the second half of the sixteenth century in some countries, seemed to be able to get by in Latin when approached by travellers anxious to obtain directions or other basic information.[21] One case in point was reported by Coryat, who while in Germany early in the seventeenth century met a peasant who was 'both learned and & unlearned':

Learned because being but a wood-cleaver (for he told me that he was the Jesuits wood-cleaver of Mentz) he was able to speake Latine. A matter as rare in one of that sordid facultie as to see a white Crowe or a blacke Swanne. Againe he was unlearned, because

---

[18] All three quotations from Howell, *Instructions*, 21.
[19] Chiara Campolongo, 'L'importanza della lingua senese nella percezione degli stranieri nei secoli XVII e XVIII', unpublished dissertation, Università degli Studi di Siena, 2011–12, 17.
[20] Burke, *Languages and Communities*, 47.   [21] Mączak, *Travel*, 14.

the Latin which he did speake was such incongruall and disjointed stuffe, such anti-priscianisticall eloquence, that I thinke were grave Cato alive he should have more cause to laugh if he should heare this fellow deliver his minde in Latin, then when he saw an Asse eate thistles.[22]

While travelling in Germany, Coryat was stopped by robbers, but by speaking in basic Latin – if we are to believe his diary entry – he succeeded in convincing them that he was a mendicant friar, and even managed to obtain some coins from them. Coryat was travelling alone and on foot, the best way to meet other passers-by, and wrote about a number of people he was able to speak Latin with. One was a pilgrim, 'a very simple fellow, who spake so bad Latin that a country Scholler in England should be whipped for speaking the like'.[23] In Lyons he met another pilgrim: 'I had a long discourse with him in Latin'.[24] He even met a Turk who 'spake sixe or seven languages besides the Latin, which he spake very well ... I had a long discourse with him in Latin of many things'.[25] On the other hand, the English churchman Peter Heylyn was dis-appointed by the ignorance of some members of the clergy on the Continent: 'When I had lost myself in the street in Paris, and wanted French to enquire homeward, I used to apply myself to some of these reverend habit. *But O seclum insipiens & infacetum!* You might as easily have wrung water out of the flint, as a worde of Latine out of their mouths.'[26] On another occasion he met a canon at Orléans:

Perceiving me to speak to him in a strange tongue, for it was Latine, he very readily asked me this question, Num potestis loqui Gallia? Which when I denyed, at last he broke out in another interrogatory, viz. Quam diu fuistis in Gallice? To conclude, having read over my Letter, ... he dismissed me with this cordiall ... Ego negotias vestras curabo.[27]

When Edward Lhwyd and his companion were arrested as spies and impri-soned in Brest in Normandy (1700), they drew up a petition in Latin requesting to be interrogated. But they were told that the most senior official, the *Intendant de la Marine,* 'was not conversant in Latin'.[28]

On the other hand, Parkes recounts the frequency with which a Frenchman, Albert Jouvin de Rochefort, known as Jorevin, while travelling in seventeenth-century England, had recourse to use Latin with parsons and soldiers alike:

In Latin, the fellow-traveller he meets at the cross-roads puts him on his way; in Latin the parson, hastily summoned by the landlord of the 'Stag' or the 'Angel', finds out his requirements, and settles him for the night; and in the same universal medium a 'late

[22] Coryat, *Crudities*, II, 269.   [23] Ibid., I, 165.   [24] Ibid., I, 211.   [25] Ibid., I, 212.
[26] Peter Heylyn, *The Voyage of France or a Compleat Journey Through France* (London, 1673), 191.
[27] Ibid.   [28] Quoted in Lough, *France Observed*, 12.

commander in the low countries', summoned in like fashion, broaches conversation, though, to delude the good hostess, with the air of speaking French.[29]

This was certainly not the impression of other travellers, such as the Transylvanian statesman Miklós Bethlen, a frequent visitor to the English Royal Court, who commented in 1663 that in England there was no use for spoken Latin as a lingua franca. More seriously, he was surprised that even Oxford professors were reluctant to converse in Latin, and priests regarded 'the speaking of Latin as a real torture!'[30] Such inconsistent reports about spoken Latin in England could reflect different individual experiences but also diverse levels of tolerance for peculiar pronunciations. There is evidence that many travellers found Latin spoken with a foreign accent not just odd but quite inaccessible.

Over the course of the seventeenth century, the insistence that Latin was of practical importance to the new generation of Europeans was received by some sectors of the educated elite with less sympathy than in the previous century, and some travellers began to record their frustrations.[31] The reports in many travel writings about the inconsistent use of Latin abroad could be explained by the authors' intentions to make the point that their difficulties conversing in Latin did not depend so much on the limitations of their own competence but rather on regional variations in the language. Given the enormous variety of speakers' backgrounds, and of simplifications to Latin through its international use, most travellers were interested in providing evidence of what they managed to achieve using Latin rather than relating episodes that indicated their failure. James Boswell possessed some rudiments of German but not enough to dispel the suspicions of soldiers at a castle gate in Prussia when he asked: *Vie veel troopen hebt der Furst?* ('How many troops does the Prince have?'). They took him to the principal guard, where the Scottish traveller was asked: *Dominus forsitam loquitur Latine?* ('Perhaps my Lord speaks Latin?'). Fortunately, there was a soldier-interpreter who, after listening to his defence, translated this for the Burgmaster, who let him go.[32]

As the Grand Tour evolved in the eighteenth century and modern languages began to prevail over Latin, the use of Latin as a lingua franca, which was resorted to for essential enquiries on the road, gave way to employing the

---

[29] Joan Parkes, *Travel in England in the Seventeenth Century* (Oxford, 1925), 288.
[30] Quoted in Tóth, *Literacy and Written Culture*, 136.
[31] Comparisons between learning French by imitation in France and studying Latin in grammar schools were often made during the century. Lambley reports that in 1654, Richard Carew was surprised that 'he learnt more French without rules in three-quarters of the year in France than he had learnt Latin in more than thirteen years' strenuous study of grammar', in *The Teaching and Cultivation of French*, 340.
[32] James Boswell, Letter from Coswig, 24 September 1764, in Pottle (ed.), *Boswell on the Grand Tour, Germany, etc.*, 105.

classical language to stress a change in mood. Again, James Boswell recounted one such instance when he wished to emphasise how thrilled he was. He was in Rome viewing antiquities in the house of Cicero along with his Scottish friend, the antiquarian Morison. Suddenly he caught sight of a statue that closely resembled the Roman philosopher:

I was seized with enthusiasm. I began to speak Latin. Mr Morison replied. He laughed a bit at the beginning. But we made a resolution to speak Latin continually during this course of antiquities. We have persisted, and every day we speak with greater facility, so that we have harangued on Roman antiquities in the language of the Romans themselves.[33]

Another example comes from Dr Johnson, indulging in a playful mood in Paris, where he was persuaded to buy a fashionable new French outfit. To counterbalance this extravagant decision, he refused to speak anything but Latin in the shop.[34] These two examples of switching into Latin by two famous friends in Rome and in Paris – the two capitals of the Grand Tour – underscore the end of an era. In the second half of the eighteenth century, switching into Latin could function as an act of identity evoking a distant past in the presence of sympathetic friends but it was no longer a language of communication.

Regional Variations

The use of Latin showed some marked regional and social peculiarities, especially in its spoken form. In particular, while the Latin used in the ecclesiastical and civil domains showed a high degree of standardisation – especially in the fields of justice, administration and diplomacy – national and municipal records reflected the local vernaculars. Indeed, ecclesiastical Latin was intermingled with local vernaculars and evolved into a folk model. This kind of popular Latin is known to many language historians; for example, Tóth mentions 'half understood Latin' in Hungary,[35] and the Italian Gian Luigi Beccaria refers to 'the Latin of those who do not know it'.[36] Burke confirms that 'Macaronic sermons', in the sense of Latin alternating with passages in vernacular, were quite common in many countries, including Italy and in France, from the end of the Middle Ages.[37]

---

[33] James Boswell, in Brady and Pottle (eds.), *Boswell on the Grand Tour, Italy etc.*, 65.
[34] Woodruff, 'From London to Paris', 46. n.77. Johnson's reputation for speaking Latin in France survived but so did a set of famous couplets he composed in French describing his first impressions of the country: '*A Calais Trop de frais. Saint-Omer Tout est cher. Arras Hélas! A Amiens On n'a rien'.* ['In Calais Too many expenses. In Saint-Omer Everything is dear. Arras Alas! At Amiens There is nothing.']
[35] Tóth, *Literacy and Written Culture*, 134.
[36] Gian Luigi Beccaria, *Sicuterat. Il latino di chi non lo sa* (1999; 2nd ed., Milan, 2001).
[37] Burke, *Languages and Communities*, 50.

Folk Macaronic or Popular Latin was more widespread in Catholic countries, where liturgical Latin was the language of the church. On the other hand, literary Macaronic Latin – in the sense of the cross-fertilisation of many languages or varieties (classical Latin, Medieval Latin and the vernacular) – became quite common everywhere. We have examples of its literary use not only in Italy, where it first emerged in the early sixteenth century,[38] but also in other European countries as far apart as Spain and Germany, Scotland and France.[39] Neighbouring regions often showed the same simplifications in Latin. For example, it is interesting that Andrew Boorde's 1540 book *Introduction of Knowledge*, which includes lists for each country of the most common phrases, renders the expression of respect 'How do you fare?' with *Quo modo stat cum vostro corps?* for both Italian and Spanish.[40]

It was not only at the folk level that Latin was evolving in order to meet the needs of ordinary people, who were often semi-literate. Also at the elite level, where Latin was needed to transmit knowledge without misunderstandings or ambiguities, professionals and scholars increasingly felt that the resources of the language were more appropriate for a bygone civilisation. After Latin became a language without native speakers, its various adaptations strongly reflected regional realities – not only the simplicity of the vernaculars but also the need to create neologisms capable of expressing new meanings. These elite and folk innovations contributed to the emergence of different types of Latins which were highly stigmatised by the humanist supporters of the unity of scholastic Latin. Such varieties, some even in the form of pidgins, played an important local role in allowing inter-regional communication, so long as regional variation from the common core did not affect mutual intelligibility.

Humanists had long been aware of these varieties of Greek and Latin and the fact that their evolution and spread often led to diverse models for learners. Yet many travellers who went abroad to study classics wrote of their surprise at some lecturers' different ways of speaking these classical languages. In the seventeenth century, Latin still firmly retained its international currency as an academic language, so the normal assumption by a travelling scholar was that he would be able to follow lectures and disputations in famous universities all over Europe. But this was not everyone's experience.

John Lauder, one of Scotland's leading jurists, arrived in France in 1664 with a view to specialising in law. He spent his first year at Poitiers and noted the odd pronunciation of Greek used by one of his professors.[41] His disappointment with the Latin spoken abroad was even greater as this was used as a medium of instruction more frequently than Greek. Lauder then moved to Paris, remarking

---

[38] See the works of Ivano Paccagnella, especially *Il fasto delle lingue: plurilinguismo letterario nel '500* (Rome, 1984).
[39] Burke, *Languages and Communities*, 133–4.   [40] Quoted in Bates, *Touring in 1600*, 51.
[41] Lauder, *Journals*, 124.

in his diary that Greek was not the only problem there either, and more linguistic difficulties arose from his disputations in Latin with French academics: 'The accent the French gives in Latin is so different from ours that sometimes we would not have understood some of them (for most part I understood them well enough), nor some of them us.' Lauder was keen to get to the root of the problem, and while attending dictated lectures, he realised that the French even used different Latin terms for punctuation marks.[42] Yet he was probably luckier than some of his English colleagues as his Scottish pronunciation of Latin apparently was much nearer to that of a Frenchman than an Englishman's would have been.[43] The French were known for the way they pronounced *u* and *r*, and 'the peculiar pronunciation of Latin grated upon the ear', to quote a Hungarian traveller in Paris.[44]

A century earlier, the English humanist Roger Ascham apparently sank into a state of despair while travelling on the Continent when he realised that his pronunciation of Latin was incomprehensible in Germany and the Netherlands.[45] The Scotsman Lauder had come to the conclusion that it was not the English but the French pronunciation of Latin that was wrong, and many students from England thought exactly the same. John Heylyn, who settled in Orléans, admired the academic organisation of the German students there: 'they have here a corporation, and indeed do make among themselves a better University than the University', but he was critical about the way they spoke Latin, commenting that they should learn to speak it 'more congruously'.[46] Such a provincial perspective on the use of Latin seems to conflict with the international spirit of a lingua franca but the comments and reactions of these young scholars must be seen in the context of people who studied ancient languages as an intellectual discipline rather than as a medium of communication.

Students of classical Latin were taught to respect the language as being incomparably superior to any modern tongue, and they were diligently trained in logic and rhetoric. Such an education did not serve to make them equally aware of the properties and limits of the lingua franca as a tool for travellers. Once they realised that the pronunciation of Latin varied from country to country because each nation taught it differently, everyone had to make their own decision about which model to follow. A traveller's experience which highlights such inconsistencies comes from Thomas Coryat, a Latinist with a taste for creating picturesque neologisms drawing on the resources of Latin. Towards the end of his Italian journey, he wrote about his observations of how Latin was spoken in Italy. His first remark concerned the rules of address:[47]

---

[42] Ibid., 123.   [43] Bates, *Touring in 1600*, 49.   [44] Tóth, *Literacy and Written Culture*, 138–9.
[45] Reported in Mączak, *Travel*, 140.   [46] Heylyn, *The Voyage of France*, 294 and 296.
[47] The four excerpts from Coryat *Crudities*, II, 59–60.

I observed a strange phrase both in this City and all other Italian cities where I was, that whensoever any Italian doth discourse in Latin with a stranger or any man else, he will very seldome speake to a man in the second person. As for example he will not say, *Placet ne tibi*: but *Placet ne domination! tuæ* or *vestræ*. So that they doe most commonly use that circumlocution, even to the meanest person that is.

His second comment addressed a specific variation in the pronunciation of Latin:

The Italian when he uttereth any Latin word wherein this letter i is to be pronounced long, doth alwaies pronounce it as a double e, viz as ee. As for example: he pronounceth feedes for fides: veeta for vita: ameecus for amicus, &c. but where the i is not to be pronounced long he uttereth it as we doe in England, as in these wordes, impius, aquila, patria, Ecclesia: not aqueela, patreea, Eccleseea. And this pronounciation is so generall in all Italy, that every man which speaketh Latin soundeth a double e for an i.

Exceptionally, Coryat did not side with his compatriots in criticising other national pronunciations of Latin. Instead, he decided to abandon what he had been taught back home and adopt a more international approach, in line with that of the majority of Continental travellers:

Neither is it proper to Italy only, but to all other nations whatsoever in Christendome saving to England. For whereas in my travels I discoursed in Latin with Frenchmen, Germans, Spaniards, Danes, Polonians, Suecians, and divers others, I observed that every one with whom I had any conference, pronounced the i after the same manner that the Italians use.

Alongside differences in pronunciation, there were also local neologisms, regional simplifications and variations in pragmatic acts such as rules of address, all of which increased the complexity of using Latin as lingua franca. Invariably, determination to communicate was needed by interlocutors from different linguistic backgrounds to compensate for the reduced standardisation of the spoken Latin found on the road. An illustration of such real-life situations comes from fictional literature. Vicente Gómez Martínez-Espinel, a Spanish writer of the Golden Age and a classical scholar and a traveller himself, who was once taken prisoner by Mediterranean pirates, included what is possibly an autobiographical adventure in his picaresque novel from 1618, *Marcos de Obregón*. The book's Spanish hero secured his passage on a boat on the river Po in Italy, together with a German, an Italian and a Frenchman, and in order to pass the time with the other travellers, he convinced them to speak Latin. But they soon gave this up as their pronunciation varied too greatly.[48]

The impoverishment of spoken Latin accelerated in the second half of the seventeenth century and became even more rapid towards the end. Once Latin was viewed as being associated with the past and its speakers with pedantry,

[48] Quoted in Bates, *Touring in 1600*, 49.

French was well on its way to becoming the new lingua franca. A modern language appeared better equipped to enable people from all parts of Europe to exchange ideas about contemporary issues with ease and without misunderstandings.

The Emergence of French

While Latin retreated to being used in written domains, the advantages of using French as a lingua franca gradually surfaced. In diplomatic circles, the hegemony of Latin clung on, as its high level of standardisation was unrivalled by any language used within a specific national community. Yet the evolution of international relations rendered oral communication more important than diplomatic correspondence, and this militated in favour of a living language rather than one without native speakers. In addition, the notion of civilisation itself was shifting from a focus on the past to contemporary models. Once the lure of modern life replaced the idealised heritage of the classical world, the social elites and the most educated classes in Europe thought that the best models of civility could be found in the language spoken within modern French society.

In the second half of the seventeenth century, many diplomats and political envoys still spoke Latin regularly, although occasionally the language of international treaties included Italian and Spanish, as at the Congress of Westphalia (1677–78). But with the heightened status of French only half a century later, treaties began to be drawn up solely in French. The Treaty of Vienna, signed on 18 November 1738, was one of the last treaties written in Latin. French increasingly became the language spoken not only between diplomats but also in courts – as happened in Germany – as well as among the regent class (patricians) in the Dutch Republic and even within the Russian Empire.[49] France was looked upon more and more as the repository of all that was refined in manners and style, whose court promoted models of behaviour, elegance and luxury that other European courts sought to imitate. As Europe grew more cosmopolitan, other factors contributed to French being assigned the role of the new language of international communication. Books aimed at a wide readership as well as learned periodicals intended for academic circulation were printed in French, and science academies began to operate exclusively in the language. From the circles of the intellectual elites to the salons of the *beau monde*, the younger generation felt that a modern language was best suited to establishing cultural exchanges as well as conducting polite conversation across frontiers. All these functions contributed to French being accepted as the lingua franca of Europe after the second half of the seventeenth century.

---

[49] Burke, *Languages and Communities*, 86.

In the meantime, priorities in language education were changing throughout Europe. The study of Latin was still seen as a discipline that trained the mind so competence in a modern language which enabled learners to hold a conversation abroad grew in academic status and educational value. This change in perceptions was captured well in the second half of the eighteenth century by Richard Hurd's *Dialogues on the Uses of Foreign Travel Considered as a Part of an Englishman's Education* (1764), which involves the two apocryphal figures, Locke and Shaftsbury. The *Dialogues* do not represent the views of its characters' real namesakes, 'as Hurd speaks with the voice of the 1760s not that of the 1690s'.[50] Locke expresses reservations about the benefits of travel and a genteel education, favouring instead the spirit of citizenship and public integrity. Shaftsbury, reflecting the predominant sentiment of the time, stresses the qualities of being a 'citizen of the world', saying his idea of a gentleman was 'a man who can converse not only in English but in the universal language of the time, French'.[51]

Certainly most British travellers in the eighteenth century boasted about whatever level of competence they had in French, and their diaries and correspondence are full of references to the use of the new lingua franca as the medium required by international convention. The following is from a letter written by James Boswell to Baron von Wachtendonck, Grand Chamberlain of the Court of Mannheim in 1764. What seems surprising today, but was in keeping with the spirit of the time, is the profusion of apologies for his imperfect use of French, while not a single word was expended on making amends for his lack of German, the native language of his Highness and of the country that welcomed him:

Sir: – Although my French is still far from good, I cannot refrain from expressing the infinite gratitude I owe his Highness the Elector Palatine for the courtesies with which I have been honoured at his court. I hope, Sir, that you will have the goodness to excuse my French. My expression will perhaps be imperfect. But my feelings are very clear. Be assured, Sir, that they come from the heart.[52]

Indeed, James Boswell was interested in picking up the language of the many countries he visited during his Grand Tour. Everywhere he went, he endeavoured to talk with men, especially great men, and of course with women, particularly willing women. By the time he arrived in Italy, he had gained sufficient experience of French. But, like many other British travellers at the

---

[50] Cohen, *Fashioning Masculinity*, 60. The author observes that 'it is precisely because of the anachronisms that the *Dialogues* highlight the shifts that have taken place in the conception of the gentleman since the late seventeenth century'.
[51] Ibid., 100.
[52] James Boswell, Letter to Baron von Wachtendonck, Grand Chamberlain of the Court of Mannheim, 8 November, 1764 [original in French]. In Pottle (ed.), *Boswell on the Grand Tour, Germany and Switzerland, 1764*, 172.

time who headed to the Italian peninsula, he had no Italian, and the only language he could count on using was the new lingua franca. The fact that French was the normal currency in the appropriate social circles in Italy was confirmed by William Patoun, who planned a tour for Lord Brownlow. To reassure his master about practical comforts, appropriate introductions and pleasurable social activities, Patoun diligently included the linguistic profiles of the local nobility, and especially those of the *femmes de salon*, in the cities where they intended to stop. For Bologna he wrote: 'The Bolognese Nobility are civill in general with Strangers. The Countesses Marulli and Lignani two sisters are the greatest patronesses of the English, and both speak French.'[53] For Parma he stated: 'The present Prince is a Minor . . . the first Minister . . . by his great Merit has raised himself to the Honours and Posts he now enjoys. He is of French extraction, and speaks the Language perfectly.'[54] Finally, in Rome: 'The Princess Juistiniani is one of the Clifford Family, and a Daughter of the Countess Mahoni at Naples. She speaks only Italian but understands French.'[55]

By the early nineteenth century, the French language was well established as the natural successor to Latin. The language of diplomacy would no longer be divided between an obsolete language of academic prestige and a living language which was à la mode and rich in modern intellectual subtleties. This is confirmed by the records of the Congress of Vienna (1815) but it is interesting to learn that a minority of representatives in the *corps diplomatique* present at that meeting argued that this supranational linguistic role should have been assigned to Italian, which in those days was still a language without a nation:

The union of different nations necessarily requires one common language, and the French still maintains its universality, being nearly the one in which the English can make themselves understood by the Russians, Poles, Germans and the French. The ladies regard it as the natural language of gallantry, and those who have wished to introduce the Italian in its stead form but a minority.[56]

Italian and Other Languages

The emergence of French as the European lingua franca was a slow process because of competition with Latin but in the early stages of this transition – from the beginning to the middle of the seventeenth century – Italian was a close challenger for the position. This is mainly due to the fact that during the Renaissance Italy, more than any other country in Europe, was seen as a modern extension of the classical world. Moreover, the political fragmentation of the Peninsula worked in favour of, rather than against the elevation of Italian to the position of a lingua franca for Europe. Tuscan was a highly

[53] Patoun, 'Advice on travel', xliii.   [54] Ibid., xlii.   [55] Ibid., xlvi.
[56] From an article of the weekly paper *Examiner,* quoted in Wykes, *Abroad,* 151.

developed vernacular and a prestigious literary language, and the fact that it had gained universal prestige among the political powers of the Peninsula – Piedmont, Genoa, Venice, Rome, Naples and Sicily – made it attractive to other nations.

After the Renaissance, Italian was also used in many European courts, and the most culturally aware elites were keen to adopt Italian etiquette, manners and fashions in order to promote a cosmopolitan image. When it became appropriate for an aspiring young courtier to study modern languages, knowledge of Italian and of its Renaissance authors grew in value, while Latin – its natural antecedent – was beginning to be side-lined. In the middle of the sixteenth century, William Thomas, author of the *History of Italy* (1549), wrote in the appended *Principal Rules of the Italian Grammar* (1550): 'You shall almost find no part of the sciences, no part of any worthy history, no part of eloquence, nor any part of fine poesy, that ye have not in the Italian tongue.'[57] Fifty years on, Ben Jonson pointed out in his play *Volpone* (1606) that Italians are 'the only known men of Europe! Great general scholars, excellent physicians, most admir'd statesmen, profess'd favourites, and cabinet councellors to the great princes; The only languag'd men of all the world'.[58] Fifty years further ahead, Giacomo Fantuzzi, the Italian traveller who set out from Ravenna to explore the Continent with the intent of meeting and conversing with people of the Protestant faith, found that French was commonly used in Germany, all along the river Rhine, and especially in Cologne. But if we are to believe his memoirs, 'in all courts outside Italy, Italian language is more widely spoken than any other language'.[59]

French came to rival Italian around the middle of the seventeenth century, after more than a century of the most direct descendant of Latin being used as a lingua franca. This was a time when Latin was already being perceived as less suitable for conversations, and when cultural conformism accelerated French's functional competitiveness over Italian. There were many reasons for this. France's absolute monarchy and the dominance of its foreign policies abroad convinced many well-educated people, like James Howell, that it was Cardinal Richelieu's intention to turn the language spoken by the leading European power into the language of Europe.[60] At the same time, the growing use of French in Europe began to challenge the position of Italian in the Mediterranean and the Levant. Because of the limited spread of Latin in

[57] Thomas, *The History of Italy*, in Parks (ed.), 'Introduction', xvii.
[58] Ben Jonson, *Volpone*, Act II, scene II, in John D. Rea (ed.) (New Haven/London/Oxford, 1919), 42.
[59] Giacomo Fantuzzi, *Itinerario di … da Ravenna nel partire di Polonia del 1652*, cc.229–30, Archivio Segreto Vaticano, Miscellanea Armadia XV, 80; quoted in Mączak, *Viaggi e viaggiatori*, Italian translation of *Travel*, 417.
[60] James Howell, *Ecclesiastical Affairs*, III (London, 1685); quoted in Burke, *Languages and Communities*, 86.

those regions, and the fact that people there who knew Latin spoke it with difficulty, it was Italian that had initially spread among the elites in the capitals, and among merchants and mariners in the city-ports.[61]

We have already seen that as late as 1673, Giovanni Torriano, the author of the successful *Introduction to the Italian Tongue*, specified in the book's subtitle that the dialogues were 'most useful for such as desire the speaking part, and intend to travel into Italy, or the Levant' (see Chapter 3). Fifty years earlier, Thomas Coryat arrived in Constantinople in 1613 with the intention of visiting the Sultan (officially called by the Italian honorific *Gran Signor*), and was able to use his Italian all the way from Italy to the capital of the Ottoman Empire, taking in stopovers in North Africa and the Levant, including Aleppo.[62] The Italian-based lingua franca (with elements of Turkish, Arabic and Greek), spoken in that region well into the seventeenth century, is described by James Howell in his *Instructions for Forreigne Travell* (1642):

There is alſo a Mongrell *Dialect* compoſed of *Italian* and *French*, and ſome *Spaniſh* words are alſo in it, which they call *Franco*, that is uſed in many of the *Iſlands* of the *Ægean Sea*, and reacheth as farre as *Constantinople*, and *Natolie*, and ſome places in *Afrique*, and it is the ordinary ſpeech of Commerce 'twixt *Christians, Jeewes, Turkes, and Greeks* in the Levant.[63]

In James Howell's explanation of the spread of this pidgin, one can almost identify Coryat's itinerary to the capital of the Ottoman Empire. Some years ago a linguist of Maltese origin, Joseph Cremona, demonstrated that Italian was also 'the chief diplomatic language between Europeans and Turks in the whole of the vast Ottoman Empire for much of the sixteenth century, the whole of the seventeenth and most of the eighteenth'.[64] Algiers and Tunis were extremely active commercially in the seventeenth century, attracting merchants from most European nations, especially France, England and the Low Countries. Cremona, who studied the archives of the chanceries of the two North African cities, found that a high variety of Italian was always used as a lingua franca between linguistically different commercial partners, while French was used only when all the signatories to a contract were French. However, a switch took place at some point: 'It is only when we reach the end of the seventeenth century, after about 1690, that the proportion of French and Italian documents is reversed.'[65]

---

[61] Bates, *Touring in 1600*, 48.
[62] R. E. Pritchard, *Odd Tom Coryate, The English Marco Polo* (Stroud, 2004), 194.
[63] Howell, *Instructions*, 53.
[64] Joseph Cremona, 'Italian-Based Lingua Francas around the Mediterranean', in Anna Laura Lepschy and Arturo Tosi (eds.), *Multilingualism in Italy, Past and Present* (Oxford, 2002), 26.
[65] Ibid., 27.

As for the nature of the low variety of Italian, called the *lingua franca* or *franco* by Cremona[66] and *franco piccolo* by Bates,[67] until recently the predominant view was that it was a hybrid tongue. But it was so heavily based on Italian that most foreigners found the two languages almost indistinguishable. For example, Coryat and Hakluyt did not seem aware of the difference when they encountered it in the Levant. However, the Italian traveller Pietro Della Valle found it was not difficult to tell them apart – of course, he was a native speaker of Italian, and also a linguist with a fine ear for languages.[68] Having acquired a good knowledge of Turkish and a little Arabic while in Constantinople, Della Valle was also aware that there was more than one version of Italian spoken around the Mediterranean.[69]

According to Cremona, different versions of a Mediterranean lingua franca fell between two poles: one was Tuscan-based Italian, a language used for writing, with 'substantial numbers of Gallicisms and other -isms and generally including many Italian dialect features'.[70] This mixed variety was used by the consulates and chanceries, and it enabled merchants and businessmen to understand each other when speaking or writing. At the other end of the spectrum, there was a pidgin, also based on spoken Italian, which had evolved from Venetian and Genoese and even Tuscan at different times. It was often called *Sabir* (from Italian *sapere* 'to know' [to speak and understand]), and it enabled interlocutors to communicate when they had no language in common.[71] This was the simplest manifestation of 'foreigners' Italian', used by illiterate people so never written down, and it is sometimes considered a distinct linguistic entity. Jocelyne Dakblia, who studied its main features, comments: 'La pauvreté de la langue assurait sa richesse fonctionelle, son caractère élémentaire et neutre ou neutralisé qui assurait l'efficace de ce parler'. ['The poverty of the language ensured its functional richness, its elementary neutral or neutralised character guaranteed the efficacy of this lingo.'][72] Some contemporary French and Italian playwrights placed this language in the mouths of their Turkish, Arab or Levantine characters for comic effect. One was Molière, and this dialogue from *Le bourgeois géntilhomme* (Act iv, scene v)[73] is a nice illustration of such a conversation:

---

[66] Ibid., 25.   [67] Bates, *Touring in 1600*, 50.   [68] Ibid.
[69] Cremona, 'Italian-Based Lingua Francas', 25–6.   [70] Ibid., 28.
[71] The most comprehensive study is Guido Cifoletti's *La lingua franca mediterranea* (Padua, 1989), which includes a dictionary, a survey of exemplary passages of various natures and a section of literary texts.
[72] Jocelyne Dakhlia, 'La langue franque, langue du marchand en Mediterranée?', in Gilbert Buti, Michèle Janin-Thivosand Olivier Raveux, *Langue et langages du commerce en Méditerranée et en Europe à l'époque moderne* (Aix-en-Provence, 2013), 161.
[73] Being a kind of simplified Italian, its nouns had no inflections and verbs were reduced to their infinitives. Molière, *Le bourgeois gentilhomme*, Act. IV, scene X, Maurice A. Gerothwohl (ed.) (London, 1902), 63.

Le Mufti
Se ti sabir,
Ti respondir;
Se non sabir,
Tazir, tazir.

Mi star Mufti:
Ti qui star ti?
Non intendir:
Tazir, tazir.

While diverse regions of the Levant introduced elements of Turkish and Arabic into the language, in North Africa *Sabir* progressively evolved by incorporating elements from Occitan, Catalan, and above all Spanish.[74] It is quite likely that the rare European travellers to the Levant, such as Coryat and Hakluyt, heard both the lower and the higher registers of this contact variety and simply referred to it all as 'Italian', *tout court*. However, John Campbell, who wrote *The Travels and Adventures of Edward Brown*, when describing a trip in the province of Alexandria, Egypt, makes specific mention of a mixed language spoken by the local guides with foreign visitors:

The Adventure was this: When I had the Occasion to go abroad, I hired always the Ass of an old Arab or, as they are called there, Bedouin, who spoke a sort of Lingua franca and with whom I could, though not without some Difficulty, converse.[75]

In the sixteenth century, Castilian too became an international language. Books written in Castilian or translations from that language were in wide circulation, not only in Italy – which was largely under Spanish rule – but also in France, the Low Countries and England. Spanish literature was greatly admired, and the reputation of some of Spain's scholars and political leaders spanned the Continent, while Spanish arts and politics dominated spirituality during the country's Golden Age. But the waning of Spanish intellectual hegemony in Europe accompanied, if it did not precede, the decline of Spanish military might, and Castilian was never widely used as a supranational language outside Spain's occupied territories.[76]

German experienced a similar destiny, in that it was widely studied and commonly spoken by the educated elites in eastern Europe, especially in the first half of the eighteenth century.[77] But its diffusion throughout that region

---

[74] See Alan D. Corré (ed.), *A Glossary of Lingua Franca* (5th ed.) (Milwaukee WI, 2005), www .uwm.edu-corre/franca/go.html (accessed 10 December, 2006); see especially Mikael Parkvall, 'Forward', unpaginated.

[75] John Campbell, *The Travels and Adventures of Edward Brown* (London, 1739), 209. However, Pine-Coffin classifies this work as 'a fiction, purporting to be an autobiography', *British and American Travel*, 107.

[76] Jocelyn Nigel Hillgarth, *The Mirror of Spain, 1500–1700: The Formation of a Myth* (Ann Arbor, 2000), 4.

[77] Black, *The British Abroad*, 80.

was never sufficient to create the conditions for it to become a supranational lingua franca. That was because Latin was preferred in the multilingual Habsburg Empire as being politically neutral, and indeed for that reason it remained the official language of Hungary as late as 1844.[78] However, the cultural and political impetus for using French also spread through that part of Europe, including to the great courts of Austria, Bohemia and Poland, which diffused the fashion of the new lingua franca across the region.

English had no place in the competition for a European lingua franca. The language was not widely studied on the Continent during the early modern period, and less so in France than in Italy. Thomas Coryat, who was a keen chronicler of the languages spoken by travellers on the road, was impressed by an Irishman, a Franciscan friar on his way from Amiens to Paris: this friar 'spake passing good English', enabling them to have a conversation on 'politique and state matters of England'.[79] For most of the seventeenth and eighteenth centuries, English spoken outside England was relegated to use by the community of English students, traders and businessmen. The Loire Valley was the main enclave of the language in France, and some local people were fluent enough in English to be able to provide competitive services to these travellers. In Italy, the city of Leghorn was known to be awash with Englishmen using the port to ship their purchases of artwork and books back to England. Edward Wright, who was in Leghorn in 1722–22, reported: 'There are so many English always there and so many of our merchant ships use that port, that our language is understood by many natives of that place; so that even in walking along the streets, one should not speak that in English, which he would not care to have a Livornine hear.'[80] This traffic must have had quite a linguistic impact on the city; in a grammar book written by Pleunus, dated 1702, one of the dialogues includes the sentence 'Everyone speaks English at Leghorn.'[81]

Although English could not rival French as a language spoken in European salons amongst the local aristocracy, its use did spread once the community of English expatriates grew in Italy, particularly after the Napoleonic wars. These Englishmen entertained each other with *conversazioni*, balls and even tea parties *à l'Angloise*.[82] Henry Matthews reported in 1817:

The English abound so much in Florence, that a traveller has little occasion for any other language. At all the hotels, there is some one connected with the house that can speak

---

[78] Tóth, *Literacy and Written Culture*, 131.

[79] Coryat, *Crudities,* I, 168. After the conquest of Ireland by the Tudor dynasty and the imposition of English law, language and culture, Irish monolingualism was confined to the less-educated classes. The friar that Coryat met was obviously a well-educated man, given the nature of their conversation.

[80] Wright, *Some Observations,* II, 374.

[81] Quoted in Pizzoli, *Le grammatiche di italiano*, 64 n.89.

[82] Reported in Trease, *The Grand Tour*, 203.

English. English shops abound with all sorts of knick-knacks, from Reading sauce to Woodstock gloves; and the last new novels stare you in the face at the libraries.[83]

By the first quarter of the nineteenth century, the beau monde in Italy spoke French and English in the salons, especially in Rome and in Florence. While the success of French in Rome was due to the attitude of the local aristocracies, who were keen to pass themselves off as international, the flourishing of English in Florence was due to the reluctance of most émigrés to learn Italian.[84]

---

[83] Matthews, *The Diary of an Invalid*, 39–40.

[84] The lifestyle and the romantic vision of Italy among the British settlers in Tuscany towards the end of the Grand Tour are examined by Hamilton in *Paradise of Exiles*, and by Sweet in her more recent and insightful *Cities and the Grand Tour*, especially 65–98.

Part III

Contrasts and Collisions

The Latin Family Tree

How the decline of Latin could affect the formation of the new vernaculars became one of the favourite topoi after the Renaissance. Scholars had long been aware that classical Latin differed from its regional and social offshoots and even its original and most elegant variant – Ciceronian Latin – was limited in distribution. As for the vernaculars, the dominant belief during the Renaissance was that the language of Italy was the natural progeny of Latin. This was not only an academic theory: it was also a popular opinion based on the first-hand testimony of many travellers as reported even in the English translation of the Wycliffe Bible (1382–95):

And Austin [St Augustine], and more Latins expounded the bible, for many parts, in Latin, to Latin men, among which they dwelt, and Latin was a common language to their people about Rome and beyond, and on this half, as English is common language to our people, and yet this day the common people in Italy speak Latin corrupt, as true men say, that have been in Italy.[1]

If the decline of Latin generated its numerous varieties, the direct cause was the process of deterioration initiated by contact with populations from outside Latinised Europe. One author, Thomas Campion, who was not a linguist but a literary theorist and a poet, explained in the opening of his *Observations in the Art of English Poesy* (1602) that once the classical language had lost its superior qualities, these were recouped through the efforts of poets writing in Italian, the only language that was Latin's direct descendant:

Learning, after the declining of the Romaine Empire and the pollution of their language through the conquest of the *Barbarians*, lay most pitifully deformed ... In those lack-learning times, and in barbarised *Italy*, began that vulgar and easie kind of Poesie which is now in use throughout most parts of Christendome, which we abusively call Rime, and Meeter, of *Rithmus* and *Metrum*, of which I will now discourse.[2]

---

[1] Reported in Gamberini, *Lo studio dell'italiano*, 21.
[2] Thomas Campion, *Observations in the Art of English Poesie* (London, 1602), in G. Gregory Smith (ed.), *Elizabethan Critical Essays*, 2 vols. (Oxford, 1904), II, 329.

A change in perspective was marked by Edward Brerewood in his book *Enquiries Touching the Diversity of Languages and Religions Through the Cheife Parts of the World* (1614), which ran to five editions in English, in addition to two translations into French and two more into Latin. The author did not accept the notion that the vernaculars derived from a deteriorated version of Latin but saw them instead as having evolved from pre-existing languages that Latin had already come into contact with. A similar view was adopted by James Howell in his *Instructions*, where he put forward the idea that the Latin language spread widely but that it absorbed rather than eliminated the local languages. James Howell, who travelled widely on the Continent as a tutor and as a member of diplomatic delegations, acquired a deep knowledge of many countries from Spain to Denmark and became fluent in many modern languages. His *Instructions for Forreine Travell* (1647) is a small book that pays great attention to the subject of language diversity. In the section about the origin and relationships of the languages he encountered on his continental journeys, Howell summarises the Latin family tree:

> It is all very behooffull, that he have a passable understanding of the *Latine* tongue, whereof the *Italian*, the *Spaniſh* and the *French*, are but as it were of the family Tree; they are but *Dialects* or *Daughters*, and having gain'd the good will of the *Mother*, he will quick prevayle with the *Daughters*.[3]

Howell's description is consistent with the common seventeenth-century perception found along the Grand Tour itinerary that the decline of Latin led to the rise of modern vernaculars. This view utilised notions of Latin's superiority and the subsequent damage to its vitality. Many academic and pedagogic materials presented such opinions couched in terminology such as purity vs. corruption, perfection vs. decadence, congruous vs. polluted, noble vs. barbarous, which set the tone of the argument for several generations. Discussions about the Romance language family were based on the belief that Latin's decay was at the root of the corrupt nature of its vernaculars. This idea emerged during the Renaissance and shaped opinion until the end of the eighteenth century. Other related themes were the corruption of Latin through contact with other languages, the loss of its plain, clear, superior forms, its denaturalisation once it became polluted by foreign idioms and spoken with barbarous diction, and the inferiority of the new vernaculars.[4]

---

[3] Howell, *Instructions*, 18.

[4] The sociolinguist James Milroy explains: 'Histories of a language and language family trees become ... part of the process of legitimisation. If a language can be shown to possess a known history, this strengthens the sense of lawfulness of a language,' 'Sociolinguistics and ideologies in language history', in M. Hernández-Campoy and J. Camilo Conde-Silvestre (eds.), 571–84.

According to Howell, the relationship of the Romance languages to Latin stems from the stronger presence of Roman colonies in what eventually became the most Romanised parts of Europe, i.e. Italy, France and Spain:

But one may juſtly aſke why the *Latine tongue* could receive no growth at all amongſt the *Brittaines*, who were ſo many hundred years under the *Roman* government, and ſome of the *Emperors* living and dying amongſt them? To this it may bee anſwered, that in *Brittaine* we reade of no more than *foure* colonies that were ever planted; but in *Spaine* there were 29, and in *France* 26.[5]

Views about the relationship of Latin to modern vernaculars showed a great deal of continuity throughout the seventeenth century: they all stressed the decay of the classical language, its corruption by barbarian populations and changes causing this loss of purity. But at the turn of the century, the causes of these changes and the outcomes of these mutations came to be presented in a more positive light. If Latin was the superior mother tongue of modern vernaculars, it had itself developed from other tongues. These contributed to the locally diversified but still flourishing Latin varieties, and this linguistic impact from outside Europe helped shape and enrich the new vernaculars. The work of William Wotton, in his *Reflections Upon Ancient and Modern Learning* (1694), expounds a mitigated position in the dispute between the purity of the classical language and the imperfection of vernaculars:

Modem *Tuscan* with the Ancient *Latin*: where, though their affinity is visible at first Sight in every Sentence, yet one sees that that derived Language actually has a Sweetness and Tunableness in its Composition that could not be derived from its Parent since nothing can impart that to another which it has not it self. And it shows likewise, that a Barbarous People, as the *Italians* were when mingled with the *Goths* and *Lombards*, may, without knowing or minding Grammatical Analogy, form a Language so very musical that no Art can mend it.[6]

Broadly speaking, discussions on the origin, rise and relationships of modern vernaculars can be divided into three phases.[7] The first phase began during the Renaissance, when humanists attributed to Italian the privileged position of being a model language that had developed from Latin and inherited most of its qualities. The second phase emerged at the end of the seventeenth century and became dominant for most of the following century; all the vernaculars were seen at this time as having an equal number of limitations and fine qualities. These two phases covered most of the early modern period and included the

---

[5] Howell, *Instructions*, 55.
[6] William Wotton, *Reflections Upon Ancient and Modern Learning* (London, 1705), 24–5.
[7] Richard Foster Jones, *The Triumph of the English Language* (Stanford, 1953). Richard J. Watts and Peter Trudgill in the 'Introduction' to their edited book *Alternative Histories of English* (London, 2002) make the important point that 'the history of English leads novices in the field to the belief that a history of English is equivalent to a history of the standard language', 1–3.

best part of the Grand Tour. Indeed, some Grand Tourists must have been aware of the dialectal fragmentation of the popular Latin spoken in medieval times as many travellers resorted to describing the vernaculars using vivid but pejorative images, which were not very dissimilar to the metaphors expressed by the authors quoted above. It is only during the third phase, in the late eighteenth century, that some of the major prejudices disappeared in the wake of new theories that were critical of purism, among which Melchiorre Cesarotti's position was the most innovative.[8]

Varieties, Dialects and Minority Languages

One linguistic border no Englishman could ignore lay between England and the Continent. In the recollections of many Grand Tourists, the stormy waters of the Channel gave a premonition of the linguistic and cultural shock waiting for them on the other side. As one Englishman put it as soon as he disembarked in Calais in 1775: 'the difference of dress, dialect, manners and persons struck us exceedingly'.[9] Another conspicuous language change occurred between major cities in France and especially in Italy. For the best part of the Grand Tour, Switzerland was not included in the itinerary, and the only reason for going near the Alps was to get to the other side as quickly as possible, which explains why there were few remarks about the various languages encountered there. On the whole, when language transitions were smooth and not marked by sizeable geographical boundaries such as bodies of water or mountains, they were less noticeable and not worthy of remark. But there were a number of travellers with a fine ear for the distinctive features of local speech who were interested in the linguistic variations encountered during a journey across gentler countryside. Certainly, even for those without a fine ear for distinctions, many travelling from Italy northwards into Germany were impressed by the boundary between Italian- and German-speaking communities that cut right across the mountainous city of Trent, made famous by the Council that condemned the Protestants (1545–63). This was a matter of great surprise for a widely travelled foreigner like the English physician

---

[8] Cesarotti based his theory on principles that were 'almost contrary to the dominant ones' ('quasi direttamente opposte alle precedenti'). For him no language was pure, perfect or even elegant or barbarous; all languages are born from uncontrollable forces, but never generated by private or public authorities; and no language is spoken uniformly within a nation, where 'i colti, i nobili hanno . . . un dialetto diverso da quello del volgo' ('the learned people and upper-classes have a dialect different from that of the common people').Melchiorre Cesarotti, *Saggio sopra la lingua italiana* (1785); reprinted in Emilio Biagi (ed.), *Dal Muratori al Cesarotti* (Milan/ Naples, 1960), 306.

[9] Quoted in Black, *The British Abroad*, 17.

Edward Browne, as it was for the Italian Bernardo Bizoni, who started his journey from Rome some fifty years earlier in 1606.[10]

In the many areas visited along national borders, tourists sometimes reported that bilingualism was a widespread phenomenon, and some were surprised to note that at times this involved language mixing while at other times it did not. The few travellers who had the opportunity to investigate the domains of use of each language discovered that they were socially marked, especially in urban centres, and this, too, was a matter of surprise. For example, Marquis Malaspina, while journeying from Italy to France in 1786, stopped in the city of Turin, where he heard the urban nobility speaking French and Italian, although both 'malparlato' ['badly spoken'], while the common people used a dialect that was 'duro e villanesco' ['hard and rustic'] called *giargone*[11] (from the Latin onomatopoeic root *garg*, designating the throat and nearby organs, and by extension their function[12]). Other tourists reported similar situations of language contact in frontier areas. For example, on his journey from Bologna to Paris, Sebastiano Locatelli observed that when in Asti, a city some 50 kilometres from Turin, he began to hear a significant amount of French used by the gentry and townspeople alongside an Italian dialect that was spoken by the lower classes. On his return journey to Italy via a different route through Simplon, Locatelli was less surprised to note that the local variety of French used in the Swiss mountains south of Brig was influenced by Italian pronunciation, just like in the Savoy region which he had crossed on his way out.[13]

Travellers' observations about linguistic transitions between regions or over frontiers were often reported either because of their practical implications or as a source of surprise. Faced with an unexpected change of language before reaching a frontier, or with sudden exposure to a mixture or multitude of languages, the reaction was proportionate to the traveller's curiosity and spirit of enquiry. Thomas Coryat wrote of his genuine astonishment at the greatly unexpected linguistic landscape he encountered when he walked into St Mark's Square, Venice. In the early seventeenth century, Venice had the most multiethnic and multilingual concentration of people of Europe and as soon as the Englishman set foot in the famous square, he felt overwhelmed: 'Here you may both see all manner of fashions of attire, and heare all the languages of Christendome, besides those that are spoken by the English barbarous Ethnickes.'[14] Having heard amongst the number of unfamiliar and exotic tongues one he thought he recognised, the polyglot Coryat could not turn down the opportunity to test his own competence, acquired through the study

---

[10] Browne, *A Brief Account,* and Bernardo Bizoni, *Europa Milleseicentosei, Diario di viaggio di Bernardo Bizoni*, in Anna Banti (ed.) (Milan, 1942), are both quoted in Mączak, *Travel*, 110.
[11] Malaspina is quoted in D'Ancona, 'Francia e Italia nel 1786', 277.
[12] The etymology of 'jargon' is from the *Trésor de la Langue Française Informatisé.*
[13] Locatelli, *Viaggio di Francia*, 283.   [14] Coryat, *Crudities*, I, 314.

of classical languages, by holding a conversation with a speaker of modern Greek: 'He spake the purest and elegantest naturall Greeke that ever I heard, insomuch that his phrase came something neere to that of Isocrates, and his pronunciation was so plausible, that any man which was skillfull in the Greeke tongue, might easily understand him.'[15] Thomas Coryat was a classical scholar and a good linguist but the linguistic toolkit of most travellers typically included adjectives with loaded connotations, such as *pure, correct* and *refined*, or their antitheses *bastard, corrupt* and *barbarous*. Indeed, a number of texts written by travellers with references to language diversity contain comments on rustic speech, simply because this was the first type language they came across during most of their journey. But denigration of rural speech was less typical of humanist travellers in the early modern period than of the authors who wrote later travel accounts.

Michel de Montaigne, who held the belief that rural speech was more conservative and preserved archaic and pure forms of the language 'since the peasants converse less with foreigners', was not unusual among scholars in the sixteenth century, and sometimes this belief survived until the seventeenth as Peter Burke states,[16] quoting a variety of sources including the Italian Vincenzio Borghini, the Swede Georg Stiernhielm and the German Gottfried Wilhelm Leibniz . More typical of the Grand Tour experience was the journey undertaken by Sebastiano Locatelli, who travelled almost a century later with a party of friends. While in France, it seemed quite natural for them to make the observation that the rustic language of a peasant girl contrasted so much with her gentle appearances that 'quando apriva la bocca per parlare si faceva riconoscere contadina' ['when she opened her mouth to speak she showed she was a countrywoman'].[17]

While the old academic belief suggested that social isolation was reflected in the purity of language, by contrast a view which was common among later tourists was that the linguistic contamination found in linguistic enclaves derived from the influence of one or more dominant languages which had corrupted the local tongue. This reversed the notion of remoteness as a factor leading to archaic purity, and indeed a noticeable curiosity developed among Grand Tourists about the similarities shown by speech communities oppressed by neighbouring languages. After Edward Lhuyd's visit to Brittany, he offered interesting observations on the state of the Armorican (Breton) language: 'The Cornish is much more corruptly spoken than the Armorican, as being confin'd to half a score parishes towards the Land's End; whereas Armorican is the common language of a country almost as large as Wales.' As for intelligibility between these languages, he explains in another piece of correspondence:

---

[15] Ibid., I, 367.   [16] Burke, *Languages and Communities*, 23.
[17] Locatelli, *Viaggio di Francia*, 140.

'Their Language is much the same with the Cornish; and both so near to the Dialect of South Wales: that in a months time at farthest a Welshman may understand their writings; but as to the speaking part their affinity creates some confusion.' Edward Lhuyd was a Welshman and, as a keen linguist interested in social varieties of language, he had something to say about the speech of ordinary citizens, the dialect of the lower classes, and their stigmatisation: '[Breton] Tis spoken at least for a Hundred miles, and their Gentry and Merchants speak it in their Great Towns; but much more corruptly than ours in N. Wales.' He also admitted that in Brittany the minority language was losing ground to French: 'they seem to have been much more discourag'd by the Mounsieur's jeering them than those of sense and Education are among us'.[18]

Lhuyd's observations, sharpened by his own Welsh-English bilingual perspective, were not typical. Most travellers in the seventeenth century, even if curious about variations in the great and small languages they came across, were not particularly interested in other social groups nor very curious about the diversity found within the same speech community. Their remarks usually focused on vocabulary, dialects and accent in order to either note connections to a particular language family or to justify problems of comprehension. It was later, in the eighteenth century, that some highly motivated travellers became more interested in local varieties and regional dialects. Their curiosity was partly stimulated by the new taste for comedies rich in social satire, which were especially popular in Italy, where the idiosyncrasies of spoken varieties were maximised to achieve comical effects. The playwright Carlo Goldoni, who was born and brought up in Venice, piloted this naturalistic form of theatre. Of course, by the eighteenth century the Italian city in the lagoon was less multilingual than in the previous century but there were still many varieties of the local Venetian language spoken by the natives with a wide range of social variation. As the mobility of tourists greatly increased during the heyday of the Grand Tour, someone realised that the rich flavour of life in the 'glittering jewel in the showcase of eighteenth-century Europe' could not be complete without a description of its complex linguistic diversity. The *1793 Guide de l'Italie*, a kind of Michelin Guide of the time published in French by Hans Ottokar Reichard, included a short attempt to explain the situation to the modern tourist:

Le *Vernacolo Veneziano* eſt le langage des affaires, celui de la ſociété, quelquefois celui des Muſes. Mais un *Illuſtriſſimo* parle tout autrement que ſon *Lacchè*; et une *Zentil Donna*, n'a pas le même ſtyle que ſes *Maſſare*, ſervantes inférieures aux *cameriere*. Le vénetien du barreau n'eſt pas celui des merchands, et les *Gondolieri* ont auſſi leur idiome à part, ainſi que les artiſans.[19]

---

[18] All three quotations from Lough, *France Observed*, 15.
[19] Reichard, *Guide de l'Italie*, section X5, unpaginated.

[The Venetian Vernacular is the language of business, of social interaction, and sometimes of literary accomplishment. But a distinguished gentleman speaks completely
differently from his servant; and a lady of distinction does not perform in the same style
as her housekeepers, servants of lower rank than chambermaids. The Venetian of
a barrister is not the same as that of a merchant, and the gondoliers have their own
jargon, like the artisans.]

Impressions of Languages and Their Speakers

Familiarity with grammars and textbooks discussing the Latin language family
certainly shaped the perceptions of many travellers at home and informed their
observations about linguistic diversity abroad. However, preconceptions
entrenched in widespread beliefs are not easy to shake off, and the resistance
met by the relativism of innovative linguists like Cesarotti is no exception. The
anti-purism trend did not immediately change the views of Grand Tourists,
many of whom continued to comment on the linguistic diversity of nation states
and the properties of their languages, with or without reference to their distance
from Latin. One case in point is the Anglo-Irish Catholic priest John Chetwode
Eustace, who wrote *A Tour Through Italy* in 1813. This was one of the most
widely read books about the Grand Tour, reaching its seventh edition by 1841
but it still included the conventional wisdom that Latin's decay was the origin
of the inferiority of modern languages. His conclusion reflected the typical
vision of the life cycle of Latin, whereby purity is associated with integrity, and
corruption with language contamination:

Its decline was as rapid as its progress. The same century may be said to have witnessed
its perfection and its decay. The causes that produced this decay continued to operate
during ten or even twelve centuries with increasing activity, during which Latin was first
corrupted, and then repolished and softened into modern Italian.[20]

The inclination to attribute the specific properties of different languages to the
nature of its speakers was well rooted in the tradition of European thinking. At
first, it emerged as admiration for the superiority of classical languages, then it
evolved into a competitive comparison between the modern vernaculars, which
was gradually overlaid with the stereotypical image of their nations. The two
views spread simultaneously among the general public and specialists alike and
set into motion a debate rich with national variations. Many contemporary
popular clichés about language belong to the tradition of the *blason*, defined by
Burke as 'the genre in which one group – more or less playfully – insults
others'.[21] Eustace's book, which remained popular for as long as fifty years at

---

[20] John Chetwode Eustace, *A Classical Tour Through Italy* (London, 1813; 7th ed. 1841), 3 vols.,
      III, 244.
[21] Burke, *Languages and Communities*, 29.

the end of the Grand Tour, is a good example of an endorsement of the unchallenged belief that the properties of classical languages reflected the superiority of their civilisations:

the language of the ancient Romans is a manly and majestic dialect, full, expressive, and sonorous, and well adapted to the genius and the dignity of a magnanimous and imperial people. Inferior in some respects, but in the qualities just mentioned superior to Greek, it corresponded well with its object, and was the vehicle, first of the edicts of the conquerors, and then of jurisprudence, philosophy, and the sciences in general; that is, it became the grand instrument of civilisation, the universal language, and the parent of all the more refined dialects of Europe.[22]

Eustace focused his comments on the idiosyncrasies of the major languages in relation to the national characters of their speakers, although he was careful to present them using the passive impersonal: 'and *it has* consequently *been remarked* [my emphasis] that Italian is soft and musical; Spanish, stately; French, voluble; German, rough; and English short and pithy'.[23] The idea that the greatness of ancient languages was rooted in the achievements of classical civilisations originated in the Renaissance, but when this concept was applied to modern languages, it generated a whole range of stereotypes and clichés. Burke quotes the humanist Giovanni Pontano, who claimed that 'Boastful speech delights the Spaniards, colorful and complicated language the Greeks; the conversation of the Romans was grave, that of the Spartans brief and rough, of the Athenians fulsome and stilted, of the Carthaginians and Africans shrewd and dry.'[24] Two hundred years on, Diderot still believed that the rhetorical qualities of Italian (and English) were the same as those of classical languages – 'pour persuader, émouvoir et tromper' – while the more rational properties of French were better suited 'pour instruire, éclarer et convaincre'.[25] While many Europeans felt the close connection between Latin and Italian, the strikingly different flavour of the two languages could not be better represented than by these remarks in Goethe's autobiography:

My father taught my sister Italian in the same room in which I had to commit Cellarius to memory. As I was soon ready with my task, and was yet obliged to sit quiet, I listened with my book before me, and very readily caught the Italian, which struck me as an *agreeable softening* of Latin. [my emphasis; other translations give 'amusing variation'][26]

The three centuries of the Grand Tour in early modern Europe provided a fertile field for drawing generalisations about some of the most diverse features of languages: from their complexity for learners to their effectiveness in different

---

[22] Eustace, *A Classical Tour,* II, 434.   [23] Ibid.
[24] Burke, *Languages and Communities,* 26–7.   [25] Quoted in Folena, *L'italiano in Europa,* 12.
[26] Johann Wolfgang von Goethe, *The Auto-biography of Goethe. Truth and Poetry: From My Own Life,* translated by John Oxenford (London, 1848), 21.

functions, from their unique resources in specific domains to their qualities of harmony and musicality. Since these properties were associated with perceptions about national characteristics that were widespread at the time, the clichés about languages closely reflected common stereotypes about these nations. In the best tradition of the *blasons*, the variety of anecdotes they generated tell us more about how people viewed other nations than about how the languages functioned.

Indeed, during the best part of the Grand Tour, folk and elite perceptions about languages and their speakers mingled together. When humanists began to praise the language that their own works were written in, the aim was to demonstrate the qualities of their native vernacular – it was as good as Latin or Greek, if not better – and occasionally to play down the merits of other languages.

At the beginning of the seventeenth century, the continuity between Greek, Latin and Italian was under attack, the image of the Italian language began to change and the competition between French and Spanish acquired a sharper edge. The Spaniard Carlos García said that 'the French generally speak much and loudly, while the Spaniards always speak little and low'.[27] In the Golden Age another Spaniard, Pedro Mexia, declared that 'Castillian does not need to concede the advantage to any other language,'[28] contrasting it with Italian and French, the only two other serious rival languages. James Howell, the Anglo-Welsh writer with much experience of France and Spain, reinforced this view, adding some details in his meticulous style:

Go to their Speech, the one Speakes oft, the other feldome; the one Fast, the other flowly; the one mangleth, cuts off, and eates many Letters, the other pronaunceth all; the one contracts and enchaines his words, and fpeakes prefsingly and fhort, the other delights in long breathed Accents, which he prolates with fuch paufes, that before he be at the period of his Sentences, one might reach a Second thought: The ones Mind and Tongue go commonly together (and the firft comes fometimes in the arreare) the others Tongue comes flagging a fourlong after his mind in fuch a diftance, that they feldome or never meet and juftle one another.[29]

Some of the clichés mentioned by travellers were more explicit about the merits and defects of specific languages, while other anecdotes were concerned more with the character of their speakers. A popular story, which is still going strong today, concerns Charles V, the sovereign whose empire was one 'on which the sun never sets', claiming that 'he spoke Spanish with his God, Italian to courtiers, French to his ladies, and German to his horse'[30]. The French Jesuit writer

[27] Burke, *Languages and Communities*, 27.   [28] Ibid., 68.   [29] Howell, *Instructions*, 33.
[30] Harald Weinrich, in 'Sprachanekdoten um Karl V', identifies the earliest version of this anecdote in 1601, written in *De locutione* by Girolamo Fabrizi d'Acquapendente, and traces variants in France, Germany, England and Russia. On the topic of the proverbial multilingualism of the emperor, Weinrich reconstructed that he had Spanish as a native language, some

Dominique Bouhours famously expanded this *blason* to include non-European languages: 'Les Chinois, et presque tous les peuples de l'Asie, chantent; les Allemands râlent; les Espagnols déclament; les Italiens soupirent; les Anglais sifflent. Il n'y a proprement que les Français qui parlent. ['The Chinese, and almost all people from Asia, sing; the Germans bray; the Spaniards declaim, the Italian sigh, the English whistle. There is no one but the French who speak'].[31] Another version of the same anecdote was presented by Roger de Rabutin, Comte de Bussy: 'l'Allemand hurle, l'Anglois pleure, le François chante, l'Italien joue la farce et l'Espagnol parle' ['The Germans shout, the English cry, the French sing, the Italians play the buffoon and the Spaniards speak.'][32] It is interesting that the two last versions differ in the stereotype for Italians: in one they 'sigh' while in the other they 'play the buffoon'. The latter cliché is certainly linked to the *Commedia dell'arte* in the seventeenth century, when European indoor theatres and market squares were invaded by troupes of Italian actors, eliciting comments such as that of the musicologist François Raguenet: 'Car les Italiens naissent tous comédiens . . . et leurs Bouffons valent ce que nous avons jamais vu de meilleur, en ce genre, sur nos théâtres' ['For Italians are all born comedians . . . and their buffoons are better than anything of the kind we have seen in our theatres.'][33]

During the seventeenth century, the political power and cultural prominence of *grand siècle* France became very influential everywhere, preparing the way for the unrivalled dominance of the French language in Europe over the other *langues de culture* – English, Spanish and Italian. Voltaire praised French 'par la marche naturelle de toutes ses constructions, et aussi par sa prosodie, est plus proper qu'aucune autre (langue à la conversation)' ['The natural flow of its phrasing, along with its prosody, makes it more suited than any other (language of conversation).'] But the philosopher did not disdain the operatic qualities of Italian: 'l'italien, par des voyelles beaucoup plus répétées, sert peut-être encore mieux la musique efféminée' ['Italian, with its much more frequent vowels, is perhaps more suited to effeminate music.'][34]

Following the Encyclopaedists, the relationship between the *génie de la langue* and the *caractère de la nation* led to more rational distinctions being drawn between languages, characterised by an *ordo naturalis* and an *ordo artificialis.* The former relied on logical coordination to convey rational arguments; the latter allowed flexible constructions more suitable for general impressions.[35] Voltaire,

Italian but not enough to give a speech, French as the language of his court, while he confused German with Flemish and his Latin if any, was poor; *Wege der Sprachkultur*, 181–92.
[31] Quoted in Folena, *L'italiano in Europa*, 221–2.   [32] Ibid., 222–3.   [33] Ibid., 225.
[34] Ibid., 223.
[35] The misconception that the syntax of French closely matches the order of natural logic has been recently discussed and challenged by Antony Lodge in 'French is a logical language', in Laurie Bauer and Peter Trudgill (eds.), *Language Myths* (New York, 1998), 23–31.

who was very aware of the imperfection of all languages, because of their diverse nature, often referred to the disadvantages of French and the advantages of Italian and English: 'Quelle profusion d'images chez les Anglais et chez les Italiens! Mais ils sont libres, ils font de leur langue tout ce qu'ils veulent' ['The English and Italians have such an abundance of images! But they are at liberty to do what they want with their language'].[36] However, as confirmation of the volatile nature of all stereotypes, the musical quality of Italian, which sounded so *plaisante* to most ears in the eighteenth century (also called the *siècle galant et libertin*), seemed quite unattractive to others. This was the case for the French journalist Antoine Rivarol, whose *Universalité de la langue française* (1786) became famous for the declaration that 'ce qui n'est pas clair n'est pas français' ['If it is not clear it is not French'], while reserving for Italian the comment that it was 'presque insupportable dans une bouche virile' ['barely tolerable when spoken by a man'].[37]

Diversity and Patois in France

Like most states that were composite entities in early modern Europe, France's linguistic diversity was conspicuous and consisted of dialects that were quite different from *le français littéraire et officiel* as well as a number of minority languages, including sister languages of French, and unrelated languages that had survived in part due to their isolation. Today we can say that the coexistence of French, its dialects and minority languages was rooted in the history of France. But during the period under consideration, perceptions of linguistic heterogeneity are a challenge to interpret for two reasons. One is the inconsistent use of terminology to classify a complex linguistic heterogeneity; the second is that notions such as language, dialect and accent carried very different connotations from today. Today, as in the past, when a vernacular is viewed as a language it is accorded greater respect than a dialect by both its speakers and listeners. But if the term *dialect* can be used in a neutral sense today, referring to a variety that identifies a person's regional background, in the early modern period both *dialect* and *patois* carried negative connotations that tended to overshadow the neutral sense of 'local use'. Burke reminds us that as early as 1690, the famous *Dictionnaire universel* by Antoine Furetière defined patois as 'a corrupt and crude language' rather than as regional or provincial variety.[38] Many travellers boasted about their knowledge of the linguistic divisions abroad, but seldom if ever investigated this diversity through the area's local history or questioned the accuracy of the terms heard in everyday use. Normally they resorted to guidebooks or acquired information

[36] Quoted by Folena, *L'italiano in Europa*, 400.
[37] Antoine Rivarol, *De l'universalité de la langue française* (1786), in Th. Suran (ed.) (Paris, 1930), 197.
[38] Burke, *Languages and Communities*, 36.

from local informants. Indeed, among many travellers in France, there was a noticeable inability to draw distinctions in what today we call a 'linguistic landscape', as many referred indiscriminately to dialects or patois, whether they were talking about French varieties north of the Loire or minority languages in the Occitan area south of the river, or indeed to isolate minority languages.

Robert Dallington, who set out on a journey through France and Italy in 1596, spoke of the diverse 'dialects' of France, 'where the Picard speaks one, the Norman another, the Britton his, the Gascoigne his, the Provençall and Savoyard theirs, the Inlanders theirs'.[39] However, it is interesting that soon after Dallington's journey, some Anglo-Welsh travellers with a solid bilingual background were able to establish more refined distinctions between the languages across the Channel. One was Edward Lhuyd, already mentioned in the section 'Varieties, Dialects and Minority Languages', who made accurate remarks about the state of the Breton language when he visited Brittany.[40] Another was James Howell, as can be seen in this passage from his *Instructions*, where he indulged in the most meticulous classification:

The French have three dialects, the Wallon (vulgarly called among themselves *Romand*) the Provencall, (whereof the Gascon is a sub-dialect) and the speech of Languedoc: They of Bearne and Navarre speak a Language that hath affinity with the Bascuence or the Cantabrian tongue in Biscaie, and amongst the Pyrenean mountaines: The Armorican tongue, which they of Low Brittaine speake (for there is *your Bas-Breton,* and the *Breton-Brittonant* or *Breton Gallois,* who speaks French) is a dialect of the old Brittish as the *word Armorica* imports, which is a meere Welsh word, for if one observes the Radicall words in that Language they are the same that are now spoken in Wales, though they differ much in the composition of their sentences, as doth the Cornish.[41]

What is lacking even in the early reports by most travellers who showed a genuine curiosity for language is information about the domains in which the different languages were used, i.e. for the diglossic situations in communities where some or even all speakers achieved bilingual competence. Clearly, some of the travellers' observations reflected personal experiences of communicating with people who spoke a regional variety different from the high-prestige language used by the elites, a situation they had been familiar with in Britain before departure. Normally Grand Tourists, who were careful to select their contacts from among the upper ranks of society, had regular access to the most prestigious variety of French, *le français littéraire et officiel*, which was the language acquired by that social group, if not through schooling then via

[39] The passage is quoted by Lough in *France Observed*, 15, and comes from *A Method for Travel* (1605), [VI], pages not numbered. This is the first edition of *The View of Fraunce* (London, 1604), reprinted by the Shakespeare Association (Oxford, 1936), which includes general comments on French, but no reference to dialects and other languages of France, see V 3 verso.
[40] Lough in *France Observed*, 15,   [41] Howell, *Instructions*, 48–9.

daily use in an exclusive environment.[42] But in rural areas, social isolation and endemic poverty lived hand-in-hand with the rustic patois of the peasants. Whenever foreign visitors came into contact with rural people either because they were interested in talking to country folks or because they required assistance on the road, they noted a strong difference in accent and often reported that they were completely defeated by the dialect.

John Locke was always being drawn into talking to peasants in the fields. While enquiring about the local types of grapevines, asking why some were tall and staked while others lay close to the ground, he noted: 'The reason of this different way of culture I could not learne of the work men for want of understanding Gascoin'. Lough, who relates this instance showing Locke's 'boundless curiosity' to talk to all kinds of people, found it 'somewhat puzzling' that a year later in Montpellier, Locke could recount 'conversations with a great variety of people who almost certainly spoke nothing but their Occitan dialect'.[43] Since Locke did not indicate any surprise while recollecting these episodes, it is likely that he expected to encounter even greater variation there between rural speakers and town dwellers. In southern France, it was quite likely that a speaker of Occitan living in a city such as Montpellier was able to adapt his or her language in order to communicate with a speaker of Parisian French but possibly the same facility was beyond the reach of speakers of a rural patois. Philip Skippon, travelling in 1663, confirmed the rustic nature of the language and the isolation of rural people in southern France:

The language of the vulgar is call'd Patois, very difficult for strangers and those born about Paris to understand, being a mixture of French, Spanish, and Italian, as may be observ'd by the following words and phrases therein: 'Peccare! Ah Paura! Ques à quo. A Dieu Seas, Dieus vous le donne. Cavalisco. Pottone. Fullou. Fumèe. Fringare. Scarabigliato. Cad. Began'.[44]

As for the provinces north of the Loire, there are even fewer references to these dialects of French. Peter Heylyn described the Norman dialect as follows:

It differth from Parisian, and more elegant French, almost as much as the English spoken in the North, doth from that of London or Oxford. Some of the old Norman words it still retaineth, but not many. It is much altered from what it was in the time of the Conqueror, few of the words in which our laws were written being known to them.[45]

Like most other travellers, John Lauder of Fountainhall, the author of *A New Journey* (1665–7), was aware of the linguistic divide between the northern area

---

[42] Apparently the 'salon' variety of French, which was made famous by the *école de politesse* inaugurated by Madame de Rambouillet in Paris, was a language much controlled in its pronunciation but in nothing else as it was used for speaking not writing ('ces arbitres du goût n'écrivaient guère, et parlaient seulement'), Brunot, *Histoire,* III, 169.

[43] Quoted in Lough, *France Observed,* 17.   [44] Skippon, 'An account', 716.

[45] Heylyn, *The Voyage of France,* 33.

of France and the southern region where another Romance language was spoken along with its dialects. He too identified the Gascons as speakers of a language different from French: 'Their language is a Dialect of the Spanish, but very Corrupt, as also is what French they speak, both in the Words and Accent; for they commonly pronounce the (b) like a (v), and the (v) like a (b).' But having identified the Loire as the boundary between the two linguistic areas, he offered incorrect observations about the various dialects: 'the dialect of bas Poictou … differs from that they speak in Gascoigne, from that in Limosin, from that in Bretagne, though all 4 be but bastard French'.[46]

Another rather confused picture of the linguistic landscape in France comes from the travel journal of Locatelli. The Italian priest, who was keen to enrich his diary with some discussion about the Latin family tree, wrote: 'Parlando in generale della lingua francese, dirò ch'essa è un rampollo della lingua italiana e latina, perché resosi signori del paese i Romani, v'introdussero le loro leggi e mutarono alquanto l'idioma degli abitanti' ['Speaking in general about the French language, I would say that it is a descendent of Italian and Latin, because when the Romans went to the country, they introduced their laws and changed the speech of the inhabitants' (note that *rampollo* means 'toddler', rather than 'sister' or 'daughter')].[47]

As time passed, most travellers noticeably started paying more attention to the bilingual competence of speakers in areas of language diversity, and travel books increasingly included comments on what language speakers used, with whom and where.[48] This had previously been usual for travellers who were bilingual themselves, like the Anglo-Welsh tourists. But it also became common among Italian travellers who came from a far more linguistically diverse reality than that of France, and indeed than most other parts of Europe. Marquis Malaspina, who arrived at Chambéry in Savoy – 'a portion of France' – in 1786, noted that the local population, who had their own dialect, spoke French with a 'perfect' accent, and he actually claimed that their pronunciation was better than that of Parisians. This was an effect of the spread of education in urban areas of eighteenth-century France, whereby dialect speakers learnt the literary and official French to a high degree of accuracy as the language of schooling. This was confirmed by Malaspina's further observations when he was in Marseille: 'In that town like everywhere else in Provence, good French was common, although it needed to be learned as a foreign language.'[49]

---

[46] Lauder, *Journals*, 61.   [47] Locatelli, *Viaggio di Francia*, 52.

[48] The linguistic sensitivity for multilingualism demonstrated by some women travellers was often a challenge to the received views on language purity and linguistic homogeneity that many male travellers indulged in in their reports. This topic will be further discussed in Chapter 9.

[49] Malaspina, *'Francia e Italia nel 1786'*, in D'Ancona (ed.), 251 and 276.

Italian Multilingualism

The Italian peninsula presented a more complex multilingual situation than France. Some minority languages had survived in either geographical or political isolation (or both) from neighbouring areas (Friulian, Ladin and Sardinian). In the north, where linguistic boundaries did not coincide with geographic or political borders, various minority languages belonging to the Romance, Germanic and Slavic families were spoken. There were also historic minorities in the centre and south who had preserved ancestral languages dating back to old immigrant settlements (Greek, Albanian, Croatian; and Catalan from the fourteenth century in Sardinia). In addition to minority languages, multilingualism was rooted in the historical background of a country that was not politically unified until 1861, and whose fragmented nature had maintained this linguistic diversity. Romance languages traditionally referred to as 'dialects' were widely spoken in everyday situations, giving a strong linguistic identity to different areas of the Peninsula.[50]

In the early days of the Grand Tour, travellers who were interested in finding out about the linguistic situation abroad before their departure were not necessarily aware that the Italian peninsula accommodated such linguistic diversity. What made quite a difference was the publication of *Instructions* by James Howell, who travelled to Italy in 1618; in his booklet, he stated quite explicitly that 'these varieties of Dialects in France and Spaine, are farre less in number to those of Italy'. The Anglo-Welsh writer also spelt out the connection between Italian political divisions and linguistic diversity:

And truly a wonder it is to see how in so small an extent of ground, which take all dimensions together, is not so big as England, there should be so many absolute and potent Princes by Sea and Land, which I believe is the cause of so many Dialects in the Italian tongue, which are above ten in numbers ... and all these have several Dialects and Idioms of Speech, and the reason I conceive to be, is the multiplicity of Governments, there being in Italy, one Kingdome, three Republiques, and five or six absolute Principalities, beside the Pope-dome, and their Lawes ... being different, their Language also growth to be.[51]

Howell had a pronounced interest in understanding linguistic diversity, and his account of Italian multilingualism is unusually insightful for the time. By contrast, a keen historian like John Chetwode Eustace, who wrote about Italy almost two centuries later, did not have much to add to Howell's description.

---

[50] In the north, there were Piedmontese, Ligurian, Lombard, Emilian and Venetian. The central area, in addition to Tuscan – the language of the literary tradition – had Umbrian and the dialects of northern Latium and the Marches. Further south, the most prominent dialects were Abruzzese, Neapolitan, Pugliese, Calabrese and Sicilian.

[51] Howell, *Instructions*, 53.

The Irish Catholic author of *A Tour Through Italy*, which became a bestseller of its genre, clearly had a more direct interest in antiquities than in language:

That a country subject to so many vicissitudes, colonised by so many different tribes, and convulsed by so many destructive revolutions, should have not only varied its dialects but sometimes totally changed its idiom, must appear natural and almost inevitable: we are only surprised when we find that in opposition to the influence of so many causes, Italy has retained, for so long a series of ages, so much of one language, and preserved amidst the influx of so many barbarous nations uttering such discordant jargons, the full harmonious sounds of its native Latin.[52]

Montesquieu, who travelled on the Continent early in the eighteenth century and was a keen observer of political and historical events, did not share Eustace's surprise that Italy had retained one major language. He was able to delineate the causes and effects of its unique situation with great lucidity: 'Il me semble que ce qui fait que la langue italienne a été fixée, c'est qu'il n'y a pas une cour commune, d'où les changements soient acceptés par la ville et les provinces. Il faut donc aller à la règle générale: qui sont les bons auteurs' ['It seems to me that what has codified the Italian language was not a common core of rules whose changes are adopted in urban centres as much as in the provinces. Instead one must refer to general models which are those of good authors.'][53]

The comments made by Howell, Eustace and Montesquieu, though differing in time, space and emphasis, share the view that of all the great languages of Europe, Italian had emerged from the most complex and fragmented context. However, the same awareness was not accessible to most observers, who travelled quickly and stopped briefly even when visiting major cities such as Turin, Milan, Venice, Bologna, Florence, Rome and Naples, following an itinerary that was a journey through a linguistic mosaic. As Serianni points out, most Grand Tourists were either unable to see the extent of linguistic differences in Italy or were disinclined to pay attention to it.[54]

Indeed, the increasing inclination of Grand Tourists was to view language just like another manifestation of the typical Italian contrast between splendour and decadence – a dichotomy that divided the once glorious country, now famous for its excesses. At one end of the spectrum lay the musical sublimity of the Tuscan language, monitored for its archaic standards and purified through the efforts of conservative academies, above all the *Accademia della Crusca*, whose name describes the separation of the wheat from the chaff. At the other end was the everyday language of ordinary people, referred to as dialects like everywhere else in Europe, even though 'dialects' in the Italian context is a term that 'refers to sibling tongues, each descended independently

---

[52] Eustace, *A Classical Tour*, III, 244.   [53] Quoted by Serianni, 'Lingua e dialetti', 71.
[54] Ibid., 60.

from Latin'. To most ears they sounded like a corruption of pure Italian, the Tuscan language which, as Hester Piozzi Thrale put it, 'is the one closer to that Italian which foreigners learn'.[55]

For travellers arriving from France, the two gates into Italy were Turin and Genoa, the former much esteemed for its elegant court, the latter for the beauty of its women. As mentioned by Jérôme Lalande, the 'hybrid' nature – as it seemed to them – of Piedmontese sounded disappointing to the ears of visitors who had learned the Tuscan variety. The Italian Malaspina called it *giargone*, 'a hard and rustic dialect'; the Spaniard Moratín claimed it was 'un compuesto de toscano y francés' ['a mixture of Tuscan and French']; the Frenchman Audebert criticised it 'car ... il y a des mots et façons de parler estranges, avec une prununciation Francoyse qui siet très mal à la langue italienne' ['because ... there are strange words and manners of speaking, with a French pronunciation which sits ill with the Italian language']; the Englishman William Hazlitt condemned it as 'a bad imitation of the French', and the moderate Stendhal said that it 'n'est pas plus Italien que français' ['it is no more Italian than French'][56]. In the first half of the eighteenth century, the historian Edward Gibbon remarked that the language of Genoa was 'the very worse Italian dialect', while the journalist Guyot de Merville called it 'fort méchant Italien' ['very bad Italian'].[57]

No better comments were bestowed on the Lombard dialect, whose accent also sounded quite off-putting: 'Le parler Lombard est fort mauvais et laid, à cause qu'il ne pronounce la moitié du mot laissant aultant à dire qu'il en dit, de sorte que l'on n'entent la terminason' ['The Lombard dialect is very ugly and corrupt, as half of the word is not pronounced, and one cannot hear their endings.'] The same judgment can be found in connection with the dialect of Bologna: 'A Bologne ... ilz ne prononcent qu'à la moitié leurs mots et ne font jamais ouir la derniere sillabe' ['At Bologna ... they only pronounce half of the words and they never make the last syllable heard.'][58] Philip Skippon remarked that in Milan 'the people ... leave out the last vowels of words', and in Bologna 'the vulgar speak Italian very corruptly, cutting their terminating vowels off and huddling their words together'.[59] This feature of many northern Italian dialects was a cause for regret among many foreigners as to them pronouncing the final vowel gave Italian its musical quality. Of all the dialects, that of Bergamo, near Milan, had been considered by far the worst since the time of Thomas Coryat: he attributed its ugliness to the rusticity of the inhabitants, and

[55] Piozzi Thrale, *Observations*, I, 118.
[56] Ibid, 81. Audebert is quoted in Olivero (ed.), *Nicolas Audebert, Voyage d'Italie*, II, 65.
[57] Serianni, 'Lingua e dialetti', 81.
[58] Nicolas Audebert, *Voyage d'Italie* in Adalberto Olivero (ed.), 2 vols. (Rome, 1981), II, 65.
[59] Skippon, 'An account', 563.

was pleased to find a Latin reference in support of his opinion from the poet Thomas Edwards: 'Bergomum ab incolta dictum est ignobile lingua'.[60]

Of all dialects of Italy, the one that was much praised in spite of its phonetic and structural distance from Tuscan was that of Venice. Travellers seemed to appreciate a wide variety of its phonetic features, which some described meticulously. Certainly, its musical quality was reinforced by the benevolent prejudice during the early modern period that Venice, even more than Rome, was a fascinating destination, offering an exciting social life, unique exhibitions of arts and music, and was famous for its low cost of living as well as its attractive and willing women. Longfellow stated that the qualities of the Venetian dialect were shared by educated people and all sectors of the local speech community: 'I have not yet heard a harsh sound – even among the common people.'[61] The Swiss historian Jacques-Augustin Galiffe indulged in a long and detailed description of its admired sounds:

The Venetian dialect is extremely agreeable to the ear; there is something infantine in the pronunciation, which is full of grace. The *g,* for example, is almost always pronounced z; they say *doze* for *doge; zorno* for *giorno; zoco* for *gioco.* Sometimes it is pronounced like a y, as *venio* for *vengo; linguajo* for *linguaggio,* ecc. They do not pronounce the c like the Tuscans, but like the French and English. *Sc* is not sounded like the English *sh,* but like *ss;* they say *conosso* for *conosco; lasso* for *lascio; zz* is turned into *ss,* as *delicatessa* for *delicatezza,* ecc.[62]

The special interest of foreign travellers in the language of Venice is witnessed by the discovery of a grammatical sketch of Venetian, 'Un Rudiment Venetien', published in Dieppe in 1781. It appeared in the sixth volume of the *Lettres écrites de Suisse, d'Italie, de Sicile et de Malthe* by Jean-Marie Roland de la Platière, the future home secretary of France who explained: 'J'ai cherché dans plusieurs Villes d'Italie, une Grammaire et un Dictionnaire où je pusse m'instruire des principes de cette Dialect; il m'a été impossible de trouver nulle part, ni l'une ni l'autre; et l'on m'a assuré, dans Vénise meme, qu'il n'en existe pas'.[63]

South of Rome, most travellers were impressed by the dialect spoken in Naples, which many reports described as being diversified into many

---

[60] Coryat, *Crudities,* II, 56. See also Thomas Edwards, *Cephalus and Procris, Narcissus* (1595?) rpt. (London, 1882), 70.

[61] Letter from Venice, December 17,1828, *Life of Henry Wadsworth Longfellow,* Samuel Longfellow (ed.), 3 vols. (Chicago, Illinois, 2003), I, 154.

[62] Quoted in Cartago, *Ricordi d'italiano,* 40, n.12.

[63] Anna Laura Lepschy 'Remarques sur le vernacolo veneziano' in 'Un "Rudiment Vénitien" del Settecento', in *Atti dell'Istituto Veneto,* CXXII, 1964, 453–81; reprinted in collaboration with Giulio Lepschy in *L'amanuense analfabeta,* 227–56. The authors explain that the 'Rudiment' is not only an important document for the history of cultural relations between France and Venice, it is also one of the first descriptive sketches in any Italian dialect and certainly the first in Venetian, 252.

subdialects. It is true that Naples in the early modern period was the third largest city in Europe after London and Paris but this in itself would not account for such substantial variations in its urban dialect. Possibly travellers were noticing different sociolects, which were characteristic of discrete districts in large cities, also found in Venice. For example, Stendhal commented: 'Il y a [en 1817] vingt patois different en Italie. A Naples, cela va jusqu'à avoir des dialects particuliers pour chaque quartier de la ville ... Le roi ne parle que napolitain; je trouve qu'il a raison: pourquoi ne pas être soi-même' ['There are (in 1817) twenty different patois in Italy. In Naples there is one characteristic of each quarter of the city ... The king speaks just Neapolitan; I think he is right: why should he not be himself.']⁶⁴ On occasions when Tuscan, the literary lingua franca, was felt to be too impersonal and speakers preferred to stick to their respective dialects, communication was still possible as long as the interlocutors were well educated and literate. Giacomo Casanova took advantage of such an opportunity when Pope Benedetto XIV, the liberal and much-loved reformer of the mid-eighteenth century, invited the Venetian aristocrat to meet him in Rome; Casanova recalled: 'He ... remarked that, instead of trying to address him in Tuscan, I could speak in the Venetian dialect, as he was himself speaking to me in the dialect of Bologna.'⁶⁵

Whenever travellers came across regional languages and local vernaculars, their attitude was one of disorientation but they seldom seemed interested in understanding the roots of this variation. Very few showed even mild curiosity about local expressions: they were much more attracted by recurrent features, even in local languages, which seemed symptomatic of the national character. One linguistic characteristic that was reported by quite a few visitors to different Italian regions was the habit of generating derivatives of endearment. The Frenchman Nicholas Audebert in his *Voyage d'Italie* (1574–8) says of the citizens of Bologna: '[ils] sont fort libres en faire de diminutif de diminutif, comme de *Fante, fantino, fantesino et fantenisello*' ['they have the great facility to form a diminutive from a diminutive, like from *Fante* (boy)'].⁶⁶ The German Philipp Joseph von Rehfues in his *Briefe aus Italien während der Jahre 1801–1805* (1809) noted that the richness of the Italian language also can

---

⁶⁴ Stendhal, *Rome, Naples et Florence* (Paris, 1826, reprinted 1987), 157. Stendhal had an unusual and well-informed perspective on Italian dialects and was not a great admirer of spoken Tuscan. See Marina Geat, 'Stendhal e la questione della lingua italiana: tra realtà storica e metafora metastilistica', in Stefano Gensini (ed.), *'D'Uomini Liberamente Parlanti': La Cultura Linguistica Italiana dell'Età dei Lumi e il Contesto Intellettuale Europeo* (Rome, 2002), 385–438. Jacques-Augustin Galiffe made a similar point: 'The Neapolitan dialect [or dialects, for there is some difference in every parish, and perhaps even in every family] is much more disagreeable to the eye, than to the ear'. Quoted in Serianni, 'Lingua e dialetti ', 84–5.

⁶⁵ Giacomo Casanova, *Mémoires*, in Robert Abirached and Elio Zorzi (eds.), 2 vols. (Paris, 1958), II, 226.

⁶⁶ Audebert, *Voyage d'Italie*, II, 65.

be seen in the pejorative expressions for 'woman' (*donna*): 'und wie reich und kurz sie das Wort *Donna* z.B. in *Donnetta, Donnicciuola, Donnaccia, Donnone, Donnuccia, Donnicina*, und *Donnina* verändert' ['and how rich and precise are the modifications of a word such as woman (*Donna*), for example, in little woman, contemptible little woman, shameless hussy, big strong woman, pretty woman, easy woman, and vulgar woman'].[67]

There is a reason for the attention of travellers in Italy being captured more by the diversity of dialects rather than the survival of minority languages.[68] The Italian dialects, whether rural or urban, were vibrant everywhere, their differences in sonority were highly audible and their specific features quite noticeable, even to foreigners who didn't have a good ear for language. Minority languages tended to be confined to areas which were far from major urban centres and very distant from the standard itinerary of most travellers. Until the nineteenth century, visitors to Italy were mostly interested in the centres of classical civilisation, the historical cities that contributed to the ideal of Italian humanism and the Renaissance. Much later, at the beginning of the Romantic era, the image of another Italy, both savage and picturesque, lured some travellers to extend their journeys south of Rome in search of a primitive society. One of the pioneers in this type of tourism was Henry Swinburne, whose adventures took him to Sicily and Calabria in 1777, where he encountered the conspicuous Greek and Albanian communities.[69]

A case of surprising indifference about minority languages involved the German aristocrat Lambert Friedrich von Corfey, who was travelling with his brother through Italy in 1698–1700, heading for Malta. Having arrived in Sicily, they were fortunate enough to witness a traditional swordfish catching session but in their recollection of the complex ritual, the travellers simply noted down the fact that one of the crew climbed the mast and uttered a few words that 'according to some are in corrupt Greek'.[70] They made no reference

---

[67] Quoted in Harro Stammerjohann, 'In viaggio attraverso gli italiani', *Italiano e Oltre*, XII (1997), 60. The last two expressions had both physical and metaphorical meanings, the latter definitely suggesting sexual availability. Robert Dallington made a similar point when he admired Tuscan for 'its way with diminutives'; see John Gallagher, "Ungratefull Tuscans", teaching Italian in early modern England', *The Italianist*, 36, 3, 408.

[68] Philip Skippon is a noticeable exception when he reports on the Romansh spoken in the Engadine Valley:
'all the inhabitants are of the protestant religion, speak an old language called Romauntsh *[sic]* (which is also spoken by the other Grisons) compounded of high Dutch, Italian, Spanish, French and their own idiom; they have several dialects of it, and those in the lower speak differently from those in the upper Egadine *[sic]*. The new testament and psalms are printed in this language, which the ministers preach in . . . Most of the people understand and speak Italian well, being near the Valteline, where Italian is spoken altogether', 'An account', 695–6.

[69] Henry Swinburne, *Travels in Two Sicilies*, 2 vols. (London, 1783).

[70] Lambert Friedrich Corfey, *Reisetagebuch 1698–1700*, in H. Lahrkamp (ed.) (Munster, 1977), 57, my translation.

at all to the fact that Greeks had been living for centuries in many areas of southern Italy, from the time of the ancient colonies of Magna Graecia in the eighth century BC to the Byzantine Greek migrations in the fifteenth century.

At this time the swordfish season opens. One of the crew climbs the mast and utters a few words, that according to some are in corrupted Greek. The sailors themselves do not know what they mean and they keep them secret, passing them down to their sons like a precious dowry. With these words they attract the fish, that are then speared with harpoons.

The disappointment of a linguist who expects more details about the story and more excitement from the traveller would be justified, until doubt arises that the narrator was not actually present at the scene but only heard about it or even read about it somewhere.[71] Indeed, the same experience of the Sicilian swordfish catch was reported by other travellers. One was Antonio Maria Lupi in 1735:

The fisherman ... always faces the Ionian sea, from where the swordfish come; as soon as he sees some he begins to sing a certain song to attract them. I do not know if that is superstitious or playful. It must be a very old song as it is in Greek language. If the fisherman will explain to me, I would write it down for you.[72]

Another was Patrick Brydone in 1773, who elaborated substantially on the episode:

The Sicilian fishermen (who are abundantly superstitious) have a Greek sentence which they make use of as a charm to bring him near their boats. This is the only bait they use, and they pretend that it is of wonderful efficacy, and absolutely obliges him to follow them; but if unfortunately he should overhear them speak a word of Italian, he plunges under water immediately, and will appear no more.

Yet another was Joseph Antoine de Gourbillon in 1819, who did not believe 'l'historiette du voyageur anglais' ['the little story of the English *[sic]* traveller'] and called Brydone an 'observateur de boudoir' ['armchair observer'] for his allegedly naïve report that fishermen use a Greek song or phrase to attract swordfish and that the fish would swim away as soon as they heard an Italian word. His argument was that 'les pêcheurs messinois ne parlent ni italien ni grec: ils parlent sicilien, comme les pêcheurs du pays de Brydone, parlent probablement irlandais' ['The Messina fishermen speak neither Italian nor

---

[71] Philip Skippon, a meticulous observer of all kinds of unusual habits and traditions, while travelling from Malta to Italy in 1663 was quite honest about his experience and did not report what he did not see. 'Here we stay'd almost two hours, but could not see any of the sword-fish (Pesce spade) taken, but saw the fishing boats, and were informed of the manner of fishing.' Skippon, 'An account', 615.

[72] Antonio Maria Lupi is quoted in Carlo Rota, *Viaggiatori italiani in Sicilia nell'età dei lumi* (Messina, 2011), 21.

Greek: they speak Sicilian, just as the fishermen from Brydone's country speak Irish'].

Certainly the sword-fishing sessions near Messina must have been one of the many *topoi* revisited by European travellers as it is quite remarkable that in this small selection of travellers, one was German, another Italian, the third a Scot and the last French.[73]

---

[73] Patrick Brydone, *A Tour Through Sicily and Malta*, 2 vols. (London, 1773) (rpt. Edinburgh 1840), 78. Joseph Antoine de Gourbillon, *Voyages critique à l'Etna en 1819*, 2 vols. (Paris, 1820), I, 259.

8   Instances of Language Contact

Manifestations and Attitudes

The simplest definition of language contact is the interaction between two languages at a societal or individual level. The effect of language contact for individuals entails a speaker of one language adopting elements of another, whether intentionally or unintentionally. Grand Tourists were constantly exposed to situations where different languages intermingled with their mother tongue, and this provided regular opportunities for mixing language features, deliberately or not. As for the actual linguistic forms, some types of contact resulted in the traveller adopting the foreign language wholesale, while other kinds merely involved borrowing foreign words and phrases into the mother tongue, perhaps with adaptations. However, what we know about such occurrences comes solely from the records provided by the travellers themselves, and this evidence cannot be fully trusted. This is why a discussion about the manifestations of language contact needs to deal with a meaningful classification of the phenomena as much as with the interpretation of attitudes involved.

Peter Burke explains that in early modern Europe, all countries experienced new words coming in from abroad, waiting to be accepted by the establishment.[1] The importation of words during the Renaissance was encouraged by the favourable attitude to Italian culture found throughout Europe. Many Italian terms became naturalised in other languages, specifically in the fields of music, trade, visual arts, food, customs, social activities and military matters. However, the historian adds that periodic attempts to defend the integrity of national languages produced a so-called anxiety of contamination.[2] For instance, beginning with the Renaissance, there were several campaigns against the 'Italianisation' of European languages, including by Henri Estienne in France and by Roger Ashman in England. At that time, the condemned neologisms followed the fashion for 'courtsanisms' (like the word *courtesan* itself), which had been borrowed from Italian before

---

[1] Burke, *Languages and Communities*, 158.   [2] Ibid., 152–3.

the appearance of Thomas Hoby's translation of the famous *Cortigiano* (*The Book of the Courtier*) by Baldassare Castiglione.[3]

Likewise, in the seventeenth and eighteenth centuries, due to the influence of France in many social and intellectual domains, French borrowings began to be explicitly acknowledged as an enhancement to European languages. A survey of *Gallicisms en Anglais* carried out by Ferdinand Brunot shows that it was not only fashionable salon life that enriched English language with lexical imports. His classification includes a vast repertoire of French loan words from a wide range of domains:

family life (*sans-souci,* 1781, H. Walpole *Lett.* VIII, 65); nature (*avalanche,* 1766, Smollett, *Trav.,* XXXVIII, 337); housing (*valet de place,* 1750, Chesterfield, *Lett.* (1774), II, XIII, 52); food (*gourmand* [*gourmet*], 1758, Chesterfield, *Lett.,* 22 Sept. (1774), II, CXX, 427); clothing (*négligée,* 1756, *Connoisseur,* no. 134, IV, 231); hair-style (*chignon,* 1783, *Lady's Mag.,* XIV, 121); health (*migraine,* 1777, H. Walpole, *Lett.,* vol. VI, 444); materials (*papier-maché,* 1753, Mrs Delany, Life and Corr., III, 260); trade (*depreciation,* 1767, Franklin, *Wks.* (1887), IV, 90); church (*dévot,* 1702, W. J. Bruyn's, *Voy. Levant,* XI, 156); intellectual life (*critique,* 1702–21, Addison, *Dial. Medals, Wks.,* 1721, I, III, 532); the arts (*goût,* 1717, Berkeley, *Tour in Italy, Wks.,* 1875, IV, 523); architecture (colonnade, 1718, Lady M. W. Montagu, *Lett.,* II, 68); pastimes (*vaudeville,* 1739, H. Walpole, *Let. to R. Weat.,* 18 June); travel (hôtel, 1765, Smollett, *France and Italy,* XXXIX, *Wks.,* V, 551); science (manometer, 1706, Varignon, *Mem. de l'Acad. Royale des Sciences.,* 300, 1730, Bailey [fol]); social life (*civilisation,* 1772, Boswell, *Johnson,* XXV); government (*bourgeois,* 1704, Addison, *Italy* (1733), 281 [previous appearance in 1674]); and diplomacy (*carte blanche,* 1707, Ld Raby, in Hearne *Collect.* (1886), II, 43).[4]

This is just a sample of the survey provided by the French historian but it shows that many writers who introduced foreignisms, which soon became assimilated into the English language, were Grand Tour travellers. Diarists like Walpole, Chesterfield, Smollett, Berkeley, Boswell and Lady Montagu contributed to the naturalisation of French terms in English through writing diaries or correspondence during their travels. Brunot, however, distinguishes borrowings which were useful for expanding English vocabulary ('expressions d'origine française [qui] abondent') from foreign terms some writers adopted occasionally ('mot éphémère') for reason of laziness or snobbery ('par paresse, par snobisme aussi').[5]

[3] Chaney, *Quo Vadis?* 63 and 91 n.27. See also Peter Burke, *The Fortunes of the Courtier* (Cambridge, 1995).
[4] In Brunot's *Histoire,* he discusses the phenomenon and provides a long list of borrowings with details of the sources which, at the time of publication of the study (1934–5), corresponded to first attestations given in the OED; III, 293–323.
[5] Scott and Machan in *English in its Social Contexts* point out that 'target changes due to conscious borrowings from a more prestigious speech community are initiated by the upper middle classes', and later explain that 'Perhaps the social class that is most crucial to the eventual acceptance and solidification of a linguistic innovation is the (upper) middle class', 17 and 18.

Indeed, when the importation of linguistic fashions and cultural models from France was à la mode, some scholars voiced their apprehension about the unregulated contamination of English language with French words. Joseph Addison himself, writing in *The Spectator* (1711), regarded it as being quite desirable that 'certain Men might be set apart, as Superintendants of our language, to hinder any Words of a Foreign Coin from passing among us . . . in particular *French* Phrases from becoming Current in this Kingdom'. Another authoritative voice was Samuel Johnson who, although not in favour of a language academy, in the Preface to his *Dictionary* admitted that a desirable initiative would be 'to stop the license of translatours, whose idleness and ignorance . . . will reduce us to babble a dialect of France'.[6]

The positive attitudes of most travellers to foreign borrowings were in startling contrast to the voices of their contemporaries writing from home. Unlike many purists, travellers who were multilingual themselves adopted foreign vocabulary unconsciously as natural innovators and conduits of language contact. The following passage from Richard Lassels (1635) makes this point almost passionately as he rejects the suspicion of affectation aimed at those who adopt foreign words in their narratives:

> Others will say, I affect a world of exotick words not yet naturalised in England: No, I affect them not; I cannot avoyd them: For who can speak of Statues, but he must speak of Niches? Or of Churches, wrought Tombes, or inlayd Tables; but he must speak of Coupolas; of bassi rilievi and of pietre commesse? If any man understand them not, its his fault, not mine.[7]

The concerns of authors writing from home was different, especially when focused on safeguarding the linguistic resources of their native language against the tendency of using modish expressions from a high-prestige foreign language. Certainly, negative attitudes towards foreign languages were typical of early modern Europe, a time when borrowings were seen as an external influence that could damage linguistic integrity and standardisation. On the other hand, positive attitudes towards foreign borrowings were typical on the Grand Tour, an experience inspired by the desire to acquire and share knowledge which, by definition, could not be fully realised without opportunities for linguistic contact and language mixing.

The attitudes of English travellers to foreign borrowings did vary over time but showed a substantial amount of continuity. Their initial tendency was to flaunt their knowledge of Latin, throwing in aphorisms and proverbs to display what they had learned from that classical heritage. During the early days of the Grand Tour, the inclination of some travellers was to naturalise or translate exotic expressions from diverse vernaculars discovered during their journey.

---

[6] Samuel Johnson, *A Dictionary of the English Language* (London, 1755).
[7] Lassels, *The Voyage of Italy*, preface, unpaginated.

But in the eighteenth century, most travellers felt quite comfortable in displaying familiarity with borrowings in their original form, almost as if to stress the inadequacy of equivalents in the native language. Two European travellers who lived in different centuries showed how a positive attitude to multilingualism always inspired the practice of mixing languages. One was the English travel writer Fynes Moryson, a translator and a solid supporter of foreign imports: 'The English language ... being mixed is therefore more and not less to be esteemed.'[8] The other was the great musician Wolfgang Amadeus Mozart, who achieved such special effects through mixing Italian, French and Latin with German that his correspondence has been described as a 'linguistic polyphony'.[9]

Status and Sources

When the passion for foreign borrowings emerged at the height of the Grand Tour, the cohabitation of conservative attitudes with cosmopolitanism had an impact on how language innovations were received. Some fashionable foreignisms brought back by travellers from France and Italy carried different connotations. Examples of mismatched connotations can be found by examining the borrowings *castrato* and *cicisbeo*, which become current in English from 1718 and 1763 respectively (see Chapter 2, section on 'Shocking Foreign Customs').[10] The two terms were normally used by foreign travellers while in Italy, and *castrato* in particular spread quickly back in England when the fashion for hiring Italian singers became a common practice. But Italians did not normally use that term, preferring *virtuoso* or *musico,* which were felt to be more respectful towards that distinguished professional figure. Likewise, *cavalier servente* was preferred in Italy to refer to the male companion of a married woman acting with the approval of her husband.[11] The term *cicisbeo* was definitely pejorative but it became popular with foreign travellers, especially because of their disapproval of the practice. It is interesting that *cicisbeo* was the Italian word that Grand Tourists transcribed with the most inconsistent spelling: viz. 'chichisbee', 'cicisbay', 'tetis bey' and 'sicisbeism'.[12] There

---

[8] Quoted in Burke, *Languages and Communities*, 122.   [9] Folena, *L'italiano in Europa*, 434.
[10] The *Oxford English Dictionary* gives the first attestation of *cicisbeo* as the work of Mary Wortley Montagu, Letter of 28 August 1837, II. 75: 'The custom of cecisbeos [1966 ed.: Tetis beys] ... I know not whether you have ever heard of those animals', and for *castrato,* John Brown, *Dissertation on Poetry and Music* (1763) v. 63: 'An Italian Castrato (who hath laboured at this Refinement through his whole Life)'.
[11] Smollett, who was a severe critic of the habit, does say that 'every married lady in this country has her cicisbeo or servente', Letter XXVII, 237.
[12] Respectively: the Earl of Cork, quoted in Pine-Coffin, *British and American Travel*, 47; Boswell, quoted in Trease, *The Grand Tour*, 173; Mary Wortley Montagu, quoted in Hudson, *The Grand Tour*, 78; Maugham, *The Book of Italian Travel*, 71. Other spellings and derivatives

could be more than one reason for this: the word was not seen in writing, and it could be heard mainly from the mouths of foreign speakers who mispronounced it.

Another revealing issue surrounding the origin of borrowings in travel writing is their status in the original language; i.e. whether travellers' attention was directed to the whole linguistic landscape of the foreign country or merely focused on the social circle of speakers using overtly prestigious forms. Although many travellers showed a curiosity for popular expressions, and quite a few had ears well tuned to the distinctive characteristics of local speech, not many recorded instances of borrowings from local dialects. Serianni stresses that the main reason for this was the fact that travellers did not move within the social milieu where French patois and Italian dialects predominated.[13] In Italy, for example, where even members of the upper classes were dialect speakers, they felt it rude not to accommodate their language to the literary Italian known by foreigners.[14] Visitors who experienced prolonged exposure to dialects did not see the point of adopting such expressions, with the noticeable exception of Venetian terms – Venice was well known for the monolingualism of the local aristocracy, and most visitors felt an affection for this local language anyway.[15] When Venetian borrowings appear in travel writing from this period, the expressions are used to describe some local reality and carry no negative force, probably because foreigners were quite unaware of their provincial currency. Examples include *cortezana* (a well-educated prostitute); *zentildonna* (a noblewoman); *barcaroli* (rowers); *remulcio* (a boat with four or six rowers); *marangora* (St Mark's bell); *mattutin* (early morning church bell); *morbin* (spirit of fun); *pestrin* (milk bar).[16]

It is interesting that the tendency not to adopt words or phrases from Italian dialects was also found among Italian travellers, who nonetheless seemed keen to adopt borrowings from abroad. When visiting cities outside their region, those Italians who co-opted a word or sentence from the area's dialect did so to add colour to the description of a local custom. For example, when Canon Giuseppe De Conti from Casale Monferrato was in Naples, he quoted the saying *Agio beduto lo mio caro Napoli: adesso songo contento* ('I have seen

---

include *chichisbee* (Earl of Cork); *cicisbay* (James Boswell); *cicisbeism* (William Hazlitt); *cicisbeatore* and *cicisbeoship* (Horace Mann).

[13]   See Serianni, 'Lingua e dialetti', especially 66–74.

[14]   See, for example, the quotations by Stendhal in Chapter 7, and by Hester Piozzi Thrale at the end of this chapter.

[15]   See Ronnie Ferguson, 'Primi influssi culturali italo-veneti sull'inglese'. la testimonianza dei venezianismi in Florio, Coryate e Jonson', in Eugenio Burgio (ed.), *Il veneto: tradizione, tutela, continuità*, Atti del Convegno, Venice 11–12 February 2011, *Quaderni Veneti*, II, 2012, 57–82.

[16]   Christopher Hibbert in *Cities and Civilizations* (London, 1987) gives these examples. Byron noted the term *morbin*, heard in Venice from a gondolier who had lost his 'passion' for memorising new songs.

my beloved Naples: now I am happy'), and employed two characteristic exclamations from that town: *Ah t'aggio capito!* ('Now I've got it!'), and *Mannaggia li morti tuoi!* ('Your damned dead!').[17]Colloquial expressions from dialects were, of course, problematic to spell if their pronunciation did not match the phonetic system of literary Italian, the language of all textbooks and works of literature. When borrowings came from literary Italian, the spelling could be checked in bilingual dictionaries and some conversation manuals.

While foreign borrowings are the most obvious manifestation of language contact, the challenge of dealing with the orthographic representation of foreign sounds was of no little concern to travellers. Reconstructing the journey of specific foreign borrowings is beyond the scope of this book but it is worth noting that the naturalisation of most loans was realised through spelling that was sometimes different from both the original and the form that was to become standard in English. It is characteristic that the way many endings of foreign loan words are spelt looks Anglicised or alternatively Frenchified or Italianised. In a chapter that deals with language contacts, such unorthodox spellings are frequent, and some of the most idiosyncratic ones have been given in parentheses without the usual warnings (viz., *sic*). As regards this point, in 1817 William Stewart Rose made a curious observation about the controversial spelling of Italianisms by English travellers:

the particular in which I consider the English are perverse, beyond other nations, is that they change the accent and termination of Italian words upon no principle whatever; but of two sounds usually prefer the wrong, though this may be as little analogous to the genius of their own language as the right. Thus GROTTA is changed into GROTTO, ROTUNDA into ROTONDO, while GOZZO the sister island of Malta is transmogrified into GOZA, and the soubriquet of the Venetian painter CANALETTO into CANALETTI.[18]

Another interesting case is that of toponyms, which were invariably misspelt in most travel writing. This is another and possibly less visible manifestation of linguistic contact but one whose oddities need to be fully appreciated. Mączak points out that the misspelling of place names is a distinctive feature of travel in early modern Europe ('Bassompierre, like all travellers, distorted names hopelessly').[19] But not all cases of misspelling should be dismissed as the product of carelessness. Ernest S. Bates mentions the hopeless rendering of names on maps: 'As for sixteenth-century maps, they seem meant for gifts

---

[17] De Conti, *Viaggio d'Italia*, 159 and 183.
[18] William Stuart Rose, Letter XII, Abano, September 1817, *Letters from the North of Italy*, 2 vols. (London, 1819), I, 142.
[19] François Bassompierre (1579–1646) was a highly educated man, and was ambassador to Spain, Switzerland and England on behalf of Henry IV of France; see Mączak, *Travel*, 243.

rather to an enemy than to a friend'.[20] He also points out that in each different region of a country, travellers need to seek the help of local people. The consequent problems of phoneticism, or pronunciation, according to him, was that: 'the tourists' own evidence as to this is more valuable, as being more authentic, when an Englishman writes 'Landtaye' for 'Landtage' and 'Bawre' for 'Bauer'.[21]

The phenomenon needs to be understood not only in the context of a non-standardised spelling of toponyms at the time, but also in view of the problems when noting down spoken place names, especially when pronounced with an unfamiliar accent. Sometimes the foreign words heard from the mouths of local people were jotted down in a hurry in order to render the sounds using the orthographic tools of another language. These attempts were thought to be useful to other travellers because they helped to convey a more accessible phonetic shape to those who were not comfortable with the sounds of the particular foreign language. Both published and unpublished travel accounts are full of forms that approximate the actual sound of names in the foreign language; but if the different renderings helped the travellers to remember the pronunciation, it is also clear that the authors were seldom worried about the spelling. The sample below shows how erratically even well-educated Englishmen spelt the names of minor destinations along the most typical itineraries to and from Rome:

> WILLIAM LITHGOW: Loreto → *Loretta*, Recanati → *Riginati.*
> FRANCIS MORTOFT: San Antimo → *St. Anthony*,
> Acquapendente → *Compendente*, Montefiascone → *Monte fiasco*,
> Ronciglione → *Ronga lyon*, Monterosi → *Monterese.*
> BANASTER MAYNARD: Torrenieri → *Torniery*, Radicofani → *Radico Fany*,
> Ponte a Rigo and Centino → *Pontecentino*, Monterosi → *Monte-Rosse*,
> Baccano → *Boccano.*
> WILLIAM PATOUN: Rimini → *Riminsi*, Sinigallia → *Seneguglia.*
> SAMUEL ROGERS: Ronciglione → *Ronciliogno.*

If in many cases the misspelt names served the purpose of reproducing the local pronunciation for the benefit of foreigners, there were also instances which led to unfortunate misunderstandings, for example when bills of exchange enabling travellers to collect their money were dispatched to the wrong city. This was the case for Sir George Courthop, who travelled to Geneva in search of a merchant called Wright, to whom the payment instructions for his money had been addressed. Mączak, who related the episode, explained that the transfer order was sent not to Geneva but to Genoa (in Italian, Genova).[22]

Naturally, examples of language contact reported by travellers by and large involved productive rather than receptive skills. Misunderstandings also

---

[20] Bates, *Touring in 1600*, 53.   [21] Ibid., 61.   [22] Mączak, *Travel*, 90.

provide important (and no less fascinating!) insights but they tend to rarely be recorded in these tourists' writings, so the few examples available are valuable. A rather nice instance appears in the Italian playwright Carlo Goldoni's *Mémoires,* written in French in 1783. Goldoni recalled a dangerous situation, which had no unfortunate consequences, and his motivation in reporting the occasion of his misunderstanding is quite clear. On the one hand, he wished to stress his rudimentary knowledge of French at the time he was moving to Paris to take up the important position of playwright-in-residence at the *Comédie Italienne.* On the other hand, he wanted to recreate the atmosphere of tension as he crossed the stormy waters around Nice aboard a fragile felucca, having decided to avoid the usual route through the Alps and risk the long and dangerous journey by sea. Goldoni was delighted to report his adventure, not only because he was travelling for work and not touring for pleasure but also because he was already fifty-four:

A hurricane took us away from the harbor, and we nearly perished while rounding the Cap de Noli. A comic incident mitigated my fear. There was in the felucca a Provencal Carmelite, who mispronounced Italian just as I mispronounced French. This monk was terrified when he saw coming towards us one of those mountains of water which threatened to submerge us. He shouted at the top of his voice: la voilà, la voilà: in Italian we say 'la vela' for 'la voile' ('sail'). I believed that the Carmelite wanted the sailors to tie up the sails; so I wanted to let him know that he was wrong, and he argued that what I was saying did not make any sense; During our dispute the Cape was rounded, we reached the harbor; I then had the time to acknowledge my mistake, and the good faith to acknowledge my ignorance.[23]

'Survival' Borrowings

Travel made knowing foreign languages a natural aim but even those travellers who did not manage to learn a language abroad left some evidence that they had picked up something from other tongues. This is shown by the number of foreign words or phrases appearing in virtually every travel account, serving a variety of functions. When writing letters, especially to their families, young travellers might throw in foreign words as evidence of their progress in learning a language, while when writing to friends such new vocabulary may have been intended to signpost newly discovered knowledge. Other travellers may have introduced foreign elements into their writing to embellish their narratives or even to serve as memorable landmarks in the reconstruction of events.

Of course, there were travellers who passed no comments about a newly encountered language and followed the remarkable example of the German

---

[23] Goldoni, *Mémoires de Carlo Goldoni pour server à l'histoire de sa vie*, 2 vols. (Paris, 1821), II, 50 [my translation of the original French].

Franz von Gaudy, whose travel kit for Italy included three key words: *sicuro!* (sure!) to express agreement or satisfaction; *domandate troppo!* (you ask too much!) to refuse an expensive service; and the exclamation *aeh!* to give the impression he was showing interest in the conversation.[24] If all men who participated in the Grand Tour had been like those who ignored language issues and never bothered to learn a foreign word, there would be little scope for studying language contact. But such cases were unusual, and even the small sample of borrowings collected for this study provide plenty of valuable information.

This section focuses on the most frequent foreign words and phrases borrowed by Englishmen on their route to destinations in France and Italy. Such items indicate what the basic survival language on the road included, and at first glance they appear to be quite different from the type of vocabulary found in the conversation manuals consulted before starting a trip or purchased during the journey. Interactions on the road for people travelling with friends, guides, tutors or interpreters did not require 'survival language' in the literal sense. On the other hand, the opportunities available to a travelling party to practise a foreign language with strangers were minimal, given the anxiety to reach the next safe destination. Certainly, one can imagine that all kinds of linguistic practices were at work while tourists were on the road. Some travellers would have tried imitating the sounds produced by a native speaker; others rehearsed the pronunciation of foreign words with companions; many must have tested new vocabulary on coach drivers, inn keepers and cicerones.

Travellers' phrase books from all eras have the prerogative to include words and dialogues that may occur on a journey but the sequence and register they are presented in hardly reflects those needed to 'survive'. Indeed, our travellers tended to remember a word which was unfamiliar because of its sounds and spelling but which reminded them of a traumatic experience better than vocabulary from the artificial dialogues of conversation manuals. What also needs to be borne in mind is that the language models provided in conversation manuals represented the 'polite' language of foreign instructors, whereas the 'survival' language actually needed on the road was the type suitable for basic communication with common people. A case reported by the Scottish architect Robert Adam in 1754 shows how this affected real-life situations. Adam met a beautiful young woman at a coffee house in Pisa, and she promised him a visit to her own *palchetto,* or theatre box, the next day. Ignorant of the local language, Adam took along his good friend Charles Hope, 'who gibbers Italian' and was soon in close conversation with the beautiful lady, whilst Adam uttered not a word: 'When she spoke to me in Italian I answered in French, she understanding one word in ten I said and I the same of her

---

[24] Quoted in Serianni, 'Lingua e dialetti', 70.

conversation . . . Next night . . . we went to the opera and I made a language of my own, half English, half French and a little sprinkling of Italian – to her amusement.'[25]

The next section presents a sample of borrowings (given in italics) that certainly made an impression on many Englishmen journeying on the Continent at the height of the Grand Tour, since they appear in their travel accounts. They are presented in the order they were likely to have been picked up when on the road in France and then in Italy on a journey to the two main continental destinations: Paris and Rome. Some foreign words and phrases were useful for dealing with the emergencies in an alien environment, while others became memorable through the effort of describing unfamiliar situations, which sometimes were in dramatic contrast with one's education and expectations.

After crossing the Channel and disembarking at Calais, the guards at the local *douane* did not have the time or will to instruct the tourists in the French language while searching their *portmanteaux* and standing around with their hands in their pockets. The true adventure began the following day when transportation to Paris was negotiated either on a public *diligeance,* or in a private carriage – a *cabriolet* or *calèche,* or a *carosse de remise* with horses *de louage.* Fortunately, the *Liste générale des postes de France* quoted distances and prices. Once they reached Paris, visitors needed to report to the *Bureau du Roi,* the Customs House, where a large number of individuals surrounded this building, offering services as temporary *valets,* either *valets de place* or *valets de chambre.* Some young visitors travelled on the Loire river using the public *bateau de poste* or a smaller *coche d'eau,* or in a *diligeance par eau* or *char-à-banc* (both pulled by horses walking on a tow path), and helped by some *laquet* (or *laquais*) *de place.* Most young lads lodged with private families, while others stayed at *pensions,* where *patrons* looked after their *pensionnaires* very well; their *garçons,* or even better the *filles du patron,* could teach the young Englishman a number of skills, including the language. The main task before departing for Italy was choosing a *voiturin* (or *voitoirine, voiturier*), the stage coach driver, with an *avant-courier* riding the lead horse. The hope was that this escort could provide the full range of services needed, including interpreting during negotiations at each stopover. One means of preventing disasters was offering him a tip, ironically called a *baisemain* (hand kissing). No inn was equipped for nobles with their servants, and sharing a room was quite common. The three key words for items required in a bedroom were *armoire* (wardrobe), *paillasse* (bed), *chèse-percée* (commode). Potential intruders included *filles* and *femmes de chamber,* previously encountered working in the *cuisine* or serving at the table. The *patron de la maison* was often their father, who was also the

---

[25] Letter by Robert Adam from Pisa, quoted in John Fleming (ed.), *Robert Adam and His Circle, in Edinburgh & Rome* (Cambridge MA, 1962), 128.

traitueur or *rotisseur*. Food and accommodation on the road left much to be desired, and many travellers managed communication *à la table* with two simple words: *manger!* or *changer!* The climax of this part of the journey occurred when they arrived at the Alps, where all carriages stopped at *la poste aux asnes* ('donkey post'), where the *voiture* was dismantled and the pieces transported by mules, while passengers were hastily transferred onto a *chaise à porteurs* or a *traineau* pulled by *marons* (guides).

Having reached the other side of the Alps, the customs experience was even more traumatic. A *biglietto* or *carta di sicurezza* (the bill of health) was required for all travellers who passed through the French *cordon sanitaire*. Most states in Italy implemented a *quarantine* when travellers lacked the *bollettino di sanità,* and every frontier required a new passport. Another necessary piece of paper was the *lasciapassare* issued by the *dogana,* stating that the transported goods were not contraband. From Genoa, or alternatively Turin, an Italian journey continued by *calesse* (or *calesso*), with a newly employed *vetturino*, plus a messenger called a *procaccia* or *procaccio*, both more than ready to ask for a *buonamano* or *bona mancia* (a good tip) at every *cambiatura* (post), as was the *staliere* (groom) himself. Tips and bribes sometime warded off attacks by *banditti* and secured a decent *albergo,* or *camera locanda,* while avoiding *vile hosterias*. Padova (Padua) was a compulsory stop for those who wanted to study at or just pay a visit to its famous university. From there, an excursion along the Brenta river, surrounded by the *villas* and *giardini* built by the nobility for their summer *villeggiatura*, was the best introduction to Venice. Passengers boarded an elegant *burchio* or *burchiello (burcello),* which once in the *laguna* was pulled via a tow rope by another boat, a *remulcio*, rowed by several *barcaroli* (*barkerolls*).

As soon as terra firma was left behind at Fusina, the city of Venice emerged from the sea, displaying her best panorama. At the entrance to the *Canal Reggio,* visitors suddenly saw *gondolas* steered skilfully by *gondoliers* through a crowd of other boats – *bichonis, piotes, tartanes* and many other types. At sunset, the *balustrades* of the *palazzo* would take on the colours of the dying light, while at sunrise it was possible to spot nobles winding their way home after a night spent in *casinos* or *cafès*, or in the *ridotti* of theatres, where men and women gambled until morning. In almost every *campo*, there were *magazzeni, mercà, boteghe, pestrini* or milk bars. Florence and Siena were the next popular destinations on the *Giro* of Italy, the former renowned for its artistic treasures, the latter for its sublime language. But of all Italian towns, it was Rome that attracted most tourists, for the social contrasts within the city, and its imperial glory emerging from the squalor of the miserable *campagna* stretching around it. After a drive of four or five days in the *carrozza* (or *caroch*) from Siena, on bad roads and endless *cambiatura*, the *vetturino* would stop at a *belvedere* to show the *vista* from the top of a hill, shouting *Ecco Roma!*

Figure 8.1 *The grand tourist approaching Venice in 1764.* Illustration from an unknown print in *Grand Tour: A Journey in the Tracks of the Age of Aristocracy,* edited by R. S. Lambert, London, Faber and Faber (1935)

No other city could boast such a fine approach as Rome: once across the Tiber at *Ponte Molle* and through the *Porta del Popolo,* the two grand streets stretching out from there – the *Via del Babuino* (*Strada Baboine or baboina*) and the *Corso* or (*Via del Corso*) – conjured up the magnificence of Rome. One could catch sight of *cupolas, piazzas* with their *porticos* and *colonnades, giardini inglesi* and *castelli d'acqua*; the venerable city was blessed with a profusion of water and rushing streams (*giochi d'acqua*). Unfortunately, foreign convoys were soon spotted and surrounded by a crowd of *servitori di piazza, ruffians* and *facchini* shouting *Signore! Signore!* The Roman aristocracy introduced the Italian fashion of promenading (*passaggio* or *passeggio*) along the famous *Via del Corso*. They paraded especially during feast days and festivals, which at the beginning of the seventeenth century included 150 religious days, in addition to the *feste popolari* of the *rione* (district). The rest of the time, the nobility and clerics enjoyed *festinos* (parties), sometimes enjoying games of cards, other times engaging in *conversazioni* (*conversaziones, converzationi*), sometimes watching a performance by an *improvvisatore* or by an *orchestra* accompanying *castrato* singers, who were particularly famous in Rome. The Carnival was the most famous of all festivals, complete with its *palio* (horse race), *confetti* and thousands of paper lanterns or *girandole*.

After Rome, the temptation was to visit Naples, the most important Italian capital of a great kingdom with the biggest population in Italy. The main attraction was to hire a *corricolo* in town and visit the *grottos*, then venture on to Vesuvius, the Italian *volcano* famous for its *lava* and finally to the Greek ruins at *Paestum* (*Pesta*). But a source of huge anxiety there was the *aria cattiva* or *malaria* (bad air). In the heyday of the Grand Tour, many travellers felt that a last sojourn in Paris would provide a finishing touch to their education and provide them with more social confidence when entering international circles. Once in Paris, new attire was necessary – silk breeches and coloured stockings 'to prevent your being stared at as a stranger'– and many abandoned their old-fashioned dress *à l'Anglaise*. A Parisian *friseur à la mode* would complete the new look with the characteristic head *bien poudré,* made famous by the many dandies portrayed in caricatures at the Macaroni Club in London.

A useful impression of how foreign borrowings can play a practical role in a context free from overtones of irony or snobbery comes from *Advice on Travel* (*c.*1766), a short text of fifteen pages written by the Scotsman William Patoun, an experienced tutor and painter sent by his master to plan a trip to Italy.[26] *Advice* is a succinct guide, peppered with French and Italian terms for no purpose other than to make useful information accessible to his client with a view to helping him make the best use of his time with various people and in different places. The sample of sentences below shows how the insertion of foreign terms (which I have put in italics) served an instrumental purpose,

---

[26] For a discussion on the preparation of this Grand Tour (1768), see Ingamells, *British and Irish Travellers,* 747.

without any pretence of exoticism. This is a selection of sentences enriched by practical loans, with only one polite expression from international French (in the last line):

I thought the Terms [of the *Viturino*] high but they were the best I could make; a *Milord anglois* being in question . . . Sardinian Customs will open and search your Baggage. In order to prevent their tumbling . . . tell them that their *Manica* [*sic*, for 'mancia'] or fee will depend upon their treatment . . . The best Inn in Parma is the Post House. There is a *Valeti de Place*, who commonly attends there to conduct Strangers about the City. You may give him and other *Cicerones* of the livery at the rate of 3 Pauls p day. The great Objects of art to be admired at Parma are the great Theatre, and the Works of Carrigio (*Correggio*) . . . The English seldom make a long stay at Bologna . . . The Bolognese Nobility are civill in general to Strangers. The Countesses Marulli and Lignani two Sisters are the great patronesses of the English, and both speak French. The latter is a handsome Woman but a great *Coquet*. A *valet de place* will be necessary in Rome . . . Some Oeconomical Friend may possibly recommend to your Lordship to travail some parts of this road by *Cambiatura* which is saving of near one third in Postage . . . The English give three Pauls to each Postillion per post. They are the most resolute *ruffians* in all Italy . . . You pay over and above for Fire &c and often there is a separate Article in the Bill *perlincommodo* for the trouble you put them to . . . The Postillions at least shall go without their *Manica* . . . and often indeed on *Maigre-days*, nothing can be had on the road . . . The *Villigiatura* of a great family in Italy, is a thing worth seeing . . . Your Lordship may stay at Rome on your return from Naples, without fear of the *Malaria* till the end of May if you chuse it . . . As your Lordship by this time will be *pratico del paese* I can say little relating to Florence that could be of Material Service . . . You leave your Chaise on *Terra Firma* and proceed by Water to Venice . . . If your Lordship should be at Venice during the great heats, I would recommend a long Ash Coloured Silk Cloak, called *Tabaro* to you . . . A *Demisaison* Velvet is a most useful genteel Coat, for Autumn and Spring . . . An *Ecritoire* which will hold your Money as well as paper, is to be had likewise at Pari . . . *Manche the de dentelle* d'Harzard are to be had very reasonable at Paris, and will save you a great deal . . . I would humbly recommend to your Lordship to study a little Architecture at Rome . . . Go to the Belvedere at Night and see the Apollo and Lacoon by torch light. *Il vaut bien la peine.*[27]

Exotic Loan Words

This chapter has so far considered 'survival' borrowings that reflect practical needs but much of the autobiographical materials left by travellers, especially diaries and letters, are rich with words that have more to do with the perception of an unfamiliar reality than with contingencies of the journey.[28] Though the

---

[27] Patoun, 'Advice on travel', xxxix–lii.
[28] The distinction between 'survival' borrowings and other foreignisms is not supported by theoretical notions. However, Sarah G. Thomason makes a similar distinction (specifying that it is only a rough, practical one) between borrowings of basic and non-basic vocabulary in more general contact situations, *Language Contact: An Introduction* (Edinburgh, 2001), 71–2.

boundaries of this distinction are fuzzy, the context in which a foreignism is inserted almost invariably clarifies the actual purpose of the loan: i.e. if it was adopted for personal convenience or as a marker of cultural difference. In the latter case, foreign words or phrases can have an allusive function, maximising the exotic flavour of their writing and achieving certain overtones.

Indeed, most Grand Tourists sent home not only comments about memorabilia and sightseeing but also witty observations of foreign customs in order to make indelible impressions on families and friends. In the following passage, a traveller is complaining about hospitality in the 'private pensions' between destinations in France and he decorates his letter with French words intended to add a touch of irony to his recollection:

> The *inn* having but one fire place we were altogether a goodly company of men women children hogs and poultry … No sooner in bed than two numerous families, ancient inhabitants of the place, with that politeness so conspicuous in the French payd their respects to me. I am certain that not a *Puce* [flea] or a *Punaise* [bedbug] neglected showing me how sensible they were of the honor we had done them.

As discussed in Chapter 5, the correspondence of many young men included references to local beauties encountered on the journey. In one case the report indicated that a lady of distinction of international reputation was actually the 'most saucy insolent coquette I ever saw'. In another case, when the intention was to de-emphasise the status of the relationship, a tourist specified that his new lady 'whose background was not an exalted one', was no '*amant du Coeur*' but '*flamme passegère*' with whom the '*affair of convenience*' left no trace. A traveller more inclined to concentrate on social issues observes: 'The distinction between noblesse et bourgeoisie in France and … have strong effects upon the national manners. They give the noblesse an exclusive right to pride with poverty: they give to the bourgeoisie an exclusive right to wealth with *grossièreté* [vulgarity].'

Excerpts from Italy show a number of Italian terms of colourful flavour with which travellers peppered their travel writing to express the reasons for appreciation or, vice versa, complaint, typical of so many reports. A positive comment is that of John Durant Breval in 1720: 'Florence is the City of the World, next to Rome, where a *Dilettante* may best entertain himself.' For Lawrence Stern, the jolly atmosphere of a Neapolitan Carnival is most effectively described by a string of borrowings: 'they attended operas – punchinellos – festinos and masquerades'.[29] In 1817 Henry Matthews was clearly pleased with the reception he found in Italy, and remarked: 'We are in high favour, and *Inglese* is a passport every where.' A definitely sarcastic remark is that of Lady Miller, leaving Broni near Pavia in 1770: 'we found the host thought himself

---

[29] Quoted from Percy Fitzgerald, *The Life of Laurence Sterne* (London, 1906), 317.

a *gallant uomo*, in not charging more than seventeen French livres for our supper'. Finally, John Chetwode Eustace was indulging in a commonplace when he observed that: 'it is generally believed beyond the Alps, that it was impossible to walk the streets of Naples without feeling or witnessing the effects of a *stiletto*'.[30]

Travellers who inserted such foreign loans into letters and journals did so neither as a faithful reconstruction of the event nor as evidence of familiarity with the donor language. They felt that using idiomatic expressions without offering a translation or an English equivalent added a special flavour which was capable of conveying to readers some of the sense of exoticness they had experienced. In some cases, these foreign imports ceased to be evocative for the traveller after some time and left no lasting footprint in the language. But quite a number of such loan words have stood the test of time and have entered into common use, becoming standard expressions that epitomise the habits and peculiarities of foreign cultures.[31]

Below is a selection of loans that have entered English and other languages, probably because their country of origin was known and admired in certain fields (i.e. French etiquette and politeness; Italian arts, opera and pleasures of life). Originally, these words were known only to a restricted group of English speakers, travellers and socialites who were well acquainted with French and Italian lifestyles. Although incorporated into the English language, some still bear witness to their foreignness and are distinctively exotic; others have lost their neutral connotation and have acquired ironic overtones.

Petit-Maître, Coquette, Coquetry

One meaning of *petit-maître* is 'a minor master, especially in the fine arts' but in another sense it is used as a derogatory expression: the OED defines it as 'an effeminate man; a dandy, a fop'. The historian Brunot reports that many observers of the theatre scene in London in the second half of the eighteenth century, including Grosley and Chesterfield, reported that a *petit-maître* was the typical character epitomising the French aristocracy: 'un Marquis François', whose ridiculous airs and pretension 'font beaucoup rire les Anglois'.[32] The

---

[30] The examples with French loans are taken from Black, *The British Abroad* (pp. 143, 200, 194, 202), and those with Italian from Cartago, *Ricordi d'italiano* (pp. 136, 163, 150, 220).

[31] There is a wealth of research that examines how foreignisms reveal cultural features and attitudes from specific domains linked to a specific nation. In the early modern period, the few Spanish loan words had to do especially with formality and ceremoniousness, and borrowings from languages like Dutch and German tended to be drawn from popular rather than 'learned and polite' vocabulary. French and Italian imports reflected a privileged life and elitist values. See Charles Barber, *Early Modern English* (Worcester and London, 1976), 178–81.

[32] Brunot, *Histoire*, VIII, 240–1.

oldest attestation dates from 1711, in an article by J. Addison for *The Spectator*: 'All his Men were *Petits-Maîtres*, and all his Women *Coquets*.'[33]

The definition of *coquette* given by the OED is: 'A woman (more or less young), who uses arts to gain the admiration and affection of men . . . a woman who habitually trifles with the affections of men; a flirt.' Its first attested use dates from 1611 as a citation word in R. Cotgrave's *Dictionarie of the French & English Tongues*. The word *coquetry,* defined as a 'coquettish act' in the OED, first appeared in 1748 in a book by Tobias Smollett: 'I was guilty of a thousand coquetries'.[34] Frances Brooke wrote in her *History of Emily Montagu* (1769): 'Continental women had "different mores,' so that 'coquetry is dangerous to English women, because they have sensibility; it is more suited to the French, who are naturally some of the salamander kind'.[35]

Bon Ton, Ton, Tonish

The definition of *bon ton* is 'Good style, good breeding; polite or fashionable society; the fashionable world.' Its first known use in writing was in 1747 by Lord Chesterfield:[36] 'Leipsig is not the place to give him that *bon ton*, which I know he wants.' The meaning of *ton*, of French origin, as given by the OED is: 'The fashion, the vogue, the mode; fashionable air or style.' Its first attestation was in 1769 in *Lloyd's Evening Post*, 18–20 December, 589: 'The present fashionable *Ton* (a word used at present to express every thing that's fashionable) is a set of French puppets.' Fanny Burney wrote ironically in 1778: 'Don't we all know that you lead the *ton* in the beau monde?'[37]

As for the derivative *tonish*, meaning 'having "ton" fashionable, modish, stylish', the OED gives 1778 as its first attestation. The word became fashionable and was used, among others, by Fanny Burney in her diary and correspondence in 1780: 'Do you know now that notwithstanding Bath Easton is so much laughed at in London, nothing here is more tonish than to visit Lady Miller, who is extremely curious in her company, admitting few people who are not of rank or of fame, and excluding of those all who are not people of character very unblemished.'[38]

Savoir Vivre, Savoir Faire, Nonchalance

The OED defines *savoir vivre* as 'knowledge of the world and the ways of society; ability to conduct oneself well; worldly wisdom, sophistication'. The

---

[33] *The Spectator*, no. 83 (1711), 5.   [34] Tobias Smollett, *Roderick Random* (London, 1853), 207.
[35] Frances Brooke, Letter to Miss Rivers, January 28, in *History of Emily Montagu* (Toronto, 2008), 132.
[36] Ld. Chesterfield, Letter 1 December 1932 (modernised text) III, 1061.
[37] Fanny Burney, *Evelina*, Letter LXXXII (London and New York, 1840), 366.
[38] Fanny Burney, *Diary and Letters of Madame d'Arblay*, 4 vols. (London, 1842) I, 364.

dictionary gives its first know use in 1745 from the pen of David Fordyce: 'Eugenio ... is acquainted with their Savoir-vivre, the Art of Living, upon which they pique themselves so much'.[39]

The dictionary definition of *savoir faire* is 'knowledge of the correct course of action in a particular situation, know-how'. The OED specifies that its meaning is now restricted to 'the ability to act or speak appropriately in social situations'. Its first attested use in English was in 1788, in Robert Bage's work *James Wallace*, III, 269: 'I have a very great opinion of your *savoir faire*, especially in the articles of sugar and rum; but for your savoir vivre – none.'

For *nonchalant*, the OED offers the definition 'calm and casual; (deliberately) lacking in enthusiasm or interest; indifferent, unconcerned. Usually of a person, or a person's demeanor or actions, but also in extended use of a literary or artistic style'. The first written attestation was in 1734 by Roger North: 'To be *non chalant* and insipid in such Matters.'[40] The word *nonchalance*, meaning 'The condition of being nonchalant', appeared earlier, in 1678, and spread in the second half of the eighteenth century. Fanny Burney used it in 1774: 'All the sisters then poured forth the Incense of Praise upon this Ode, to which he listened with the utmost nonchalance.'[41]

Connoisseur, Cognoscente

A *connoisseur* is 'one who knows, one versed in a subject' according to the OED, or in a second sense, 'a person well-acquainted with one of the fine arts, and competent to pass a judgement in relation thereto; a critical judge of art or of matters of taste'. The first attested use was in 1719, and George Berkeley in *Alciphron* (1732) explains with a hint of sarcasm that 'Commendation of Honour and Good-nature: but the former of these, by *Connoisseurs*, is always understood to mean nothing but Fashion.'[42] Black quotes a traveller in 1783 who said: 'I by no means pretend to be a *connoisseur*, either in painting or sculpture, but at the same time, they give me great pleasure.'[43]

The Italian word *cognoscente* means 'knowing man'. The OED defines it as 'One who knows a subject thoroughly; a connoisseur: chiefly in reference to the fine arts' and gives 1777 as its first attestation. Philip Francis used the word in his *Hints to a Traveller* published in 1772: 'To a man really curious in the polite arts, Rome alone must be an inexhaustible fund of entertainment; but what can be more disgustful, than to see our young people give themselves the airs of *cognoscenti*.'[44]

---

[39] David Fordyce, *Dialogues Concerning Education*, 2 vols. (London, 1745) II, 330.
[40] Roger North, *Examen*, 2 vols. (1734) v. II, iv, §146, 310.
[41] Fanny Burney, *Early Journals & Letters*. 5 vols. (1990) II, 35.
[42] George Berkeley, *Alciphron* (New Haven, 1803), v, xxvii, 234.
[43] Black, *The British Abroad*, 273.   [44] Quoted in Black, *The British Abroad*, 266.

Bravo, Bravissimo, Primadonna

In Italian, the literal meaning of *bravura* is 'bravery', but in English it is used in the domain of music to refer either to a passage requiring great skill, or to a brilliant performance. For *bravo*, the OED offers the definitions 'Capital! excellent! well done!'. The dictionary cites 1761 as its first attestation, in G. Colman's *Jealous Wife* (I.11): 'That's right – I am Steel – Bravo!-Adamant-Bravissimo!' The pair of words was also used in a French text by the Marquis De Sade about the performance of a castrato: 'J'en fus révolté . . . lesquels cependent occaisonnent aussitot, . . . des hurlements de plaisir à l'unisson, rendus par des "*Bravo! . . . Bravissimo!*".[45] The suffix that marks the superlative was remarked on by several travellers in Italy, among them Walter Savage Landor, who called Italy the nation of the '*issimi*'.[46] As already mentioned in Chapter 2, Oliver Goldsmith referred to himself jokingly as 'the Dullissimo Maccaroni'.

English borrowed the term *primadonna* from Italian in its original sense, 'The leading female singer in an opera company; a female opera singer of great skill and renown.' In this meaning it was first attested in 1754 in A. Drummond's *Travels II*, 52: 'Signora Ronchetti, the prima donna or heroine of the piece, would charm a listening world: she sings with so much ease.' But the term also took on a second more figurative meaning, which the OED defines as: 'a person who has the highest standing or who takes a leading role in a particular community or field. Also: a self-important or temperamental person'. It was first used in this sense in 1834 by Charlotte Brontë: 'The wife of Northangerland, the prima donna of the Angrian Court.'[47]

Fresco, Al Fresco

Fresco evokes a recurrent image of Italy as a hot country, where one must try to escape the sun during the hottest hours. The meaning of *fresco* or *al fresco* given by the OED is 'in the fresh or cool air', and the English sense is 'in the open air; outdoors', as the expression was imported especially with reference to dining outside. The first attested use in the OED dates from 1620 in Nathaniel Brent's translation of Paolo Sarpi's *History of the Council of Trent*: 'There being a custome amongst the people of Paris, in the Summers evenings, to goe out of the Suburbs of S. Germain in great multitudes, to take the *fresco*.'[48] Many travellers used the word in their writing: '*Fresco* at the table' (Lassels, 1635); 'take the *fresco* from the sea' (Evelyn, 1644); 'and came to mount

---

[45] de Sade, *Voyage d'Italie*, 68.   [46] Quoted in Serianni, 'Lingua e dialetti', 65.
[47] 'A peep into a picture book', in *Twelve Adventurers* (1925), 168.
[48] Nathaniel Brent, *The Historie of the Councel of Trent* [translation of Paolo Sarpi's *Historia del concilio Tridentino*] (London, 1620), v. 410.

Pausillipus, a promontory; about which, in the summer evenings, the nobility take the fresco or air in their felucca's' (Skippon, 1732); 'a door at the end of the channel which lets in the *fresco*' (John Ray, 1663); 'we dined *al Fresco*' (Sir James Smith, 1786); 'the pedestrians of all classes and ages, all coming forth *per pigliar il fresco*' (Lady Sydney Morgan, 1819).[49]

Dolce Far Niente

In the OED, the pleasing inactivity expressed by the saying *dolce far niente* ('sweet to do nothing') is defined as 'delightful idleness'. The first attestation was in 1814 in Byron's *Letters* (3 August): 'Making the most of the "dolce far-niente" [at Hastings].'[50] It soon became a national stereotype, although some writers like Mary Shelley adopted it in a rather mild form: 'The more I see the inhabitants of this country, the more I feel convinced that they are highly gifted with intellectual powers and possess all the elements of greatness. They are made to be a free, active, enquiring people. But they must cast away their *dolce far niente*.'[51] Early nineteenth-century commentaries on Italy often alluded to the *dolce far niente* but some accounts were sympathetic about how the warmth of the south created indolence in its inhabitants. Anna Jameson was one such traveller-narrator. She was inclined to designate 'southern indolence as a source of pleasure accessible to the traveler as well as to the Italians themselves',[52] and she claimed that 'All my activity of mind, all my faculties of thought and feeling, and suffering, seemed lost and swallowed up in an indolent delicious reverie, a sort of vague and languid enjoyment, the true "*dolce far niente*" of this enchanting climate.' A Mrs Blessington went even further: 'I shall journalise no more; but merely write down, whenever in the humour, what occurs, or what I see. *O the dolce far niente of an Italian life!* Who can resist its influence? Not I, at least.'[53] As time passed, travellers took this stereotype less seriously. Charles Dickens adopted it in a rather comic sense in the description of a northern landscape: 'perfect Italian cows enjoying the *dolce far niente* all day along'.[54]

Code-Switching

Many travel accounts include not only single words in a foreign language but also phrases and sentences, such as exclamations, remarks, commands,

---

[49] Skippon, 'An account', 601. All other quotations about this item are from Cartago, *Ricordi d'Italiano*, 146.
[50] George Gordon Byron, Letter to Mr Moore, Hastings, August, 1814, in Thomas Moore's *Letters and Journals of Lord Byron: with Notices of His Life*, 17 vols. (Paris, 1833), I, 407.
[51] Mary Wollstonecraft Shelley, *Rambles in Germany and Italy in 1840, 1842, and 1843* (1844) 2 vols. (Folcroft-Pennsylvania, 1975), I, 86.
[52] Jameson, *Diary*, 274.   [53] Blessington, *The Idler in Italy*, II, 119.
[54] Dickens, *Pictures from Italy*, 23.

questions and expressions of approval or disapproval. However, the division between borrowing and code-switching is not absolute, nor is the difference between a switch in language that calls attention to the unfamiliar and one that emphasises cultural diversity. An appropriate distinction is that code-switching in a travel narrative is different from the practice of alternating two languages in real life. In ordinary communication, a single word can quite naturally trigger a change of language, while code-switching in travel writing involves a premeditated change of emphasis. Typically, foreign phrasing is used when there is the need to signal a change of mood vis-à-vis a situation, an idea or attitude that expresses a quite different vision of the world.

A conversation between Arthur Young and a French peasant in a rustic area near Bézier in the Languedoc-Roussillon provides a good example of how switching to another language can suddenly create the right climax to a story. Young was a campaigner for the rights of agricultural workers, and his intention here was to emphasise the state of indigence to which the rural population was reduced in a rich country like France. Switching between the two languages at a crucial point served to stress the peasant's incredulity, in preparation for Young's conclusion:

The other day a Frenchman asked me, after telling him I was an Englishman, if we had trees in England? – I replied that we had a few. Had we any rivers? – Oh, none at all. *Ah ma foi c'est bien triste!* This incredible ignorance, when compared with the knowledge so universally disseminated in England, is to be attributed, like every thing else, to government.[55]

Unlike indirect speech, which focuses more on the content of what was said, repeating something verbatim tends to emphasise the emotional impact of that part of a conversation. Thus, the difference between code-switching and single borrowings also concerns the position of the writer vis-à-vis the participants. If the insertion of a single word indicates the novelty of an object or the singularity of a situation, the alternation of longer stretches in foreign languages can signal to readers that the authors themselves were struck by that aspect of the conversation. In this sense, code-switching, more than a single borrowing can be a more effective marker of personalisation. It underscores the fact that authors experienced the same emotional or cultural impact they expect to recreate in their readers. Travel accounts have always made use of language alternations for this rhetorical purpose. But it was especially in the eighteenth century, at the peak of the Grand Tour, that some writers resorted to code-mixing as a strategy to underscore cultural alterity.[56]

---

[55] Young, *Travels in France*, 55.
[56] Herbert Schendl explains that code-switching in written texts has only emerged recently as a research field and reminds us of Suzanne Romaine's distinction between its different functions: as a marker of personalisation vs. objectivisation. The former can point to the writer being

French and Italian phrases or sentences which were scattered among the pages of travel accounts served different functions in a narrative depending on the context as shown in the categories and examples below. But in all the examples, we can assume the narrators felt that without the recourse to the original language, the momentum of the narrative would be lost or the attitudes of those emotionally involved would not be faithfully reconstructed.

Reproducing written language: There are a number of inscriptions found on buildings and monuments which were transcribed by travellers in their written accounts. However, these cannot be considered examples of code-switching but rather cases of language alternation. The authors who used them in their original form rather than in translation did so with the intent of emphasising a comic message or a curious warning. Thomas Coryat, who loved inscriptions in all languages, could not resist quoting an amusing one in French found near Lyon: 'At the South side of the higher court of mine Inne . . . there is written this pretty French poesie: *On ne loge ceans à credit: car il est mort, les mauvais paieurs l' ont tué*'. He goes on to decipher it: 'The English is this: Here is no lodging upon credit: for he is dead, ill payers have killed him.'[57]

Foreign phrases with and without translation: Some travel writers offered a translation after inserting a foreign expression, as in the passage above, and when this related to spoken rather than written language, the repetition of the content increased the emphasis on cultural distance. Patrick Brydone achieved this effect when reporting on a drinking session with merry company in Sicily. A Canon, referring to someone called Pontio (like Pontius Pilate) who had fallen drunk under the table, groaned out: 'Ah, Signor Capitano, sapeva sempre che Pontio era un gran traditore'- 'I always knew that Pontius was a great traitor!'[58] In other cases, especially when the meaning was obvious, the translation was not provided as in this passage from Mrs Piozzi Thrale: 'Italians seem to me to have no feeling of cold; they open the casements – for windows we have none – now in the winter, and cry, "*Che bel freschetto!*" while I am starving outright'[59] (where starving means 'freezing cold'). Here, the original exclamation involved such a famous Italian phrase (see *fresco* and *al fresco*) that a rendition in English was felt unnecessary.

French as a lingua franca: Code-switching into Italian usually happened during interactions in Italy, and those in French normally occurred in France. However, in the eighteenth century, quite a number of French expressions trickled into other languages because of its status as an international language, and indeed some French phrases were heard or used by travellers outside of France. The following examples were all recorded in Italy. The first is an idiomatic expression for a person

emotionally involved with the message, 'Multilingualism¸ code-switching and language contact', in Hernández-Campoy and Conde-Silvestre (eds.), 529.

[57] Coryat, *Crudities*, I, 213.   [58] Brydone, *A Tour Through Sicily,* 53.
[59] Piozzi Thrale, *Observations*, I, 92.

of distinction, used by William Beckford: 'Indeed, Sir, no *Monsieur comme il faut* ever left the Spa in such dudgeon before.'[60] The second is the phrase *pour passer le temps*, used in a sarcastic passage by Mary Wortley Montagu: 'I am assured here that it was an expedient ... to find employment for those young men who were forced to cut one another's throats *pour passer le temps*.'[61] The third example comes from the already discussed *Advice* by William Patoun, who was writing from Italy: 'Go to the Belvedere at Night and see the Apollo and Lacoon by torch. *Il vaut bien la peine*.'[62]

Foreigner talk: In addition to Grand Tourists throwing in phrases and expressions from French or Italian, they also included in their written accounts amusing verbatim instances of 'foreigner talk' in English with people they encountered who had a poor command of English. A nice example of this is provided by Charles Dickens, whose English cook had regular interchanges with the Genoese by speaking 'with great fluency in English (very loud: as if the others were only deaf, not Italian)'. His cook's way of 'talking at' foreigners inspired the author of *Little Dorrit* in his portrayal of one of his famous characters, who actually uses classic 'foreigner talk':

Mrs Plornish was particularly ingenious in this art; and attained so much celebrity for saying 'Me ope you leg well soon', that it was considered in the Yard but a very short remove indeed from speaking Italian. Even Mrs Plornish herself began to think that she had a natural call towards that language.[63]

Reporting their own speech: While reports of direct speech usually involved interactions with other participants, some authors noted down their own internal dialogues in a foreign language. An example comes, again, from Charles Dickens while in Italy, where 'he was drawn to the life of Italy's people and streets more than to its monuments and works of art'. In April 1846, Dickens had learned enough Italian to report: 'I talk to all the Italian Boys who go about the streets with Organs and white mice, and give them mints of money *per l'amore della bell'Italia*.' Here Dickens's sudden code-switch emphasises his sympathy for the humble people living in dire urban conditions which contrasted so starkly with the grandiose buildings and beauty of the country admired by other travellers of the time.[64]

---

[60] Beckford, Letter vii, Spa, 6 July 1780, in *Dreams, Waking Thoughts, and Incidents in a Series of Letters from Various Parts of Europe*. www. biblioteca virtual universal.

[61] Montagu, *Letters and Works*, I, 386.   [62] Patoun, 'Advice on travel', lii.

[63] Charles Dickens, *Little Dorrit* (New York, 1883), 308.

[64] The phenomenon of itinerant children sent out onto the streets to beg by their poor parents was common in Italy, though Dickens was referring here to those begging in the streets of London, a practice strongly opposed by philanthropic associations and the medical profession. The reference to the interests of Charles Dickens in Italy comes from John Bowen, 'Dickens and the figures of *Pictures from Italy*', in Clare Hornsby (ed.), *The Impact of Italy*, 200. The quotation is from Michael Hollington, 'The European context', in Sally Ledger and Holly Furneaux (eds.), *Charles Dickens in Context* (Cambridge, 2011), 43–50.

Another case of code-switching during an author's reconstruction of his memories of a journey to Italy can be found in a story recounted by Dickens's old friend, the poet Samuel Rogers, in a passage where he recalls an emotional visit to the house of the great Italian poet Ariosto at Ferrara. Here his code-switching was not intended to convey an attitude of cultural superiority or alterity, but rather a sense of emotional identification: 'His chair, plainer than Petrarch's, entire, & very low & easy. Sat in it. Would I could have said *'Ed io sono anche &c'.* (The editor's interpretation is: 'would I could have said that I also am such a poet?')[65]

Language switches could also involve idiomatic expressions heard from passers-by or modes of address suitable for titled people, kinship terms, and expressions of endearment or formulae of respect used with different professions and social positions. It is interesting that when these appeared in a narrative in Italian, it was always to signal exaggeration or melodramatic circumstances. When used in dialogues with or between French people, the author tended to be stressing politeness and good manners.

Italian:

Viva il Compare et viva la Comare ['May our good-man and good-wife prosper'] (Drummond)

Figlia mia, che domandate? ['My child, what is your request?'] (Burney)

Anime sante di purgatorio! ['Hallowed souls in purgatory!'] (Piozzi Thrale)

Ah figliuolo indegno! Siamo rovinati! ['Ah base child! We are in ruins!'] (Smollett)

Eccellenza! Assoluzione in articulo mortis! ['Your excellency! Absolution at the point of death!'] (Swinburne)

Ecco il vero Pulcinella ['Here is the true Punchinello'] (Sharp)

French:

En cet état ['as the French say' (= in that state)] (Piozzi Thrale)

Ah monsieur – ça c'est la politesse ['Ah monsieur, these are good manners!'] (Burney)

Oh le charmant – c'est il qui l'a fait! ['Oh very charming –is he who did it?'] (Rogers)

Avec bonne grace ['On great style'] (Wharton)

Ah! Il y a assez de belles choses ['Ah! There are plenty of beautiful things'] (Walpole)

De grâce, Messieurs, laissez-moi en paix ['If you please, Messieurs, leave me in peace'] (Carlyle)

---

[65] Samuel Rogers, *Italy* (1830) in John Rigby Hale (ed.), *The Italian Journal of Samuel Rogers, with an Account of Rogers' Life and of Travel in Italy in 1814–1821* (London, 1956), 183.

Proverbs and popular sayings presented in the original language could also function to attract the attention of readers to situations where it was felt more appropriate to conjure up everyday scenarios by using the local language. Like stereotypes that highlight national characteristics, such expressions were inserted to elucidate the hyperbolic dimension of Italian passions or the sophisticated nature of French manners. Even when writers were not interested in representing an exotic situation, nor signalling approval or disapproval, the foreign expressions functioned to add colour to a picturesque description of the actors and actions observed. More often than not, however, the intention of the writer was to create an ironic effect by exemplifying how distant these foreign phrases were from the more composed English perspective:

Italian:

Servire et non gradire ['To serve well and get no thanks'] (Wake)
Dio me ne libere [sic]! ['God deliver me from it!'] (Smollett)
È battezzato come noi ['He has been christened as well as ourselves'] (Piozzi Thrale)
Non scordatevi mai dei vostri amici ['Do not speak ill of your friends'] (Brydone)
I pensieri stretti ed il viso sciolto ['Honest thoughts and guarded looks'] (Henry Wotton)
Si fa sempre aspettare ['Always keeps people waiting'] (Craven)

French:

Courage le diable est mort! ['Courage, the devil is dead!'] (Coryat)
Beaucoup de fantaisie, mais rien de solide ['Very imaginative, but nothing substantial'] (Young)
Le lebeche raccomode le tems [sic] (instead of *temps*) ['The Lebeche settles the weather'] (Smollett)
Sacre Dieu je suis mort ['My God, I am dead!'] (anonymous author of *A New Journey*)
A force d'en avoir vu ['After seeing so many of them'] (Walpole)
Coute qui coute ['At all costs'] (Piozzi Thrale)

As the fashion for tourism evolved, so did the tendency of travellers to portray in a more naturalistic way the picturesque image of a distant country. When the otherness of foreign people needed to be represented with dramatic tones, recounting interactions with natives afforded the opportunity to show sympathy with the locals. Italian immoderation offered quite sensational opportunities in this respect as the two customs of monasticism and cicisbeism were known abroad as causes of improper restraint.[66] The following quotations spell out to an English audience the two extremes of restriction and licence imposed upon Italian women. The first, from *Some Observations* by Edward Wright, relates a friend's encounter with a nun in a convent. Here the original language clearly conveys a strong sense of pity:

Wright tells the story of an acquaintance who, when visiting a convent, encounters a nun 'detain'd there contrary to her Inclinations': the unhappy woman 'came, in a perfectly frantic manner, into the *Parlatorio*, tearing her Hair, and making hideous Complaints, and crying, *Pregate Dio per mi' [sic] son' disperata*. "Pray God for me, I am in Despair"'.[67]

The other example comes from an interesting conversation Hester Piozzi Thrale reported in her *Observations and Reflections* when she asked an Italian friend about her view of cicisbeism. It would have been very surprising to the English readership of the time, most of whom believed women in Italy would be corrupted by this unnatural habit, that her friend far from condemned this practice. The passage is perfused with gentle humour aimed at capturing the sympathy of female readers:

'*Mr. Such-a-one* sat much with me at home, or went with me to the Corso; and I *must* go with some gentleman you know: and the men are such ungenerous creatures, and have such ways with them: I want money often, and this *cavaliere servente* pays the bills, and so the connection draws closer – *that's all*'. And your husband! said I – 'Oh, why he likes to see me well dressed; he is very good natured, and very charming; I love him to my heart'. And your confessor! cried I. – 'Oh, why he is *used to it* – in the Milanese dialect – è *assuefaà*'.[68]

Both dialogues emphasise the discrepancy between local customs in Italy and the outlook of the travellers and their readers who, by the end of the eighteenth century, consisted of men and women in much less unequal proportions. It seems appropriate to bring the chapter to a close on this note, especially because the next will be devoted to the issue of the diverse perspectives of male and female travel writers. This is a topic which concerns language and gender, something that has been the subject of many investigations, although it has not been researched much in the context of the Grand Tour.[69]

---

[66] See Chard, *Pleasure and Guilt*, especially 91–3.   [67] Wright, *Some Observations*, I, 229.
[68] Piozzi Thrale, *Observations*, I, 101.
[69] An outstanding exception is Rosemary Sweet, who remarks in her 2012 book: "neither Dolan, *Ladies of the Grand Tour,* nor Kathryn Walchester, *Our Own Fair Italy: Nineteenth-Century Women's Travel Writing and Italy 1800–1844* (Bern, 2007), engages with the question of how and why the feminine experience differed from the masculine", 20 n.61. Another essential publication on gendered perspectives during the Grand Tour is Paula Findlen, Wendy Wassying Roworth and Catherine M. Sama (eds.), *Italy's Eighteenth Century: Gender and Culture in the Age of the Grand Tour* (Stanford, 2009).

9   Women Travellers and Gender Issues

Exclusion

This chapter looks at the life and travels of some of the women who participated in the last phase of the Grand Tour. Until then, the common assumption had been that young ladies' preparation for adult life would focus on the family, and travel did not play a role in this, as they had no career to prepare for.[1] Since women's education was home-oriented, their integration into adult life involved acceptance of a husband's authority and did not call for personal experience of the world. In recent times, some historians have produced substantial evidence and detailed references supporting the view that women's domestic vocation denied them the independence that freedom of travel presupposed.[2]

One of the early traditional opinions on this topic was voiced by Georgius Loysius, who claimed in his *Pervigilium Mercurii* (1644) that 'Nature herself desires that women should stay at home', which he underscored by the explanation that 'It is true throughout the whole Germany that no woman unless she is desperately poor or "rather fast" desires to travel.'[3] Indeed, for the best part of the early modern era in Europe, it was rare for women to undertake a journey for leisure or education and leave records of their travels. Mączak mentions two early

---

[1] A famous exception is the Italian journey of Lady Catherine Whetenhall, which was planned as a pilgrimage. Second daughter of John Talbot, 10th Earl of Shrewsbury, whose estates were confiscated in 1647, this young Catholic Royalist, who married Thomas Whetenhall, expressed the strong desire to visit Rome and the Santa Casa of Loreto with her husband, and with Richard Lassels acting as a guide, on the occasion of the Holy Year in 1650. During the journey, Lady Catherine became pregnant and eventually died in Padua. According to Edward Chaney, who carried out extensive research on Lassels' *Voyage of the Lady Catherine Whetenhann from Brussels into Italy in the Holy Yeare, 1650,* the Catholic priest and guide for the young couple was 'concerned that his friend and patron should not be described as having acted irresponsibly in agreeing to the expedition in the first place'; *The Grand Tour*, 81–2.

[2] See: Cohen, *Fashioning Masculinity;* Elizabeth Garms-Cornides, 'Esiste un *Grand Tour* al femminile?' in Dinora Corsi (ed.), *Altrove: Viaggi di donne dall'antichità al Novecento* (Rome, 1999), 175–200; Dolan, *Ladies of the Grand Tour*; and Donatella Abbate Badin, 'Tre primedonne del Grand Tour: Lady Montagu, Hester Thrale e Lady Morgan', in Claudio Sensi and Patrizia Pellizzari (eds.), *Viaggi e pellegrinaggi fra Tre e Ottocento* (Alessandria, 2008), 331–82.

[3] Georgius Loysius, *Privilegium Mercurii* (Frankfurt, 1644), 8.

240

books by women which earned them considerable success. Both wrote about their travels to Spain, which was not a typical destination. One was Lady Fanshawe, who gave birth at least seventeen times, and whose husband was the English ambassador to Madrid after the Civil War.[4] Another was the Frenchwoman Madame d'Aulnoy, whose travel diary about Spain enjoyed some forty-three editions in five different languages, in spite of the fact that she had never been to the country. According to Mączak, the desperate conditions of travel in that country, together with the fact that these ladies of distinction recounted journeys to an unusual destination, explain the success of their publications. Mączak goes on to state that, once comfort and safety on the road improved, travelling became a more pleasurable experience for women as well as men, and this was what eventually led to an increase in their numbers.[5]

The intellectual climate of the Enlightenment, with its stress on reason and individualism rather than tradition, was not a minor factor in challenging the customary view of women's place being in the home. At the time, the most liberal sectors of British society were the first to question the concept that women's domestic virtues were a prerequisite for the health of the nation. When women realised that they had the wealth and ability to attain the same intellectual distinction as men, they became more vocal about their aspirations. Traditionally, young ladies were sent to boarding schools for a brief experience of formal education, or they were educated at home by a tutor or governess. A change in educational perspective occurred when modern languages came to be more practical than Latin for communication abroad, although this introduced further divisions between the sexes. In Britain, modern languages gradually grew to be a favourite subject for women; but this was difficult to reconcile with the emphasis on gentlemen receiving linguistic training for a political or academic career.

The study of foreign languages in principle no longer appeared unbecoming for ladies but its practical effects needed to be carefully monitored, as 'it could create an undesirable, unpatriotic and cosmopolitan mentality'.[6] Italian was seen as the new fashionable language because of international recognition of the country's music. But it was the French language, associated with the cultural life of Parisian salons, that inspired intellectuals of both sexes to imitate the conversation circles of the *beau monde* across the Channel. As late as the second half of the eighteenth century, Hester Chapone, a writer of conduct books for women (the first in 1773), felt the need to endorse this change in climate with the argument that 'dancing and the knowledge of the French tongue are now so universal, that they cannot be dispensed with in the education of a gentlewoman'.[7]

---

[4] Mączak, *Travel*, 142.   [5] Ibid., 141.   [6] Dolan, *Ladies of the Grand Tour*, 44.
[7] Hester Chapone, *Letters on the Improvement of the Mind, Addressed to a Young Lady*, 2 vols. (Dublin, 1773), new ed. (Philadelphia, 1786), 715.

However, the inclination of young ladies to advance their knowledge of foreign languages was still viewed with circumspection. Quite apart from the fact that the conversational method of language learning had not completely replaced the grammatical approach, girls who wanted to study French at home or at school were told that their knowledge of a foreign language was best applied to reading rather than speaking, and instruction was planned accordingly.[8] If a young lady was keen to show her accomplishment in speaking French, it was considered more seemly to do so in private salons rather than in public spaces.

Among the young ladies who expressed frustration about being excluded from wider social circles, there were some who later became famous travellers. First, they acquired competence and skills in areas which would normally be denied to them by the patriarchal world they lived in. Then they sought new types of knowledge, with a view to liberating themselves and engaging in public intellectual activities. When they finally made the decision to go abroad, they did so with a view to writing travel accounts that contained an alternative vision of the world that did not follow the traditions of the Grand Tour. This change began at the height of the Grand Tour and left such an indelible mark that it effectively accelerated its decline, as explained below.

Travel for Self-Realisation

It is not a coincidence that all the women who became famous travellers pursued self-education intensively, and quite a few studied classics while becoming fluent in one or more European languages. The first of these accomplished ladies was Mary Wortley Montagu, who is often credited with inspiring subsequent generations of women. Daughter of Evelyn Pierrepont, Earl of Kingston-upon-Hull, she received her initial education at home from a governess she deeply despised. Lady Mary was intellectually ambitious, and in order to take control of her own education, she made use of the library in her father's mansion and taught herself Latin, fully aware that this language was traditionally reserved for men.[9] Hester Piozzi Thrale also grew up as a precocious linguist before becoming the most famous of all the female writers of the eighteenth century. Although born to an impoverished family of the gentry, she was raised by enlightened parents and given an education that

---

[8] Cohen, *Fashioning Masculinity*, 65.

[9] Mary Wortley Montagu gave an account of this when she met the literary scholar Joseph Spence in Rome in 1741: 'When I was young I was a great admirer of Ovid's Metamorphoses, and that was one of the chief reasons that set me upon the thoughts of stealing the Latin language. Mr Wortley was the only person to whom I communicated my design, and he encouraged me in it. I used to study five or six hours a day for two years in my father's library; and so got that language, whilst everybody else thought I was reading nothing but novels and romances.' Quoted in 'Introductory anecdotes' in Montagu, *Letters and Works*, II, 53.

included etiquette, horsemanship, Spanish, Italian, Latin and rhetoric. As a leading literary figure, she became involved in Samuel Johnson's prestigious circle, and she continued to commit herself to studying new languages and improving her proficiency. After her death, Reverend Edward Mangin remarked that 'she not only read and wrote Hebrew, Greek and Latin, but had for sixty years constantly and ardently studied the Scriptures and the works of commentators in the original languages'.[10]

Mary Hamilton was another member of the social circle acquainted with Dr Johnson and his friends. While governess to the daughters of George III, she became one of the most prolific diarists, writing almost 2,500 letters. She, too, was a linguist as a young lady, and at the age of sixteen she let her cousin and guardian, William Napier, into a secret: she was teaching herself Latin. Once informed of this, her mother-in-law, Mrs Dickenson, advised her not 'to study as to hurt your health, remember that we are creatures formed for society'.[11] Two other young ladies of distinction who were closely connected to writers and intellectuals of the time were Mary Berry and her sister Agnes, called 'twin wives' by Horace Walpole. This politician and man of letters remained their close friend from the time they set up a fashionable salon, which became famous in London society. Mary and her younger sister remained unmarried, and the former admitted to treating travel as 'the route to the improvement of the mind, to becoming distinguished and to preparing herself and her sister for society'.[12]

Increasingly, the model set by distinguished ladies like Mary Montagu, Hester Piozzi Thrale, Mary Hamilton and Mary Berry of being in charge of one's own linguistic education at home raised expectations among young ladies of being able to use their foreign languages abroad, which implied freedom to travel. Indeed, most of these women found it objectionable that their knowledge of modern languages should be restricted to reading activities at home, when this should have made it possible for them to engage in interactions abroad and communicate with real people. But such a project would have interfered with their domestic responsibilities. For many women during the second half of the eighteenth century, the quest for a change of culture or a better climate covered a hidden agenda of escaping an arranged marriage or other type of social imposition. Access to the Continent would provide a chance for them to break free and build a new life based on a better understanding of others and more respect for themselves.

---

[10] Quoted in Dolan, *Ladies of the Grand Tour*, 45.
[11] Letter from Mrs Dickenson to Mary Hamilton, 12 November 1772, Mary Hamilton Papers (Box 4, Folder A4, Interim Box List, Page 1 of 19), November 2008 online edition, University of Manchester Collections.
[12] Quoted in Dolan, *Ladies of the Grand Tour*, 26.

The most usual form of travel writing adopted by women was correspondence: letters to relatives or female friends, with a view to sharing personal information, observations and comments on the new realities they encountered abroad.[13] There was already an established tradition in personal travel correspondence of including digressions on historical, social and political aspects of the foreign countries visited. This format was uncontroversial as long as the narrative was free from self-assertions, something that would have been interpreted as insolent in a woman. In reality, once women started publishing their travel writing under titles such as *Letters, Diary* or *Tour*, this genre evolved rapidly and began to include not only travel accounts characterised by narrative distance but also memoirs charged with personal emotions and subjective opinions.

From the second half of the eighteenth century, many women became keen readers of this genre of narrative; and some women writers targeted their own publications specifically at a female readership. In Germany, where there were also many women travellers, the poetess Elisa von der Recke made the point in her posthumously published diary that her travel book was written 'solely for persons of my sex, who, like myself have not had an education, but nevertheless keep in their own heart a special passion for antiquities'.[14] A typical offering for this new readership was the *Traveller's Companion for Conversation in Travelling and in the Different Situations of Life* (1819) by the prolific writer Stéphanie Félicité, Comtesse de Genlis, who penned conversations in four languages, including dialogues aimed at women giving birth abroad. In the first half of the nineteenth century, the number of travel books written by English women increased visibly, with twenty new works published in the decade between 1838 and 1848.[15] This confirmed that the travel book genre was evolving beyond being a guide, a diary or evidence of a young gentleman's educational progress. Travel writing was diversifying, and the contribution of women was transforming it dramatically from its manifestation during the heyday of the Grand Tour, when travel books were laden with the historical or artistic preoccupations of their male authors.

At the twilight of the Grand Tour, women writers aired a variety of fresh interests and inspirations in their new forms of travel narrative. The fact that most British women travellers did not regard Italy as a museum of antiquities

---

[13] Ways of posting and receiving letters in the eighteenth century were more varied and informal than today but rarely if ever did writers express concern that their letters would not reach the intended destination. The Post Office service in Lombard Street in London sent letters to Paris twice a week. In Italy, the system was considered inefficient so many relied on couriers or even friends. Another common and reliable system was to send letters through a bank. See James T. Boulton and T. O. Macloghlin (eds.), *News from Abroad: Letters Written by British Travellers on the Grand Tour*, 1728–1771 (Liverpool, 1998), especially 16–18.

[14] Quoted in Garms-Cornides, 'Esiste un *Grand Tour* al femminile?', 182.

[15] Pine-Coffin, *British and American Travel*, 221–46.

but rather as a hospitable land of refuge from domestic oppression and social ostracism, certainly encouraged them to analyse the nature of social relations more objectively. Those who had moved abroad in search of an alternative way of life became conscious that accommodating to differences was easier when they, as outsiders, were willing to listen to locals of both genders and all classes. The attitude of Lady Montagu towards the institution of cicisbeism in Italy, considered scandalous elsewhere, is quite instructive. She first encountered it in Genoa in 1718, after a lengthy residence in Turkey as the wife of the British Ambassador, and she explained that the same custom was quite normal at the Ottoman Court in Constantinople. Accordingly, she viewed the Italian cicisbei, their ladies and the husbands through a rational mind and described it using measured words:

The fashion began here, and is now received all over Italy, where the husbands are not such terrible creatures as we represent them. [Cicisbei] are gentlemen who devote themselves to the service of a particular lady (I mean a married one, for the virgins are all invisible, and confined to convents): they are obliged to wait on her to all public places, such as the plays, operas, and assemblies (which are here called Conversationes) ... but the husband is not to have the impudence to suppose this any other than pure platonic friendship. 'Tis true they endeavour to give her a cicizbei of their own chusing; but when the lady happens not to be of the same taste, as that often happens, she never fails to bring it about to have one of her own fancy.[16]

A sympathetic description of this Italian custom was something most British men were unwilling to accept; but it showed how better insights into cultural diversity could be gained by casting aside the prejudices of those who looked on with horror at the surface of this foreign custom. Of course, Mary Montagu knew very well that adultery was far from unusual among the English aristocracy although it was much less publicised. Having a mistress was a normal habit for upper-class men in England, and wives were expected to hide their emotions when faced with their husbands' infidelity. Their humiliation was common, while divorces were extremely rare. But if a woman undertook an extra-marital affair, it was grounds for divorce and resulted in public condemnation. As most marriages were arranged for economic benefit, English women could take little initiative in establishing relationships before their marriage and had little freedom afterward. Those who wanted to speak out about this situation back home, like Lady Montagu, were probably aware that in other countries adulterous liaisons were quite usual. But in those days, when women were held to 'different mores', their dalliances were veiled behind euphemisms. For example, *coquetry* was a well-known French term imported into English, referring to flirtatious behaviour. Germans borrowed the term *gallantry* from

---

[16] Letter from Lady Montagu to the Countess of Mar, Genoa, 28 August 1718, *Letters and Works*, II, 76.

French and also turned it into a euphemism – adultery by wives must have been alive and well there if this comment by an appalled Duchess of Northumberland is anything to go by: 'The Comtesse Fugger who is not reckon'd one of the worst told Mrs Cressener that the Grand Ecuyer . . . was her 49th Gallant.'[17] Mary Montagu herself wrote about the normal habit of ladies of distinction in Germany having a lover as well as a husband:

> Here are neither coquettes nor prudes. No woman dares appear coquette enough to encourage two lovers at a time, and I have not seen any such prudes as to pretend fidelity to their husbands . . . In one word, 'tis the established custom for every lady to have two husbands, one that bears the name, and another that performs the duties; and . . . it would be a downright affront and publicly resented if you invited a woman of quality to dinner without at the same time inviting her two attendants of lover and husband, between whom she always sits in state with great gravity.[18]

Otherness Revisited

The custom of engaging in adulterous behaviour in public was often criticised in men's accounts of their travels in Italy, although some travellers left it unmentioned and others reported it without disgust. The observers who exhibited the most shock drew attention to the fact that these liberties taken by married women and their male companions in Italy could set a bad example for British women.[19] It is interesting, however, that no male observers tried to get to the roots of this social habit to understand why the Italian nobility spent more time socialising with women than did their counterparts in Britain. The chief reason was that unlike in other countries, the Italian aristocracy was not allowed to participate in the affairs of state or to take up offices in the army or the navy because those positions were occupied by natives of the two main foreign powers, Habsburg Spain (1559–1714) and Habsburg Austria (1714–96).

It was not until women voiced a radically innovative view on this topic that readers of travel books began to appreciate this social practice as a harmless indulgence. Not only was it seen as conducive to good social relations between the sexes but female readers who kept an open mind appreciated the Italian custom as morally better than their own country's domestic hypocrisy. This was the position taken by Hester Piozzi Thrale:

[17] Dolan, who quotes it, explains that gallant means 'lover', since 'gallantry was a borrowed French euphemism for amorous behaviour'. Dolan, *Ladies of the Grand Tour*, 94.
[18] Letter from Lady Montagu to Lady K. Rich, Vienna, 20 September 1716, in *Letters and Works*, I, 244.
[19] Quoted in Black, *The British Abroad*, 43.

We have all heard much of Italian cicisbeism; I had a mind to know how matters really stood; and took the nearest way to information by asking a mighty beautiful and apparently artless young creature, not noble, how that affair was managed, for there is no harm done I am sure, said I: 'Why no', replied she, 'no great harm to be sure: except wearisome attentions from a man one cares little about' . . . The certainty that the worst, whatever that worst may be, meets your immediate inspection, gives great repose to the mind: you know there is no latent poison lurking out of sight . . . and talking freely with women in this country [Italy], though you may have a chance to light on ignorance, you are never teized by folly.[20]

What appeared to male travellers as a manifestation of moral degradation and social awkwardness was seen by women travellers as a different realisation of male and female roles in society. Recent research on gender in the context of the Grand Tour has shown that in order to arrive at this new viewpoint, the traveller needed to adopt an anthropological perspective avant la lettre. The new approach was that observations made abroad needed to be based on interpretation, not condemnation, of the foreign reality. Although this innovative attitude was decisively transgressive in origin, it soon became usual amongst the most socially aware travellers. Chloe Chard has been the main advocate of this view in her work on the traversal of cultural boundaries by women travellers.[21] She claims that women writers during the Grand Tour did not enrich their travel accounts with feminine topics, nor did they condemn outright male perceptions and justify female attitudes in foreign countries. But they were the first to seriously examine customs and manners that differed from those back home with sharp and unprejudiced perseverance.

Mary Montagu was aware of being the first woman to challenge criticisms of foreign customs perpetuated by her male compatriots. She was so conscious of her new approach that she used uncompromising words to announce it: '[This] is so different from what I had always heard and read, that I am convinced either the manners of the country are wonderfully changed, or travellers have always related what they have imagined and not what they saw.' She also criticised the superficial knowledge of Italy based on other books 'that are antiquated or confined to trite observations' written by people who 'after a tour . . . think of themselves qualified to give exact accounts of the customs, policies, and interests of the dominions they have gone through post'.[22] Her

[20] Piozzi Thrale, *Observations*, I, 100.
[21] Chard's most relevant work is *Pleasure and Guilt on the Grand Tour* (1999). Parts of some chapters in the book also appeared in 'Crossing boundaries and exceeding limits: destabilisation, tourism, and the sublime' in Chloe Chard and Helen Langdon (eds.), *Transports: Travel, Pleasure, and Imaginative Geography, 1600–1830* (New Haven and London, 1996), and in 'Comedy, antiquity, the feminine and the foreign: Emma Hamilton and Corinne', in Hornsby (ed.), *The Impact of Italy* (2000).
[22] Letter from Lady Montagu to the Countess of Bute, Genoa, 8 December 1759, *Letters and Works*, III, 189.

argument that readers deserve accurate accounts was based on a declaration of honest intent: 'a very long stay, a diligent enquiry, and a nice observation, are requisite even to a moderate degree of knowing a foreign country'.[23]

Cultural diversity was a major field of discussion throughout the second half of the eighteenth century, and the social customs of foreigners became a favourite *topos* for comparing diverse visions of otherness. Indeed, the whole concept of otherness was beginning to be influenced by the Romantic movement. Another Italian custom which many English visitors commented on with amazement and incredulity was the art of poetic improvisation. Tourists reported on these impromptu performances in great detail and seemed impressed by the actors' versatility but nevertheless found them quite unnatural and awkward. Most commentaries focused on the erratic emotions portrayed by the men and women improvisers, their sudden changes in pose and voice quality that emphasised their anomalous, almost disturbed personalities. Like cicisbeism, improvisation was viewed as unnatural, a foreign custom that evoked a sense of absurdity, something that could only be attributed to having a nature radically alien to that of the rational English mind. This view was challenged by Hester Piozzi Thrale in her 1789 book *Observations and Reflections*, based on the diary she wrote with the intention of publishing it once back home. She voiced resentment not only at the lack of understanding of the tradition but also the fact that this was often combined with mockery. Her argument was that the art of improvisation was made both natural and successful in Italy by the sense of empathy between performers and spectators. She stressed that this was not an unnatural faculty but an act of free creativity which was welcomed in Italy, but not elsewhere, because of a more genuine sense of respect found there:

I have already asserted that the Italians are not a laughing nation: were ridicule to step in among them, many innocent pleasures would soon be lost; and this [improvisation] among the first. For who would risque the making impromptu poems at Paris? *pour s'attirer persiflage in every Coterie comme il faut?*[24] Or in London, at the hazard of *being taken off, and held up for a laughing-stock at every print-seller's window? ...* Different amusements, like different sorts of food, suit different countries; and this is among the efforts of those who have learned to refine their pleasures without so refining their ideas as to be able no longer to hit on any pleasure subtle enough to escape their own power of ridiculing it.[25]

Lady Mary Montagu and Hester Piozzi were both committed to publicising their conviction that no social custom was unnatural but rather just peculiar to different cultures. Both writers offered commentaries on foreign realities which covered a number of *topoi* that previous authors had presented within the

---

[23] Ibid.   [24] 'To draw upon one's self the ridicule of every polite assembly.'
[25] Piozzi Thrale, *Observations*, I, 240.

dichotomy of good and evil: for example, rectitude vs. corruption; masculinity vs. effeminacy; honesty vs. lax morals; industry vs. idleness. Hester Piozzi in particular was determined to revisit commonplaces that had contributed to the success of travel literature in the past, and she even challenged some of the most popular myths about Italy, specifically its warm climate, and Italians' degenerate taste in food:

(a) The praises of Italian weather, though wearisomely frequent among us, seem however much confined to this island for aught I see; who am often tired with hearing their complaints of their own sky, now that they are under it: always too cold or too hot, or a sciroc wind, or a rainy day, or a hard frost, che gela fin ai pensieri ['which can freeze even your thoughts'].[26]
(b) The Italians retain their tastes for small birds in full force; and consider beccafichi, ortolani, &c. as the most agreeable dainties: it must be confessed that they dress them incomparably ... Here the most excellent, the most incomparable fish I ever eat ... besides the calamaro, or ink-fish [squid], a dainty worthy of imperial luxury ... Figs too are here in such Perfection ...; small, and green on the outside, a bright full crimson within, and we eat them with raw ham, and truly delicious is the dainty. By raw ham, I mean ham cured, not boiled or roasted.[27]

In the attempt to make the best of her experience abroad and to analyse the preconceptions of her compatriots, Hester Piozzi always adopted a conciliatory tone, explaining in Italian 'Che c'è in tutto il suo bene e il suo male' ['There is good and bad in everything'] and that 'I will write my Travels & publish them – why not? 'twill be difficult to content the Italians, & the English, but I'll try- & 'tis something to do.'[28] Indeed, Piozzi Thrale was determined to make the most of what she called her 'demi-naturalisation' (her own term) after her marriage with an Italian and departure from London. This 'insider view' and her 'sympathetic and engaging personality' contributed to establishing a less prejudiced and more sympathetic image of contemporary Italy.[29]

The travel books by Montagu and Piozzi Thrale gave an unprecedented firsthand portrayal of life abroad, one not available in previous accounts which included opinions and commonplaces that were often taken from other books of proven success. Instead, these women's narratives used a personal approach, based on the description of an unusual custom followed by the appraisal of its social dynamics, or vice versa. Chard quotes a good example of this strategy of mingling together perspectives 'from the position of spectator to that of spectacle'[30] in a passage from Lady Montagu. The story unfolds in Sophia,

---

[26] Footnote: 'which freezes even one's fancy'. Piozzi Thrale, *Observations*, 'Venice' I, 190.
[27] Ibid., Genoa, 1 November 1784, 55.   [28] Piozzi Thrale, *Observations*, II, 382.
[29] See Abbate Badin, 'Tre primedonne del Grand Tour', especially 350–6.
[30] Chard, *Pleasure and Guilt,* 157.

then part of the Ottoman Empire, when as a foreign visitor she enters the women's baths, finding some two hundred women 'in the state of nature . . . without any beauty or defect concealed'. These women should have gazed with curiosity at Lady Montagu, dressed in her travelling habit, 'a riding dress [that] certainly appeared very extraordinary to them', but this is not what happened:

> Yet there was not one of them that showed the least surprise or impertinent curiosity, but received me with all the obliging civility possible. I know no European court where the ladies would have behaved themselves in so polite a manner to such a stranger . . . none of those disdainful smiles and satirical wispers, that never fail in our assemblies when any body appears that is not dressed exactly in the fashion. They repeated over and over to me, 'Guzel, pec guzel', which is nothing but *Charming, very charming*.[31]

Investigations into otherness were close to the interests of female travellers, and today this is appreciated as the most innovative feature of their travel narratives. Most women writers did not like to limit their observations through detachment: they wanted to become insiders in the foreign community. This, too, was atypical for the times as male travellers felt strongly attached to the position in which they were often portrayed in traditional iconography, i.e. standing on the top of a hillside looking down at a city. Women did not want to place themselves above things or at a distance. They felt empathetically attracted to foreign environments and sought out social interactions before reporting their observations and reflections.

Language Insights

At the end of the eighteenth century, most young British men still travelled for the purpose of acquiring knowledge, although many indulged in the social adventures available on the Continent: theatres and salons in France; and casinos, opera houses and coffee houses in Italy.[32] Educated ladies travelled to gain a different experience of modern life, and while they wanted to be exposed to the glorious cultural legacies of France and Italy, they were not particularly attracted by social adventures. Mary Montagu could not be more outspoken about the difference: 'They [male travellers] return no more instructed than they might have been at home by the help of a Map,' and 'The Boys only remember where they met with the best Wine or prettyests

---

[31] Mary Wortley Montagu from Constantinople, 1 April 1717, in *Letters and Works*, I, 285.

[32] When in Rome, Smollet reported that 'No Englishman above the degree of a painter or cicerone frequents any coffee-house.' The comment was both unjustified and unfair: many coffee houses around Piazza di Spagna, the English quarter, were very popular with Grand Tourists, and among the painters and ciceroni of the time there were some distinguished Scotsmen and Englishmen of high birth. See also Chapter 7.

Women, and the Governors (I speak of the most learned amongst them) have only remark'd Situations and Distances, or at most Status and Edifices.'[33]

As women developed alternative ways of portraying cultural diversity, many female writers felt this offered them the opportunity to subvert commonplaces and challenge established views of foreign countries.[34] Now they had the chance to capture the interest of readers, many of whom were growing disenchanted with an old-fashioned view of the world. Rather than indulge in writing about topics of a domestic nature, such as clothing, music, etiquette and food, women needed to display their views and emotions about the new forms of human behaviour they felt naturally attracted to. Contrasts and comparisons with foreign cultures became the single focus of their narratives, particularly with respect to the conditions of women in foreign societies with regard to marriage, sexuality and femininity. As published observations about everyday behaviour increased, so did attention to manifestations of language use by speakers of both sexes and diverse classes.

Lady Montagu was well positioned to write about language issues. As a precocious child, she had learned Latin and Greek and spoke French, Italian and German fluently but later she also learned colloquial Turkish in Constantinople. Having maintained her deep interest in languages throughout her life, she often discussed the linguistic education of young people, as in this letter addressed to the Countess of Bute:

There are two cautions to be given on this subject: first, not to think herself learned, when she can read Latin, or even Greek. Languages are more properly to be called vehicles of learning than learning itself, as may be observed in many schoolmasters, who, though perhaps critics in grammar, are the most ignorant fellows upon earth. True knowledge consists in knowing things, not words. I would no farther wish her a linguist than to enable her to read books in their originals, that are often corrupted, and are always injured, by translations.[35]

Lady Mary was also a severe judge of her own linguistic competence, as revealed in this letter, where she confesses how worried she is about the lack of practice in her native tongue after living in a foreign environment for so long:

I am in great danger of losing my English. I find 'tis not half so easy to me, to write in it as it was a twelvemonth ago. I am forced to study for expressions, and must leave off all other languages, and try to learn my mother tongue. Human understanding is as much limited as human power or human strength. The memory can retain but a certain number of images; and this as impossible for one human creature to be perfect master of ten

---

[33] Correspondence between Lady Montagu and Countess of Bute, Genoa, 8 December 1759, in *Letters and Works*, III, 188.

[34] See also Mary F. McVicker, *Women Adventurers, 1750–1900. A Biographical Dictionary with Excerpts from Selected Travel Writings* (Jefferson NC and London, 2008).

[35] Correspondence between Lady Montagu and Countess of Bute, 28 January 1753, in *Letters and Works*, II, 226.

different languages, as to have in perfect subjection ten different kingdoms, or to fight against ten men at a time: I am afraid I shall at last know none as I should do.[36]

Her awareness of multilingualism benefited a great deal from the extraordinary language situation in the highly cosmopolitan district of Pera in Constantinople, where she resided:

I live in a place that very well represents the tower of Babel: In Pera they speak Turkish, Greek, Sclavonian, Walachian, German, Dutch, French, English, Italian, Hungarian; and what is worse, there are ten of these languages spoken in my own family. My grooms are Arabs, my footmen, French, English and German, my nurse an Armenian; my housemaids Russians; half a dozen other servants, Greeks; my steward, an Italian; my janizaries, Turks; so that I live in the perpetual hearing of this medley of sounds, which produces a very extraordinary effect upon the people that are born here; for they learn all these languages at the same time, and without knowing any of them well enough to write or read in it. There are very few men, women, or even children, here, that have not the same compass of words in five or six of them. I know myself of several infants of three or four years old, that speak Italian, French, Greek, Turkish, and Russian, which last they learn of their nurses, who are generally of that country.[37]

Being interested in the agglomeration of languages in her environment, Lady Montagu developed a sensible idea of what a speaker could achieve under those circumstances. But she did not miss the opportunity to reflect on the language situation back home and draw some sharp conclusions: 'This seems almost incredible to you, and is, in my mind, one of the most curious things in this country, and takes off very much from the merit of our ladies who set up for such extraordinary geniuses, upon the credit of some superficial knowledge of French and Italian.'[38]

Hester Piozzi Thrale experienced a great deal of success with her unconventional travel writing fifty years later. In her diary *Observations and Reflections*, she covered much of the same ground as previous male travellers but her revisitation of old themes connected with Italy, the country she eventually adopted as her home, is neither superficial nor matter-of-fact. Her aim was always to defend local forms of socialisation against the prejudice shown by previous observers. In this passage on the linguistic diversity of Italian cities, she does not trot out the usual myths about linguistic purity but offers accurate perceptions about social diversity, combined with a keen sense of her participation in local life.

The States of Italy being all under different rulers, are kept separate from each other, and speak a different dialect; that of Milan full of consonants and harsh to the ear, but abounding with classical expressions that rejoice one's heart, and fill one with the oddest but most pleasing sensations imaginable. I heard a lady there call a runaway nobleman

---

[36] Letter from Lady Montagu, Pera at Constantinople, 16 March 1718. Ibid., I, 351–2.   [37] Ibid.
[38] Ibid.

Profugo ['refugee'] mighty prettily; and added, that his conduct had put all the town into orgasmo grande. All this, however, the Tuscans may possibly have in common with them. My knowledge of the language must remain ever too imperfect for me to depend on my own skill in it; all I can assert is, that the Florentines appear, as far as I have been competent to observe, to depend more on their own copious and beautiful language for expression, than the Milanese do; who run to Spanish, Greek, or Latin for assistance, while half their tongue is avowedly borrowed from the French, whose pronunciation, in the letter u, they even profess to retain.[39]

In Venice she turned to the *topos* of the Venetian dialect, which she also found surprisingly pleasant: 'At Venice, the sweetness of the patois is irresistible; their lips, incapable of uttering any but the sweetest sounds, reject all consonants they can get quit of; and make their mouths drop honey more completely than it can be said by any eloquence less mellifluous than their own.'[40] But when she felt that her observations about the social spread of the Venetian language needed to be supported by some evidence, she provided a humorous vignette about a local countess who was willing to speak to foreigners in her fluent French but was so inadequate in Tuscan that she slipped into Venetian in every other word. This sketch very effectively summarises the special linguistic situation in Venice as well as the unique language situation in Italy:

At Venice the men of literature and fashion speak with the same accent, and I believe the same quick turns of expression as their Gondolier; and the coachman at Milan talks no broader than the Countess; who, if she does not speak always in French to a foreigner, as she would willingly do, tries in vain to talk Italian; and having asked you thus, alla capi? which means ha ella capita? laughs at herself for trying to toscaneggiare, as she calls it.[41]

By observing not only men of literature and ladies of distinction but humble people as well, Piozzi noticed what most men did not and shared it with her readers with passion and delicate charm. She engaged in conversations with servants, interviewed men and women of lower ranks in public places, and paid attention to the lifestyle of foreign women as no traveller had done before. Her diary, rich in details about ordinary people and their social conditions, was originally designed to capture the interest of female readers but it ended up introducing new elements of authenticity and vitality to narrative representations of a foreign country. When Piozzi turned to another linguistic *topos* – the unpleasant sound of the Bologna dialect – she rapidly shifted the focus of her observations from the ugliness of its sounds to the gentle behaviour of a humble *laquais de place*:

The Bolognese dialect is detested by the other Italians, as gross and disagreeable in its sounds . . . The Laquais de Place who attended us at Bologna was one of the few persons I had met then, who spoke a language perfectly intelligible to me. 'Are you a Florentine, pray friend, said I?' 'No, madam, but the combinations of this world having led me to

---

[39] Piozzi Thrale, 24 June 1785, *Observations*, I, 314.   [40] Ibid.   [41] Ibid.

talk much with strangers, I contrive to tuscanise it all I can for their advantage, and doubt not but it will tend to my own at last.'[42]

This episode is followed by a note that reflects more than a sympathetic appreciation of the relaxed relationship between servants and their employers in Italy – it demonstrates the awareness of someone who realises that people from another culture usually show social respect differently. For example, people of different ranks may speak the same language with the same eloquence and maintain their dignity, something that should not be a cause of astonishment, or worse, derision:

Such a sentiment, so expressed by a footman, would set a plain man in London a laughing, and make a fanciful Lady imagine he was a nobleman disguised. Here nobody laughs, nor nobody stares, nor wonders that their valet speaks just as good language, or utters as well-turned sentences as themselves. Their cold answer to my amazement is as comical as the fellow's fine style–é battizzato ['he has been baptised'], say they, come noi altri ['as well as we'].[43]

End of a Male Institution

The most critical comments about male attitudes to the wider world during the degenerate waning years of the Grand Tour came from the pen of Lady Montagu. While describing her social life in Rome and Venice, and obviously anxious to receive a worthwhile visitor, she wrote the following to her friend Lady Pomfret:

The winter I passed at Rome there was an unusual concourse of English, many of them with great estates, and their own masters: as they had no admittance to the Roman ladies, nor understood the language, they had no way of passing their evenings but in my apartment, where I had always a full drawings room. Their governors encouraged their assiduities as much as they could, finding I gave them lessons of economy and good conduct; and my authority was so great, it was a common threat amongst them.[44]

Lady Montagu had lived away from England long enough to hold an unbiased opinion of cultural differences and she certainly did not believe that the conduct of young Englishmen abroad was a great credit to her country. Writing from Italy in 1740, she was beginning to witness behaviour that would destabilise the credibility of the Grand Tour. The young aristocrats sent abroad to learn about men and manners often returned more corrupt than when they left, having engaged in licentious activities abroad which they did not have the courage to seek out back home. In another letter addressed to Lady Pomfret,

---

[42] Ibid.   [43] Ibid.
[44] Correspondence between Lady Montagu and the Countess of Bute, Rome, 3 June 1753, in *Letters and Works*, III, 61.

this time from Venice in 1740, a surprised Lady Montagu offered a range of detailed comments about the comportment of the young English boys there, from their monolingual complacency to their fashion for turning into *petits-maîtres* under the close supervision of their governors:

You may imagine . . . I am impatient to hear good sense pronounced in my native tongue; having only heard my language out of the mouths of boys and governors for these five months. Here are inundations of them broke in upon us this carnival, and my apartment must be their refuge; the greater part of them having kept an inviolable fidelity to the languages their nurses taught them.

Their whole business abroad (as far as I can perceive) being to buy new cloaths, in which they shine in some obscure coffee-house, where they are sure of meeting only one another; and after the important conquest of some waiting gentlewoman of an opera Queen, who perhaps they remember as long as they live, return to England excellent judges of men and manners. I find the spirit of patriotism so strong in me every time I see them, that I look on them as the greatest blockheads in nature; and to say truths the compound of booby and petit-maître makes up a very odd sort of animal.[45]

Travel on the Continent, which used to be considered an educational experience that would fashion a gentleman, was now at risk of contaminating English integrity with exaggerated French politeness and Italian extravagance. The Grand Tour was becoming increasingly debased, even though some observers of this social convention, such as Dr Johnson, were never convinced that the average young traveller could really benefit from this essential part of an education:

The greater part of travellers tell nothing, because their method of travelling supplies them with nothing to be told. He that enters a town at night and surveys it in the morning, and then hastens away to another place, and guesses at the manners of the inhabitants by the entertainment which his inn afforded him, may please himself for a time with a hasty change of scenes, and a confused remembrance of palaces and churches; he may gratify his eye with variety of landscapes, and regale his palate with a succession of vintages: but let him be contented to please himself without endeavouring to disturb others. Why should he record excursions by which nothing could be learned, or wish to make a show of knowledge, which, without some power of intuition unknown to other mortals, he could never attain.[46]

Of course, even late in the eighteenth century there were some refined young men and art connoisseurs on the Grand Tour but most travellers were turning into curious wanderers, displaying neither artistic taste nor their best behaviour. James Boswell was atypical, as he prided himself on having developed the former: 'I have almost finished my tour of Italy . . . and I have acquired taste to a certain degree,' he wrote to Rousseau in 1765. But he did not keep secret from his male friends the great enjoyment he found in the latter: 'my desire to know the world made me

---

[45] Correspondence between Lady Montagu and the Countess of Pomfret, Venice, in *Letters and Works,* II, 234.
[46] Samuel Johnson, *The Idler* (1760), in *The Works of Samuel Johnson*, 12 vols. (Liverpool, 1820), VII, 385.

resolve to intrigue a little while in Italy, where the women are so debauched that they are hardly to be considered moral agents, but as inferior beings'[47].

By 'little intrigues' Boswell actually meant 'experiments in comparative morality' a common entertainment during the later stage of the Grand Tour but we have little evidence of this, as not many travellers wrote about their exploits with Boswell's audacity. Many young men certainly made a spectacle of themselves during their tour, in front of audiences that they themselves usually considered to be a spectacle. As discussed above, Chard argued that the reversal of the relationship between spectator and spectacle can add a new dimension to our understanding of the Grand Tour. Along these lines, a precious document exists, found by Ilaria Bignamini, which divulges local gossip in the city of Venice while the arrival of a royal visit was awaited.[48] With the whole city busy carrying out grandiose preparations for the arrival of this visitor, who was famous for his libidinous behaviour, the local men responded with a song inspired by the preventive measures necessary to protect the chastity of their women:

Odoardo Fratell dell Rè d'Inghilterra	Edward, brother of the King of England
vien a Venezia con un gran corteggio	arrives in Venice with a great following
doppo haver visto Roma, Parma, e Reggio	after having visited Rome, Parma, and Reggio
Turin, e tanti altri gran Paesi.	Turin, and many other grand places
I Veneziani Splendidi, e Cortesi	The Venetians, splendid, and courteous
i ghe prepara un Trattamento Reggio	have prepared a princely reception for him
e de vera amicìzia i se fà preggio	and of real friendship they are keen
darghe i Segni piu vivi, e piu palesi.	to give him the most vivid and sincere signs.
Per far feste, Regatte, e Recreazion	Organising receptions, regattas, and recreations
è in motto, e in allegria ogni Persona	everybody is joyfully active.
Solo i morosi xe in agitazion	Only lovers are in a state of agitation;
Savendo che ghe piase assae la Donna	and since they know how much he likes the female sex
i pensa alle morose con rason	they are considering, wisely enough
de metterghe un Luchetto sulla mona.	locking the vaginas of their beloved.

---

[47] Boswell, Letter of Thursday 10 January 1765, in *Boswell on the Grand Tour, Italy. etc.*, 28.

[48] Ilaria Bignamini, 'The Italians as spectators and actors: the Grand Tour reflected', in Clare Hornsby (ed.), *The Impact of Italy*, 39. Bignamini, who died prematurely in 2001, was one of the most active historians of the golden age of the Grand Tour. She gathered a massive archive of materials dealing especially with excavations, art and archaeology in Rome, which she published with Clare Hornsby, *Dealing and Digging in Eighteenth-Century Rome*, 2 vols. (New Haven, 2010).

Quite apart from the erosion of moral behaviour displayed by many young lads on the Grand Tour, historians argue that it was the French Revolution which destroyed its underlying cultural and political premises. Others point out that the end of the Grand Tour coincided with the age of the railway, a means of transportation that involved a rate of speed incompatible with the leisurely routine of slower travellers. The young aristocrats required a longer time to savour foreign differences in order to become acquainted with different realities. One must also realise that the education of the aristocracy relied on a consensus about what was necessary for the elite to learn. In addition, the ideal of gentlemanly education required a tacit agreement between men and women. Although the main goal of participating in a Grand Tour was not questioned by women for a long time, its credibility faded when male travellers became more inclined towards earthly pleasures than intellectual accomplishment. At the same time that men themselves were destabilising the institution, women felt attracted by a different form of travel experience – one that could function as a transgression of their own domesticity, while elevating their personal dignity and social respect.[49]

Reflecting on politics abroad was traditionally considered to be the remit of men. The sudden emergence of women travellers interested in this area caused further transgressions of gender distinctions. At the turn of the century, many liberal-minded British women were quite outspoken regarding individual rights and freedoms. Some were even sympathetic to the aims of the French Revolution, and felt that principles such as *liberté, égalité et fraternité* should apply to the situation of all women. Lady Morgan, the Irish writer, was the first woman to profess a strong passion for politics while she was a tourist in Italy. Like Madame de Staël's novel *Corinne*, her book *Italy* was composed with the intention of combatting old prejudices against Italy trotted out by previous travellers. Her Romantic representation of the country made her book a very popular travel guide during the first half of the nineteenth century. Unlike Mary Montagu and Hester Piozzi, Lady Morgan did not focus on the social dimensions of daily life but on the political roots of national conflicts as in this passage about people in Naples:

It is a calumny against Providence and solecism in philosophy, to assert that there are nations so marked by physical tendencies to evil, so instinctively devoted to particular vices, that they remain unredeemable by good laws, incorrigible by wise institutes. . . . It has been the fashion to accuse the Neapolitans o£ an inherent viciousness, over which external circumstances could hold no control; but the prejudice has only obtained currency in European opinion, since that country has been the slave of Spain.[50]

---

[49] The issue was thoroughly discussed by Cohen, *Fashioning Masculinity*, 63, and more recently by Sweet, *Cities and the Grand Tour*, especially 1–64.
[50] Morgan, *Italy*, III, 239.

Lady Morgan's book alienated those who were not sympathetic to the idea of a women being engaged in politics. But her work challenged the view that some nations were superior and others inferior.

The Romantic ideal of Italy inspired much of the pro-unification ideology about the country circulating in Europe. The spirit of unification was beginning to find its way into the most liberal quarters in England, too, and men like Byron and Shelley shared a great deal of Lady Morgan's political outlook. While Byron's Canto IV of *Childe's Harold Pilgrimage* (1818) and Shelley's *Ode to Naples* (1820) were two Romantic works which sought to promote the cause of unifying Italy among the liberal sections of British society, Lady Morgan's view about Italian decadence and the right to self-determination were inspired by her strong radical ideology.[51] The image of Italy that dominated the Grand Tour – of a Peninsula composed of a constellation of diverse states – still held a fascination for much of British society in the nineteenth century. A good example of this is a quote from Edward Bulwer Lytton, the politician author of the popular novel *The Last Days of Pompeii*: 'Italy, Italy . . . listen not to the blind policy which would unite all your crested cities, mourning for their republics, into one empire.'[52]

While Lady Montagu and Hester Piozzi transgressed the boundaries of the permissible, Lady Morgan challenged the image of Italy as either a tourist playground or an artist's heaven. She claimed that, as a country exploited through international politics, Italy had much more to offer than its ancient history, and her vision marked a turning point in the experience of modern travellers. This, too, Chloe Chard argues, contributed to a change in the way tourists approached foreign travel around the third decade of the nineteenth century. Eventually travellers' attitudes split into two directions, she explains, 'both of which still play a crucial part in determining the ways in which encounters with the foreign can be described or imagined today'. The first is what she calls the 'Romantic view of travel', which involves 'the discovery or realisation of the self through the exploration of the other'.[53] The second approach is that of the modern tourist who indulges in trivial gratifications; recognising the risks of a confrontation with 'the other' keeps the traveller at a safe distance. This new attitude was best summarised by Anna Jameson in her 1826 book *Diary of an ennuyée,* and it was soon to become the typical way of dealing with cultural diversity in the age of modern tourism:

---

[51] See Donatella Abbate Badin, 'Lady Morgan in Italy: a traveller with an agenda', *in Studi irlandesi. A Journal of Irish Studies*, 6 (2016), 127–48.

[52] Quoted in Frank Salmon, 'The impact of the archaeology of Rome on British architects and their work c.1750–1840', in Hornsby (ed.), *The Impact of Italy*, 242.

[53] Chard, *Pleasure and Guilt*, 11.

Let the modern Italians be what they may, – what I hear them styled six times a day at least, – a dirty, demoralised, degraded, unprincipled race, centuries behind our thrice blessed, prosperous, and comfort-loving nation in civilisation and morals; if I were come among them as a resident this picture might alarm me; situated as I am a nameless sort of person, a mere bird of passage, it concerns me not.[54]

In the finest days of the Grand Tour, travellers learned through preparation and observation, as Jennifer Craik pointed out, 'by looking or visually taking in the vistas and splendor of the continental culture . . . which facilitate international relations by making contacts and learning foreign languages'. In stark contrast, the modern tourist mainly concentrated on passive entertainment, with 'a marked preference for the eye over the ear and the increasing predominance of sightseeing'.[55] The difference between 'observations' and 'sightseeing' is crucial, in that the first suggests an act of engagement, while the latter involves little more than passive exposure. The new tendency now is to 'do' the sights as quickly as possible. The emergence of the colloquial use of 'to do' in the sense of 'doing a tour' or 'visiting a place', reflecting a substantially new attitude, was first attested in 1817. In that year Lord Byron stated with great irony that 'having "done" Constantinople, I must also "do" t'other place [Rome]'.[56]

---

[54] Jameson, *Diary of an ennuyée*, 309.
[55] Jennifer Craik, 'The culture of tourism', in Chris Rojek and John Urry (eds.), *Touring Cultures: Transformations of Travel and Theory* (London, 1997), 113–36.
[56] Lord George Gordon Byron, Letter to Hobhouse, Venice, 19 December 1816, in John Murray (ed.), *Byron's Correspondence* (Cambridge, 1922), II, 28.

10   Conclusion

The origin of the Grand Tour is rooted in a period of European history when modern vernaculars were increasing in social prestige, having challenged the international position of Latin as the common language of religion, education and culture. This led to a degree of consolidation in a number of languages, in terms of structural homogeneity and consistency of pronunciation and spelling. Indeed, the status and functionality of such languages was greatly buttressed by the printing press during the Renaissance, which contributed to promoting the vernaculars within the boundaries of emerging nation-states. But the functional stability and phonetic consistency of these privileged vernaculars were still very distant from the standardisation they went on to achieve as national languages in the nineteenth century. This is why the mosaic of languages observed by some travellers in early modern Europe, consisting of a few privileged vernaculars and many low-status varieties, was not much different from the linguistic landscape experienced by the final generation of Grand Tourists almost three centuries later.

Given this complex linguistic situation, most travellers who arrived on the Continent from England for the first time faced two disconcerting experiences. One involved linguistic transitions because Europe had not succeeded in aligning military and political frontiers with linguistic boundaries. Another cause for travellers' disorientation was the linguistic diversity within each country. The patchwork of regional languages and dialect variations sounded so removed from the linguistic models which travellers were vaguely familiar with through literature and education that they felt they were dealing with separate languages rather than variants of the same language. This situation was common to every nation and to most regions, from rural communities that retained a rustic dialect to the cities where different accents were hard for outsiders to understand, especially when the language was spoken by uneducated people.

In order to better appreciate the evolution of travellers' attitudes to language and their perceptions of linguistic situations abroad, it is helpful to distinguish between common and specific features of two separate chronological phases. The first phase includes the beginning of the Grand Tour, a period still influenced by post-Renaissance culture, which was marked by a new linguistic awareness. This came about not only because a number of people began to study modern European vernaculars but also because of the growing consciousness about social and linguistic differences. At this time, a common belief was that different languages revealed their speakers' natures, something that could be easily observed and appreciated abroad. But there was also a novel faith in linguistic purity, which was no longer seen as being dependent on natural factors but rather on human design and initiatives.[1] Although a desire for purity implies discriminating against others, the early phase of the Grand Tour was actually a time of cultural curiosity and linguistic exuberance. Most travellers viewed foreign languages as a tool for engaging in civil interactions and intellectual exchanges abroad, and many were proud of their multilingual performances. Travel memoirs from this phase show no evidence that cross-linguistic experiences were limited by inhibitions about speaking a foreign language as if this constituted unnatural behaviour. Rather, travellers felt a sense of achievement in being able to utilise unfamiliar sounds and new structures to communicate and gain knowledge.[2]

This was the typical attitude of the civilised Renaissance man, who valued freedom of expression and adopted a playful attitude towards models of foreign behaviour, and thus also had a proclivity to improvise in foreign languages in order to communicate. There was no sense of anxiety about correctness – typical of later generations – that restricted their interactions, inhibited their performance or resulted in taciturnity. This natural inclination of early travellers, who were keen observers of language use abroad, encouraged their linguistic creativity and fashioned them into unashamed agents of language contact. Indeed, some diaries report the writer's efforts to emulate other cultures, sometimes to hide their national origin, or even pass themselves off as a native speaker of another language. After all, this was not a pretention beyond the reach, especially in situations of poorly standardised languages, where 'foreigner talk' would have sounded no stranger in form and pronunciation than the native speech of someone from another region.

The early eighteenth century was the turning point leading into the second phase, which began when travellers became conscious that English was a rich and vigorous language, something which affected attitudes towards non-standard varieties of English at home and speakers of other languages abroad. This is also the time when British people were becoming more class conscious, and aspirations for a purified language was spreading among intellectual circles

[1] Roy Harris and Talbot J. Taylor, *Landmarks in Linguistic Thought: The Western Tradition from Socrates to Saussure* (London and New York, 1989), 86.
[2] Williams, 'Sixteenth-century anticipations', 69–101. Discussing the English language during the Elizabethan period, the author stressed that 'the late sixteenth-century was the most inventive period in the history of English', 72.

and the social elite. Since travellers at that time were all from the highest ranks of society, they were either witnesses to or even supporters of initiatives for language codification and prescription. One aspect of the 'standard language culture' was that linguistic regulation meant relegation of non-standard varieties to subordinate positions.[3]

The language attitudes many Britons took abroad from that time on included a new self-consciousness about speech and a strong sense of anxiety about correctness. As they were now concerned about linguistic models of polite social behaviour, their efforts went into using the right language with the right people. The spirit of improvisation typical of the post-Renaissance gave way to a new sense of language as a marker of social and cultural identity. At the same time, the ideology of a 'pure' language, and the belief that members of polite society in any nation have the monopoly of it, informed their views of language everywhere. Effectively, the way English speakers used and viewed language at home inspired the attitudes of travellers towards the hierarchies of language in France and Italy.

France was a fashionable destination, whether for long period of study in the Loire region, or a short term of residence in Paris, or a combination of the two experiences prior to embarking on a Grand Tour. Before leaving home, travellers were issued with warnings against the *formes gasconnes ou normandes* and were familiar with the notion that 'polite' French was to be found in cities, especially the capital, where townspeople were in contact with the court, the chancery and their entourages and, like in England, were able to participate in this culture.[4] France also had the advantage of a language academy which regulated the purity of *le français littéraire et officiel* and strove to ensure that regionalisms and foreign words did not contaminate the national language.

Neither the young men who proceeded to France with some knowledge of French nor those who went as complete beginners expected to learn the 'right' language just by living in the country and picking it up from the natives. This was how merchants claimed to learn French by ear but they ended up acquiring the type of jargon suitable only for tavern talk[5]. Families of distinction who sent their offspring to learn French in France needed to secure introductions to the appropriate sources of polite conversation, in the suitable salons, usually with the assistance of experienced tutors. Since the seventeenth century, when

---

[3] James Milroy defines 'the culture of standard language' at the time of the incipient standardisation of English. He explains that it was based on two criteria: the prestige of the social group who used it and the uniformity of its structure. The former was seen as a natural characteristic of their class, while the latter was recognised as a property of language that maximises flexibility; in 'Sociolinguistics and ideologies in language history', 571–84.

[4] On the other hand, Paris, like London, was becoming less of an ideal reference for language purity, being a great centre of cultural life where social mobility tended to lead to the melding of a variety of forms and pronunciation. See Burke, *Languages and Communities*, especially 98–9.

[5] Lambley, *The Teaching and Cultivation of French,* 323.

Madame de Rambouillet became famous with her *école de politesse*, the salon life of the capital set linguistic models that were imitated throughout the country.[6] There, the foreign visitor could come across not only the exclusive models of social elegance but also the refined linguistic expressions that were used at the court of Versailles.

The linguistic outlook of early modern Europeans was one in which English, French and Italian, as well as Dutch, Spanish and Portuguese, were recognised as established languages.[7] Each had its own literature, history and grammar and, with the exception of Italian, each was backed by the authority of an independent state.[8] Italy was not a united country at that time and had no royal court, chancery or capital promoting models of 'good' language until the middle of the nineteenth century. This situation had significant linguistic consequences for Italy, not least the fact that its domestic multilingualism was not comparable to that of established nation-states. Indeed, when English travellers crossed the Alps, they found that in Italy the division between 'polite' language and its 'vulgar' alternatives did not quite match what travellers had been brought up with in England and observed in France.

There was, of course, the internationally renowned literary Italian, a language that could be acquired through study, as many travellers did before embarking on their journeys. For example, *Orlando Furioso* by Ariosto pro-vided the ideal source for the 'right' model of Italian throughout the era of the Grand Tour, and many travellers indeed made references to it.[9] But the problem was that the author modelled his language on the great poets of the *Trecento* (the fourteenth century), following the prescriptions laid down by the Italian language academy (*Accademia della Crusca*), whose aim was to crystallise and perpetuate the prestigious models of the classical written tradition. Naturally this literary language, like a modern version of Latin, had no native speakers, neither among the literati nor the upper classes. Indeed, it was a taught, written language that was rarely spoken, while the local regional languages were spoken but not usually written, with the exception of Tuscan.

Of course, one way in which the Italian elite could be differentiated from the lower classes was through literacy and knowledge of literature.[10] But apart from their ability to read and write, their spoken command of literary Italian varied according to local circumstances. Moreover, some members of the social elite were semi-literate or even illiterate. Thus, throughout the Italian peninsula the nobility, the intellectual elite and wealthy middle-class citizens

---

[6] Janet Holmes, *Women, Men and Politeness* (London, 1995). See also Brunot, *Histoire*, III, 170.
[7] As Burke explains, in Germany, like in Italy, 'the centrifugal tendencies being as strong as or stronger than the centripetal ones', *Language and Communities*, 109.
[8] Harris and Taylor, *Landmarks*, 86.   [9]   Richardson 'Varie maniere di parlare', 85.
[10] Brian Richardson, 'The Italian of Renaissance elites in Italy and Europe', in Anna L. Lepschy and Arturo Tosi (eds.), 5–23.

alike were quite relaxed about using their regional dialects, which they all had learned in childhood and continued to speak in most contexts, from everyday conversation to polite interactions in the salons. Indeed, there was a strong sense of language loyalty in most historical cities outside Tuscany. In addition, local vernaculars came in high-status and low-status variants that signalled social differences: they were linguistic microcosms that mirrored a national context where a privileged language coexists with its lower-prestige alternatives. Thus, unless an educated Italian needed to resort to Tuscan for cultural or commercial purposes, the only common language on the Peninsula that was so strongly associated with its literary status was felt to be an unnatural language rather than one of social distinction.[11]

Of course, we read in travel works that members of the upper classes used literary Italian with foreign visitors for reasons of social politeness. But it was also true that in eighteenth-century Italian salons, hosts and guests alike opted for French, which was felt to be more natural as well as more exclusive[12]. Moreover, before the unification of Italy, the Tuscan language used by the social elite was not consistent with the literary model found in grammar books; rather, it was a hybrid type of interregional language mixed with forms from the local dialect.[13] When the Italian upper classes used this hybrid language rather than 'pure' literary Italian, they were quite unaware of its social stigma and were not even embarrassed about speaking it. It was indeed quite natural for them to switch between the two codes, either by 'dialectising' polite literary expressions to make them sound more natural or by emphasising a concept using Tuscan during a conversation in dialect.[14] As for the question which language variety travellers aimed at learning in Italy and what they actually acquired during their Italian tour through such a complex linguistic mosaic, there is a short and a longer answer. The short answer is that throughout the era of the Grand Tour, the Italian learned by travellers was spoken by Italians themselves as a lingua franca, not as a native language. The longer answer is that since Italian did not have a single codified form like French, travellers of distinction who relied on prestigious individuals

[11] Stendhal understood well the situation of dialect vs. language in Italy, and his view about Italian multilingualism is epitomised by a comment about Naples: 'The king speaks just Neapolitan; I think he is right: why should he not be himself'. See Chapter 7.
[12] The autobiography of the dramatist and poet Vittorio Alfieri (1749–1803) is most illustrative about the conventional use of French by the Italian elite. An Italian aristocratic himself, Alfieri felt so inadequate about his knowledge of literary Italian that he decided to study it formally and even spent time at Siena, where he could 'find the best language and few foreigners' ('dove si parla meglio, e vi son pochi forestieri'), *Vita di Vittorio Alfieri scritta da esso* (Florence, 1822), 89.
[13] Richardson, 'The Italian of Renaissance elites', 19.
[14] A good example of the former switching is mentioned by Hester Piozzi Thrale in her conversation with a young Italian lady about the practice of cicisbeism: 'And your confessor! cried I'. – 'Oh, why he is *used to it* – in the Milanese dialect – è *assuefaà*' (see Chapter 8).

for their linguistic models encountered a great deal of variation between regions, and even more between the cities which were proud of their diverse identities.

Foreigners in Italy were of course interested in the theatre; they enjoyed comedies in France that satirised the behaviour of different social classes but could not find such productions in Italy.[15] Certainly, the same pretentions of social climbers existed in Italy but this could not be expressed through a common everyday language, as the country did not have one for all regions. Thus, Italian comic theatre, throughout the seventeenth century and the best part of the eighteenth, was regional and itinerant: comedians needed to adapt the language of their plays to different audiences, often eliciting mixed reactions.[16] The *Comédie-Française* ridiculed the affectations of the lower classes when they imitated refined language. In the Italian *Commedia dell'Arte*, the characters – nobles and commoners alike – were all speakers of the local dialect, with either serious or satirical intent, depending on the location of the performance. Literary Tuscan, which was considered too refined and quite artificial outside Tuscany, was invariably spoken by two stock characters – the *Innamorati* – whose unreal manner of speaking was ridiculed in this form of popular theatre. It is doubtful whether such nuanced multilingual performances could be comprehended by foreigners. Some Grand Tourists made explicit criticisms of these comedies, and this is not surprising considering that the English had the reputation of being a nation of demanding theatre-goers who expected to understand every aspect of the language used by actors on the stage.[17]

Some English travellers were even more disconcerted by another linguistic mismatch: the singular performances by uneducated people, such as peasants or gondoliers, who were able to recite or sing the pure Tuscan of Ariosto's and Tasso's stanzas. But of all performances, the most amazing were those by improvisers[18]. Some were well-educated artists who recited impromptu verses on a given theme in salons and even the courts, using an impressive command

---

[15] The popularity of the modern playwright Carlo Goldoni grew throughout the best part of the eighteenth century and co-existed with the *Commedia dell'Arte*, whose masks and intrigues he set out to replace with more credible characters and real-life situations. See Franco Fido, *Guida a Goldoni: teatro e societa nel Settecento* (Torino, 1977).

[16] This type of interaction was witnessed and reported on with some surprise by Skippon, 'An account', 510. There are many works on the multilingualism of the *Commedia dell'Arte* published in Italian, amongst which is the excellent *Il Linguaggio del caos* by Folena, where he defines this popular genre as the 'greatest legacy of Italian theatre to Europe'. For a shorter essay in English, see Arturo Tosi, 'Histrionic transgressions', in Michael Caesar and Marina Spunta (2006) (eds.), *Orality and Literacy in Italian Culture* (London, 2006), 18–31.

[17] This is stressed by Brunot, who reported on and analysed the behaviour of Englishmen in French theatres: 'les Anglais ne goûtaient pas ce qu'ils suivaient difficilement' ('The English did not enjoy what they were not able to fully understand'); *Histoire*, VIII, 253.

[18] Richardson discusses the language of itinerant performers and urban improvisers in *Varie maniere di parlare*, 83–5.

of the literary language. Many were humble street artists, charlatans[19] who had memorised some scenarios from literary sources as their art took them from place to place. Sometimes their language was ornate or even magniloquent but their audiences did not seem to mind, although they could not fathom much of it. Of course, the ideal context for literary Italian was the opera, with its librettos written in a majestic form of Tuscan, reminding the tourists of stock phrases in conversation books for learning Italian as a foreign language.[20] But the most shocking experience of all must have been the discovery that in Venice, which had one of the oldest Italian aristocracies, the distinguished Senators spoke Venetian, and when their sophisticated ladies used French in the salons, they felt unashamed to confess they were not as comfortable speaking Italian.[21]

English women were the first travellers who, focusing on the apparently anomalous social and linguistic customs of Italy, expressed attitudes that challenged the established view of their male compatriots. To account for this unexpected linguistic behaviour of the Italian aristocracies, they pointed out that Italy was not a country where noblemen worked for the court or the chancery, like in Britain, as such official positions were usually granted by the ruling foreign powers to their own compatriots. With the exception of Venice, where the nobility actually spoke Venetian even in the Senate, the Italian elite were not in a position to be recipients or providers of good models of a language of wider social acceptability. The political division of the Peninsula also accounted for the linguistic situation in pre-unified Italy, which was not comparable to that of the nation-states of Europe.[22]

As already discussed in previous chapters, the state of decay of Italy, in contrast with examples of its former glory, became a favourite *topos* of the Grand Tour. Quite a number of travellers echoed one another in arguing that the social and linguistic anomalies in Italy were caused by its cultural decadence, which led to its political decline, rather than vice versa. Indeed, Italy was identified by foreigners as a country with endless cases of 'violated decorum':

---

[19] In early modern times, the meaning of *charlatan* in English was closer to the original Italian: 'a mountebank or Cheap Jack who descants volubly to a crowd in the street'. The subsequent meaning, 'an assuming empty pretender to knowledge or skill; a pretentious impostor', developed later, as documented in the OED. See also Richardson, 'Varie maniere di parlare', 84.

[20] Opera students were advised to learn to read and pronounce Italian perfectly, as one of their leading instructors stressed with the comment 'not having been born in Tuscany being no excuse for ignorance'; in Barbier, *The World of the Castrati*, 61.

[21] See Chapter 7. For a comprehensive overview of the linguistic situation of Venice, see Ronnie Ferguson, *A Linguistic History of Venice* (Olschki, 2007).

[22] The Austrian Prince von Metternich, one of Europe's leading politicians, famously described Italy as a 'geographical expression'. But despite being an agglomeration of separate states, the Catholic religion was extremely influential in everyday Italian life, for example in maintaining a common system of timekeeping that fixed the start of the day at sunset.

for example, a nobleman using the language of the uneducated masses in the salons, or commoners such as servants daring to speak to their masters using the prestige language. Women travellers were right to suggest that this notion of decorum came from a vision of linguistic hierarchies that their male counterparts took from Britain.[23] They re-addressed the question and challenged the common male expectation that speakers should stay within their linguistic boundaries. Hester Piozzi Thrale found this form of non-elite bilingualism quite natural in a country whose languages were associated with different social roles. Indeed, quite a few British women set out to demonstrate that the linguistic patterns of social prestige were not the same abroad as in Britain and while the linguistic behaviour of Italians was unusual, it was not due to their national character but to their political circumstances.

This is why at the height of the Grand Tour in the second half of the eighteenth century, women found themselves in a better position to come to the realisation that diverse forms of human behaviour were not necessarily inferior to those found in their own society. By recounting foreign men's behaviour without criticism, reporting on foreign women's customs in a way that accorded them dignity and describing social linguistic habits that were different from those at home, women travellers contradicted the conclusions of a number of well-established male travel writers. Moreover, female travellers strove to establish intimacy with other women through sharing their diaries and letters, and these became precedents for new perceptions about cultural diversity. All this threatened the status of travel as a masculine pursuit of adventure as well as calling into question some of the most conventional accounts that purported to demonstrate British superiority.

---

[23] See Williams, 'Sixteenth-century anticipations', especially 76–7.

References

Primary Sources

Addison, Joseph, Letters to Guardian, *The Works of Joseph Addison*, 3 vols. (New York, 1837).

Addison, Joseph, *Remarks on Several Parts of Italy etc in the Years 1701, 1702, 1703* (London, 1705) rpt. 2 vols. (1721) and (1745).

Addison, Joseph, *The Spectator*, 83 (1711).

Akin, Lucy, *The Life of Joseph Addison*, 2 vols. (London, 1843).

Alfieri, Vittorio, *Vita di Vittorio Alfieri scritta da esso* (Florence, 1822).

Alison, Archibald and Patrick Fraser Tytler, *Travel in France, During the Years 1814–1815*, 2 vols. (Edinburgh, 1815). Altieri, Ferdinando, *A New Italian Grammar*, etc. (Leghorn, 1756).

Andrews, John, *A Comparative View of the French and English Nations in their Manners, Politics and Literature* (London, 1785).

Anonymous, [James Douglas Robinson], *'Mems' of a Ten Weeks' Continental Trip* (London, 1852).

Ascham, Roger, *The Scholemaster* (1570) (London, New York, Toronto and Melbourne, 1909).

Audebert, Nicolas, *Voyage d'Italie* in Adalberto Olivero (ed.), 2 vols. (Rome, 1981).

Bacon, Francis, 'Of travel' (London, 1597) rpt. in *The Essays or Counsels, Civil and Moral of Francis Bacon* (Chicago, 1883), 87–90.

Baretti, Joseph, [Giuseppe] *An Account of the Manners and Customs of Italy: With Observations on the Mistakes of Some Travellers with Regard to That Country*, 2 vols. (London, 1768).

Baretti, Giuseppe, *Dizionario Italiano, ed Inglese* (Livorno, 1828).

Baretti, Giuseppe, in Luigi Piccioni (ed.), *La scelta delle lettere familiari* (Bari, 1912).

Barlow, Thomas, *A Trip to Rome, at Railways Speed* (London,1836).

Barrow, John, *Tour on the Continent by Rail and Road in the Summer of 1852* (London, 1853).

Beckford, William, *Dreams, Waking Thoughts, and Incidents in a Series of Letters from Various Parts of Europe*, www. biblioteca virtual universal.

Beckford, William, *Italy with Sketches of Spain and Portugal*, 2 vols. (London, 1834).

Berkeley, George, *Alciphron* (New Haven, 1803).

Bertelli, Francesco, *Theatro delle città d'Italia* (Padova,1629).

Binos, Abbé de, *Voyage par l'Italie, en Égypte, au mont Liban et en Palestine*, 2 vols. (Paris, 1787).

Bizoni Bernardo, *Europa Milleseicentosei, Diario di viaggio di Bernardo Bizoni*, Anna Banti (ed.) (Milan, 1942).

Blessington, Countess of, *The Idler in Italy*, 3 vols. (London, 1839–40).

Boorde, Andrew, *Fyrst Boke of the Introduction of Knowledge* (London, 1547).

Boyer, Abel, *The Complete French Master for Ladies and Gentlemen* (London, 1761).

Boswell, James, *Boswell in Holland 1763–1764*, in Frederick A. Pottle (ed.) (New York-London, 1928).

Boswell, James, *Boswell on the Grand Tour, Germany and Switzerland, 1764*, in Frederick A. Pottle (ed.) (New York, Toronto and London, 1928).

Boswell, James, *Boswell on the Grand Tour, Italy, Corsica, and France 1765–1766*, in Frank Brady and Frederick A. Pottle (eds.) (New York, Toronto and London, 1955).

Boswell, James, in Frederick A. Pottle and Charles H. Bennett (eds.), *Boswell's Journal of the Tour of the Hebrides with Samuel Johnson, L.L.D.* (New York, 1936).

Boswell, James, *The Life of Samuel Johnson*, (1791) 2 vols. rpt. (London, 1907).

Brerewood, Edward, *Enquiries Touching the Diversity of Language and Religions Through the Cheife Parts of the World* (London, 1614).

Brooke, Frances, *History of Emily Montagu* (Toronto, 2008).

Brosses, Charles de, *Lettres familières écrites d'Italie en 1739 et 1740*, 2 vols. (Paris, 1904).

Browne, Edward, *A Brief Account of Some Travels in Divers Parts of Europe, etc.* (London, 1673).

Browne, Thomas, *Sir Thomas Browne's Works, Including His Life and Correspondence* in Simon Wilkin (ed.), 4 vols. (London, 1836).

Brydone, Patrick, *A Tour Through Sicily and Malta*, 2 vols. (London, 1773) rpt. (Edinburgh, 1840).

Burckhardt, Jacob, *Der Cicerone: Eine Anleitung zum Genuss der Kunstwerke Italiens* (Basel, 1855).

Burnet, Gilbert, *Travels: Or Letters Concerning an Account of What Seemed Most Remarkable in Switzerland, Italy,* Some Parts of Germany etc. in the Years 1685 and 1686 (Rotterdam, 1686–7).

Burney, Fanny: see Madame D'Arblay.

Byron, George Gordon, *Letters and Journals of Lord Byron: With Notices of His Life*, by Thomas Moore (ed.), 17 vols. (Francfort, 1830) rpt. (Paris, 1833).

Byron, George Gordon, *Lord Byron's Correspondence*, in John Murray (ed.), 2 vols. (Cambridge, 1922).

Cambry, Jacques, *Voyage Pittoresque en Suisse et en Italie*, 2 vols. (Paris, 1801).

[Campbell, John] *The Travels and Adventures of Edward Brown, Esq. Formerly a Merchant of London* (London, 1739).

Campion, Thomas, *Observations in the Art of English Poesie* (London, 1602) in G. Gregory Smith (ed.), *Elizabethan Critical Essays*, 2 vols. (Oxford, 1904).

Carew, Richard, *Epistle on the Excellency of the English Tongue* (1586) rpt. (London, 1769).

Casanova, Giacomo, *Mémoires* in Robert Abirached and Elio Zorzi (eds.), 2 vols. (Paris, 1958).

Casotti, L., *A New Method of Teaching the Italian Tongue to Ladies and Gentlemen* (London, 1709).

Castiglione, Baldassare, *Il libro del Cortegiano* (Torino, 1965).

Cesarotti, Melchiorre, *Saggio sopra la lingua italiana* (1785) rpt. in Emilio Biagi (ed.), *Dal Muratori al Cesarotti* (Milan, Naples, 1960), 304–468.

Chapone, Hester, *Letters on the Improvement of the Mind, Addressed to a Young Lady* (Dublin,1773), new ed. (Philadelphia, 1786).

Chesterfield, Philip Dormer Stanhope (Earl of), *Letters to His Son, 1737–1768*, (1774), (Philadelphia, 1874).

Chesterfield, Philip Dormer Stanhope (Earl of), *The Letters of Philip Dormer Stanhope, Earl of Chesterfield, with the Characters*, 3 vols. (London, 1892).

Corfey, Lambert Friedrich, *Reisetagebuch 1698–1700*, in H. Lahrkamp (ed.) (Munster, 1977).

Colsoni, Francesco, *The New Trismagister or the New Teacher of Three Languages etc . . .* (London, 1688).

Comenius [Jan Amos Komenský], *Janua Linguarum Reserata* (Leszno, 1631).

Coryat, Thomas, *Coryat's Crudities: Hastily Gobled Up in Five Moneths Travells in France, Savoy, Italy, Rhetia . . . Helvetia . . . Some Parts of High Germany and the Netherlands* (London, 1611) rpt. 2 vols. (Glasgow, 1905).

Coyer, M. [Abbé], *Voyages d'Italie et de Hollande*, 2 vols. (Paris, 1775).

Cowper, William, *The Progress of Errors* (1782) rpt. in *The Poems* (Boston, 1860).

Coxe, Henry [pseudonym of John Millard], *Picture of Italy* (London, 1815).

Dallington, Robert, *A Method for Travell: Shewed by Taking the View of Fraunce as it Stoode in the Yeare of our Lord 1598* (London, 1605). Second edition of *The View of Fraunce 1604* rpt. by the Shakespeare Association (Oxford, 1936).

Dallington, Robert, *A Survey of the Great Dukes State of Tuscany: In the Yeare of Our Lord 1596* (London, 1605). Da Ponte, Lorenzo, *Memorie di Lorenzo Da Ponte da Ceneda Scritte da Esso*, 3 vols. (Nuova Yorca [New York], 1829).

D'Arblay Madame [Fanny Burney], *Early Journals & Letters*, 5 vols. (1990).

D'Arblay Madame [Fanny Burney], *Memoires of Dr. Burney*, 3 vols. (London, 1832).

Davy, Humphry, *Consolations in Travel* (London, 1830).

De Conti, Giuseppe, *Viaggio d'Italia. Un manoscritto del Settecento*, in Barbara Corino (ed.) (Novara, 2007).

Dickens, Charles, *Little Dorrit* (New York, 1883).

Dickens, Charles, *Pictures from Italy* (London, 1846) (rpt. Mineola, New York, 2016).

Dryden, John, 'An essay of dramatic poesy' (1668) in D. D. Arundell (ed.), *Dreyden and Howard* (Cambridge, 1929).

Edwards, Thomas, *Cephalus and Procris, Narcissus* (1595) rpt. (London, 1882)

Eustace, John Chetwode, *A Tour Through Italy*, 2 vols. (London, 1813), 7th ed., *A Classical Tour Through Italy*, 3 vols. (London, 1841).

Evelyn, John, *Memoirs Illustrative of the Life and Writings of John Evelyn, Comprising His Diary from 1641 to 1705/6, and a Selection of His Familiar Letters*, William Bray (ed.), 2 vols. (London, 1818).

Evelyn, John, *The Diary of John Evelyn*, in E. S. de Beer (ed.), 5 vols. (Oxford, 1955).

Florio, John, *Firste Fruites; Which Yeelde Familiar Speech, Merie Prouerbs, Wittie Sentences, and Golden Sayings* (London, 1578).

Florio, John, *Second Fruites* (London, 1591).

Fordyce, David,*Dialogues Concerning Education*, 2 vols. (London, 1745).

Fordyce, James, *Sermons to Young Women*, 2 vols. (London, 1770).

Forsyth, Joseph, *Remarks on Antiquities, Arts and Letters, During an Excursion in Italy in the Years 1802 and 1803* (4th ed. London, 1835).

Fox, Charles James, *Memorials and Correspondence of Charles James Fox*, in John Russell (ed.), 2 vols. (Philadelphia, 1853).

Franco, Veronica, *Poems and Selected Letters*, in Ann Rosalind James and Margaret F. Rosenthal (eds.) (Chicago, 1998).

Gailhard, John, *The Compleat Gentleman, or, Directions for the Education of Youth as to Their Breeding at Home and Travelling Abroad* (London, 1678).

Gibbon, Edward, *Gibbon's Journey from Geneva to Rome: His Journal from 20 April to 2 October 1764*, Georges Alfred Bonnard (ed.), (London, 1961).

Gibbon, Edward, *Memoirs of My Life and Writings*, Henry Morley (ed.) (London, 1891).

Gibbon, Edward, *Private Letters of Edward Gibbon (1753–1794)*, Rowland E. Prothero (ed.), 2 vols. (London, 1895).

Goethe, Johann Wolfgang von, The Auto-biography of Goethe. *Truth and Poetry: From My Own Life*, trans. John Oxenford, (London, 1848).

Goldoni, Carlo, *Mémoires de Carlo Goldoni pour server à l'histoire de sa vie*, 2 vols. (Paris, 1821).

Goldsmith, Oliver, *The Life of Oliver Goldsmith*, in James Prior (ed.), 2 vols. (London, 1837).

Goldsmith, Oliver, *The Miscellaneous Works of Oliver Goldsmith*, in James Prior (ed.), 4 vols. (London, 1837). Gourbillon, Joseph Antoine de, *Voyage critique à l'Etna en 1819*, 2 vols. (Paris, 1820).

Gray, Thomas, *The Works of Gray*, John Mitford (ed.), 2 vols. (London, 1835).

Grimani, Gasparo, *Ladies' New Italian Grammar* (London, 1788).

Guazzo, Stefano, *La civil conversazione* (Brescia, 1574).

Guerrini, Pietro, *Il Viaggio in Europa di Pietro Guerrini (1682–1686)*, 2 vols. (Florence, 2005).

Heine, Heinrich, *Heine's Pictures of Travel*, in Charles Godfrey Leland (ed.) (Philadelphia, 1879).

Henley, John, *The Compleat Linguist. Or, an Universal Grammar of All Considerable Tongues in Being. A Grammar of the Italian Tongue*. 2 vols. (London, 1719–21).

Heylyn, Peter, *The Voyage of France or a Compleat Journey Through France* (London, 1673).

Hill, Brian, *Observations and Remarks in a Journey Through Sicily and Calabria, in the year 1791* (London, 1792).

Hillgarth, Jocelyn Nigel, *The Mirror of Spain, 1500–1700: The Formation of a Myth* (Ann Arbor, 2000).

Hoby, Thomas, *The Book of the Courtier* (New York, 1906).

Hoby, Thomas, *The Travels and Life of Sir Thomas Hoby, 1547–1564*, in Edgar Powell (ed.) (London, 1902).

Holmes, Dalkeith, *A Ride on Horseback to Florence Through France and Switzerland* (London, 1842).

Hollyband, Claudius, [Claude de Sainliens] *The French School-Master* (London, 1573).

Howell, James, *Epistolae Ho-Elianae: The Familiar Letters of James Howell*, 4 vols. (London, 1892).

Howell, James, *Instructions for Forraine Travell* (London, 1642).

Inglis, Henry David, *Solitary Walks Through Many Lands* (London, 1828).

Jameson, Anna, *Diary of an ennuyée* (London, 1826).

Johnson, James, *Change of Air* (London, 1831).

Johnson, Samuel, *A Dictionary of the English Language* (London, 1755).

Johnson, Samuel, *The Idler, The Works of Samuel Johnson*, 12 vols. (Liverpool, 1820).

Johnson, Samuel, *The Lives of the Most Eminent English Poets with Critical Observations on Their Works*, 3 vols. (London, 1801).

Jonson, Ben, *Volpone*, John D. Rea (ed.) (New Haven/London/Oxford, 1919).

Keysler, John George, *Travels Through Germany, Bohemia, Hungary, Switzerland, Italy and Lorrain*, 4 vols. (London, 1756) rpt. 1760.

Knight, Phillipina Lady, *Lady Knight's Letters from France and Italy 1776–1795*, Lady Elliott-Drake (ed.) (London, 1905).

Lalande, Joseph J., *Voyage d'un François en Italie, fait dans les années 1765 & 1766*, 8 vols. (Paris, 1786).

La Martinière, Antoine Augustin Bruzen de, *Le grand dictionnaire géographique: historique et critique* (Amsterdam and Rotterdam, 1732).

Lassels, Richard, *The Voyage of Italy or a Compleat Journey Through Italy, in Two Parts* (Paris, 1670).

Latrobe, Charles James, *The Pedestrian* (London, 1830).

Lauder, John, *Journals of Sir John Lauder, Lord Fountainhall, with His Observations on Public Affairs and Other Memoranda, 1665–1676*, in Donald Crawford (ed.) (Edinburgh, 1900).

Lithgow, William, *Rare Adventures and Painful Peregrinations by W. Lithgow* (London, 1609), rpt. 1906.

Locatelli, Sebastiano, *Viaggio di Francia*, in Luigi Monga (ed.), CIRVI: Centro Interuniversitario di Ricerche sul Viaggio in Italia (Torino, 1991).

Locke, John, *Some Thoughts Concerning Education* (1693) in R. H. Quick (ed.) (Cambridge, 1892).

Longfellow, Henry Wadsworth, *Life of Henry Wadsworth Longfellow with Extracts from His Journal and Correspondence*, Samuel Longfellow (ed.), 3 vols. (Chicago, Illinois, 2003).

Loysius, Georgius, *Privilegium Mercurii* (Frankfurt, 1644).

Mabillon, Jean, *Mabillon Correspondence inedited de Mabillon et de Montfaucon avec l'Italie*, in M. Valery (ed.), 3 vols. (Paris, 1846), vol. III.

Martinelli, Vincenzo, *Lettere Familiari e Critiche* (Londra, 1751).

Matthews, Henry, *The Diary of an Invalid* (London, 1820).

Mauger, Claude, *French Grammar* (London, 1688).

Misson, François Maximilien, *A New Voyage to Italy*, 2 vols. (London, 1695).

Molière, [Jean-Baptiste Poquelin], *Le bourgeois gentilhomme*, in Maurice A. Gerothwohl (ed.) (London, 1902).

Montagu, Mary Wortley, *Letters and Works of Lady Mary Wortley Montagu*, in Lord Wharncliffe (ed.), 3 vols. (London, 1837).

Montaigne, Michel de, *Journal de voyage en Italie par la Suisse et l'Allemagne en 1580–1581* (Paris, 1774), rpt. in François Rigolot (ed.) (Paris, 1992), trans., *The Journal of Montaigne's Travels in Italy by Way of Switzerland and Germany in 1580 and 1581*, William George Waters (ed. and trans.) 3 vols. (London, 1903).

Montesquieu, Charles de, *Voyages de Montesquieu* (Paris, 1774), 2 vols. (Bordeaux, 1894–6).

Moore, John, *A View of Society and Manners in Italy with Anecdotes Relating to Some Eminent Characters*, 2 vols. (London, 1781).

Morgan, Lady (Sidney), *Italy*, 3 vols. (London, 1821).

Mortoft, Francis, *Francis Mortoft: His Book. Being His Travels Through France and Italy 1658–1659*, in Malcom Letts (ed.) (London, 1925).

Morton, Harriet, *Protestant Vigils* (London, 1826).

Moryson, Fynes, *Itinerary Written by Fynes Moryson Gent.* (London, 1617) 4 vols., rpt. (Glasgow, 1907–8).

Mulcaster, Richard, *The First Part of the Elementarie* (1582: facsimile repr., Menston, 1970).

Munday, Antony, *The English Romayne Lyf*e (1581), rpt. (London, 1925).

Nashe, Thomas, *The Unfortunate Traveller* (London, 1594).

North, Roger, *Examen*, 2 vols. (1734).

Northall, John, *Travels Through Italy* (London, 1766).

Nugent, Thomas, *The Grand Tour; Or, a Journey Through the Netherlands, Germany, Italy, and France*, 4 vols. (London, 1778).

Palmer, Joseph, *A Four Months' Tour*, 2 vols. (London, 1776).

Patoun, William,'Advice on travel in Italy', in John Ingamells (ed.), *A Dictionary of British and Irish Travellers in Italy, 1701–1800* (New Haven and London, 1997) xxxix–lii.

Piale, Luigi, *Rome Seen in a Week* (Rome, 1853).

Piozzi Thrale, Hester Lynch, *Observations and Reflections Made in the Course of a Journey Through France, Italy and Germany*, 2 vols. (London, 1789).

Platière, Jean Marie Rolande de la, *Lettres ècrtites de Suisse d'Italie et de Sicile*, 2 vols. (Lyon, 1781).

Pleunus, Arrigo, *A New, Plain, Methodical and Compleat Italian Grammar, Whereby You May Very Soon Attain to the Perfection of the Italian Tongue* (Livorno, 1715).

Pope, Alexander, *The Dunciad*, Book IV, in John Butt (ed.), *The Poems of Alexander Pope* (London, 1963).

Pope, Alexander, *Imitations of Horace*, 2 vols. (Edinburgh, 1764).

[Port Royal] *A New Method of Learning the Italian Tongue* (London, 1750).

Ray, John, *Observations Topographical, Moral, & Physiological: Made in a Journey Through Part of the Low-Countries, Germany, Italy, and France* (London, 1673).

Raymond, John, *An Itinerary Containing a Voyage Made Through Italy, in the Year 1646 and 1647* (London, 1648).

Reichard, Hans Ottokar de, *Guide de l'Italie, 1793*, rpt. (Paris, 1971).

Reynolds, Joshua, *Discourses*, in *Sir Joshua Reynolds's Discourses*, Edward Gilpin Johnson (ed.) (Chicago, 1891).

Rivarol, Antoine, *De l'universalité de la langue française* (1786), Th. Suran (ed.) (Paris, 1930).

Rogers, Samuel, 'Italy' (1830) in John Rigby Hale (ed.), *The Italian Journal of Samuel Rogers, with an Account of Rogers' Life and of Travel in Italy in 1814–1821* (London, 1956).

Roots, William, *Paris in 1814, or, a Tour in France after the First Fall of Napoleon*, Henry A. Ogle (ed.) (Newcastle-Upon-Tyne, 1909).

Rose, William Stewart, *Letters from the North of Italy* (London, 1819).

Ruskin, John, *Praeterita* (1886) rpt. in 2 vols. (London, 1907).

Sabellico, Marco Antonio, *Enneadis* (1504).

Sade, Donatien Alphonse François de, *Voyage d'Italie or a Critical, Historical and Philosophical Dissertation on the Cities of Florence, Rome and Naples, 1775–6* (Paris, 1995).

Sharp, Samuel, *Letters from Italy: Describing the Customs and Manners of That Country, in the Years 1765, and 1766 etc.* (London, 1768).

Shelley, Mary Wollstonecraft, *Rambles in Germany and Italy in 1840, 1842, and 1843* (1844) 2 vols. (Folcroft – Pennsylvania, 1975).

Shelley, Percy Bysshe 'Letter to Leigh Hunt', from Naples 20 December 1818, in *Letters from Percy Bysshe Shelley to J. H. Leigh Hunt*, in Thomas James Wise (ed.), 2 vols. (London, 1894).

Seymour, Michael Hobart, *A Pilgrimage to Rome* (London, 1848).

Skippon, Philip, 'An account of a journey', in Awnsley and John Churchill (eds.), *A Collection of Voyages*, 6 vols. (London, 1732), vol. VI.

Smith, Adam, *The Wealth of Nations* (London, 1776) in Dugald Stewart (ed.), *The Works of Adam Smith*, 5 vols. (London, 1811).

Smith, J. *Grammatica quadrilinguis, or Brief Instructions for the French, Italian, Spanish, and English Tongues* (London,1674).

Smollett, Tobias, *Roderick Random* (London, 1853).

Smollett, Tobias, *Travels Through France and Italy*, Thomas Seccombe (ed.) (London, 1907) rpt. (London, 2010).

Snow, Robert, *Journal of a Steam Voyage down the Danube to Constantinople* (London, 1842).

Staël, Mme de, *Corinne, or Italy*, trans. Sylvia Raphael, (Oxford, 1998).

Stendhal, *Promenades dans Rome* (Paris, 1866).

Stendhal, *Rome, Naples et Florence* (Paris, 1826) rpt. (1987).

Sterne, Laurence, *A Sentimental Journey Through France and Italy* by *Mr Yorick* (London, 1768) rpt. in Gardner D. Stout, Jr (ed.) (Berkeley and Los Angeles,1967).

Strutt, Arthur John, *A Pedestrian Tour in Calabria & Sicily* (London, 1842).

Strutt, Elizabeth, *A Spinster's Tour in France* (London, 1828).

Swinburne, Henry, *Travels in Two Sicilies*, 2 vols. (London, 1783).

Talfourd, Thomas Noon, *Vacation Rambles* (London, 1845).

Terry, Edward, *The Travels of Mr Thomas Coryat*, in *The English Acquisition in Guinea & East India*, by R. B. (London, 1700).

Thomas William, *The Historie of Italie* (London, 1549) rpt. in G. B. Parks (ed.), *The History of Italy* (Ithaca NY, 1963).

Tommaseo, Niccolò, *Dizionario della Lingua Italiana* (1861–74).

Torriano, Giovanni, *Italian Reviv'd or the Introduction to the Italian Tongue* (London, 1673).

Torriano, Giovanni, *The Italian Tutor* (Cambridge, 1640).

Torriano, Giovanni, *New and Easie Directions for Attaining the Thuscan Italian Tongue* (Cambridge, 1639).

Trollope, Frances Milton, *A Visit to Italy*, 2 vols. (London, 1842).

Uvedale, Thomas, *The New Italian Grammar: Or, the Easiest and Best Method for Attaining That Language* (London, 1711).

Veneroni, Giovanni [Jean de Vigneron], *The Complete Italian Master; Containing the Best and Easiest Rules for Attaining That Language* (London, 1763) trans. of *Maître Italien* (Lyon, 1729).

Veneroni, Giovanni, *Short Specimen* (London, 1760).

Veryard, Ellis, *An Account of Divers Choice Remarks, etc. Taken in a Journey Through the Low-Countries, France, Italy, and Part of Spain; with the Isles of Sicily and Malta* (London, 1701).

Villemarest, Catherinet de, *The Heremit in Italy* (London, 1825).

Vivès, Jean Luis, *Exercitatio Linguae Latinae* (Venice, 1539).

Walpole, Horace, *Letters of Horace Walpole*, 4 vols. (Philadelphia, 1842).

Walpole, Horace, *Letters of Horace Walpole Earl of Orford to Sir Horace Mann*, 4 vols. (London, 1843).

Weatherhead, George Hume, *A Pedestrian Tour Through France and Italy* (London, 1834).

Wilkinson, Joshua Lucock, *The Wanderer* (London, 1798).

Wilmot, Catherine, *An Irish Peer on the Continent (1801–1803), Being a Narrative of the Tour of Stephen, 2nd Earl Mount Cashell, Through France, Italy, etc.* in Thomas U. Sadler (ed.) (London, 1920).

Wotton, Henry, *The Life and Letters of Sir Henry Wotton*, in Smith, Logan Pearsall (ed.), 2 vols. (Oxford, 1907).

Wotton, William, *Reflections Upon Ancient and Modern Learning* (London, 1705).

Wreford, Henry, *Rome Pagan and Papal* (London, 1846).

Wright, Edward, *Some Observations Made in Travelling Through France, Italy &c. in the Years 1720, 1721 and 1722* (London, 1730).

Young, Arthur, *Travels in France During the Years 1787, 1788 and 1789* (London, 1892).

Secondary Sources

Abbate Badin, Donatella, 'Lady Morgan in Italy: a traveller with an agenda', *Studi irlandesi: A Journal of Irish Studies*, 6 (2016), 127–48.

Abbate Badin, Donatella, 'Tre primedonne del Grand Tour: Lady Montagu, Hester Thrale e Lady Morgan', in Claudio Sensi and Patrizia Pellizzari (eds.), *Viaggi e pellegrinaggi fra Tre e Ottocento* (Alessandria, 2008), 331–82.

Babeau, Albert, *Les Voyageurs en France: depuis la Renaissance jusqu'à la Révolution* (Tours, 1928).

Barber, Charles, *Early Modern English* (Worcester and London, 1976).

Barber Morrison, Helen (ed.), *The Golden Age of Travel* (London, 1953).

Barbier, Patrick, *The World of the Castrati. The History of an Extraordinary Operatic Phenomenon* (Paris, 1989), trans. (London, 1996) rpt. 2001.

Barefoot, Brian, *The English Road to Rome* (Upton-upon-Severn, Worcs.,1993).

Barthes, Roland, *L'Empires des signes* (Geneva, 1970).

Bartlett, Kenneth R, 'Travel and translation: The English and Italy in the sixteenth century', *Bollettino del C.I.R.V.I* (Centro interuniversitario di Ricerche sul viaggio in Italia), XV, 29–30, I–II (1994), 53–71.

Bates, Ernest Stuart, *Touring in 1600. A Study in the Development of Travel as a Means of Education* (New York, 1911).

Bayley, Susan N., 'The English Miss, German *Fräulein* and French *Mademoiselle*: foreign governesses and national stereotyping in nineteenth- and early twentieth-century Europe', *Journal of the History of Education Society*, 43, 2 (2014), 160–86.

Beccaria, Gian Luigi, *Sicuterat. Il latino di chi non lo sa* (1999, II ed., Milan, 2001).

Bertrand, Gilles, *Le Grand Tour revisité: pour une archéologie du tourisme: le voyage des français en Italie, milieu XVIIIe siècle-début XIXe siècle* (Rome, 2008).

Bignamini, Ilaria, 'The Italians as spectators and actors: the Grand Tour reflected' in Clare Hornsby (ed.), *The Impact of Italy, The Grand Tour and Beyond* (London, 2000), 29–47.

Bignamini, Ilaria and Clare Hornsby, *Dealing and Digging in Eighteenth-Century Rome*, 2 vols. (New Haven, 2010).

Bizzocchi, Roberto, 'Italian morality and European values in the eighteenth century' in Paula Findlen, Wendy Wassyng Roworth, Catherine M. Sama (eds.), *Italy's Eighteenth Century: Gender and Culture in the Age of the Grand Tour* (Stanford, 2009), 35–55.

Black, Jeremy, *The British Abroad: The Grand Tour in the Eighteenth Century* (New York, 1992).

Blunden, Edmund, 'From Paris to Geneva', in Lambert (ed.), *Grand Tour*, 55–69.

Boulton, James T. and T. O. Macloghlin (eds.), *News from Abroad: Letters Written by British Travellers on the Grand Tour, 1728–1771* (Liverpool, 1998).

Boutier, Jean,'Compétence internationale, émergence d'une "profession" et circulation des savoirs. Le tuteur aristocratique dans l'Angleterre du XVIIe siècle', in Maria-Pia Paoli (ed.), *Saperi in Movimento* (Pisa, 2009), 149–77.

Bouton, Charles-Pierre, *Les Grammaires Françaises de Claude Mauger à l'usage des Anglais* (Paris, 1972).

Bowen, John, 'Dickens and the figures of *Pictures from Italy*', in Clare Hornsby (ed.), *The Impact of Italy* (London, 2000), 197–217.

Bowron, Edgard Peters and Joseph J. Rishel (eds.), *Art in Rome in the Eighteenth Century* (London, 1997).

Brennan, Michael G. (ed.), *The Origins of the Grand Tour, The Travels of Robert Montagu, Lord Mandeville, 1649–1654, William Hammond, 1655–1658, Banaster Maynard, 1660–1663* (London, 2004).

Brizay, François, *Touristes du Grand Siècle: Le voyage d'Italie au XVIIe siècle* (Paris, 2006).

Brunot, Ferdinand, *Histoire de la langue française des origines à 1900*, 13 vols. (Paris, 1934–5) rpt. 1966–79.

Burke, Peter, *The Art of Conversation* (Cambridge, 1993).

Burke, Peter, *The Fortunes of the Courtier: The European Reception of Castiglione's Cortegiano* (Cambridge, 1995).

Burke, Peter, *Languages and Communities in Early Modern Europe* (Cambridge, 2004).

Buzard, James, 'The Grand Tour and after (1660–1840)', in *The Cambridge Companion to Travel Writing* (Cambridge, 2002), 37–52.

Caesar, Michael and Marina Spunta (eds.), *Orality and Literacy in Modern Italian Culture* (London, 2006).

Campolongo, Chiara, 'L'importanza della lingua senese nella percezione degli stranieri nei secoli XVII e XVIII', unpublished dissertation, Università degli Studi di Siena, 2011–12.

Cartago, Gabriella, *Ricordi di italiano. Osservazioni intorno alla lingua e italianismi nelle relazioni di viaggio degli inglesi in Italia* (Bassano del Grappa, 1990).

Chaney, Edward, *The Evolution of the Grand Tour: Anglo-Italian Cultural Relations since the Renaissance* (London, 1998).

Chaney, Edward, (ed.), *The Grand Tour and the Great Rebellion: Richard Lassels and the 'Voyage of Italy' in the Seventeenth Century* (Geneva, 1985).

Chaney, Edward, 'Quo Vadis? Travel as education and the impact of Italy in the sixteenth century', in Edward Chaney, *The Evolution of the Grand Tour*, 58–101.

Chard, Chloe, 'Crossing boundaries and exceeding limits: destabilisation, tourism, and the sublime' in Chloe Chard and Helen Langdon (eds.), *Transports: Travel, Pleasure, and Imaginative Geography, 1600–1830* (New Haven and London, 1996), 117–49.

Chard, Chloe, *Pleasure and Guilt on the Grand Tour* (Manchester, 1999).

Chard, Chloe and Helen Langdon (eds.), *Transports: Travel, Pleasure, and Imaginative Geography, 1600–1830* (New Haven and London, 1996).

Cifoletti, Guido, *La lingua franca mediterranea* (Padova, 1989).

Cohen, Michèle, *Fashioning Masculinity. National Identity and Language in the Eighteenth Century* (London and New York, 1996).

Corré, Alan D. (ed.), *A Glossary of Lingua Franca*, I ed. 1997 (5th ed.) (Milwaukee -Wi, 2005), http://www.uwm.edu-corre/franca/go.html (accessed 10 December 2006).

Cremona, Joseph, 'Italian-based lingua francas around the Mediterranean', in Anna Laura Lepschy and Arturo Tosi (eds.), 24–30.

Craik, Jennifer, 'The culture of tourism', in Chris Rojek and John Urry (eds.), *Touring Cultures: Transformations of Travel and Theory* (London, 1997), 113–36.

Dakhlia, Jocelyne, 'La langue franque, langue du merchand en Méditerranée?', in Gilbert Buti, Michèle Janin-Thivos and Olivier Raveux (eds), *Langues et langages du commerce en Méditerranée et en Europe à l'époque moderne* (Aix-en-Provence, 2013), 149–61.

D'Ancona, Alessandro, 'Francia e Italia nel 1786: Nella Relazione del viaggio di G.B. Malaspina', *Nova Antologia*, 16 December 1891, rpt. in Alessandro D'Ancona (ed.), *Viaggiatori e avventurieri* (Florence, 1974), 243–84.

Dolan, Brian, *Ladies of the Grand Tour* (London, 2001).

Engel, William Edward, 'Knowledge that counted: Italian phrase books and dictionaries in Elizabethan England', *Bollettino del C.I.R.V.I.*, 31–32, 1995, XVI, fasc. I–II, 117–128.

Fedalto, Giorgio, 'Stranieri a Venezia e a Padova', *Storia della Cultura Veneta*, 3/1, *Dal primo Quattrocento al Concilio di Trento*, Girolamo Arnaldi and Manlio Pastore Stocchi (eds.), (Vicenza,1980), 501–14.

Ferguson, Ronnie, *A Linguistic History of Venice* (Olschki, 2007).

Ferguson, Ronnie, 'Primi influssi culturali italo-veneti sull'inglese: la testimonianza dei venezianismi in Florio, Coryate e Jonson', in Eugenio Burgio (ed.), *Il veneto: tradizione, tutela, continuità*, Atti del Convegno, Venice, 11–12 February 2011, *Quaderni Veneti*, II, 2012, 57–82.

Fido, Franco, *Guida a Goldoni: teatro e società nel Settecento* (Torino, 1977).

Findlen, Paula, Wendy Wassying Roworth, and Catherine M. Sama (eds.), *Italy's Eighteenth Century: Gender and Culture in the Age of the Grand Tour* (Stanford, 2009).

Finegan, Edward, 'Style and standardisation in England: 1700–1900', in Tim William Machan and Charles T. Scott (eds.), *English in Its Social Context: Essays in Historical Sociolinguistics*, (Oxford, 1992), 102–30.

Fitzgerald, Percy, *The Life of Laurence Sterne* (London, 1906).

Fleming, John (ed.), *Robert Adam and His Circle, in Edinburgh & Rome* (Cambridge MA, 1962).

Folena, Gianfranco, *L'italiano in Europa. Esperienze linguistiche del Settecento*, (Torino, 1983).

Folena, Gianfranco. *Il Linguaggio del caos. Studi sul plurilinguismo rinascimentale* (Torino, 1991).

Ford, Brinsley, '*James Byres: Principal antiquarian for the English visitors in Rome'*, *Apollo*, 99 (June 1974).

Fosi, Irene, *Papal Justice: Subjects and Courts in the Papal State, 1500–1750*. Eng. trans. Thomas V. Cohen (Washington DC, 2011).

Fumaroli, Marc, *La République des Lettres* (Paris, 2015).

Gallagher, John, 'The Italian London of John North: cultural contact and linguistic encounter in early modern England', *Renaissance Quarterly*, 70 (2017), 88–131.

Gallagher, John, '*Language and education on the grand tour of Sir Philip Perceval, 1676-9'*, in Helmut Glück, Mark Häberlein and Andreas Flurschütz da Cruz (eds.), *Adel und Mehrsprachigkeit in der Frühen* Neuzeit. *Ziele, Formen und Praktiken des Erwerbs und Gebrauchs von Fremdsprachen* (Wolfenbüttel, 2019).

Gallagher, John, '"Ungratefull Tuscans": teaching Italian in early modern England', *The Italianist*, 36:3 (2016), 392–413.

Gamberini, Spartaco, *Lo studio dell'italiano in Inghilterra nel '500 e nel '600* (Messina-Firenze, 1970).

Garms-Cornides, Elizabeth, 'Esiste un *Grand Tour* al Femminile?' in Dinora Corsi (ed.), *Altrove: Viaggi di donne dall'antichità al Novecento* (Rome, 1999), 175–200.

Gasperin, Vilma de, 'Rules and grammars of Italian in eighteenth-century England: the case of Giuseppe Baretti', *The Italianist* 36, 3 (2016), *500 Years of Italian Grammar(s), Culture, and Society in Italy and Europe: From Fortunio's Regole (1516) to the Present*, Helena Sanson and Francesco Lucioli (eds.), 429–46.

Geat, Marina, 'Stendhal e la questione della lingua italiana: tra realtà storica e metafora metastilistica', in Stefano Gensini (ed.), '*D'Uomini Liberamente Parlanti'. La Cultura Linguistica Italiana dell'Età dei Lumi e il Contesto Intellettuale Europeo* (Rome, 2002), 385–438.

Giddey, Ernest, 'Le condizioni materiali e spirituali del viaggio in Italia alla fine del XVI e del XVII secolo', in Giorgio Botta (ed.), *Cultura del viaggio. Ricostruzione storico-geografica del territorio* (Milan, 1989), 63–83.

Hamilton, Olive, *Paradise of Exiles: Tuscany and the British* (London, 1974).

Hans, Nicholas, *New Trends in Education in Eighteenth Century* (London, 1966).

Harris, Roy and Talbot J. Taylor, *Landmarks in Linguistic Thought: The Western Tradition from Socrates to Saussure* (London and New York, 1989).

Hernández-Campoy, Juan Manuel and Juan Camilo Conde-Silvestre (eds.), *The Handbook of Historical Sociolinguistics* (New York, 2014).

Hibbert, Christopher, *Cities and Civilizations* (London, 1987).

Hibbert, Christopher, *The Grand Tour* (London, 1987).

Hibbert, Christopher, *Rome: The Biography of a City* (London, 2001).

Hollington, Michael, 'The European context', in Sally Ledger and Holly Furneaux (eds.), *Charles Dickens in Context* (Cambridge, 2011).

Holmes, Janet, *Women, Men and Politeness* (London, 1995).

Hornsby, Clare, 'Introduction, or why travel?' in Clare Hornsby (ed.), *The Impact of Italy, The Grand Tour and Beyond* (London, 2000), 1–25.

Horodowich, Elizabeth, *Language and Statecraft in Early Modern Venice* (Cambridge, 2008).

Howard, Clare, *The English Travellers of the Renaissance* (London-New York, 1914).

Hudson, Roger, (ed.), *The Grand Tour 1592–1796* (London, 1993).

Hulme, Peter and Tim Youngs (eds.), *The Cambridge Companion to Travel Writing* (Cambridge, 2002).

Ingamells, John (ed.), *A Dictionary of British and Irish Travellers in Italy, 1701–1800* (New Haven and London, 1997).

Johnson, Donald R., 'Addison in Italy', *Modern Languages Studies*, 6 (Spring 1976), 32–6.

Jones, Richard Foster, *The Triumph of the English Language* (Stanford, 1953).

Ketton-Cremer, R. W. *Thomas Gray: A Biography* (Cambridge, 1955).

Kirby, Paul Franklin, *The Grand Tour in Italy (1700–1800)* (New York, 1952).

Lambert, Richard Stanton, (ed.), *Grand Tour: A Journey in the Tracks of the Age of Aristocracy* (London, 1935).

Lambley, Kathleen, *The Teaching and Cultivation of the French Language in England During Tudor and Stuart Times* (Manchester, 1920).

Lepschy, Anna Laura, 'Un "Rudiment Vénitien" del Settecento', *Atti dell'Istituto Veneto*, CXXII, 1964, 453–81; rpt. in collaboration with Giulio Lepschy in *L'amanuense analfabeta e altri saggi*, (Florence, 1999), 227–56.

Lepschy, Anna L. and Arturo Tosi (eds.), *Multilingualism in Italy: Past and Present* (Oxford, 2002).

Letts, Malcom, 'Cologne and the journey to the coast', in Richard Stanton Lambert (ed.), *Grand Tour: A Journey in the Tracks of the Age of Aristocracy* (London, 1935), 137–52.

Letts, Malcom, 'Germany and the Rhineland', in Richard Stanton Lambert (ed.), *Grand Tour: A Journey in the Tracks of the Age of Aristocracy* (London, 1935), 119–36.

Letts, Malcom (ed.), 'Introduction', in *Francis Mortoft: His Book Being His Travels Through France and Italy 1658–1659* (London, 1925), XIII–XXIV.

Lodge, Antony, 'French is a logical language', in Laurie Bauer and Peter Trudgill (eds.), *Language Myths* (New York, 1998), 23–31.

Lough, John, *France Observed in the Seventeenth Century by British Travellers* (Stocksfield, 1985).

Lovell Ernest, J. Jr., *Lady Blessington's Conversations of Lord Byron* (Princeton, 1969).

Machan, Tim William and Charles T. Scott (eds.), *English in Its Social Context: Essays in Historical Sociolinguistics* (Oxford, 1992).

Mączak, Antoni, *Travel in Early Modern Europe* (Cambridge, 1995).

Marenco, Franco, 'Introduzione', in Franco Marenco and Antonio Meo (eds.), *Thomas Coryat, Crudezze, 1608*, It. trans. (Milan, 1975).

Martelli, Francesco, 'Introduzione', *Il Viaggio in Europa di Pietro Guerrini (1682–1686)*, 2 vols. (Florence, 2005).

Martin, Philip W., *Byron: A Poet before His Public* (Cambridge, 1982).

Maugham, H. Neville, *The Book of Italian Travel (1580–1900)* (New York, 1903).

Mazur, Peter, *Conversion to Catholicism in Early Modern Italy* (Abingdon, 2016).

Maxwell, Constantia, *The English Traveller in France, 1698–1815* (London, 1932).

McVicker, Mary F., *Women Adventurers, 1750–1900. A Biographical Dictionary with Excerpts from Selected Travel Writings* (Jefferson NC and London, 2008).

Mead, William Edward, *The Grand Tour in the Eighteenth Century* (Boston/New York, 1914).

Milroy, James, 'Sociolinguistics and ideologies in language history', in M. Hernández-Campoy and J. Camilo Conde-Silvestre (eds.) (2014), 571–84.

Monga, Luigi (ed.), *Discours viatiques de Paris à Rome et de Rome à Naples et Sicile (1588–1589)*, CIRVI (Centro Interuniversitario di Ricerche sul Viaggio in Italia) (Torino, 1983).

Nauert, Charles G. Jr., *Humanism and the Culture of Renaissance Europe* (Cambridge, 1995).

Paccagnella, Ivano, *Il fasto delle lingue: plurilinguismo letterario nel '500* (Rome, 1984).

Padley, George Arthur P., *Grammatical Theory in Western Europe (1500–1700). Trends in Vernacular Grammar* (Cambridge, 1988).

Parkes, Joan, *Travel in England in the Seventeenth Century* (Oxford, 1925).

Parks, George, *The Middle Ages (to 1525)*, vol. I, *The English Traveler to Italy* (Stanford, 1954).

Parkvall, Mikael, 'Forward', in Alan D. Corré (ed.), *A Glossary of Lingua Franca* (5th ed.) (Milwaukee WI, 2005), unpaginated.

Pine-Coffin, R. S., *Bibliography of British and American Travel in Italy to 1860* (Florence, 1974).

Pizzoli, Lucilla, *Le grammatiche di italiano per inglesi (1550–1776): Un'analisi linguistica* (Florence, 2004).

Pritchard, R. E., *Odd Tom Coryate: The English Marco Polo* (Stroud, 2004).

Reid, Loren, *Charles James Fox: A Man for the People* (Columbia, 1969).

Reinert, Sophus A. 'Mapping the Economic Grand Tour: traveling and international emulation in Enlightenment Europe', *Harvard Business School Working Papers*, 17–005 (2016).

Richardson, Brian, 'The Italian of Renaissance elites in Italy and Europe', in Anna L. Lepschy and Arturo Tosi (eds.), 5–23.

Richardson, Brian, "Varie maniere di parlare": aspects of learning Italian in Renaissance Italy and Britain', in Vilma de Gasperin (ed.), *Ciò che potea la lingua nostra: Lectures and Essays in Memory of Clara Florio Cooper*, special supplement of *The Italianist*, 30 (2010), 78–94.

Ricci, Giovanni, 'Cataloghi di città, stereotipi etnici e gerarchie urbane nell'Italia di antico regime', *Storia Urbana*, VI, 18 (1982), 3–33.

Rigby, Hale John (ed.), *The Italian Journal of Samuel Rogers, with an Account of Rogers' Life and of Travel in Italy in 1814–1821* (London, 1956), 19–128.

Rosenthal, Margaret, *The Honest Courtesan: Veronica Franco, Citizen and Writer in Sixteenth-Century Venice* (Chicago, 1992).

Rota, Carlo, *Viaggiatori italiani in Sicilia nell'età dei lumi* (Messina, 2011).

Rubiés, Joan-Pau, 'Instructions for travellers: teaching the eye to see', *History and Anthropology*, 9, 2–3 (1996), 139–90.

Salmon, Frank, 'The impact of the archaeology of Rome on British architects and their work *c*.1750–1840', in Clare Hornsby (ed.), *The Impact of Italy: The Grand Tour and Beyond* (London, 2000), 219–43.

Sánchez-Jáuregui, María Dolores and Scott Wilcox (eds.), *The English Prize: The Capture of the Westmorland, an Episode of the Grand Tour* (New Haven, 2012).

Schendl, Herbert, 'Multilingualism, code-switching, and language contact in historical sociolinguistics', in Hernández-Campoy and J. Camilo Conde-Silvestre (eds.), *English in Its Social Context: Historical Sociolinguistics* (New York, 2014), 520–33.

Scott, Charles T. and Tim William Machan, 'Sociolinguistics, language change, and the history of English', in Tim William Machan and Charles T. Scott (eds.), *English in Its Social Context: Essays in Historical Sociolinguistics* (Oxford, 1992), 3–27.

Serianni, Luca, 'Lingua e dialetti d'Italia nella percezione dei viaggiatori sette-ottocenteschi', *Italianistica*, 26 (1997), 471–90, rpt. in Luca Serianni, *Viaggiatori, Musicisti, Poeti, Saggi di Storia della Lingua italiana* (Milan, 2002), 55–88.

Sherman, William, 'Stirrings and searching' (1500–1720), in Peter Hulme and Tim Youngs (eds.), *The Cambridge Companion to Travel Writing* (Cambridge, 2002), 17–36.

Simonini, Rinaldo, Charles S. Jr, 'The Italian pedagogy of Claudius Holyband', *Studies in Philology*, XLIX (1952), 144–54.

Stagl, Justin, 'The methodising of travel in the 16th century: a tale of three cities', *History and Anthropology*, 4, (1990), 303–38.

Stammerjohann, Harro, 'In viaggio attraverso gli italiani', *Italiano e Oltre*, XII (1997), 56–62.

Stoye, John, *English Travellers Abroad 1604–1667* (1952), rpt. (New Haven, 1989)

Strien, C. D. van, *British Travellers in Holland During the Stuart Period: Edward Browne and John Locke as Tourists in the United Provinces* (Leiden, 1993).

Sweet, Rosemary, *Cities and the Grand Tour: The British in Italy, c.1690–1820* (Cambridge, 2012).

Thomason, Sarah, G., *Language Contact: An Introduction* (Edinburgh, 2001).

Thorne, E. H., 'Italian teachers and teaching in eighteenth century England', *English Miscellany*, 9 (1958), 143–58.

Tosi, Arturo, 'The *Accademia della Crusca* in Italy: past and present', in Bernard Spolsky (ed.), *Language Academies and Other Language Management Agencies*, special issue of *Language Policy*, 10, 4 (2011), 289–303.

Tosi, Arturo, 'Histrionic transgressions: the Dario Fo-*Commedia dell'arte* relationship revisited', in Michael Caesar and Marina Spunta (eds.), *Orality and Literacy in Italian Culture* (London, 2006), 18–31.

Tóth, István G., *Literacy and Written Culture in Early Modern Europe* (1996), Eng. trans. (Budapest, 2000).

Trease, Geoffrey, *The Grand Tour* (London, 1967).

Vicentini, Alessandra, 'English language and cultural stereotypes in the eighteenth century: the first grammars of English for Italian learners', *Quaderni del CIRSIL*, (Centro Interuniversitario della Storia degli Insegnamenti Linguistici), 8–9, (2009–10), 2–18.

Walchester, Kathryn, *Our Own Fair Italy: Nineteenth-Century Women's Travel Writing and Italy 1800–1844* (Bern, 2007).

Waquet, Françoise, *Le latin ou l'empire d'un signe, XVIe–XXe siècle* (Paris, 1998).

Warneke, Sara, *Images of the Educational Travellers in Early Modern England* (Leiden, 1995).

Watts, Richard J., 'Language myths', in Juan M. Hernández-Campoy and J. Camilo Conde-Silvestre (eds.), (2014), 585–606.

Watts, Richard J. and Peter Trudgill, *Alternative Histories of English* (London, 2002).

Weinrich, Harald, 'Sprachanekdoten um Karl V' in *Wege der Sprachkultur* (Stutgart, 1985), 181–92.

Westrienen van, Anna Frank, *De Groote Tour* (Amsterdam, 1983).

Williams, Joseph M. "O! when degree is shak'd": sixteenth-century anticipations of some modern attitudes towards usage', in Tim William Machan, and Charles T. Scott (eds.), *English in Its Social Context: Essays in Historical Sociolinguistics* (Oxford, 1992), 69–101.

Wilson, Mona, 'The decline of the Grand Tour', in Richard Stanton Lambert (ed.), *Grand Tour: A Journey in the Tracks of the Age of Aristocracy* (London, 1935), 153–67.

Woodruff, Douglas, 'From London to Paris', in Richard Stanton Lambert (ed.), *Grand Tour: A Journey in the Tracks of the Age of Aristocracy* (London, 1935), 35–53.

Wykes, Alan, *Abroad: A Miscellany of English Travel Writing 1700–1914* (London, 1973).

Index of Names

Subject Index

Latin (cont.)
  epithets of Italian cities, 46
  family tree, 191–4, 205
  folk model, 175
  grammar, 170
  in the theatre, 73
  international language, 169, 170, 260
  language without a speech community, 168
  langue vivante, 100
  lingua franca, 57, 62, 128, 168, 170, 172, 174, 177, 186
  literary, 176
  multipurpose language, 168–70
  no longer language of elites, 54
  opera, 136
  phonetic variations of, 137
  regional variations of, 175–9
  to denote a change in mood, 175
  written and spoken, 170–5
Latium, 206
Lausanne, 45, 102, 115, 116, 117, 127
learned societies, 133
Leghorn (Livorno), 2, 118, 186
Leipzig, 43, 116, 117, 166
Letts, M., 167
Levant, 57, 81, 93, 182, 183, 184, 185, 215
Leyden, 47
libraries, 34
libretti, 83, 87, 98, 159, 266
Ligurian, 206
Lille, 114
Limosin, 205
lingua franca, 54, 57, 82, 123, 136, 168, 210, 235
linguistic affectations, 136, 216, 265
linguistic boundaries and frontiers, 194, 195, 205, 206, 260, 266, 267
linguistic contact, *see also* borrowings
  and language mixing, 195
  and receptive skills, 220
  in frontier areas, 195
  Latin and pre-existing languages, 191–2
  pidgin or hybrid language, 183, 184, 264
  seen as corruption, 192
linguistic corruption, 196, 198, 202, 208
linguistic landscape, 203
linguistic purity, 16, 192, 194, 196, 198, 252, 261, 262
linguistic variations, *see also* language status
  and decorum, 267
  and domains, 203
  and evolution, 206
  and homogeneity, 200, 202
  derivatives of endearment, 210

high-status and low-status variants, 264
Latin phonetic variations, 16, 177
local varieties, 197
Macaronic Latin, 176
non-standard English, 261
regional languages, 175–9, 197, 202, 260, 263–5
rustic language, 196
standard language culture, 262
literary language, 263, 264, 265, 266
literati, 35
literature, 34, 67, 84, 88, 94, 117, 133, 134
Loire Valley, 17, 19, 31, 59, 116, 117, 123, 125, 126, 128, 129, 130, 131, 132, 135, 186, 196, 203, 204, 205, 223, 262
Lombard dialect, *206*, 208
Lombardy, 39
London, 2, 16, 18, 33, 34, 64, 66, 79, 87, 90, 92, 93, 94, 97, 101, 102, 119, 130, 133, 226, 229, 243
lone travellers, 107, 163, 173
Loreto, 220
Lough, J., 19, 204
Low Countries and United Provinces, 42, 126
Lucca, *36*, 49
Luxembourg, 42
Lyons, 140, 173

Macaroni Club, 226
macaroni/maccaroni, 66, 232
Macaronic sermons, 175
Mączak, A., 20, 47, 110, 115, 116, 138, 147, 149, 152, 157, 171, 172, 219, 220, 240, 241
Madrid, 241
Magna Graecia, 212
malaria, 226
male speech and behaviour, 149
Maltese, 59
manners, foreign, 62, 67
Mannheim, 44, 180
Mantua, *53*, 53, 145, 146
maps, 219
Marseilles, *1*, 45, 205
Maxwell, C., 19, 35
Mead, W.E., 19
mementos, 141
memoirs, 150, 163, 182, 244, 261
memorabilia, 228
Mentz (Mainz), 58, 172
Merchant of Venice (Shakespeare, 1596), 29
Mermaid Club, 57
Metz, 26
middle classes, 35, 40, 83, 85, 99, 263
Middle East, 56

Siena (cont.)
    municipal identities, 39, 131
    tea drinking, 64
    theatre, 120
    transport, 224
    university, 118, 131, 134, 172
    women in, 158
sightseeing, 228, 259
signs and gestures, 160
Simplon, 195
Sinigallia, 220
sketchbooks, 59
Slovenian, 109
social isolation, 196
social roles, 267
social satire, 265
socialisation, 20, 110, 116–21, 126, 165
socially marked domains of language use, 195
sociolects, 210
soldiers, 150, 172, 173, 174
solo travellers, 107, 163, 173
Sophia, 249
Spain and the Iberian Peninsula
    and the New World, 42
    castrati, 79
    cicisbei, 75
    language in, 200
    Latin in, 170, 176
    not on main route, 2
    pilgrims, 5
    power in Italy, 43, 257
    problems of travelling to, 42
    Romance languages, 193
    sexual habits, 78
    stereotypes, 27, 29
    theatre, 73
    women in, 241
    women travellers in, 241
Spanish
    and national characteristics, 199, 200
    as international language, 185
    as national language, 263
    contact with Italian, 185
    dialects of, 205
    education in, 81
    in international treaties, 179
spelling, 217, 219, 260
spoken language
    code-switching, 235
    education in, 85, 93, 94
    pidgins, 184
    regional dialects, 263
    women, 242
sponsorship, 12, 17, 107, 122
standard itinerary, *1*, 108, 116, 220, 223

standard language and standardisation, 132,
    133, 175, *193*, 207, 216, 219, 260,
    261, 262
steamboats, 14, 114
Stoye, J., 17, 130
Stuttgart, 44
superlatives, 232
Sweet, R., 21
Switzerland
    accomodation standards, 114
    and the Grand Tour, 42, 44
    as a barrier, 42, 109, 194
    as alternative route, 2
    as an attraction, 45
    French language, 102, 115, 126
    German in, 145, 163
    language variations, 109
    pronunication in, 195
    roads, 44
swordfish, Sicilian, 212

table d'hôte, 115
textbooks, 92, 93–8, 219
theatre, 59, 72, 79, 87, 119, 154
    French, 34, 265
    gesture, 162
    Italian, 201, 265
    naturalistic, 197
    petit-maître, 229
Thirty Years' War, 122, 171
Thorne, E.H., 84
tipping, 113, 223, 224
tonish, 230
toponyms, 219
topos/topoi
    best language and worst accent, 58, 253
    Catholic extravagant festivities, 29
    foreign sexual habits, 29
    Italian decadence, 266
    language explaining human diversity, 59
    myths about Italy, 249
    new vernaculars, 191
    Sicilian swordfish, 213
    visions of otherness, 248
Torg, 47
Torrenieri, 220
Tóth, I.G., 171, 175
Toulouse, 111
Tour through Italy, 14
Tours, 1, 128
translation, 13, 94, 97, 146, 235
travel
    and purchase of artwork, 143
    bills of exchange, 220
    by public carriage, 110